The Shotgun Reference
A Guide for All Shotgun Types

Contents

1 Introduction to Shotgun Types   1
- 1.1 Shotgun 1
  - 1.1.1 Characteristics 1
  - 1.1.2 Uses 2
  - 1.1.3 Design features for various uses 3
  - 1.1.4 Types 4
  - 1.1.5 History 5
  - 1.1.6 Design factors 7
  - 1.1.7 Ammunition 12
  - 1.1.8 Legal issues 14
  - 1.1.9 See also 17
  - 1.1.10 References 17
  - 1.1.11 External links 18
- 1.2 Semi-automatic shotgun 18
  - 1.2.1 Examples of semi-automatic shotguns 18
  - 1.2.2 References 18
  - 1.2.3 See also 18
- 1.3 Automatic shotgun 18
  - 1.3.1 Design 19
  - 1.3.2 Ammunition 19
  - 1.3.3 Strengths and weaknesses 19
  - 1.3.4 Use 19
  - 1.3.5 List of automatic shotguns 19
  - 1.3.6 See also 20
  - 1.3.7 References 20
- 1.4 Double-barreled shotgun 20
  - 1.4.1 Construction 20
  - 1.4.2 Regional use 21
  - 1.4.3 See also 22

		1.4.4 References	22
	1.5	Lever action	22
		1.5.1 History	22
		1.5.2 Usage in warfare	23
		1.5.3 Advantages and disadvantages	24
		1.5.4 Calibers	24
		1.5.5 Other long gun actions	24
		1.5.6 See also	24
		1.5.7 References	25
		1.5.8 External links	25
	1.6	Pump action	25
		1.6.1 History	25
		1.6.2 Advantages	25
		1.6.3 Disadvantages	25
		1.6.4 Layout	26
		1.6.5 Operating cycle	26
		1.6.6 Trigger disconnectors	26
		1.6.7 Other long gun actions	26
		1.6.8 Type of Pump action shotgun	26
		1.6.9 References	27
2	**Semi-Automatic Shotguns**		**28**
	2.1	Akdal MKA 1919	28
		2.1.1 Related firearms	28
		2.1.2 References	28
	2.2	Baikal MP-153	28
		2.2.1 History	28
		2.2.2 Related Firearms	29
		2.2.3 See also	29
		2.2.4 References	29
		2.2.5 External links	29
	2.3	Benelli M1	29
		2.3.1 See also	29
		2.3.2 References	29
		2.3.3 External links	29
	2.4	Benelli M2	29
		2.4.1 Operation	29
		2.4.2 Users	29
		2.4.3 See also	30

	2.4.4	References	30
	2.4.5	External links	30
2.5	Benelli M3	30
	2.5.1	Background	30
	2.5.2	Variants	30
	2.5.3	Users	31
	2.5.4	See also	31
	2.5.5	References	31
	2.5.6	External links	32
2.6	Benelli M4	32
	2.6.1	History	32
	2.6.2	Design	32
	2.6.3	Users	33
	2.6.4	See also	34
	2.6.5	References	34
	2.6.6	External links	34
2.7	Benelli Raffaello	34
	2.7.1	Design details	34
	2.7.2	Operation	35
	2.7.3	See also	35
	2.7.4	External links	35
2.8	Benelli Raffaello CrioComfort	35
	2.8.1	Design details	35
	2.8.2	Operation	35
	2.8.3	See also	35
	2.8.4	External links	35
2.9	Benelli Vinci	35
	2.9.1	References	36
2.10	Beretta 1201FP	36
	2.10.1	External links	36
2.11	Beretta A303	36
2.12	Beretta AL391	36
	2.12.1	Features	36
	2.12.2	Models	36
	2.12.3	See also	36
	2.12.4	References	36
	2.12.5	External links	37
2.13	Beretta Xtrema 2	37

	2.13.1	Overview	37
	2.13.2	Technical advantages	37
	2.13.3	See also	37
	2.13.4	References	37
2.14	Browning Auto-5	37
	2.14.1	History	37
	2.14.2	Design details	38
	2.14.3	References	38
	2.14.4	External links	39
2.15	FN SLP	39
	2.15.1	References	39
	2.15.2	External links	39
2.16	Franchi AL-48	39
	2.16.1	References	39
2.17	Franchi SPAS-12	40
	2.17.1	Design	40
	2.17.2	SPAS-12, SAS-12 and LAW-12 Model Differences	41
	2.17.3	United States Importers	42
	2.17.4	U.S. Legal	42
	2.17.5	Users	43
	2.17.6	See also	43
	2.17.7	Notes	43
	2.17.8	References	44
	2.17.9	External links	44
2.18	Franchi SPAS-15	44
	2.18.1	Design	44
	2.18.2	Legality	45
	2.18.3	Users	45
	2.18.4	See also	45
	2.18.5	References	45
	2.18.6	External links	45
2.19	Heckler & Koch HK512	45
	2.19.1	Design	45
	2.19.2	Users	46
	2.19.3	References	46
	2.19.4	External links	46
2.20	Ithaca Mag-10	46
	2.20.1	Variants	46

- 2.20.2 References . . . 46
- 2.20.3 External links . . . 46
- 2.21 Manville gun . . . 46
  - 2.21.1 Manville 12-Bore Gun . . . 46
  - 2.21.2 26.5mm Manville Machine-Projector . . . 47
  - 2.21.3 37mm Manville Gas Gun . . . 47
  - 2.21.4 History . . . 47
  - 2.21.5 Related Guns . . . 47
  - 2.21.6 Notes . . . 47
- 2.22 MAUL (weapon) . . . 47
  - 2.22.1 Users . . . 48
  - 2.22.2 References . . . 48
- 2.23 Mossberg 930 . . . 48
  - 2.23.1 Design . . . 48
  - 2.23.2 References . . . 48
  - 2.23.3 External links . . . 48
- 2.24 Remington Model 11-48 . . . 48
  - 2.24.1 Design . . . 48
  - 2.24.2 Sportsman '48 . . . 49
  - 2.24.3 References . . . 49
  - 2.24.4 External links . . . 49
- 2.25 Remington Model 11-87 . . . 49
  - 2.25.1 Users . . . 49
  - 2.25.2 External links . . . 49
  - 2.25.3 References . . . 49
- 2.26 Remington Model 1100 . . . 49
  - 2.26.1 History . . . 50
  - 2.26.2 Design . . . 50
  - 2.26.3 Use . . . 50
  - 2.26.4 Users . . . 50
  - 2.26.5 Notes . . . 51
  - 2.26.6 External links . . . 51
- 2.27 Remington Model 58 . . . 51
  - 2.27.1 Design . . . 51
  - 2.27.2 Versions . . . 51
  - 2.27.3 References . . . 51
- 2.28 Remington Model 878 . . . 51
  - 2.28.1 Design . . . 51

- 2.28.2 References 52
- 2.29 Remington Model SP-10 52
  - 2.29.1 References 52
  - 2.29.2 External links 52
- 2.30 Remington Spartan 453 52
  - 2.30.1 Notes 52
- 2.31 Safir T-14 52
  - 2.31.1 See also 52
  - 2.31.2 References 52
- 2.32 Saiga-12 52
  - 2.32.1 Modifications to the basic Kalashnikov platform 53
  - 2.32.2 Common Saiga 12 configurations 53
  - 2.32.3 Variants 54
  - 2.32.4 Legal status 54
  - 2.32.5 Users 54
  - 2.32.6 See also 54
  - 2.32.7 References 54
  - 2.32.8 Sources 55
  - 2.32.9 External links 55
- 2.33 Sjögren shotgun 55
  - 2.33.1 References 55
- 2.34 SRM Arms Model 1216 55
  - 2.34.1 Design details 55
  - 2.34.2 Variants 56
  - 2.34.3 References 56
  - 2.34.4 External links 56
- 2.35 Weatherby SA-08 56
  - 2.35.1 Models 56
- 2.36 Winchester Model 1911 57
  - 2.36.1 Description and development 57
  - 2.36.2 Design and safety flaws 57
  - 2.36.3 References 57
- 2.37 List of semi-automatic shotguns 57
  - 2.37.1 See also 58
  - 2.37.2 References 58

3 Automatic Shotguns   59
- 3.1 Atchisson Assault Shotgun 59
  - 3.1.1 History 59

- 3.1.2 Ammunition ... 59
- 3.1.3 Usage ... 59
- 3.1.4 See also ... 59
- 3.1.5 References ... 60
- 3.1.6 External links ... 60
- 3.2 Daewoo Precision Industries USAS-12 ... 60
  - 3.2.1 Design ... 60
  - 3.2.2 History ... 60
  - 3.2.3 See also ... 61
  - 3.2.4 References ... 61
  - 3.2.5 External links ... 61
- 3.3 Franchi mod .410 ... 61
  - 3.3.1 References ... 61
- 3.4 Gordon Close-Support Weapon System ... 61
  - 3.4.1 Overview ... 61
  - 3.4.2 Variants ... 61
  - 3.4.3 References ... 62
- 3.5 Heckler & Koch HK CAWS ... 62
  - 3.5.1 Development ... 62
  - 3.5.2 References ... 62
  - 3.5.3 See also ... 62
  - 3.5.4 External links ... 62
- 3.6 Pancor Jackhammer ... 62
  - 3.6.1 Development ... 62
  - 3.6.2 Design ... 62
  - 3.6.3 Related developments ... 63
  - 3.6.4 See also ... 63
  - 3.6.5 References ... 63
  - 3.6.6 External links ... 63
- 3.7 Smith & Wesson AS ... 63
  - 3.7.1 References ... 63
  - 3.7.2 See also ... 63
- 3.8 Special Operations Weapon ... 64
  - 3.8.1 History ... 64
  - 3.8.2 See also ... 64
  - 3.8.3 References ... 64
  - 3.8.4 External links ... 64

4 Bolt-Action shotguns ... 65

4.1	M26 Modular Accessory Shotgun System		65
	4.1.1	Development	65
	4.1.2	Specifications	66
	4.1.3	See also	66
	4.1.4	References	66
	4.1.5	External links	66
4.2	Marlin Model 25MG		67
	4.2.1	References	67
4.3	Marlin Model 55		67
	4.3.1	Variants	67
	4.3.2	References	67
	4.3.3	External links	67
4.4	Mossberg 183		67
	4.4.1	Variants	67
	4.4.2	References	68
4.5	Mossberg 185		68
	4.5.1	Variants	68
	4.5.2	External links	68
	4.5.3	References	68

5 Bullpup Shotguns — 69

5.1	High Standard Model 10		69
	5.1.1	History and design	69
	5.1.2	Service	69
	5.1.3	Users	69
	5.1.4	See also	70
	5.1.5	External links	70
5.2	Kel-Tec KSG		70
	5.2.1	Operation	70
	5.2.2	Revisions	70
	5.2.3	See also	70
	5.2.4	References	70
	5.2.5	External links	70
5.3	Neostead		70
	5.3.1	US Debut and history	71
	5.3.2	Design and production	71
	5.3.3	Patent drawings	71
	5.3.4	See also	71
	5.3.5	References	71

6 Double-Barreled Shotguns — 72

- 6.1 Beretta 682 — 72
  - 6.1.1 References — 72
  - 6.1.2 External links — 72
- 6.2 Beretta DT-10 — 72
  - 6.2.1 References — 73
  - 6.2.2 External links — 73
- 6.3 Beretta Silver Pigeon — 73
  - 6.3.1 References — 73
  - 6.3.2 External links — 73
- 6.4 Browning Citori — 73
  - 6.4.1 Origin — 73
  - 6.4.2 Features — 73
  - 6.4.3 References — 74
  - 6.4.4 External links — 74
- 6.5 Browning Superposed — 74
  - 6.5.1 History — 74
  - 6.5.2 References — 75
- 6.6 Cynergy Shotgun — 75
  - 6.6.1 Mechanism differences — 75
  - 6.6.2 History of the design — 75
  - 6.6.3 Sources — 76
  - 6.6.4 References — 76
  - 6.6.5 External links — 76
- 6.7 Ithaca Auto & Burglar — 76
  - 6.7.1 Variants — 77
  - 6.7.2 Demise — 77
  - 6.7.3 See also — 77
  - 6.7.4 References — 77
  - 6.7.5 External links — 77
- 6.8 Paradox gun — 77
  - 6.8.1 History — 78
  - 6.8.2 References — 79
  - 6.8.3 External links — 79
- 6.9 Remington Spartan 310 — 79
  - 6.9.1 Features — 79
  - 6.9.2 See also — 79

5.3.6 External links — 71

6.9.3	Notes	79
6.9.4	External links	79
6.10	Ruger Gold Label	79
6.10.1	Features	79
6.10.2	Models	80
6.10.3	Awards	80
6.10.4	Notes	80
6.10.5	External links	80
6.11	Ruger Red Label	80
6.11.1	History	80
6.11.2	Design	80
6.11.3	Criticism	80
6.11.4	References	80
6.12	Stoeger Coach Gun	81
6.12.1	Features	81
6.12.2	Models	81
6.12.3	Notes	81
6.12.4	External links	81
6.13	Stoeger Condor	81
6.13.1	Condor Supreme	81
6.13.2	Condor Outback	81
6.13.3	Notes	82
6.13.4	External links	82
6.14	Ugartechea	82
6.14.1	Overview	82
6.14.2	History	82
6.14.3	Further Changes	82
6.14.4	References	83
6.14.5	External links	83
6.15	Winchester Model 21	83
6.15.1	Production from 1931–1959	83
6.15.2	Custom Shop Production 1960–1991	83
6.15.3	Notes	84
6.15.4	Resources	84
7	**Lever-Action Shotguns**	**85**
7.1	Martini–Henry	85
7.1.1	Overview	85
7.1.2	Operation of the Martini action	88

- 7.1.3 In popular culture 88
- 7.1.4 See also 89
- 7.1.5 References 89
- 7.1.6 External links 89
- 7.2 Winchester Model 1887/1901 89
  - 7.2.1 Overview 90
  - 7.2.2 Reproduction 90
  - 7.2.3 Portrayals in popular culture 90
  - 7.2.4 References 91
  - 7.2.5 External links 91

8 Pump-Action Shotguns — 92
- 8.1 Bandayevsky RB-12 92
  - 8.1.1 See also 92
  - 8.1.2 References 92
  - 8.1.3 External links 92
- 8.2 Benelli Nova 92
  - 8.2.1 Technical specifications 92
  - 8.2.2 Common Features 92
  - 8.2.3 Recoil Reducer 93
  - 8.2.4 References 93
  - 8.2.5 External links 93
- 8.3 Benelli Supernova 93
  - 8.3.1 Technical specifications 93
  - 8.3.2 Common Features 93
  - 8.3.3 Recoil Reducer 94
  - 8.3.4 References 94
  - 8.3.5 External links 94
- 8.4 Brixia PM-5 94
  - 8.4.1 See also 94
  - 8.4.2 External links 94
- 8.5 Ciener Ultimate Over/Under 94
  - 8.5.1 Notes 94
  - 8.5.2 References 95
  - 8.5.3 See also 95
- 8.6 Fabarm SDASS Tactical 95
  - 8.6.1 SDASS Tactical 95
  - 8.6.2 Variants 95
  - 8.6.3 Related weapons 95

- 8.6.4 References ... 96
- 8.6.5 External links ... 96
- 8.7 FN P-12 ... 96
  - 8.7.1 Design ... 96
  - 8.7.2 References ... 96
  - 8.7.3 External links ... 96
- 8.8 FN TPS ... 96
  - 8.8.1 References ... 96
  - 8.8.2 External links ... 96
- 8.9 Heckler & Koch FABARM FP6 ... 96
  - 8.9.1 History ... 96
  - 8.9.2 Design details ... 96
  - 8.9.3 Operation ... 97
  - 8.9.4 Accessories ... 97
  - 8.9.5 Variants ... 97
  - 8.9.6 Users ... 97
  - 8.9.7 See also ... 98
  - 8.9.8 Notes ... 98
  - 8.9.9 References ... 98
- 8.10 Ithaca 37 ... 98
  - 8.10.1 History ... 98
  - 8.10.2 Users ... 98
  - 8.10.3 Operation ... 98
  - 8.10.4 Versions ... 99
  - 8.10.5 Argentine variants ... 99
  - 8.10.6 Users ... 99
  - 8.10.7 See also ... 99
  - 8.10.8 Notes ... 99
  - 8.10.9 References ... 99
  - 8.10.10 External links ... 99
- 8.11 KAC Masterkey ... 100
  - 8.11.1 Users ... 100
  - 8.11.2 See also ... 100
  - 8.11.3 References ... 100
  - 8.11.4 External links ... 100
- 8.12 KS-23 ... 100
  - 8.12.1 History ... 100
  - 8.12.2 Ammunition ... 100

- 8.12.3 Variants 101
- 8.12.4 Users 101
- 8.12.5 See also 102
- 8.12.6 References 102
- 8.12.7 Further reading 102
- 8.12.8 External links 102
- 8.13 MAG-7 102
  - 8.13.1 History and design 102
  - 8.13.2 Service 103
  - 8.13.3 Proprietary ammunition 103
  - 8.13.4 Current status 103
  - 8.13.5 M7 *Dual Riot* 103
  - 8.13.6 See also 103
  - 8.13.7 References 103
  - 8.13.8 External links 103
- 8.14 Mossberg 500 104
  - 8.14.1 Basic features 104
  - 8.14.2 Model 500 options 104
  - 8.14.3 Model 500 variants 106
  - 8.14.4 Accessories and combinations 107
  - 8.14.5 Maverick Arms subsidiary 108
  - 8.14.6 Model numbers 108
  - 8.14.7 Military use 108
  - 8.14.8 See also 109
  - 8.14.9 References 109
  - 8.14.10 External links 110
- 8.15 Mossberg Maverick 110
  - 8.15.1 Overview 110
  - 8.15.2 See also 110
  - 8.15.3 References 110
  - 8.15.4 External links 110
- 8.16 New Haven 600 110
  - 8.16.1 Model numbers 111
  - 8.16.2 See also 111
  - 8.16.3 External links 111
- 8.17 Norinco HP9-1 111
  - 8.17.1 External links 111
- 8.18 Remington Model 10 111

- 8.18.1 Military use ... 111
- 8.18.2 References ... 111
- 8.19 Remington Model 17 ... 111
  - 8.19.1 References ... 112
- 8.20 Remington Model 31 ... 112
  - 8.20.1 History ... 112
  - 8.20.2 External links ... 112
- 8.21 Remington Model 870 ... 112
  - 8.21.1 Development ... 112
  - 8.21.2 Design details ... 113
  - 8.21.3 Variants ... 113
  - 8.21.4 Users ... 114
  - 8.21.5 See also ... 114
  - 8.21.6 References ... 114
  - 8.21.7 External links ... 116
- 8.22 Remington Model 887 ... 116
  - 8.22.1 Design and Features ... 116
  - 8.22.2 Remington Model 870 Comparison ... 116
  - 8.22.3 Variations ... 117
  - 8.22.4 See also ... 117
  - 8.22.5 Notes ... 117
- 8.23 RMB-93 ... 117
  - 8.23.1 Variants and commercial availability ... 117
  - 8.23.2 Users ... 118
  - 8.23.3 See also ... 118
  - 8.23.4 References ... 118
  - 8.23.5 Sources ... 118
  - 8.23.6 External links ... 118
- 8.24 Serbu Super-Shorty ... 118
  - 8.24.1 Users ... 118
  - 8.24.2 See also ... 118
  - 8.24.3 References ... 118
  - 8.24.4 External links ... 119
- 8.25 Stevens Model 520/620 ... 119
  - 8.25.1 Background ... 119
  - 8.25.2 Model 520 ... 119
  - 8.25.3 Model 520A ... 120
  - 8.25.4 Model 620 ... 120

- 8.25.5 Model 620A 121
- 8.25.6 Model 520-30 and 620A (US Military) 121
- 8.25.7 References 121
- 8.26 Stevens Model 77E 122
  - 8.26.1 References 122
- 8.27 TOZ-194 122
  - 8.27.1 Variants 122
  - 8.27.2 Notes 122
  - 8.27.3 See also 122
  - 8.27.4 External links 123
- 8.28 UTAS UTS-15 123
  - 8.28.1 Background 123
  - 8.28.2 Features 123
  - 8.28.3 Variants 123
  - 8.28.4 Critical Reception and Malfunctions 124
  - 8.28.5 See also 124
  - 8.28.6 In popular culture 124
  - 8.28.7 References 124
- 8.29 Valtro PM-5/PM-5-350 124
  - 8.29.1 See also 124
  - 8.29.2 External links 124
- 8.30 Winchester Model 1200 124
  - 8.30.1 History 125
  - 8.30.2 Description 125
  - 8.30.3 Bayonet 125
  - 8.30.4 Variants 125
  - 8.30.5 Users 125
  - 8.30.6 See also 126
  - 8.30.7 References 126
  - 8.30.8 External links 126
- 8.31 Winchester Model 1897 126
  - 8.31.1 History 126
  - 8.31.2 Description 127
  - 8.31.3 Military use 128
  - 8.31.4 World War I protests 129
  - 8.31.5 Other uses 129
  - 8.31.6 See also 129
  - 8.31.7 References 129

			8.31.8	Bibliography	130
			8.31.9	External links	130
	8.32	Winchester Model 1912			130
		8.32.1	Description		130
		8.32.2	Military use		131
		8.32.3	See also		131
		8.32.4	References		131
		8.32.5	External links		131

9 Revolver Shotguns 132

	9.1	Armsel Striker		132
		9.1.1	History	132
		9.1.2	Design and features	132
		9.1.3	Availability in the USA	132
		9.1.4	Variants	132
		9.1.5	See also	133
		9.1.6	References	133
		9.1.7	External links	133
	9.2	ENARM Pentagun		133
		9.2.1	References	133
	9.3	MTs255		133
		9.3.1	See also	133
		9.3.2	External links	133
	9.4	RGA-86		134
		9.4.1	See also	134

10 Text and image sources, contributors, and licenses 135

10.1	Text	135
10.2	Images	144
10.3	Content license	154

Chapter 1

Introduction to Shotgun Types

1.1 Shotgun

This article is about the type of gun. For other uses, see Shotgun (disambiguation).

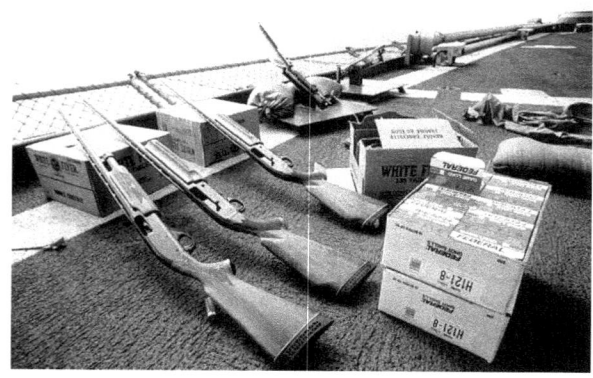

A pump-action Remington 870, two semi-automatic Remington 1100 shotguns, 20 boxes of shotgun shells, a clay trap, and three boxes of clay pigeons

A **shotgun** (also known as a **scattergun** and **peppergun**,[1] or historically as a **fowling piece**) is a firearm that is usually designed to be fired from the shoulder, which uses the energy of a fixed shell to fire a number of small spherical pellets called shot, or a solid projectile called a slug. Shotguns come in a wide variety of sizes, ranging from 5.5 mm (.22 inch) bore up to 5 cm (2.0 in) bore, and in a range of firearm operating mechanisms, including breech loading, single-barreled, double or combination gun, pump-action, bolt-, and lever-action, semi-automatic, and even fully automatic variants.

A shotgun is generally a smoothbore firearm, which means that the inside of the barrel is not rifled. Preceding smoothbore firearms, such as the musket, were widely used by armies in the 18th century. The direct ancestor to the shotgun, the blunderbuss, was also used in a similar variety of roles from self defence to riot control. It was often used by cavalry troops due to its generally shorter length and ease of use, as well as by coachmen for its substantial power. However, in the 19th century, these weapons were largely replaced on the battlefield with breechloading rifled firearms, which were more accurate over longer ranges. The military value of shotguns was rediscovered in the First World War, when American forces used 12-gauge pump action shotguns in close-quarters trench fighting to great effect. Since then, it has been used in a variety of roles in civilian, law enforcement, and military applications.

The shot pellets from a shotgun spread upon leaving the barrel, and the power of the burning charge is divided among the pellets, which means that the energy of any one ball of shot is fairly low. In a hunting context, this makes shotguns useful primarily for hunting birds and other small game. However, in a military or law enforcement context, the large number of projectiles makes the shotgun useful as a close quarters combat weapon or a defensive weapon. Militants or insurgents may use shotguns in asymmetric engagements, as shotguns are commonly-owned civilian weapons in many countries. Shotguns are also used for target shooting sports such as skeet, trap, and sporting clays. These involve shooting clay disks, known as clay pigeons, thrown in various ways.

1.1.1 Characteristics

Shotguns come in a wide variety of forms, from very small up to massive punt guns, and in nearly every type of firearm operating mechanism. The common characteristics that make a shotgun unique center around the requirements of firing shot. These features are the features typical of a shotgun shell, namely a relatively short, wide cartridge, with straight walls, and operating at a relatively low pressure.

Ammunition for shotguns is referred to in the USA as shotgun shells, shotshells, or just shells (when it is not likely to be confused with artillery shells). The term cartridges is standard usage in the United Kingdom.

The shot is usually fired from a smoothbore barrel; another

configuration is the rifled slug barrel, which fires more accurate solitary projectiles.

1.1.2 Uses

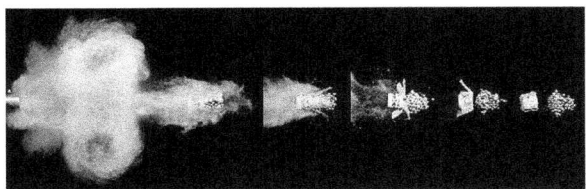

Series of individual 1/1,000,000 second exposures showing shotgun firing shot and wadding separation

The typical use of a shotgun is against small and fast moving targets, often while in the air. The spreading of the shot allows the user to point the shotgun close to the target, rather than having to aim precisely as in the case of a single projectile. The disadvantages of shot are limited range and limited penetration of the shot, which is why shotguns are used at short ranges, and typically against smaller targets. Larger shot sizes, up to the extreme case of the single projectile slug load, result in increased penetration, but at the expense of fewer projectiles and lower probability of hitting the target.

Aside from the most common use against small, fast moving targets, the shotgun has several advantages when used against still targets. First, it has enormous stopping power at short range, more than nearly all handguns and many rifles. Though many believe the shotgun is a great firearm for inexperienced shooters, the truth is, at close range, the spread of shot is not very large at all, and competency in aiming is still required. A typical self-defense load of buckshot contains 8-27 large lead pellets, resulting in many wound tracks in the target. Also, unlike a fully jacketed rifle bullet, each pellet of shot is less likely to penetrate walls and hit bystanders.[2] It is favored by law enforcement for its low penetration and high stopping power.

On the other hand, the hit potential of a defensive shotgun is often overstated. The typical defensive shot is taken at very close ranges, at which the shot charge expands no more than a few centimeters.[2] This means the shotgun must still be aimed at the target with some care. Balancing this is the fact that shot spreads further upon entering the target, and the multiple wound channels of a defensive load are far more likely to produce a disabling wound than a rifle or handgun.[3]

Vincent Hancock in the men's skeet finals at the 2008 Summer Olympics

Sporting

Some of the most common uses of shotguns are the sports of skeet shooting, trap shooting, and sporting clays. These involve shooting clay discs, also known as clay pigeons, thrown in by hand and by machine. Both skeet and trap competitions are featured at the Olympic Games.

Hunting

The shotgun is popular for bird hunting, it is also used for more general forms of hunting especially in semi-populated areas where the range of rifle bullets may pose a hazard. Use of a smooth bore shotgun with a rifled slug or, alternatively, a rifled barrel shotgun with a sabot slug, improves accuracy to 100 m (110 yd) or more. This is well within the range of the majority of kill shots by experienced hunters using shotguns.

However, given the relatively low muzzle velocity of slug ammunition, typically around 500 m/s (about 1600 feet per second), and the blunt, poorly streamlined shape of typical slugs (which cause them to lose velocity very rapidly, compared to rifle bullets), a hunter must pay close attention to the ballistics of the particular ammunition used to ensure an effective and humane kill shot.

At any reasonable range, shotgun slugs make effective lethal wounds due to their tremendous mass, reducing the length of time that an animal might suffer. For example, a typical 12 gauge shotgun slug is a blunt piece of metal that could be described as an 18 mm (.729 inch) caliber that weighs 28 grams (432 grains). For comparison, a common deer-hunting rifle round is a 7.62 mm (.308 inch) slug weighing 9.7 grams (150 grains), but the dynamics of the rifle cartridge allow for a different type of wound, and a much further reach.

Shotguns are often used with rifled barrels in locations

1.1. SHOTGUN

where it is not lawful to hunt with a rifle. Typically, a sabot slug is used in these barrels for maximum accuracy and performance. Shotguns are often used to hunt whitetail deer in the thick brush and briers of the Southeastern and upper Midwestern United States, where, due to the dense cover, ranges tend to be close - 25m or less.

Sabot slugs are essentially very large hollowpoint bullets, and are streamlined for maximum spin and accuracy when shot through a rifled barrel. They have greater ranges than older Foster and Brenneke-type slugs.

A Gurkha Contingent trooper in Singapore armed with a folding stock pump shotgun

Law enforcement

In the US and Canada, shotguns are widely used as a support weapon by police forces. One of the rationales for issuing shotguns is that, even without much training, an officer will probably be able to hit targets at close to intermediate range, due to the "spreading" effect of buckshot. This is largely a myth, as the spread of buckshot at 25 feet averages 8 inches, which is still very capable of missing a target. Some police forces are replacing shotguns in this role with carbine rifles such as AR-15s. Shotguns are also used in roadblock situations, where police are blocking a highway to search cars for suspects. In the US, law enforcement agencies often use riot shotguns, especially for crowd and riot control where they may be loaded with less-lethal rounds such as rubber bullets or bean bags. Shotguns are also often used as breaching devices to defeat locks.

Military

See also: Combat shotgun

Shotguns are common weapons in military use, particularly for special purposes. Shotguns are found aboard naval vessels for shipboard security, because the weapon is very effective at close range as a way of repelling enemy boarding parties. In a naval setting, stainless steel shotguns are often used, because regular steel is more prone to corrosion in the marine environment. Shotguns are also used by military police units. U.S. Marines have used shotguns since their inception at the squad level, often in the hands of NCOs, while the U.S. Army often issued them to a squad's point man. Shotguns were modified for and used in the trench warfare of WWI, in the jungle combat of WWII and Vietnam and are being used in Iraq, being popular with soldiers in urban combat environments. Some U.S. units in Iraq use shotguns with special frangible breaching rounds to blow the locks off doors when they are making a surprise entry into a dwelling.

Home and personal defense

Shotguns are a popular means of home defense for many of the same reasons they are preferred for close-quarters tasks in law enforcement and the military.

1.1.3 Design features for various uses

Compared to handguns, shotguns are heavier, larger, and not as maneuverable in close quarters (which also presents a greater retention problem), but do have these advantages:

- They are generally much more powerful.
- The average shooter can engage multiple targets faster than with a handgun.
- They are generally perceived as more intimidating.
- On average, a quality pump-action shotgun is generally less expensive than a quality handgun (self-loading shotguns are generally more expensive than their pump-action counterparts).
- When loaded with smaller shot, a shotgun will not penetrate walls as readily as rifle and pistol rounds, making it safer for non-combatants when fired in or around

populated structures. This comes at a price, however, as smaller shot may not penetrate deeply enough to cause an immediately incapacitating wound; those who recommend birdshot for minimizing wall penetration also suggest backing it up with a larger buckshot if the first shot fails to stop the threat.[4]

1.1.4 Types

A U.S. Marine fires a Benelli M4 shotgun during training in Arta, Djibouti, December 23, 2006.

The wide range of forms the shotgun can take leads to some significant differences between what is technically a shotgun and what is legally considered a shotgun. A fairly broad attempt to define a shotgun is made in the United States Code (18 USC 921), which defines the shotgun as "a weapon designed or redesigned, made or remade, and intended to be fired from the shoulder, and designed or redesigned and made or remade to use the energy of the explosive in a fixed shotgun shell to fire through a smooth bore either a number of ball shot or a single projectile for each single pull of the trigger."

A rifled slug, with finned rifling designed to enable the projectile to be safely fired through a choked barrel, is an example of a single projectile. Some shotguns have rifled barrels and are designed to be used with a "saboted" bullet, one which is typically encased in a two-piece plastic ring (*sabot*) designed to peel away after it exits the barrel, leaving the bullet, now spinning after passing through the rifled barrel, to continue toward the target. These shotguns, although they have rifled barrels, still use a shotgun-style shell instead of a rifle cartridge and may in fact still fire regular multipellet shotgun shells, but the rifling in the barrel will affect the shot pattern. The use of a rifled barrel blurs the distinction between rifle and shotgun, and in fact the early rifled shotgun barrels went by the name *Paradox* for just that reason. Hunting laws may differentiate between smooth barreled and rifled barreled guns.

Riot gun has long been a synonym for a shotgun, especially a short-barrelled shotgun. During the 19th and early 20th century, these were used to disperse rioters and revolutionaries. The wide spray of the shot ensured a large group would be hit, but the light shot would ensure more wounds than fatalities. When the ground was paved, police officers would often ricochet the shot off the ground, slowing down the shot and spreading pattern even further. To this day specialized police and defensive shotguns are called riot shotguns. The introduction of rubber bullets and bean bag rounds ended the practice of using shot for the most part, but riot shotguns are still used to fire a variety of less-lethal rounds for riot control.

A **sawed-off shotgun** (or "sawn-off") refers to a shotgun whose barrel has been shortened, leaving it more maneuverable, easier to use at short range and more readily concealed. Many countries establish a legal minimum barrel length that precludes easy concealment (this length is 18 inches (460 mm) in the U.S.). The sawed-off shotgun is sometimes known as a "Lupara" (in Italian a generic reference to the word "*lupo*" ("wolf")) in Southern Italy and Sicily.

Coach guns are similar to sawn-off shotguns, except they are manufactured with an 46 cm (18") barrel and are legal for civilian ownership in some jurisdictions. Coach guns are also more commonly associated with the American Old West or Australian Colonial period, and often used for hunting in bush, scrub, or marshland where a longer barrel would be unwieldy or impractical.

A **backpacker shotgun** has a short barrel and either a full-size stock or pistol grip, depending on legislation in intended markets. The overall length of these weapons is frequently less than 90 cm (35 in), with some measuring up at less than 63 cm (25 in). These weapons are typically break-action .410 "gauge" (caliber), single-barrel designs with no magazine and no automatic ejection capability. They typically employ a cylinder bore and sometimes are available in modified choke as well.

Backpacker shotguns are popular for "home defense" purposes and as "survival" weapons. Other examples include a variety of .410 / rifle "survival" guns manufactured in over/under designs. In the drilling arrangement, a rimfire or centrefire rifle barrel is located beneath the barrel of a .410 gauge shotgun. Generally, there is one manually cocked external hammer and an external selection lever to select which caliber of cartridge to fire. A notable example is the Springfield Armory M6 Scout, a .410 / .22 issued to United States Air Force personnel as a "survival" gun in the event of a forced landing or accident in a wilderness area. Variants have been used by Israeli, Canadian, and American armed forces. Shotgun-rifle combination guns with two, three, and occasionally even four barrels are available from a number of makers, primarily European. These provided flexibility, enabling the hunter to effectively shoot at flushing birds or more distant small mammals while only carrying one gun.

1.1.5 History

Confederate cavalryman

Most early firearms, such as the blunderbuss, arquebus, and musket had large diameter, smoothbore barrels, and could fire shot as well as solid balls. A firearm intended for use in wing shooting of birds was known as a **fowling piece**. The 1728 *Cyclopaedia* defines a *fowling piece* as:

> *Fowling Piece, a portable Fire Arm for the shooting of Birds. See Fire Arm.*
>
> *Of Fowling Pieces, those are reputed the best, which have the longest Barrel, vis. from 5½ foot to 6; with an indifferent Bore, under Harquebus: Tho' for different Occasions they shou'd be of different Sorts, and Sizes. But in all, 'tis essential the Barrel be well polish'd and smooth within; and the Bore all of a Bigness, from one End to another...*[5]

For example, the Brown Bess musket, in service with the British army from 1722 to 1838, had a 19 mm (.75 inch) smoothbore barrel, roughly the same as a 10 gauge shotgun, and was 157 cm (62 in) long, just short of the above recommended 168 cm (5½ feet). On the other hand, records from the Plymouth colony show a maximum length of 137 cm (4½ feet) for fowling pieces,[6] shorter than the typical musket.

Shot was also used in warfare; the buck and ball loading, combining a musket ball with three or six buckshot, was used throughout the history of the smoothbore musket. The first recorded use of the term *shotgun* was in 1776 in Kentucky. It was noted as part of the "frontier language of the West" by James Fenimore Cooper.

With the adoption of smaller bores and rifled barrels, the shotgun began to emerge as a separate entity. Shotguns have long been the preferred method for sport hunting of birds, and the largest shotguns, the punt guns, were used for commercial hunting. The double-barreled shotgun has changed little since the development of the boxlock action in 1875. Modern innovations such as interchangeable chokes and subgauge inserts make the double-barreled shotgun the shotgun of choice in skeet, trap shooting, and sporting clays, as well as with many hunters.

As wing shooting has been a prestige sport, specialty gunsmiths such as Krieghoff or Perazzi have produced fancy double-barrel guns for wealthy European and American hunters. These weapons can cost US$5,000 or more; some elaborately decorated presentation guns have sold for up to US$100,000.[7]

During its long history, the shotgun has been favored by bird hunters, guards, and law enforcement officials. The shotgun has fallen in and out of favor with military forces several times in its long history. Shotguns and similar weapons are simpler than long-range rifles, and were developed earlier. The development of more accurate and deadlier long-range rifles minimized the usefulness of the shotgun on the open battlefields of European wars. But armies have "rediscovered" the shotgun for specialty uses many times.

19th century

During the 19th century, shotguns were mainly employed by cavalry units. Both sides of the American Civil War employed shotguns. U.S. cavalry used the shotgun extensively during the Indian Wars in the latter half of the 19th century. Mounted units favored the shotgun for its moving target effectiveness, and devastating close-range firepower. The shotgun was also favored by citizen militias and similar groups.

With the exception of cavalry units, the shotgun saw less and less use throughout the 19th century on the battlefield. As a defense weapon it remained popular with guards and lawmen, however, and the shotgun became one of many symbols of the American Old West. Lawman Cody Lyons killed two men with a shotgun; his friend Doc Holliday's only confirmed kill was with a shotgun. The weapon both these men used was the short-barreled version favored by private strongbox guards on stages and trains. These guards, called express messengers, became known as shotgun messengers, since they rode with the weapon (loaded with buckshot) for defense against bandits. Passenger carriages carrying a strongbox usually had at least one private guard armed with a shotgun riding in front of the coach, next to the driver. This practice has survived in American slang; the term "riding shotgun" is used for the passenger who sits in the front passenger seat. The shotgun was a popular weapon for personal protection in the American Old West, requiring less skill on the part of the user than a revolver.

Hammerless shotguns

The origins of the hammerless shotgun are European but otherwise obscure. The earliest breechloading shotguns originated in France and Belgium in the early 19th century (see also the history of the Pinfire) and a number of them such as those by Robert and Chateauvillard from the 1830s and 1840s did not use hammers. In fact during these decades a wide variety of ingenious weapons, including rifles, adopted what is now often known as a 'needle-fire' method of igniting the charge, where a firing pin or a longer sharper needle provided the necessary impact. The most widely used British hammerless needle-fire shotgun was the unusual hinged-chamber fixed-barrel breech-loader by Joseph Needham, produced from the 1850s. By the 1860s hammerless guns were increasingly used in Europe both in war and sport although hammer guns were still very much in the majority. The first significant encroachment on hammer guns was a hammerless patent which could be used with a conventional side-lock. This was British gunmaker T Murcott's 1871 action nicknamed the 'mousetrap' on account of its loud snap action. However, the most successful hammerless innovation of the 1870s was Anson and Deeley's boxlock patent of 1875. This simple but ingenious design only used four moving parts allowing the production of cheaper and reliable shotguns.

Daniel Myron LeFever is credited with the invention of the American hammerless shotgun. Working for Barber & LeFever in Syracuse, N.Y. he introduced his first hammerless shotgun in 1878. This gun was cocked with external cocking levers on the side of the breech. He went on to patent the first truly automatic hammerless shotgun in 1883. This gun automatically cocked itself when the breech was closed. He later developed the mechanism to automatically eject the shells when the breech was opened.

John Moses Browning

One of the men most responsible for the modern development of the shotgun was prolific gun designer John Browning. While working for Winchester Firearms, Browning revolutionized shotgun design. In 1887, Browning introduced the Model 1887 Lever Action Repeating Shotgun, which loaded a fresh cartridge from its internal magazine by the operation of the action lever. Before this time most shotguns were the 'break open' type.

This development was greatly overshadowed by two further innovations he introduced at the end of the 19th century. In 1893, Browning produced the Model 1893 Pump Action Shotgun, introducing the now familiar pump action to the market. And in 1900, he patented the Browning Auto-5, the world's first semi-automatic shotgun. The Browning Auto-5 remained in production until 1998.

World wars

The decline in military use of shotguns reversed in World War I. American forces under General Pershing employed 12-gauge pump action shotguns when they were deployed to the Western front in 1917. These shotguns were fitted with bayonets and a heat shield so the barrel could be gripped while the bayonet was deployed. Shotguns fitted in this fashion became known as *trench guns* by the United States Army. Those without such modifications were known as *riot guns*. After World War I, the United States military began referring to all shotguns as *riot guns*.

Due to the cramped conditions of trench warfare, the American shotguns were extremely effective. Germany even filed an official diplomatic protest against their use, alleging they violated the laws of warfare. The judge advocate general reviewed the protest, and it was rejected because the Germans protested use of lead shot (which would have been illegal) but military shot was plated. This is the only occasion the legality of the shotgun's use in warfare has been questioned.[8]

During World War II, the shotgun was not heavily used in the war in Europe by official military forces. However, the shotgun was a favorite weapon of Allied-supported partisans, such as the French Resistance. By contrast, in the Pacific theater, thick jungles and heavily fortified positions made the shotgun a favorite weapon of the United States Marines. Marines tended to use pump shotguns, since the pump action was less likely to jam in the humid and dirty conditions of the Pacific campaign. Similarly, the United States Navy used pump shotguns to guard ships when in port in Chinese harbors (e.g., Shanghai). The United States Army Air Forces also used pump shotguns to guard bombers and other aircraft against saboteurs

A United States Marine carrying a Winchester M97 shotgun during World War II

when parked on airbases across the Pacific and on the West Coast of the United States. Pump and semi-automatic shotguns were used in marksmanship training, particularly for bomber gunners. The most common pump shotguns used for these duties were the 12 gauge Winchester Model 97 and Model 12. The break-open action, single barrel shotgun was used by the British Home Guard and U.S. home security forces. Notably, industrial centers (such as the Gopher State Steel Works) were guarded by National Guard soldiers with Winchester Model 37 12 gauge shotguns.

Late 20th century to present

Since the end of World War II, the shotgun has remained a specialty weapon for modern armies. It has been deployed for specialized tasks where its strengths were put to particularly good use. It was used to defend machine gun emplacements during the Korean War, American and French jungle patrols used shotguns during the Vietnam War, and shotguns saw extensive use as door breaching and close quarter weapons in the early stages of the Iraq War, and saw limited use in tank crews.[9] Many modern navies make extensive use of shotguns by personnel engaged in boarding hostile ships, as any shots fired will almost certainly be over a short range. Nonetheless, shotguns are far less common in military use than rifles, carbines, submachineguns, or pistols.

On the other hand, the shotgun has become a standard in law enforcement use. A variety of specialty less-lethal or non-lethal ammunitions, such as tear gas shells, bean bags, flares, explosive sonic stun rounds, and rubber projectiles, all packaged into 12 gauge shotgun shells, are produced specifically for the law enforcement market. Recently, Taser International introduced a self-contained electronic weapon which is fired from a standard 12 gauge shotgun.[10]

The shotgun remains a standard firearm for hunting throughout the world for all sorts of game from birds and small game to large game such as deer. The versatility of the shotgun as a hunting weapon has steadily increased as slug rounds and more advanced rifled barrels have given shotguns longer range and higher killing power. The shotgun has become a ubiquitous firearm in the hunting community.

1.1.6 Design factors

Action

Action is the term for the operating mechanism of a gun. There are many types of shotguns, typically categorized by the number of barrels or the way the gun is reloaded.

Break-action For most of the history of the shotgun, the break-action breech loading double was the most common type, typically divided into two subtypes: the traditional "side by side" shotgun features two barrels mounted one beside the other (as the name suggests), whereas the "over and under" shotgun has the two barrels mounted one on top of the other. Side by side shotguns were traditionally used for hunting and other sporting pursuits (early long barrelled side-by side shotguns were known as "fowling pieces" for their use hunting ducks and other birds), whereas over and under shotguns are more commonly associated with sporting use (such as clay pigeon and skeet shooting). Both types of double-barrel shotgun are used for hunting and sporting use, with the individual configuration largely being a matter of personal preference.

Another, less commonly encountered type of break-action shotgun is the combination gun, which is an over and under design with one shotgun barrel and one rifle barrel (more often rifle on top, but rifle on bottom was not uncommon). There is also a class of break action guns called *drillings*, which contain three barrels, usually two shotgun barrels of

A view of the break-action of a typical double-barrelled shotgun, shown with the action open

the same gauge and a rifle barrel, though the only common theme is that at least one barrel be a shotgun barrel. The most common arrangement was essentially a side by side shotgun with the rifle barrel below and centered. Usually a drilling containing more than one rifle barrel would have both rifle barrels in the same caliber, but examples do exist with different caliber barrels, usually a .22 long rifle and a centerfire cartridge. Although very rare, drillings with three and even four (a *vierling*) shotgun barrels were made.

A Winchester M1897, one of the first successful pump-action shotgun designs

Pump-action In pump-action shotguns, a sliding forearm handle (the *pump*) works the action, extracting the spent shell and inserting a new one while cocking the hammer or striker as the pump is worked. A pump gun is typically fed from a tubular magazine underneath the barrel, which also serves as a guide for the pump. The rounds are fed in one by one through a port in the receiver, where they are lifted by a lever called the *elevator* and pushed forward into the chamber by the bolt. A pair of latches at the rear of the magazine hold the rounds in place and facilitate feeding of one shell at a time. If it is desired to load the gun fully, a round may be loaded through the ejection port directly into the chamber, or cycled from the magazine, which is then topped off with another round. Well-known examples include the Winchester Model 1897, Remington 870 and Mossberg 500/590.

Pump-action shotguns are common hunting, fowling and sporting shotguns. Hunting models generally have a barrel between 600 and 700 mm (24"–28"). Tube-fed models designed for hunting often come with a dowel rod or other stop that is inserted into the magazine and reduces the capacity of the gun to three shells (two in the magazine and one chambered) as is mandated by U.S. federal law when hunting migratory birds. They can also easily be used with an empty magazine as a single-shot weapon, by simply dropping the next round to be fired into the open ejection port after the spent round is ejected. For this reason, pump-actions are commonly used to teach novice shooters under supervision, as the trainer can load each round more quickly than with a break-action, while unlike a break-action the student can maintain his grip on the gun and concentrate on proper handling and firing of the weapon.

Pump action shotguns with shorter barrels and little or no barrel choke are highly popular for use in home defense, military and law enforcement, and are commonly known as riot guns. The minimum barrel length for shotguns in most of the U.S. is 18 inches (460 mm), and this barrel length (sometimes 18.5–20 in (470–510 mm) to increase magazine capacity and/or ensure the gun is legal regardless of measuring differences[11]) is the primary choice for riot shotguns. The shorter barrel makes the weapon easier to maneuver around corners and in tight spaces, though slightly longer barrels are sometimes used outdoors for a tighter spread pattern or increased accuracy of slug projectiles. Home-defense and law enforcement shotguns are usually chambered for 12-gauge shells, providing maximum shot power and the use of a variety of projectiles such as buckshot, rubber, sandbag and slug shells, but 20-gauge (common in bird-hunting shotguns) or .410 (common in youth-size shotguns) are also available in defense-type shotgun models allowing easier use by novice shooters.

A riot shotgun has many advantages over a handgun or rifle. Compared to "defense-caliber" handguns (chambered for 9mm Parabellum, .38 Special, .357 Magnum, .40 S&W, .45 ACP and similar), a shotgun has far more power and damage potential (up to 10 times the muzzle energy of a .45 ACP cartridge), allowing a "one-shot stop" that is more difficult to achieve with typical handgun loads. Compared to a rifle, riot shotguns are easier to maneuver due to the shorter barrel, still provide better damage potential at indoor distances (generally 3–5 meters/yards), and reduce the risk of "overpenetration"; that is, the bullet or shot passing completely through the target and continuing beyond, which poses a risk to those behind the target through walls. The wide spread of the shot reduces the importance of shot placement compared to a single projectile, which increases the effectiveness of "point shooting" - rapidly aiming simply by pointing the weapon in the direction of the target. This allows easy, fast use by novices.

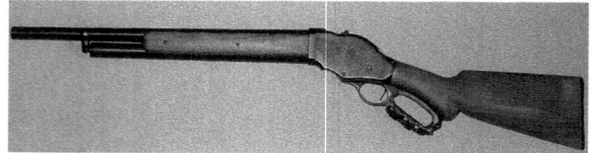

A modern reproduction of the Winchester M1887 lever-action shotgun

Lever-action Early attempts at repeating shotguns invariably centred around either bolt-or lever-action designs, drawing inspiration from contemporary repeating rifles, with the earliest successful repeating shotgun being the lever-action Winchester M1887, designed by John Browning at the behest of the Winchester Repeating Arms Company.

Lever shotguns, while less common, were popular in the late 19th century with the Winchester Model 1887 and Model 1901 being prime examples. Initially very popular, demand waned after the introduction of pump-action shotguns around the start of the 20th century, and production was eventually discontinued in 1920.

One major issue with lever-actions (and to a lesser extent pump-actions) was that early shotgun shells were often made of paper or similar fragile materials (modern hulls are plastic or metal). As a result, the loading of shells, or working of the action of the shotgun, could often result in cartridges getting crushed and becoming unusable, or even damaging the gun.

Lever shotguns have seen a return to the gun market in recent years, however, with Winchester producing the Model 9410 (chambering the .410 gauge shotgun shell and using the action of the Winchester Model 94 series lever-action rifle, hence the name), and a handful of other firearm manufacturers (primarily Norinco of China and ADI Ltd. of Australia) producing versions of the Winchester Model 1887/1901 designed for modern 12-gauge smokeless shotshells with more durable plastic casings. There has been a notable uptick in lever-action shotgun sales in Australia since 1997, when pump-actions were effectively outlawed.

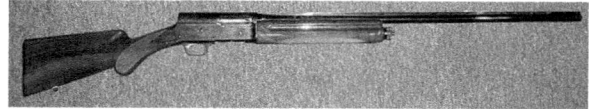

A Browning A-5 semi-automatic shotgun

Semi-automatic Gas, inertia, or recoil operated actions are other popular methods of increasing the rate of fire of a shotgun; these are generally referred to as autoloaders or semi-automatics. Instead of having the action manually operated by a pump or lever, the action automatically cycles each time the shotgun is fired, ejecting the spent shell and reloading a fresh one into the chamber. The first successful semi-automatic shotgun was John Browning's Auto-5, first produced by Fabrique Nationale beginning in 1902. Other well-known examples include the Remington 1100, Benelli M1, and Saiga-12.

Some, such as the Franchi SPAS-12 and Benelli M3, are capable of switching between semi-automatic and pump action. These are popular for two reasons; first, some jurisdictions forbid the use of semi-automatic actions for hunting, and second, lower-powered rounds, like "reduced-recoil" buckshot shells and many less-lethal cartridges, have insufficient power to reliably cycle a semi-automatic shotgun.

Bolt-action Bolt-action shotguns, while uncommon, do exist. One of the best-known examples is a 12 gauge manufactured by Mossberg featuring a 3-round magazine, marketed in Australia just after changes to the gun laws in 1997 heavily restricted the ownership and use of pump-action and semi-automatic shotguns. They were not a huge success, as they were somewhat slow and awkward to operate, and the rate of fire was noticeably slower (on average) than a double-barrelled gun. The Ishapore Arsenal in India also manufactured a single-shot .410 bore shotgun based on the SMLE Mk III* rifle. The Russian Berdana shotgun was effectively a single-shot bolt-action rifle that became obsolete, and was subsequently modified to chamber 16 gauge shotgun shells for civilian sale. The U.S. military M26 is also a bolt-action weapon. Bolt-action shotguns have also been used in the "goose gun" application, intended to kill birds such as geese at greater range. Typically, goose guns have long barrels (up to 36 inches), and small bolt-fed magazines. Bolt-action shotguns are also used in conjunction with slug shells for the maximum possible accuracy from a shotgun.[12]

Other In addition to the commonly encountered shotgun actions already listed, there are also shotguns based on the

Martini-Henry rifle design, originally designed by British arms maker W.W. Greener.

Some of the more interesting advances in shotgun technology include the versatile NeoStead 2000 and fully automatics such as the Pancor Jackhammer or Auto-Assault 12.

In 1925, Rodolfo Cosmi produced the first working hybrid prototype semi-automatic shotgun, which had an 8-round magazine located in the stock. While it reloaded automatically after each shot like a semi-automatic, it had a break-action to load the first shell. This design has only been repeated once, by Beretta with their UGB25 automatic shotgun. The user loads the first shell by breaking the gun in the manner of a break-action shotgun, then closes it and inserts the second shell into a clip on the gun's right side. The spent hulls are ejected downwards. The guns combine the advantages of the break action (they can be proven to be safe by breaking open, there are no flying hulls) with those of the semi-automatic (low recoil, low barrel axis position hence low muzzle flip).

Gauge

A United States Army soldier armed with a Mossberg 500 shotgun

Main article: Gauge (bore diameter)

The caliber of shotguns is measured in terms of *gauge* (U.S.) or *bore* (U.K.). The gauge number is determined by the weight, in fractions of a pound, of a solid sphere of lead with a diameter equal to the inside diameter of the barrel. So, a 10 gauge shotgun nominally should have an inside diameter equal to that of a sphere made from one-tenth of a pound of lead. By far the most common gauges are 12 (0.729 in, 18.5 mm diameter) and 20 (0.614 in, 15.6 mm), although .410 (= 67), 32, 28, 24, 16, and 10 (19.7 mm) gauge also exist. Ammunition manufacturer CCI produces 9 mm (.355 in.) and several other popular pistol calibers up to .45 ACP as well as .22 (5.5 mm) for firing from handguns. These are commonly called snake shot cartridges. rimfire caliber.[13] Larger gauges, too powerful to shoulder, have been built, but were generally affixed to small boats and referred to as punt guns. These were used for commercial waterfowl hunting, to kill large numbers of birds resting on the water. Although relatively rare, single and double derringers have also been produced that are capable of firing either .45 (Long) Colt or .410 shotgun shells from the same chamber; they are commonly known as "snake guns", and are popular among some outdoorsmen in the South and Southwest regions of the United States. There are also some revolvers, such as the Taurus Judge, that are capable of shooting the .45LC/.410 rounds; but as with derringers, these are handguns that shoot .410 shotgun shells, and are not necessarily considered shotguns.

The .410 bore (10.4 mm) is unusual, being measured in inches, and would be approximately 67 "real" gauge, though its short hull versions are nominally called 36 gauge in Europe. It uses a relatively small charge of shot. It is used for hunting and for skeet. Because of its very light recoil (approx 10 N), it is often used as a beginner's gun. However, the small charge and typically tight choke make it more difficult to hit targets. It is also frequently used by expert shooters because of the difficulty, especially in expensive side by side and over/under models for hunting small bird game such as quail and doves.[14] Inexpensive bolt-action .410 shotguns are a very common first hunting shotgun among young pre-teen hunters, as they are used mostly for hunting squirrels, while additionally teaching bolt-action manipulation skills that will transfer easily later to adult-sized hunting rifles. Most of these young hunters move up to a 20-gauge within a few years, and to 12 gauge shotguns and full-size hunting rifles by their late teens. Still, many who are particularly recoil-averse choose to stay with 20-gauge shotguns all their adult life, as it is a suitable gauge for many popular hunting uses.

A recent innovation is the back-boring of barrels, in which the barrels are bored out slightly larger than their actual gauge. This reduces the compression forces on the shot when it transitions from the chamber to the barrel. This leads to a slight reduction in perceived recoil, and an improvement in shot pattern due to reduced deformation of the shot.

Shot

Most shotguns are used to fire "a number of ball shot", in addition to slugs and sabots. The ball shot or pellets is for the

1.1. SHOTGUN

U.S. Marines fire their shotguns

most part made of lead but this has been partially replaced by bismuth, steel, tungsten-iron, tungsten-nickel-iron and even tungsten polymer loads. Non-toxic loads are required by Federal law for waterfowl hunting in the US, as the shot may be ingested by the waterfowl, which some authorities believe can lead to health problems due to the lead exposure. Shot is termed either birdshot or buckshot depending on the shot size. Informally, birdshot pellets have a diameter smaller than 5 mm (0.20 in) and buckshot are larger than that. Pellet size is indicated by a number; for bird shot this ranges from the smallest 12 (1.2 mm, 0.05 in) to 2 (3.8 mm, 0.15 in) and then BB (4.6 mm, 0.18 in).[15]

For buckshot, the numbers usually start at 4 (6.1 mm, 0.24 in) and go down to 1, 0, 00 ("double aught"), 000, and finally 0000 (9.7 mm, .38 in). A different informal distinction is that "bird shot" pellets are small enough that they can be measured into the cartridge by weight, and simply poured in, whereas "buckshot" pellets are so large they must be stacked inside the cartridge in a fixed geometric arrangement in order to fit. The diameter in hundredths of an inch of bird shot sizes from #9 to #1 can be obtained by subtracting the shot size from 17. Thus, #4 bird shot is 17 - 4 = 13 = 0.13 inches (3.3 mm) in diameter. Different terminology is used outside the United States. In England and Australia, for example, 00 buckshot cartridges are commonly referred to as "S.G." (small game) cartridges.

Pattern and choke

Shot, small and round and delivered without spin, is ballistically inefficient. As the shot leaves the barrel it begins to disperse in the air. The resulting cloud of pellets is known as the shot pattern, or shotgun shot spread. The ideal pattern would be a circle with an even distribution of shot throughout, with a density sufficient to ensure enough pellets will intersect the target to achieve the desired result, such as a kill when hunting or a break when shooting clay targets. In reality the pattern is closer to a Gaussian, or normal distribution, with a higher density in the center that tapers off at the edges. Patterns are usually measured by firing at a 30 inches (76 cm) diameter circle on a large sheet of paper placed at varying distances. The hits inside the circle are counted, and compared to the total number of pellets, and the density of the pattern inside the circle is examined. An "ideal" pattern would put nearly 100% of the pellets in the circle and would have no voids—any region where a target silhouette will fit and not cover 3 or more holes is considered a potential problem.

A constriction in the end of the barrel known as the choke is used to tailor the pattern for different purposes. Chokes may either be formed as part of the barrel at the time of manufacture, by squeezing the end of the bore down over a mandrel, or by threading the barrel and screwing in an interchangeable choke tube. The choke typically consists of a conical section that smoothly tapers from the bore diameter down to the choke diameter, followed by a cylindrical section of the choke diameter. Briley Manufacturing, a maker of interchangeable shotgun chokes, uses a conical portion about 3 times the bore diameter in length, so the shot is gradually squeezed down with minimal deformation. The cylindrical section is shorter, usually 0.6 to 0.75 inches (15 to 19 millimetres). The use of interchangeable chokes has made it easy to tune the performance of a given combination of shotgun and shotshell to achieve the desired performance.

The choke should be tailored to the range and size of the targets. A skeet shooter shooting at close targets might use 127 micrometres (0.005 inches) of constriction to produce a 76 cm (30 in) diameter pattern at a distance of 19 m (21 yd). A trap shooter shooting at distant targets might use 762 micrometres (0.030 inches) of constriction to produce a 76 cm (30 in) diameter pattern at 37 m (40 yd). Special chokes for turkey hunting, which requires long range shots at the small head and neck of the bird, can go as high as 1500 micrometres (0.060 inches). The use of too much choke and a small pattern increases the difficulty of hitting the target, whereas the use of too little choke produces large patterns with insufficient pellet density to reliably break targets or kill game. "Cylinder barrels" have no constriction. See also: Slug barrel

Other specialized choke tubes exist as well. Some turkey hunting tubes have constrictions greater than "Super Full", or additional features like porting to reduce recoil, or "straight rifling" that is designed to stop any spin that the shot column might acquire when traveling down the barrel. These tubes are often extended tubes, meaning they project beyond the end of the bore, giving more room for things like a longer conical section. Shot spreaders or diffusion chokes work opposite of normal chokes—they are designed to spread the shot more than a cylinder bore, generating wider patterns for very short range use. A number of recent spreader chokes, such as the Briley "Diffusion" line, actually use rifling in the choke to spin the shot slightly, creating a wider spread. The Briley Diffusion uses a 1 in 36 cm twist, as does the FABARM Lion Paradox shotgun.

Oval chokes, which are designed to provide a shot pattern wider than it is tall, are sometimes found on combat shotguns, primarily those of the Vietnam War era. They were available for aftermarket addition in the 1970s from companies like A & W Engineering.[16] Military versions of the Ithaca 37 with *duckbill* choke were used in limited numbers during the Vietnam War by US Navy Seals. It arguably increased effectiveness in close range engagements against multiple targets. Two major disadvantages plagued the system. One was erratic patterning. The second was that the shot would spread too quickly providing a limited effective zone.

Offset chokes, where the pattern is intentionally slightly off of center, are used to change the point of impact. For instance, an offset choke can be used to make a double barrelled shotgun with poorly aligned barrels hit the same spot with both barrels.

Barrel length

Shotguns generally have longer barrels than modern rifles. Unlike rifles, however, the long shotgun barrel is not for ballistic purposes; shotgun shells use small powder charges in large diameter bores, and this leads to very low muzzle pressures (see internal ballistics) and very little velocity change with increasing barrel length. According to Remington, modern powder in a shotgun burns completely in 25 (9.8425 in) to 36 (14.173 in) cm barrels.

Since shotguns are generally used for shooting at small, fast moving targets, it is important to *lead* the target by firing slightly ahead of the target, so that when the shot reaches the range of the target, the target will have moved into the pattern. On uphill shooting, this means to shoot *above* the target. Conversely, on downhill shooting, this means to shoot *below* the target, which is somewhat counterintuitive for many beginning hunters. Of course, depending on the barrel length, the amount of *lead* employed will vary for different barrel lengths, and must be learned by experience.

Shotguns made for close ranges, where the angular speed of the targets is great (such as skeet or upland bird hunting), tend to have shorter barrels, around 24 to 28 inches (610 to 710 millimetres). Shotguns for longer range shooting, where angular speeds are small (trap shooting; quail, pheasant, and waterfowl hunting), tend to have longer barrels, 28 to 36 inches (910 mm). The longer barrels have more angular momentum, and will therefore swing more slowly but more steadily. The short, low angular momentum barrels swing faster, but are less steady. These lengths are for pump or semi-auto shotguns; break open guns have shorter overall lengths for the same barrel length, and so will use longer barrels. The break open design saves between 9 and 15 cm (3.5 and 5.9 in) in overall length, but in most cases pays for this by having two barrels, which adds weight at the muzzle, and so usually only adds a couple of centimetres. Barrels for shotguns have been getting longer as modern steels and production methods make the barrels stronger and lighter; a longer, lighter barrel gives the same inertia for less overall weight.

Shotguns for use against larger, slower targets generally have even shorter barrels. Small game shotguns, for hunting game like rabbits and squirrels, or shotguns for use with buckshot for deer, are often 56 to 61 cm (22 to 24 in).

Shotguns intended for all-round hunting are a compromise, of course, but a 72 to 74 cm (28 to 29 in) barrel pump-action 12-gauge shotgun with a modified choke can serve admirably for use as one gun intended for general all-round hunting of small-game such as quails, rabbits, pheasants, doves, and squirrels in semi-open wooded or farmland areas in many parts of the eastern US (Kentucky, Indiana, Tennessee) where dense brush is less of a hindrance and the ability to have more reach is important. For hunting in dense brush, shorter barrel lengths are often preferred when hunting the same types of game.

1.1.7 Ammunition

Main article: Shotgun shell

The extremely large caliber of shotgun shells has led to a

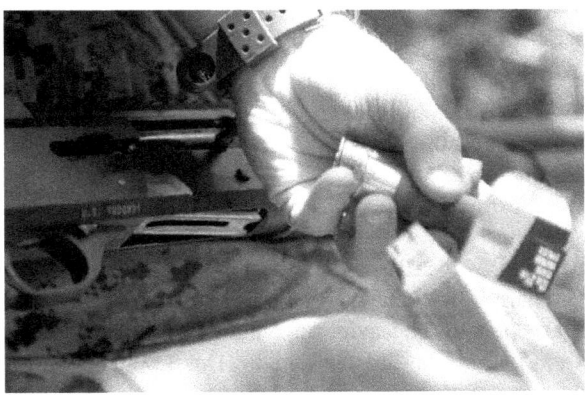

Loading 12-gauge shells

wide variety of different ammunition.

Shotshells are the most commonly used round, filled with lead or lead substitute pellets.

Of this general class, the most common subset is **birdshot**, which uses a large number (from dozens to hundreds) of small pellets, meant to create a wide "kill spread" to hunt birds in flight. Shot shells are described by the size and number of the pellets within, and numbered in reverse order (the smaller the number, the bigger the pellet size, similar to bore gauge). Size nine (#9) shot is the smallest size normally used for hunting and is used on small upland game birds such as dove and quail. Larger sizes are used for hunting larger upland game birds and waterfowl.

Buckshot is similar to but larger than birdshot, and was originally designed for hunting larger game, such as deer (hence the name). While the advent of new, more accurate slug technologies is making buckshot less attractive for hunting, it is still the most common choice for police, military, and home defense uses. Like birdshot, buckshot is described by pellet size, with larger numbers indicating smaller shot. From the smallest to the largest, buckshot sizes are: #4, (called "number four"), #1, 0 ("one-aught"), 00 ("double-aught"), 000 ("triple-aught") and 0000 ("four-aught"). A typical round for defensive use would be a 12 gauge 2 $^3/_4$ inches (7.0 cm) length 00 buck shell, which contains 9 pellets roughly 8.4 mm (.33 inch) in diameter, each comparable to a .38 Special bullet in damage potential. New "tactical" buckshot rounds, designed specifically for defensive use, use slightly fewer shot at lower velocity to reduce recoil and increase controllability of the shotgun. There are some shotgun rounds designed specifically for police use that shoot effectively from 50 yards (46 m) with a 20" diameter grouping of the balls.

Slug rounds are rounds that fire a single solid slug. They are used for hunting large game, and in certain military and law enforcement applications. Modern slugs are moderately accurate, especially when fired from special rifled slug barrels. They are often used in "shotgun-only" hunting zones near inhabited areas, where rifles are prohibited due to their greater range.

Sabots are a common type of slug round. While some slugs are exactly that—a 12-gauge metal projectile in a cartridge—a sabot is a smaller but more aerodynamic projectile surrounded by a "shoe" of some other material. This "sabot" jacket seals the barrel, increasing pressure and acceleration, while also inducing spin on the projectile in a rifled barrel. Once the projectile clears the barrel, the sabot material falls away, leaving an unmarked, aerodynamic bullet to continue toward the target. The advantages over a traditional slug are increased shot power, increased bullet velocity due to the lighter-mass bullet, and increased accuracy due to the velocity and the reduction in deformation of the slug itself. Disadvantages versus a traditional slug include lower muzzle momentum due to reduced mass, reduced damage due to smaller bullet diameter, and significantly higher per-unit cost.

Specialty ammunition

The unique properties of the shotgun, such as large case capacity, large bore, and the lack of rifling, has led to the development of a large variety of specialty shells, ranging from novelties to high tech military rounds.

Hunting, defensive, and military Brenneke and Foster type slugs have the same basic configuration as normal slugs, but have increased accuracy. The hollowed rear of the Foster slug improves accuracy by placing more mass in the front of the projectile, therefore inhibiting the "tumble" that normal slugs may generate. The Brenneke slug takes this concept a bit further, with the addition of a wad that stays connected to the projectile after discharge, increasing accuracy. Both slugs are commonly found with fins or rib, which are meant to allow the projectile to safely squeeze down during passage through chokes, but they do not increase stability in flight.

Flechette rounds contain aerodynamic darts, typically from 8 to 20 in number. The flechette provide greatly extended range due to their aerodynamic shape, and improved penetration of light armor. American troops during the Vietnam War packed their own flechette shotgun rounds, called *beehive rounds*, after the similar artillery rounds. However, terminal performance was poor due to the very light weight of the flechettes, and their use was quickly dropped.

Grenade rounds use exploding projectiles to increase long range lethality. These are currently experimental, but the British FRAG-12, which comes in both armor penetrating and fragmentary forms, is under consideration by military forces.[17]

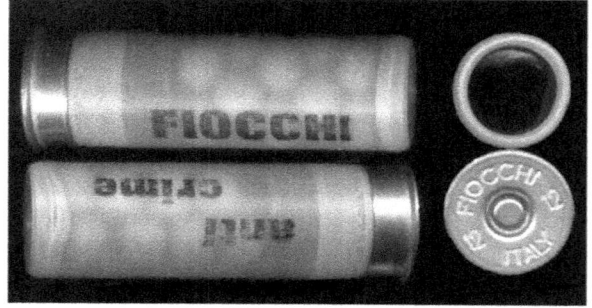

Two rounds of Fiocchi 12 gauge rubber buckshot

Less-lethal rounds, for riot and animal control
Flexible baton rounds, commonly called *bean bags*, fire a fabric bag filled with birdshot or a similar loose, dense substance. The "punch" effect of the bag is useful for knocking down targets; the rounds are used by police to subdue violent suspects. The bean bag round is by far the most com-

mon less-lethal round used. Due to the large surface area of these rounds, they lose velocity rapidly, and must be used at fairly short ranges to be effective, though use at extremely short ranges, under 3 m (9.8 ft), can result in broken bones or other serious or lethal injuries. The rounds can also fly in a frisbee-like fashion and cut the person or animal being fired at. For this reason, these types of rounds are referred to as less-lethal, as opposed to less-than-lethal.[18]

Gas shells spray a cone of gas for several meters. These are primarily used by riot police. They normally contain pepper gas or tear gas. Other variations launch a gas-grenade-like projectile.

Rock salt shells are hand loaded with coarse rock salt crystals, replacing the standard lead or steel shot. Rock salt shells could be seen as the forerunners of modern less-lethal rounds. In the United States, rock salt shells were and are sometimes still used by rural civilians to defend their property. The brittle salt was unlikely to cause serious injury at long ranges, but would cause painful stinging injuries and served as a warning. British gamekeepers have used rock salt shells to deter poachers. Rather than get into a physical confrontation, they stalk the poachers, making themselves known by a loud shout of "Run!" just before firing, to avoid hitting the now-fleeing subject in the eyes.

Rubber slugs or **rubber buckshot** are similar in principle to the bean bag rounds. Composed of flexible rubber or plastic and fired at low velocities, these rounds are probably the most common choice for riot control.

Taser International announced in 2007 a new 12 gauge **eXtended Range Electronic Projectile** or **XREP**, which contains a small electroshock weapon unit in a carrier that can be fired from a standard 12 gauge shotgun. The XREP projectile is fin stabilized, and travels at an initial velocity of 100 m/s (300 ft/s). Barbs on the front attach the electroshock unit to the target, with a tassel deploying from the rear to widen the circuit. A twenty-second burst of electrical energy is delivered to the target. This product is expected to be released to market in 2008.[19] They were used — despite still being subject to testing, in breach of the supplier's license — by Northumbria police in their standoff with Raoul Moat in 2010.

Breaching rounds, often called **Frangible**, **Disintegrator**, or **Hatton** rounds, are designed to destroy door locking mechanisms without risking lives. They are constructed of a very brittle substance that transfers most of the energy to the primary target but then fragment into much smaller pieces or dust so as not to injure unseen targets such as hostages or non-combatants that may be standing behind a breached door.

Bird bombs are low-powered rounds that fire a firecracker that is fused to explode a short time after firing.[20] They are designed to scare animals, such as birds that congregate on airport runways.

Screechers fire a pyrotechnic whistle that emits a loud whistling sound for the duration of its flight.[20] These are also used to scare animals.

Blank shells contain only a small amount of powder and no actual load. When fired, the blanks provide the sound and flash of a real load, but with no projectile.[20] These may be used for simulation of gunfire, scaring wildlife, or as power for a launching device such as the Mossberg #50298 marine line launcher.[21]

Stinger is a type of shotgun shell which contains 16-00 buck balls made of zytel, and is designed as a non-lethal ammunition ideally used in small spaces.

Novelty and other   **Bolo** rounds are made of two or more slugs molded onto steel wire. When fired, the slugs separate, pulling the wire taut creating a flying blade, which could theoretically decapitate people and animals or amputate limbs. However, many active shotgun users consider this to be overstated, and view bolo shells as being less effective than conventional ammunition. Bolo shell rounds are banned in many locations (including the US states of Florida[22] and Illinois[23]) due to concerns about their potential lethality. The round is named in reference to bolas, which use two or more weighted balls on a rope to trap cattle or game.

Dragon's Breath usually refers to a zirconium-based pyrotechnic shotgun round. When fired, a gout of flame erupts from the barrel of the gun (up to 20 ft). The visual effect it produces is impressive, similar to that of a short ranged flamethrower. However, it has few tactical uses, mainly distraction/disorientation.

Flare rounds are sometimes carried by hunters for safety and rescue purposes. They are available in low and high altitude versions. Some brands claim they can reach a height of up to 200 m (660 ft).

1.1.8 Legal issues

A homemade Lupara

Globally, shotguns are generally not as heavily regulated as rifles or handguns, likely because they lack the range of rifles and are not easily concealable as handguns are; thus, they are perceived as a lesser threat by legislative authorities. The one exception is a sawed-off shotgun, especially a Lupara, as it is more easily concealed than a normal shotgun.

Australia

Within Australia, all shotguns manufactured after January 1, 1901 are considered firearms and are subject to registration and licensing. Most shotguns (including break-action, bolt-action and lever-action shotguns) are classed as "Category A" weapons and, as such, are comparatively easy to obtain a licence for, given a legally recognised 'legitimate reason' (compare to the British requirement for 'good reason' for a FAC), such as target shooting or hunting. However, pump-action and semi-automatic shotguns are classed as "Category C" weapons; a licence for this type of firearm is, generally speaking, not available to the average citizen. For more information, see Gun politics in Australia.

Canada

Canada has three classifications of firearms: non-restricted, restricted, and prohibited. Shotguns are found in all three classes.

All non-restricted shotguns must have an overall length of 660 mm (26 in). Semi-automatic shotguns must also have a barrel length of more than 469.9 mm (18.50 in) and have a capacity of 5 shells or less in the magazine to remain non-restricted. All other shotgun action types (pump/slide, break open, lever, bolt) do not have a magazine limit restriction or a minimum barrel length provided the overall length of the firearm remains more than 660 mm (26 in) and the barrel was produced by an approved manufacturer. Shotgun barrels may only be reduced in length to a minimum of 457 mm (18.0 in). Non-restricted shotguns may be possessed with any Possession and Acquisition Licence (PAL) or Possession-Only License (POL) and may be transported throughout the country without special authorization and may be used for hunting certain species at certain times of the year.

Semi-automatic shotguns with a barrel length of less than 469.9 mm (18.50 in) are considered restricted and any shotgun that has been altered so its barrel length is less than 457 mm (18.0 in) or if its overall length is less than 660 mm (26 in) is considered prohibited.[24] Restricted and prohibited shotguns may be possessed with a PAL or POL than has been endorsed for restricted or prohibited grandfathered firearms. These shotguns require special Authorization to Transport (ATT).<ref

A RCMP officer in 2010 armed with a shotgun outfitted to fire beanbag rounds

name=""canUS95trans">"Transporting Firearms". Canada Firearms Centre. Retrieved 2008-06-21.</ref>

The Canadian Firearms Registry was a government-run registry of all legally owned firearms in Canada. The government provided amnesty from prosecution to shotgun and rifle owners if they fail to register non-restricted shotguns and rifles.[25] The long gun portion of the registry was scrapped in 2011.

See online[26] for an official Canadian list of non-restricted and restricted and prohibited firearms.

UK

In the United Kingdom, a Shotgun Certificate (SGC) is required to possess a "Section 2" shotgun. These cost £50 and can only be denied if the chief of police in the area believes and can prove that the applicant poses a real danger to the public, or if the applicant has been convicted of a crime punishable by imprisonment for a term of three years or more or if the applicant cannot securely store a shotgun (gun clamps, wire locks and locking gun cabinets are considered secure). The round number restrictions apply only to the magazine, not the chamber, so it is legal to have a single-barreled semi-auto or pump-action shotgun that holds three rounds in total, or a shotgun with separate chambers (which would need to also be multi-barrelled). For a shotgun to qualify as a section 2 shotgun, it must meet the following criteria:

(a) has a barrel not less than 24 inches (610 mm) in length and does not have any barrel with a bore more than 2 inches (51 mm) in diameter;

(b) either has no magazine or has a non-detachable magazine not capable of holding more than two cartridges;

(c) is not a revolver gun.

Prior to a SGC being issued an interview is conducted with the local Firearms Officer, in the past this was a duty undertaken by the local police although more recently this function has been "contracted out" to civilian staff. The officer will check the location and suitability of the gun safe that is to be used for storage and conduct a general interview to establish the reasons behind the applicant requiring a SGC.

An SGC holder can own any number of shotguns meeting these requirements so long as he/she can store them securely. No certificate is required to own shotgun ammunition, but one is required to buy it. There is no restriction on the amount of shotgun ammunition that can be bought or owned. There are also no rules regarding the storage of ammunition.

However, shotgun ammunition which contains fewer than 6 projectiles requires a section 1 Firearms Certificate (FAC). Shotguns with a magazine capacity greater than 2 rounds are also considered to be section 1 firearms and, as such, require an FAC to own. An FAC costs £50 but is much more restrictive than an SGC. The applicant must nominate two referees who are known to the applicant to vouch for his or her character; a new 'variation' is required for each new caliber of gun to be owned; limits are set on how much ammunition a person can own at any one time; and an FAC can be denied if the applicant does not have sufficient 'good reason'. 'Good reason' generally means hunting, collecting, or target shooting - though other reasons may be acceptable, personal defence is not an acceptable reason.

Any pump-action or semi-automatic smooth-bore gun (such as a shotgun) with a barrel length of less than 24 inches or total length of less than 40 inches is considered to be a section 5 firearm, that is, one that is subject to general prohibition, unless it is chambered for .22 caliber rimfire ammunition.[27]

President Barack Obama skeet shooting with a Browning Citori 525 on the range at Camp David.

US

In the US, federal law prohibits shotguns from being capable of holding more than three shells including the round in the chamber when used for hunting migratory gamebirds such as doves, ducks, and geese. For other uses, a capacity of any number of shells is generally permitted. Most magazine-fed shotguns come with a removable magazine plug to limit capacity to 2, plus one in the chamber, for hunting migratory gamebirds. Certain states have restrictions on magazine capacity or design features under hunting or assault weapon laws.

Shotguns intended for defensive use have barrels as short as 18 inches (46 cm) for private use (the minimum shotgun barrel length allowed by law in the United States without federal registration. Barrel lengths of less than 18 inches (46 cm) as measured from the breechface to the muzzle when the weapon is in battery, or have an overall length of less than 26 inches (66 cm) are classified as short barreled shotguns (SBS) under the 1934 National Firearms Act and are regulated. A similar short barreled weapon having a pistol grip may be classified as an AOW or "Any Other Weapon". A shotgun is defined as a weapon (with a buttstock) designed to be fired from the shoulder. The classification varies depending on how the weapon was originally manufactured.

Shotguns used by military, police, and other government agencies are regulated under the National Firearms Act of 1934; however, they are exempt from transfer taxes. These weapons commonly have barrels as short as 12 to 14 inches (30 to 36 centimetres) so that they are easier to handle in confined spaces. Non-prohibited private citizens may own short-barreled shotguns by passing extensive background checks (state and local laws may be more restrictive) as well as paying a $200 federal tax and being issued a stamp. Defensive shotguns sometimes have no buttstock or will have a folding stock to reduce overall length even more when required. AOWs transfer with a $5 tax stamp from the BATFE.

1.1.9 See also

- Antique guns
- Gun safety
- List of shotguns
- Double-barreled shotgun
- Riding shotgun
- Shotgun wedding
- Kim Rhode - five-time Olympic skeet shooter medal winner

1.1.10 References

Notes

[1] "Scattergun". Dictionary.com. Retrieved 2007-05-12.

[2] "The Box O' Truth #3 - The Shotgun Meets the Box O' Truth The Box O' Truth". *The Box O' Truth*. Retrieved 3 October 2014.

[3] "Shotgun Home Defense Ammunition, .357 SIG - A Solution in Search of a Problem?". Firearmstactical.com. Retrieved 2015-02-19.

[4] "Shotgun Home Defense Ammunition". Firearms Tactical Institute. Retrieved 19 February 2015.

[5] "Problem while searching in History of Science". Digicoll.library.wisc.edu. Retrieved 2015-02-19.

[6] "Firearms in Plymouth Colony". Plymoutharch.tripod.com. Retrieved 3 October 2014.

[7] Fjestad, S. P. *Blue Book of Gun Values*, 13th Ed.

[8] Bruce N. Canfield (May 2004). "Give Us More Shotguns!". *American Rifleman*.

[9] Archived June 13, 2013 at the Wayback Machine

[10] "Taser Xrep". Taser.com. Archived from the original on September 3, 2008. Retrieved 2008-09-05.

[11] "Mossberg & Sons | Products". Mossberg.com. Retrieved 2015-02-19.

[12] "April, 97 Browning". Gun-tests.com. Archived from the original on July 25, 2008. Retrieved 2008-09-05.

[13] "Popular Mechanics - Google Books". Books.google.com. Retrieved 2015-02-19.

[14] "410 Gauge". Chuckhawks.com. Retrieved 2015-02-19.

[15] "Popular Mechanics - Google Books". Books.google.com. Retrieved 2015-02-19.

[16] Roger H. Robinson (1973). *The Police Shotgun Manual*. Thomas. pp. 91–94. ISBN 0-398-02630-0.

[17] Archived April 13, 2008 at the Wayback Machine

[18] "NIJ : Research for Practice : Impact Munitions Use: Types, Targets, Effects" (PDF). Ncjrs.gov. Retrieved 19 February 2015.

[19] Archived April 2, 2015 at the Wayback Machine

[20] Archived February 19, 2015 at the Wayback Machine

[21] "Safety Equipment : Owner's Manual : Mossberg" (PDF). Mossberg.com. Retrieved 19 February 2015.

[22] "The 2007 Florida Statutes". Flsenate.gov. Retrieved 3 October 2014.

[23] "Public Act 92-0423 of the 92nd General Assembly". Ilga.gov. Retrieved 2015-02-19.

[24] "Prohibited Firearms". Cfc-cafc.gc.ca. Retrieved 19 February 2015.

[25] Tim Naumetz (2008-05-14). "Government extends gun-registration amnesty". Canada.com. Retrieved 2008-05-26.

[26] "Royal Canadian Mounted Police - Canadian Firearms Program | Gendarmerie royale du Canada - Programme canadien des armes à feu". Cfc-cafc.gc.ca. 2008-12-31. Retrieved 2015-02-19.

[27] "Firearms Act 1968". Legislation.gov.uk. Retrieved 3 October 2014.

Bibliography

- Bob Brister (1976). *Shotgunning, The Art and the Science*. New Jersey: New Win Publishing. ISBN 0-8329-1840-7.
- Elmer Keith (1950). *Shotguns*. Pennsylvania: The Stackpole Company. ISBN 0-935632-58-1.
- Michael McIntosh (1999). *Best Guns*. Alabama: Countrysport Press. ISBN 0-924357-79-7.
- Jack O'Connor (1965) [1949]. *The Shotgun Book*. New York: Alfred A. Knopf. ISBN 0-394-50138-1.

1.1.11 External links

- Shotgun FAQ
- Shotgun sabot separation photography
- "Shotgun Chokes and Gauges." *Popular Mechanics*, October 1947, p. 196-200. Excellent diagrams and drawings.

1.2 Semi-automatic shotgun

Benelli M4 Super 90 semi-automatic shotgun

A **semi-automatic shotgun** is a shotgun that is able to fire a shell after every trigger squeeze, without needing to manually chamber another round. These weapons use gas, blowback or recoil operation to cycle the action, eject the empty shell and to load another round.

Many semi-automatic shotguns also provide an optional manual means of operation such as by pump-action or via a charging handle.

1.2.1 Examples of semi-automatic shotguns

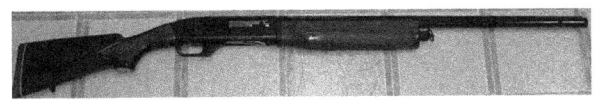

An Ithaca Mag-10 shotgun

- Akdal MKA 1919
- Armsel Striker-12
- Baikal MP-153
- Benelli M4 Super 90
- Beretta AL391
- Beretta Xtrema 2
- Browning Auto-5
- Daewoo USAS-12 (semi-automatic versions for civilian use)
- Franchi SPAS-12
- Franchi SPAS-15
- High Standard Model 10
- Ithaca Mag-10
- MTs 21-12 (*МЦ 21-12*) - first Soviet semi-automatic shotgun[1]
- Mossberg 930
- Remington 1100
- Remington 11-87
- Remington Model SP-10
- Saiga-12 ("*Сайга—12*")
- Molot Vepr-12
- Weatherby SA-08

1.2.2 References

[1] Виктор Шунков. Боевое и служебное оружие России. М., ООО "Издательство ЭКСМО", 2012. стр.479-481

1.2.3 See also

See also: Category:Semi-automatic shotguns.

- List of shotguns
- Assault weapon - certain semi-automatic shotguns are classified as assault weapons in some jurisdictions
- Automatic shotgun
- Personal defense weapon
- Semi-automatic firearm
    - Semi-automatic pistol
    - Semi-automatic rifle

1.3 Automatic shotgun

An **automatic shotgun** is an automatic firearm that fires shotgun shells and uses some of the energy of each shot to automatically cycle the action and load a new round. It will fire repeatedly until the trigger is released or ammunition runs out. Automatic shotguns have a very limited range, but provide tremendous firepower at close range.[1]

1.3. AUTOMATIC SHOTGUN

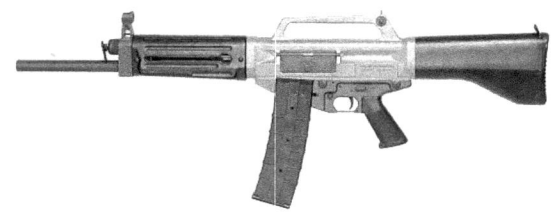

Daewoo USAS-12 automatic shotgun

1.3.1 Design

Automatic shotguns generally employ mechanisms very similar to other kinds of automatic weapons. There are several methods of operation, with the most common being gas, recoil, and blowback operated:

- Gas operation uses the pressure of the gas (created by the burning propellant) behind the projectile to unlock the bolt assembly and then move it rearward.

- Recoil operation uses the backward force applied by the projectile (due to Newton's Third Law of Motion) to retract the bolt assembly.

- Blowback operation uses the backward force to retract the entire barrel and bolt assembly, which unlock at the rear of the barrel's path.

Each of these methods use springs to return the retracted parts to their forward positions and restart the cycle.[2]

Many automatic shotguns are capable of selective fire, meaning they can fire in multiple modes (semi-automatic, three-round burst, and sometimes fully automatic).

1.3.2 Ammunition

They generally store ammunition in detachable box or drum magazines in order to decrease reloading time, whereas most pump-action and semi-automatic shotguns use underbarrel tubular magazines.

Shotguns are able to handle a wide variety of ammunition, however automatics are slightly limited because the shot must provide sufficient force to reliably cycle the action. This means that they are not compatible with low powered rounds, like most less-than-lethal ammunition. The most common ammunition used in combat shotguns is 00 buckshot, which fires about 9 metal balls and is very effective against unarmored targets.[3]

1.3.3 Strengths and weaknesses

A standard shotgun shot fires multiple small projectiles at once, increasing the chances of hitting the target. Shotguns have a short effective range of about 50–70 metres (160–230 ft), but provide a lot of firepower at close range.[1] Automatic fire enhances these effects, due to the increase in the rate of fire.

Automatics typically have much shorter barrels than pump-action shotguns (especially hunting shotguns). Barrel length contributes to tighter shot spread, so automatics have relatively wide spread.[3] Short-barreled automatic shotguns have a very high chance of hitting close range targets, and can even hit multiple targets in one area, which is ideal for combat situations. Long-barreled pump action shotguns are more accurate and have increased range, which is ideal for hunting and sporting purposes.

Automatic shotguns are generally viewed as less reliable than manual operation shotguns, because there are more moving parts and increased chances of error.[4] If any one piece fails, it will most likely halt the operation and cause damage to the weapon and/or user. Automatic weapons are also more susceptible to jamming and negative effects from dirtiness.

1.3.4 Use

Automatic shotguns are intended for use as military combat shotguns. They typically have a high rate of fire and relatively low recoil, making them ideal for engaging multiple targets in a fast paced combat situation.[1] They are able to fulfill several different combat roles, due to the wide variety of shotgun ammunition available. A single gun can be used to breach a door, clear a room, provide support with special grenade rounds, or even suppress a riot with some less-lethal rounds.[5]

Automatic shotguns have not seen much use in the United States, but have been slightly more popular in some other countries.[6]

1.3.5 List of automatic shotguns

- AAI CAWS
- Auto Assault-12
- Daewoo USAS-12
- FAS-173
- Gordon CSWS
- Heckler & Koch HK CAWS

- LW-3
- Pancor Jackhammer
- Saiga-12 (if converted to fully automatic fire)
- Smith & Wesson AS-3
- Special Operations Weapon
- Remington 7188
- SRM Arms MLE-12

1.3.6 See also

- Armsel Striker
- Combat shotgun
- List of combat shotguns
- List of shotguns
- Riot shotgun
- Semi-automatic shotgun

1.3.7 References

[1] Popenker, Maxim. "Modern Firearms — Shotguns". Retrieved February 9, 2012.

[2] Watson, Stephanie; Tom Harris. "How Machine Guns Work". howstuffworks. Retrieved February 14, 2012.

[3] Brooks, Adam; Peter Mahoney (2010). *Ryan's Ballistic Trauma: A Practical Guide* (3 ed.). Springer. p. 33. ISBN 1-84882-123-9.

[4] Coustan, Dave. "How Shotguns Work". Retrieved February 9, 2012.

[5] Morgan, Ryan. "The tactical shotgun in urban operations". Infantry Magazine. Retrieved February 14, 2012.

[6] Popenker, Max. "USAS-12 shotgun". Retrieved February 14, 2012.

1.4 Double-barreled shotgun

A **double-barreled shotgun** ("double" in context) is a shotgun with two parallel barrels, allowing two shots to be fired in quick succession.

A view of the break-action of a typical side-by-side double-barreled shotgun, with the Anson & Deeley boxlock action open and the extractor visible. The opening lever and the safety catch can also be clearly seen.

1.4.1 Construction

Modern double-barreled shotguns, often known as *doubles*, are almost universally break open actions, with the barrels tilting up at the rear to expose the breech ends of the barrels for unloading and reloading. Since there is no reciprocating action needed to eject and reload the shells, doubles are more compact than repeating designs such as pump action or lever-action shotguns.

Barrel configuration

See also: coach gun and sawed-off shotgun

Double-barreled shotguns come in two basic configurations: the **side-by-side shotgun** (SxS) and the **over/under shotgun** ("over and under", O/U, etc.), indicating the arrangement of barrels. The original double-barreled guns were nearly all SxS designs, which was a more practical design in the days of muzzle-loading firearms. Early cartridge shotguns also used the SxS action, because they kept the exposed hammers of the earlier muzzle-loading shotguns they evolved from. When hammerless designs started to become common, the O/U design was introduced, and most modern sporting doubles are O/U designs.[1]

One significant advantage that doubles have over single barrel repeating shotguns is the ability to provide access to more than one choke at a time. Some shotgun sports, such as skeet, use crossing targets presented in a narrow range of distance, and only require one level of choke. Others, like sporting clays, give the shooter targets at differing ranges, and targets that might approach or recede from the shooter, and so must be engaged at differing ranges. Having two barrels lets the shooter use a more open choke for near targets, and a tighter choke for distant targets, providing the optimal shot pattern for each distance.

Their disadvantage lies in the fact that the barrels of a double-barreled shotgun, whether *O/U* or *SxS*, are not parallel, but slightly angled, so that shots from the barrels converge, usually at "40 yards out". For the *SxS* configuration, the shotstring continues on its path to the opposite side of the rib after the converging point; for example, the left barrel's discharge travels on the left of the rib till it hits dead center at 40 yards out, after that, the discharge continues on to the right. In the *O/U* configuration with a parallel rib, both barrels' discharges will keep to the dead center, but the discharge from the "under" barrel will shoot higher than the discharge from the "over" barrel after 40 yards. Thus, double-barreled shotguns are accurate only at practical shotgun ranges, though the range of their ammunition easily exceeds four to six times that range.

SxS shotguns are often more expensive, and may take more practice to aim effectively than a *O/U*. The off-center nature of the recoil in a SxS gun may make shooting the body-side barrel slightly more painful by comparison to an OU, single-shot, or pump/lever action shotgun. Gas-operated, and to a lesser extent recoil-operated, designs will recoil less than either. More *SxS* than *O/U* guns have traditional 'cast-off' stocks, where the end of the buttstock veers to the right, allowing a right-handed user to point the gun more easily.[1]

Trigger mechanism

The early doubles used two triggers, one for each barrel. These were located front to back inside the trigger guard, the index finger being used to pull either trigger, as having two fingers inside the trigger guard can cause a recoil induced double-discharge. Double trigger designs are typically set up for right-handed users.[1] In double trigger designs, it is often possible to pull both triggers at once, firing both barrels simultaneously, though this is generally not recommended as it doubles the recoil, battering both shooter and shotgun. Discharging both barrels at the same time has long been a hunting trick employed by hunters using 8 gauge "elephant" shotguns, firing the two two-ounce slugs for sheer stopping power at close range.

Later models use a single trigger that alternately fires both barrels, called a *single selective trigger* or *SST*. The SST does not allow firing both barrels at once, since the single trigger must be pulled twice in order to fire both barrels. The change from one barrel to the other may be done by a clockwork type system, where a cam alternates between barrels, or by an inertial system where the recoil of firing the first barrel toggles the trigger to the next barrel. A double-barreled shotgun with an inertial trigger works best with full power shotshells; shooting low recoil shotshells often will not reliably toggle the inertial trigger, causing an apparent failure to fire occasionally when attempting to depress the trigger a second time to fire the second barrel. Generally there is a method of selecting the order in which the barrels of an SST shotgun fire; commonly this is done through manipulation of the safety, pushing to one side to select top barrel first and the other side to select bottom barrel first. In the event that an inertial trigger does not toggle to the second barrel when firing low recoil shotshells, manually selecting the order to the second barrel will enable the second barrel to fire when the trigger is depressed again.

One of the advantages of the double, with double triggers or SST, is that a second shot can be taken almost immediately after the first, utilizing different chokes for the two shots. (Assuming, of course, that full power shotshells are fired, at least for a double-barreled shotgun with an inertial type SST, as needed to toggle the inertial trigger.)

Regulation

Regulation is a term used for multi-barreled firearms that indicates how close to the same point of aim the barrels will shoot. Regulation is very important, because a poorly regulated gun may hit consistently with one barrel, but miss consistently with the other, making the gun nearly useless for anything requiring two shots. Fortunately, the short ranges and spread of shot provide a significant overlap, so a small error in regulation in a double will often be too small to be noticed. Generally the shotguns are regulated to hit the point of aim at a given distance, usually the maximum expected range since that is the range at which a full choke would be used, and where precise regulation matters most.

1.4.2 Regional use

The double-barreled shotgun is seen as a weapon of prestige and authority in rural parts of India, where it is known as *dunali*[2] (literally "two pipes"). It is especially common in Bihar, Purvanchal, Uttar Pradesh, Haryana and Punjab.

1.4.3 See also

- Boxlock action
- Coach gun - A style of double-barrel shotgun from the American Wild West
- Combination guns and drillings
- Double-barreled name
- Double-barreled cannon
- Double rifle
- Lupara
- Multiple barrel firearm

1.4.4 References

[1] John Barsness (July 2010), "Twin barrel myths: side-by-side vs. over-under", *Guns Magazine*

[2] *The Popular Dictionary in English and Hindustani and Hindustani and English: With a Number of Useful Tables.* Methodist Episcopal Church Press. 1881. p. 48. Retrieved 1 September 2013.

1.5 Lever action

A Winchester Model 1873 repeating rifle.

Lever action is a type of firearm action which uses a lever located around the trigger guard area (often including the trigger guard itself) to load fresh cartridges into the chamber of the barrel when the lever is worked. This contrasts to bolt-action, semi-automatic, or selective-fire weapons. Most lever-action firearms are rifles, but some lever-action shotguns and a few pistols have also been made. One of the most famous lever-action firearms is the Winchester Model 1873 rifle, but many manufacturers—notably Marlin and Savage—also produce lever-action rifles. Mossberg produces the 464 in centerfire .30-30 and rimfire .22. While the term *lever-action* generally implies a repeating firearm, it is also sometimes (and incorrectly) applied to a variety of single-shot, or falling-block actions that use a lever for cycling, such as the Martini–Henry or the Ruger No. 1.

1.5.1 History

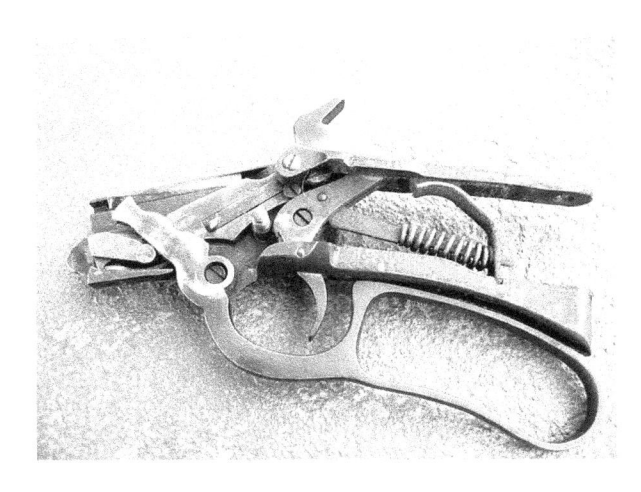

Inside of Marlin 39A receiver

The first significant lever-action design was the Spencer repeating rifle, a magazine-fed lever-operated breech-loading rifle designed by Christopher Spencer in 1860. It was fed from a removable seven-round tube magazine, enabling the rounds to be fired one after another, and which, when emptied, could be exchanged for another. Over 20,000 were made, and it was adopted by the United States and used during the American Civil War, marking the first adoption of a removable-magazine-fed infantry-and-cavalry rifle by any country.

Unlike later designs, the early Spencer's lever only served to unlock the falling-block action and load a new cartridge from the magazine; it did not cock the hammer, and thus the hammer had to be cocked after the lever was operated to prepare the rifle to fire. The Henry rifle, invented by Benjamin Tyler Henry, a gunsmith employed by Oliver Winchester in 1860, used a centrally located hammer, rather than the offset hammer typical of muzzleloading rifles, and this hammer was cocked by the rearward movement of the Henry's bolt. The Henry also placed the magazine under the barrel, rather than in the butt-stock, a trend followed by most tubular magazines since.

The Martini–Henry rifle was the main rifle of British and Empire forces from the early 1870s to the turn of the 20th century and remained in use to the end of World War I. It was used in some areas, either by civilians or by the local military, much longer. Variants copying the Martini–Henry mechanism but using more modern cartridges were also produced; as late as the 1970s a version taking the common Enfield .303 ammunition was common in Afghanistan.

John Marlin, founder of Marlin Firearms Company, New Haven, Connecticut, introduced Marlin's first lever-action repeating rifle as the Model 1881. This was chambered in rounds such as the 45/70 and 38/55. Its successor was the 1895 solid top design, which we know as the model 336 today. It also gave rise to the Marlin Model 1894, which is still in production today.

By the 1890s, lever-actions had evolved into a form that would last for over a century. Both Marlin and Winchester released new model lever-action rifles in 1894. The Marlin rifle is still in production, whereas production of the Winchester 94 ceased in 2006. While externally similar, the Marlin and Winchester rifles are quite different internally; the Marlin has a single-stage lever action, while the Winchester has a double-stage lever. The double-stage action is easily seen when the Winchester's lever is operated, as first the entire trigger group drops down, unlocking the bolt, and then the bolt is moved rearward to eject the fired cartridge.

The fledgling Savage Arms Company became well known after the development of its popular hammerless Models 1895 and 1899 (which became named the Model 99) lever-action sporting rifles. The Models 1899/99 were produced from introduction in 1899 until the expense of producing the rifle, and declining interest in lever-action rifles from the 1950s on, resulted in dropping the Model 99 from production in 2000. Unlike most Winchester and the Marlin lever-action rifles, which used a tubular magazine requiring round-nose or flat-nose bullets, Arthur Savage designed his rifle using a rotary magazine. This allowed the 99 to use cartridges with spitzer pointed bullets for increased ballistic performance. The 99 was produced in many different cartridges and several different model variations. The final models eliminated the very expensive-to-produce rotary magazine, using a detachable box magazine instead. But the 99 was still very expensive to produce when compared to the other lever-action rifles, and the Savage bolt-action rifles and economics determined the fate of the rifle.

More recently, Sturm Ruger and Company introduced a number of new lever-action designs in the 1990s, unusual because most lever action designs date from before World War II, in the period before reliable semi-automatic rifles became widely available.

1.5.2 Usage in warfare

Lever action rifles were used extensively by irregular forces during the Spanish Civil War in the 1930s. Typically, these were Winchesters or Winchester copies of Spanish manufacture.

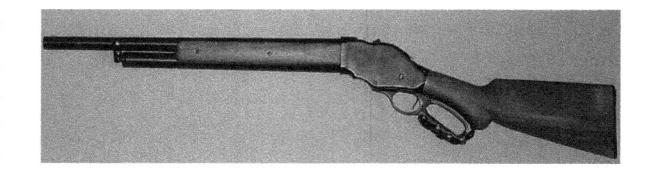

A modern reproduction of the Winchester M1887 lever-action shotgun

Lever-action shotguns

Early attempts at repeating shotguns invariably centered around either bolt-action or lever-action designs, drawing obvious inspiration from the repeating rifles of the time. The earliest successful repeating shotgun was the lever-action Winchester M1887, designed by John Browning in 1885 at the behest of the Winchester Repeating Arms Company, who wanted to market a repeating shotgun. The lever-action design was chosen for reasons of brand recognition, Winchester being best known for manufacturing lever-action firearms at the time, despite the protestations of Browning, who pointed out that a slide-action design would be much better for a shotgun. Initially chambered for black powder shotgun shells (as was standard at the time), the Model 1887 gave rise to the Winchester Model 1901, a strengthened version chambered for 10ga smokeless powder shells. Their popularity waned after the introduction of slide-action shotguns such as the Winchester Model 1897, and production was discontinued in 1920. Modern reproductions are (or have been), however, manufactured by Armi Chiappa in Italy, Norinco in China and ADI Ltd. in Australia, while Winchester continued to manufacture the .410-bore Model 9410, effectively a Winchester Model 94 chambered for .410-bore shotgun shells, until 2006.

On other applications

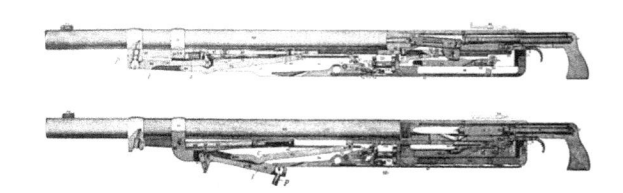

M1895 operating mechanism showing the lever in the forward (top) and rear (bottom) positions

A one-off example of lever-action reloading on automatic firearms is the M1895 Colt–Browning machine gun. This weapon had a swinging lever beneath its barrel that was actuated by a gas bleed in the barrel, unlocking the breech to reload. This unique operation gave the nickname "potato digger," as the lever swung each time the weapon fired and would dig into the ground if the weapon was not situated high enough on its mount.

The Knötgen automatic rifle is another example.

1.5.3 Advantages and disadvantages

While lever-action rifles were (and are) popular with hunters and sporting shooters, they were not widely accepted by the military. One significant reason for this was that it is harder to fire a lever-action from the prone position (compared to a straight-pull or rotating-bolt bolt-action rifle), and while nominally possessing a greater rate of fire (contemporary Winchester advertisements claimed their rifles could fire 2 shots a second) than bolt-action rifles, lever-action firearms are also generally fed from a tubular magazine, which limits the type of ammunition that can be used in them. Pointed centerfire *Spitzer* bullets, for example, can cause explosions in a tubular magazine, as the point of each cartridge's projectile rests on the primer of the next cartridge in the magazine (elastomer-tipped Hornady LEVERevolution ammunition overcomes this problem).[1] The tubular magazine may also have a negative impact on the harmonics of the barrel, which limits the theoretical accuracy of the rifle. A tubular magazine under the barrel also pushes the center of gravity forward, which alters the balance of the rifle in ways that are undesirable to some shooters. However, there are some lever rifles—such as the Winchester Model 1895, which saw service with the Russian Army in World War I—that use a box magazine. Furthermore, many of the newer lever-action rifles are capable of shooting groups smaller than 1 minute of angle, making them closer to the accuracy of most modern bolt-action rifles than in the past.

Due to the higher rate of fire and shorter overall length than most bolt-action rifles, lever-actions have remained popular to this day for sporting use, especially short- and medium-range hunting in forests, scrub, or bushland. Lever-action firearms have also been used in some quantity by prison guards in the United States, as well as by wildlife authorities/game wardens in many parts of the world.

An additional advantage over typical bolt-action rifles is the lack of handedness: lever-actions like pump-actions are frequently recommended as ambidextrous in sporting guidebooks.

1.5.4 Calibers

Most lever-action designs are not as strong as bolt-action or semi-automatic designs, and as a result, lever-action rifles tend to be generally found in low- and medium-pressure cartridges such as .30-30 Winchester or .44 Magnum, although the Marlin Model 1894 is available in three high-pressure magnum calibers; and the Winchester Model 1895, which used a box magazine, was chambered for .30-06 and other powerful military cartridges. The most common caliber is by far the .30-30, which was introduced by Winchester with the Model 1894. Other common calibers for lever-action firearms include: .38 Special/.357 Magnum, .44 Special/.44 Magnum, .41 Magnum, .444 Marlin, .45-70, .45 Colt, .32-20 Winchester, .35 Remington, .308 Marlin Express, .22 caliber rimfire, and .300 Savage. Lever-action designs using stronger, rotary locking bolts (such as the Browning BLR) or tilting block designs such as the Savage Model 99 are usually fed from either box or rotary magazines and are not limited to round nose bullet designs, as well as being able to handle a greater range of calibers than a traditional lever-action design.

Lever-action shotguns such as the Winchester Model 1887 were chambered in 10 or 12-gauge black powder shotgun shells, whereas the Model 1901 was chambered for 10 gauge smokeless shotshells. Modern reproductions are chambered for 12 gauge smokeless shells, while the Winchester Model 9410 shotgun is available in .410 bore.

1.5.5 Other long gun actions

- Bolt action
- Pump action
- Break-action
- Falling-block action
- Rolling block
- Semi-automatic rifle

1.5.6 See also

- Antique guns
- Henry Rifle
- Colt-Burgess rifle
- Marlin 336
- Mossberg model 464
- Spencer repeating rifle
- Volcanic Repeating Arms
- Winchester rifle
- Winchester M1887
- Martini–Henry

1.5.7 References

[1] John Taffin (February 2007), "Seven revolution: it's not your grandpa's .30-.30", *Guns Magazine*

1.5.8 External links

- The All-American Lever Gun - Rifle Shooter (dead link)
- Hunting with lever-action rifle (dead link)

1.6 Pump action

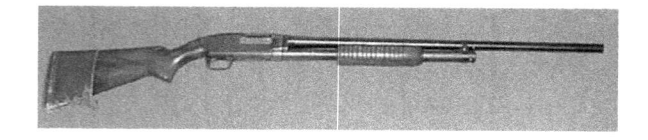

A Winchester Model 1912 12-gauge pump-action shotgun

A **pump-action** rifle or shotgun is one in which the handgrip can be pumped back and forth in order to eject a spent round of ammunition and to chamber a fresh one. It is much faster than a bolt-action and somewhat faster than a lever-action, as it does not require the trigger hand to be removed from the trigger whilst reloading. When used in rifles, this action is also commonly called a **slide action**.

Pump-action shotguns, also called "slide-action repeating shotguns" or "slide-action shotguns" are a class of shotguns that are distinguished in the way in which spent shells are extracted and fresh ones are chambered. The weapon has a single barrel above a tube magazine into which shells are inserted. New shells are chambered by pulling a pump handle (often called the fore-end) attached to the tube magazine toward the user, then pushing it back into place to chamber the cartridge (in a few cases this action is reversed). Fore-ends are replaceable, and modern ones may include a pistol grip for a more secure hold, picatinny rails, or a tactical light.

The term *pump-action* can also be applied to various airsoft guns and air guns, which use a similar mechanism to both load a pellet and compress a spring piston for power, or pneumatic guns where a pump is used to compress the air used for power. See the airgun article for information on how spring piston and pneumatic airguns work.

1.6.1 History

Modern pump-action designs are a little slower than a semi-automatic shotgun, but the pump-action offers greater flexibility in selection of shotshells, allowing the shooter to mix different types of loads and for using low-power or specialty loads. Semi-automatic shotguns must use some of the energy of each round fired to cycle their actions, meaning that they must be loaded with shells powerful enough to reliably cycle. The pump-action avoids this limitation. In addition, like all manual action guns, pump-action guns are inherently more reliable than semi-automatic guns under adverse conditions, such as exposure to dirt, sand, or climatic extremes. Thus, until recently, military combat shotguns were almost exclusively pump-action designs.

Older pump-action shotguns are often faster than modern semi-automatic shotguns, as they often did not have a trigger disconnector, and were capable of firing a new round as fast as the pump action was cycled, with the trigger held down continuously. This technique is called a slamfire, and was often used in conjunction with the M1897 in the First World War's trench warfare.

It is popularly believed that the distinctive sound of a pump action being cycled carries an inherent deterrent effect, though self-defense experts advise that this should never be relied upon.[1][2]

1.6.2 Advantages

The cycling time of a pump-action is quite short. The manual operation gives a pump-action the ability to cycle rounds of widely varying power that a gas or recoil operated firearm would fail to cycle, such as most less-than-lethal rounds. The simplicity of the pump-action relative to a semi-automatic design also leads to improved durability and lower cost. It has also been noticed that the time taken to work the action allows the operator to identify and aim on a new target, avoiding a "spray and pray" usage.

An advantage of the pump-action over the bolt-action is its ease of use by both left- and right-handed users: like lever-actions, pump-actions are frequently recommended as ambidextrous in sporting guidebooks. However, most are not truly ambidextrous, as the spent casing is ejected out the side in most designs.

1.6.3 Disadvantages

Like most lever-action rifles, most pump-action shotguns and rifles do not use a detachable magazine. This makes for slow reloading, as the cartridges have to be inserted individually into the firearm. Some pump action shotguns and rifles, such as the Zlatoust RB-12, Italian Valtro PM5 and the American Remington 7600 series use detachable box magazines.

1.6.4 Layout

A pump-action firearm is typically fed from a tubular magazine underneath the barrel, which also serves as a guide to the movable forend. The rounds are fed in one by one through a port in the receiver, where they are pushed forward. A latch at the rear of the magazine holds the rounds in place in the magazine until they are needed. If it is desired to load the gun fully, a round may be loaded through the ejection port directly into the chamber, or cycled from the magazine, which is then topped off with another round. Pump shotguns with detachable box magazines or even drums exist, and may or may not allow the magazine to be inserted without stripping the top round.

1.6.5 Operating cycle

Nearly all pump-actions use a back-and-forward motion of the forend to cycle the action. The forend is connected to the bolt by one or two bars; two bars are considered more reliable because it provides symmetric forces on the bolt and pump and reduces the chances of binding. The motion of the bolt back and forth in a tubular magazine model will also operate the *elevator*, which lifts the shells from the level of the magazine to the level of the barrel.

After firing a round, the bolt is unlocked and the forend is free to move. The shooter pulls back on the forend to begin the operating cycle. The bolt unlocks and begins to move to the rear, which extracts and ejects the empty shell from the chamber, cocks the hammer, and begins to load the new shell. In a tubular magazine design, as the bolt moves rearwards, a single shell is released from the magazine, and is pushed backwards to come to rest on the elevator.

As the forend reaches the rear and begins to move forward, the elevator lifts up the shell, lining it up with the barrel. As the bolt moves forward, the round slides into the chamber, and the final portion of the forend's travel locks the bolt into position. A pull of the trigger will fire the next round, where the cycle begins again.

Most pump-action firearms do not have any positive indication that they are out of ammunition, so it is possible to complete a cycle and have an empty chamber. The risk of running out of ammunition unexpectedly can be minimized in a tubular magazine firearm by topping off the magazine by loading new rounds to replace the rounds that have just been fired. This is especially important when hunting, as many locations have legal limits on the magazine capacity: for example, three rounds for shotguns and five rounds for rifles.

The BSA Machine Carbine used a unique pump-action that also required twisting the handguard.

1.6.6 Trigger disconnectors

Modern pump shotgun designs, such as the Remington 870 and Mossberg 500, have a safety feature called a trigger disconnector, which disconnects the trigger from the sear as the bolt moves back, so that the trigger must be released and pulled again to fire the shotgun after it closes. Many early pump shotguns, such as the Winchester 1897, did not have trigger disconnectors, and would, if the trigger were held back, fire immediately upon closing. Due to the higher rate of fire that this allows, some shooters prefer models without this feature, such as the Ithaca 37, Stevens Model 520/620, and Winchester Model 12.

1.6.7 Other long gun actions

- Shotgun
- Bolt action
- Lever-action
- Break-action
- Falling-block action
- Rolling block
- Semi-automatic rifle

1.6.8 Type of Pump action shotgun

- Franchi SPAS-12
- Ithaca Model 37
- Winchester Model 1897
- Winchester Model 1912
- Stevens Model 520/620
- NeoStead 2000
- Remington 870
- Mossberg 500
- Winchester 1200
- New Haven 600
- Remington 887 Nitro Mag
- Norinco HP9-1
- Benelli Nova
- Benelli Supernova

- Ciener Ultimate Over/Under
- Specialized types of shotgun which are often pump-action:
    - Riot shotgun
    - Combat shotgun

1.6.9 References

[1] Home Defense Shotgun at the Wayback Machine (archived December 13, 2014)

[2] Guns On Board | MaritimeSecurity.com at the Wayback Machine (archived April 23, 2012)

Chapter 2

Semi-Automatic Shotguns

2.1 Akdal MKA 1919

The **Akdal MKA 1919** is a gas operated, semi-automatic shotgun that resembles the M16 rifle and mimics the layout and placement of some of the controls. It was created by Turkish company Akdal Arms. The MKA 1919 uses a conventional gas-operated action which is located around the support tube that runs below the barrel. The return spring is also located around the same support tube which is concealed by an enlarged polymer handguard. The MKA 1919 barrel can be quickly removed from upper receiver. To charge the rifle, the charging handle on the receiver must be pulled. The upper receiver is manufactured from an aluminum alloy while the lower receiver, along with pistol grip and shoulder stock, is manufactured as one piece from impact-resistant polymer. Akdal MKA 1919 semi-automatic rifle has a 5 round detachable box magazine. It has a bolt release identical in location and function to the one on the M16. Manual safety also duplicates M16-style being located on the left side of the receiver above the pistol grip.[1] Standard sights include a front post installed on the M16-style removable base and a detachable M16A2-style carrying handle with built-in diopter sight. On the upper receiver, an integral Picatinny rail exists which will accept detachable carrying handle or optional red-dot or other optical sight attachments.

2.1.1 Related firearms

- Benelli M3
- Franchi SPAS-15
- Heckler & Koch FABARM FP6
- Fabarm SDASS Tactical
- Safir T-14
- Saiga 12
- USAS-12

2.1.2 References

[1] "Modern Firearms - Akdal MKA 1919". world.guns.ru. Retrieved 2014-09-27.

2.2 Baikal MP-153

The Baikal MP-153 is a 12 gauge gas-operated semi-automatic shotgun manufactured by the Izhevsk Mechanical Plant in Russia.[1]

The shotgun is available with 12/76mm or 12/89mm chambers and either 610, 650, 710 or 750 mm barrels.

The MP-153 is manufactured with fixed choke available as Cylinder, Modified or Full variants, or with screw in chokes with Cylinder, Improved Cylinder, Modified, Improved Modified, Full and Extra Full variants available. Normally there are 3 or 4 chokes included with multi choke variants of the shotgun and a spanner that duplicates as a choke extractor and gas screw adjustor. Screw in chokes come as lead or steel proofed versions.

2.2.1 History

Development began in 1997 of a 12/70mm unit based on the IZH-81. With increasing market demand for 12/89mm guns, further development of a gun capable of firing light skeet and trap load as well as heavier magnum game loads commenced in February 1999[2]

The developers retained characteristics from the IZH-81:-

- barrel locking by a single, retractable lug on the top of the bolt that cams into a recess cut into the barrel extension (analogous to the J.M. Browning patent and applied in Remington 870 model and its semi-auto options;
- under-barrel tube magazine.[2]

2.2.2 Related Firearms

- Baikal MP-155[3]
- Remington Spartan 453

2.2.3 See also

- List of Russian inventions
- List of Russian weaponry makers
- List of firearms

2.2.4 References

[1] "MP-153 & MP-153C Semi-Automatic Guns". Retrieved 25 February 2014.

[2] "IZH Press Release March 2011" (PDF). Retrieved 23 March 2014.

[3] "MP-155 Semi-Automatic Gun". Retrieved 25 February 2014.

2.2.5 External links

- Specification MP-153 IMZ
- eaa corp User manual
- eaa corp MP-153 Parts List

2.3 Benelli M1

The **Benelli M1 (Super 90)** is a semi-automatic shotgun manufactured by Benelli Armi S.P.A.. It is available in several versions for civilian, law enforcement and military use. It features the proprietary Benelli recoil system, known for its reliability and easy maintenance. The standard model features an aluminum alloy receiver and tubular magazine, and is available with a standard or pistol grip stocks. The M1 Super 90 can be fitted with traditional iron sights, or ghost ring diopter sights. Mounts are available for laser pointers and tactical flashlights. Due to the inertia recoil system, the M1 should use heavier loads to cycle properly but because the action is inertia driven vs. the traditional gas cycling operation it can fire and reliably cycle lighter loads.[1]

The M1 was succeeded by the Benelli M2, Benelli M3 and Benelli M4 models.

2.3.1 See also

- Benelli (firearms)
- Benelli M2
- Benelli M3
- Benelli M4
- Combat shotgun

2.3.2 References

[1] "Modern Firearms - Shotgun - Benelli M1 Super 90". Retrieved 2007-11-23.

2.3.3 External links

- Benelli M1 Owners Manual
- American Rifleman's Exploded-View Diagram of the Benelli M1 Super 90 Montefeltro Edition

2.4 Benelli M2

The **Benelli M2 (Super 90)** is a semi-automatic shotgun manufactured by Benelli Armi SpA. It is an updated version of the Benelli M1. Like its predecessor, it is available in several versions for civilian, law enforcement and military use. It features the proprietary Benelli inertia system of operation.[3]

2.4.1 Operation

The inertia recoil system was developed for the Benelli M1, M2, and M3 shotguns in the early 1980s. This short-stroke recoil system is dependent upon the force of the shotgun's rearward movement under recoil. As a result of inertia, heavier loads cycle in a shorter amount of time.[4]

The recoil spring is housed within the butt stock in the same manner as a Browning Auto-5 or Remington 1100; as a result, the shotgun can only be fired with a butt stock in place.[4]

2.4.2 Users

The M2 Super 90 is marketed as a tactical or defensive shotgun to military and police forces as well as to civilian hunters and target shooters for skeet, Sporting clays and trap shooting.[5]

Exhibition sharpshooter Tom Knapp used a Benelli M2 in many of his shooting demonstrations, breaking 10 clays in 2.2 seconds with the M2 and an extended magazine.[6]

A popular sporting variant of the Benelli M2 is the XRAIL design offered by Roth Concept Innovations. This modified magazine tube gives the shooter a 25-round magazine capacity by using 4 tubes in tandem like a revolver's cylinder.[7]

2.4.3 See also

- Benelli M3
- Benelli M4

2.4.4 References

[1] Product Page

[2] Tactical products

[3] Cutshaw, Charles Q. (28 February 2011). *Tactical Small Arms of the 21st Century: A Complete Guide to Small Arms From Around the World*. Iola, Wisconsin: Gun Digest Books. p. 329. ISBN 1-4402-2482-X.

[4] Wagner, Scott W. (28 February 2011). "The Benelli M2". *Gun Digest Book of The Tactical Shotgun*. Iola, Wisconsin: Gun Digest Books. pp. 109–112. ISBN 1-4402-1895-1.

[5] Ayoob, Massad (May 1, 2000). "SELF DEFENSE IS BIG BUSINESS". *Shooting industry – via HighBeam Research (subscription required)* .

[6] Anderson, Dennis (August 1, 2010). "Hunting extravaganza signals again that fall is coming". *Star Tribune – via HighBeam Research (subscription required)* .

[7] MacRunnels, Colleen (September 16, 2014). "Crazy Quail clay target shoot supports Special Olympics". MidWeek News.

2.4.5 External links

- Benelli M2 Owners Manual

2.5 Benelli M3

The **Benelli M3 (Super 90)** is a dual-mode (both pump-action and semi-automatic) shotgun designed and manufactured by Italian firearms manufacturer Benelli. The M3 holds a maximum of seven rounds and uses the proprietary Benelli semi-automatic system first showcased in the M1.

The M3 is notable for allowing the user the choice of semi-automatic or pump-action operation. It is reliable and versatile, and popular with military and police forces as well as civilians.

2.5.1 Background

Pump-action operation is employed when shooting less powerful shells—such as rubber bullets—that do not generate enough recoil to operate the semi-automatic mechanism. Conversely, the semi-automatic mode can be employed with more powerful shells, absorbing some of the recoil. Switching between the two modes is done by manipulating the ring located at the front of the forend grip.

The Benelli M3 also features a removable stock allowing the user to choose one of two styles, the traditional shotgun stock or a stock with a pistol grip.

The Benelli M3 is an updated version of the Benelli M1 shotgun. The M3 uses the same inertia recoil semi-automatic system as the earlier Benelli M1, but adds another Benelli-patented feature, which allows the shooter to lock the semi-automatic action and switch to the manually operated pump-action mode and back in the matter of seconds. The action type switch is located at the forward end of the forearm, and is formed as an annular knurled ring. Rotation of this ring either engages the action rods of the pump system and locks the semi-automatic recoil system, or disengages the action bars, locks the forearm and allows the inertia recoil system to operate the action automatically. This greatly improves the versatility of the shotgun, allowing it to fire low-powered ammunition (mostly of special purpose, such as less-lethal rubber or tear-gas projectiles) in the manually operated pump action mode, and to fire full power combat loads with slugs or buckshot in rapid semi-automatic mode. An underbarrel tubular magazine usually holds 8 rounds for police or military versions, or less in some civilian models.

The M3 Super 90 is available with various barrel lengths and stock options, with fixed butt and semi-pistol or pistol grips, or with top-folding butts and pistol grips. Sight options include shotgun-type open sights, rifle type open sights, ghost ring (diopter) sights and various mounts for reflex or low magnification telescope sights and tactical flashlights and laser pointers.

2.5.2 Variants

The Benelli M3 comes in several variations, most notably the M3 Super 90, which features a smaller body. There is also a shorter version—which is easier to transport—used by law enforcement officers.

While other Benelli self-loading shotguns have the recoil spring inside a tube in butt-stock, in the M3 the recoil spring is placed around the magazine tube. This is an interesting feature for weapon modification, since other shotguns (such as M1, M2 and M4) attach the butt-stock to the recoil spring tube. The M3 has a dummy tube just for stock attachment.

Benelli's M3T is an OEM variant, where the butt-stock and dummy tube have been replaced with a pistol grip and up-folding skeleton butt-sock.

Benelli's SuperNova pump-shotgun and MR1 self-loading rifle have similar butt-stock attachment to the M3, so this adds two new butt-stock options to M3.

The M3 butt-stock and dummy rod can be replaced with a "Benelli Supernova Tactical Collapsible Stock". The collapsible stock allows 5-position draw length adjustment, so a shooter can compensate the effects of thick winter clothes or body armor by adjusting the stock length. The required spare parts are: adjustment rod, pistol grip and collapsible butt-stock.

A rare modification is to replace the M3 butt-stock and dummy rod with a "Benelli SuperNova Handle Grip". The "handle grip" is just the pistol grip attached to the receiver with a screw.

2.5.3 Users

- Canada: Joint Task Force 2.[1]
- Czech Republic: The M3T Super 90 is used by special units of the Czech Armed Forces.[2] Used by operators of the 601st Special Forces Group.[3]
- Estonia: Estonian Defence Forces.[4]
- France: Select units of the French Army.[5]
- Indonesia: M3T is used by the *Komando Pasukan Katak* (KOPASKA) tactical diver group and *Komando Pasukan Khusus* (Kopassus) special forces group.[6]
- Ireland; Irish Army Ranger Wing, Garda; National Bureau of Criminal Investigation, Special Detective Unit, Emergency Response Unit.[7][8]
- Japan: M3T model used by the Maritime Self-Defense Forces.[9]
- Luxembourg: *Unité Spéciale de la Police* of the Grand Ducal Police.[10][11][12]
- Malaysia: *Pasukan Gerakan Khas* (PGK) counter-terrorism group of the Royal Malaysia Police.[13]

- New Zealand: NZ Defence Force;[14] initially introduced in Army service in 2006.[15]
- Philippines

2.5.4 See also

- Benelli (firearms)
- Benelli M1, predecessor
- Benelli M2
- Benelli M4, successor to M3, adopted by U.S. armed forces as the *M1014 Combat Shotgun*.
- Combat shotgun

2.5.5 References

[1] "Canadian Forces - Small Arms - Specialist Weapons - Index - CASR DND 101 - Visual Guide - Canadian American Strategic Review - Side Arms - Automatic Pistols - Submachine Guns - Tactical Shotguns". Casrca.nationprotect.net. Retrieved 2012-02-22.

[2] RUČNÍ ZBRANĚ AČR

[3] "601st Special Forces Group official website". 601skss.cz. Retrieved 2012-02-22.

[4] "Kaitsevägi - Tehnika - Pumppüss Benelli M3T". Mil.ee. Retrieved 2012-02-22.

[5] "Benelli M3T (Tactical) Super 90" (in French). Defense.gouv.fr. Retrieved 2012-02-22.

[6] "Kopassus & Kopaska - Specijalne Postrojbe Republike Indonezije" (in Croatian). Hrvatski Vojnik Magazine. Retrieved 2010-06-12.

[7] Leroy Thompson. "SPEC-OPS SPAS-15". Tactical Life. Retrieved 2011-05-24.

[8] "Garda College Yearbook listing weapons training on page 66" (PDF).

[9] http://www.mod.go.jp/msdf/ccf1/1ed/hyuga/topic/20100308/index.htm

[10] "Unofficial Shotguns Page, Equipment". http://USP.lu - Unofficial Website of Unité Spéciale, Officially Endorsed. Retrieved 2009-10-06. External link in |publisher= (help)

[11] "L'Unite d'Intervention de la Police Luxembourgeoise" (PDF) (in French). RAIDS Magazine. March 2006. Retrieved 2009-09-23.

[12] Lasterra, Juan Pablo (2004). "UPS Unidad Especial de la Policia Luxemburguesa" (PDF) (in Spanish). ARMAS Magazine. Retrieved 2009-09-23.

[13] "Benelli M3 Super 90 Pump-Action / Semi-Automatic Shotgun (1995)". Militaryfactory.com. 2013-03-26. Retrieved 2014-07-27.

[14] "New Shotguns for Defence" (PDF). *NZ Army News*. NZ Defence Force. September 2011. p. 5. Retrieved 31 January 2012.

[15] "Heed The Need". *NZ Army News*. NZ Defence Force. 14 November 2006. Retrieved 31 January 2012. The Army is purchasing a small number of Benelli M3 Tactical shotguns, which are expected to deploy with 1 RNZIR and 2/1 RNZIR soldiers on stability and security-type operations.

2.5.6 External links

- World Guns: Benelli M3 Super 90

2.6 Benelli M4

The **Benelli M4 Super 90** is an Italian semi-automatic shotgun manufactured by Benelli Armi SpA.

2.6.1 History

On May 4, 1998, the United States Army's Armaments Research, Development and Engineering Center (ARDEC) at Picatinny Arsenal, New Jersey issued Solicitation #DAAE30-98-R-0401, requesting submissions for a new 12 gauge, semi-automatic combat shotgun for the U.S. military. In response to the request, Benelli Armi SpA of Urbino, Italy designed and built the Benelli M4 Super 90 Combat Shotgun. On August 4, 1998, five samples of the M4 were delivered to Aberdeen Proving Ground, Maryland, and after intense testing, the M4 had beaten the competition. In early 1999, ARDEC awarded the M1014 Joint Service Combat Shotgun contract to Heckler & Koch, American subsidiary for importation of the Benelli M4 Combat Shotgun. The first units (count of 20,000) were delivered to the United States Marine Corps in 1999. During testing, the prototype was named *XM1014*, but after adoption, the 'X' was dropped, and the weapon was officially designated the *M1014*.[2]

2.6.2 Design

The M4 was the first gas-operated shotgun produced by Benelli. Its function is designed around an entirely new method called the "auto regulating gas operated" (ARGO) system. The short-stroke design uses two stainless-steel self-cleaning pistons located just ahead of the chamber to function opposite the rotating bolt, thereby eliminating the need for the complex mechanisms found on other gas-actuated automatics. The ARGO incorporates only four parts: two symmetrical shrouds containing two small steel gas pistons.

Additionally, the weapon is self-regulating for use with cartridges of varying length and power levels. It can fire 2.75 (70 mm) and 3-inch (76 mm) shells of differing power-levels without any operator adjustments and in any combination. Low-power rounds, such as less-lethal rubber pellets, must be cycled manually.

The sights are military-style ghost ring and are adjustable in the field using only a cartridge rim. The MIL-STD-1913 Picatinny sight rail on top allows use of both conventional and night-vision sights, while retaining use of the original sights.

A U.S. Marine trains with the M1014 shotgun in December 2006.

U.S. Marines armed with an M1014 shotgun raid a suspected enemy bomb factory in Fallujah, Iraq in May 2006.

The modular basis of the shotgun means many of its features can be reconfigured as needed. It allows a user to quickly exchange the various assembly groups (barrel, buttstock, forearm, etc...) without the use of tools.

Durability

Preliminary testing of the M4 suggests a high level of reliability. It can reliably function for at least 25,000 rounds without replacement of any major parts.[2][3] The steel components of the weapon feature a matte black phosphated corrosion resistant finish while the aluminum parts are matte hard-anodized. These finishes reduce the weapon's visibility during night operations.

The weapon requires little maintenance and operates in all climates and weather conditions.

Collapsible buttstock

The buttstock is collapsible on the M4 Model (designated 11707) but will not collapse on the M1014. This is because the M1014 was manufactured before the U.S. 1994 assault weapon ban expired, whereas the M11707 has been manufactured since the ban expired therefore not subject to the terms under the ban. Collapsing the buttstock shortens the weapon by almost 8 inches, allowing easier storage and transportation; furthermore, it permits better maneuverability around tight corners and over obstacles. The M4 is also available with a fixed stock (pistol grip and semi-pistol grip styles are both available). The M4 is no longer sold today with the skeleton fixed stock (model M11707) to civilians. Benelli only sells the M4 with a fixed pistol grip style tactical stock in the United States. However, the collapsible butt stock can be purchased by civilians in Canada.

Rail interface system

The rail interface system or Picatinny rail, built into the top of the shotgun accepts scopes, laser illuminators, night-vision sights, and flashlights. Most modern military firearms have similar structures.

Benelli Tactical and the M4

Benelli Tactical is a division of Beretta's Law Enforcement (LE) division. Benelli Tactical manages the sales of all Benelli tactical shotguns to law enforcement, government, and military entities. The M4 shotgun is sold in three configurations: M4 Entry with a 14 in barrel; M4 with an 18.5 in barrel; and M1014, which is an M4 with the "M1014" nomenclature on it for military usage only. M4 shotguns sold through Benelli tactical are available with the collapsible buttstock.

Benelli Tactical and Beretta LE have maintained the belief that the collapsible buttstock, while no longer illegal in the United States, is still only to be made available to law enforcement and government agencies. Benelli Tactical/Beretta LE will not sell these stocks to private individuals. Benelli Tactical does sell the stock piece for retrofitting the pistol grip stock for $150. The stock must be direct-shipped from Italy, however it and other aftermarket stocks are commercially available and not restricted by the United States.

Suggested retail price of the civilian version is around $1,899.[2][4] An NFA stamp is required to purchase or own the 14.5" barreled model only since this model is considered to be a Short Barreled Shotgun or SBS. Standard magazine capacity of the civilian version is 5+1, although it is possible to fit 6+1 and two shot extension tubes are sold by Benelli as well as some other companies. Some LE models have become available to private individuals on the secondary market.

2.6.3 Users

- Australia[2][5]
- Brazil: Used by Brazilian Army.
- Croatia: Used by Croatian Special Police Command (Lučko Anti-Terrorist Unit).[6][7]
- Georgia: in use with MIA and military special operation forces.[2][8]
- Greece: Used by Special Anti-Terrorist Unit (Greece) E.K.A.M.
- Italy: Used by special forces.[2]
- Iraq: Used by ISOF.[2]
- Ireland: Used by special forces and special police units (Army Ranger Wing, Special Detective Unit, Emergency Response Unit, Regional Support Unit).[2][9]
- Israel: Used by special forces.[2]
- Libya: Ordered 1800 before the Revolution. Used by special forces.[2][10]
- Lithuania: Used by special forces.[2]
- Malaysia: Used by Royal Malaysian Customs[11] and PASKAU counter-terrorism team of Royal Malaysian Air Force.[2]
- Malta[2]
- Moldova: Used by internal troops, bought in 2013.

- Philippines: Used by Special Action Force.
- Slovakia: Used by Special Defence Division and Intervention Group.[2][12]
- Slovenia: Used by Military Police Forces.[2][13]
- United Kingdom: Used by the British Armed Forces designated *L128A1*.[2][14]
- South Korea[2]
- United States of America: United States Armed Forces designated *M1014*,[15][16] Los Angeles Police Department (LAPD).[2][17]
- Bahrain: Used by internal troops in Bahraini uprising (2011–present) .

2.6.4 See also

- Benelli M1
- Benelli M2
- Benelli M3
- Combat shotgun

2.6.5 References

[1] "USMC Weapons". Retrieved 2009-12-26.

[2] "Benelli M4 Super 90 / M1014 JSCS Semi-Automatic Combat Shotgun (1999)". Military Factory. February 5, 2014. Retrieved 2014-12-23.

[3] "HK M4 Super 90/XM1014". Club.guns.ru. Retrieved 2008-09-08.

[4] "M4 Tactical Shotgun". Benelli USA. Retrieved 2013-10-09.

[5] "AusTender: Contract Notice View - CN192892". Tenders.gov.au. Retrieved 2013-10-09.

[6] 2nd row, 5th and 6th picture; special police member can be seen wielding a Benelli M4 shotgun with reflex sight. Zapovjedništvo specijalne policije, MUP. Retrieved October 2, 2013.

[7] "Benelli M4 Super 90 shotgun on 2nd from the right, after the SPAS-12. Photographed on September 28, 2013 on the Croatian Police Day". Commons.wikimedia.org. Retrieved 2013-10-09.

[8] http://www.hendonpub.com/law_and_order/articles/2014/01/ati_upgrades_for_benelli_m4

[9] "Garda Resources". *28 November 2012*. National Security Ireland. Retrieved 9 February 2014.

[10] Giorgio Beretta Mercoledì, 09 Marzo 2011 (2011-02-27). "L'Italia ha inviato 11mila Beretta semiautomatici al regime di Gheddafi / Notizie / Home" (in Italian). Unimondo. Retrieved 2013-10-09.

[11] Royal Malaysian Customs Academy (2010). "Royal Malaysian Customs Academy: Firing range". Royal Malaysian Customs. Retrieved 2011-08-22.

[12]

[13]

[14] "Combat Shotgun". Ministry of Defence (United Kingdom). Retrieved 2010-01-28.

[15]

[16] "Weapons & Demo". Navy SEALs. Retrieved 2013-10-09.

[17] Published on (2009-02-25). "LAPD Approves Benelli M4 Tactical for Individual Officer Purchase". Ammoland.com. Retrieved 2013-10-09.

2.6.6 External links

- Benelli M4 Website
- Benelli M4 operator's manual
- Official M4 Super 90 page
- British Forces show off Firepower
- Benelli ETHOS
- Benelli Legacy
- Benelli Montefeltro
- USMC weapons: M1014 Combat Shotgun

2.7 Benelli Raffaello

The **Benelli Raffaello** semi-automatic shotgun is manufactured by Italian arms manufacturer Benelli Armi SpA.

2.7.1 Design details

The shotgun has a relatively small number of component parts, incorporating a simple operating principle. The main features of the mechanism are the turning block bolt locking system and the cartridge feeding system (cut off).

2.7.2 Operation

Benelli's range of semi-automatic shotguns operate on the same basic principle of inertial operation, with a fixed barrel, utilizing the kinetic energy of gun recoil. This system requires no outlet for gas or barrel recoil, but operates by means of a spring freely interposed between bolt head and bolt.

During firing, due to the recoil of the gun, breech block inertia makes it move about 4 mm forward in relation to the power of the cartridge, compressing the spring. When this is fully compressed, it overcomes breech block inertia, thrusting it to the rear under residual pressure, permitting cartridge case extraction and reloading with the conventional system.

The pressure of the spring is calculated to delay the opening of the action, which occurs after the shot has left the barrel, and to regulate the different pressures produced by cartridges of varying power, with no need for braking.

2.7.3 See also

- Benelli Raffaello CrioComfort

2.7.4 External links

- Official homepage - Italy
- Official homepage - USA

2.8 Benelli Raffaello CrioComfort

Benelli Raffaello CrioComfort is the name of a semi-automatic shotgun. It is manufactured by Italian arms manufacturer Benelli Armi SpA.

2.8.1 Design details

The shotgun has a relatively small number of component parts, incorporating a simple operating principle. The main features of the mechanism are the turning block bolt locking system and the cartridge feeding system (cut off). These serve to make the **Raffaello CrioComfort** reliable and practical, easy to strip and maintain.

2.8.2 Operation

Benelli's range of semi-automatic shotguns operate on the same basic principle of inertial operation, with a fixed barrel, utilizing the kinetic energy of gun recoil. This system requires no outlet for gas or barrel recoil, but operates by means of a spring freely interposed between bolt head and bolt.

During firing, due to the recoil of the gun, breech block inertia makes it move about 4 mm forward in relation to the power of the cartridge, compressing the spring. When this is fully compressed, it overcomes breech block inertia, thrusting it to the rear under residual pressure, permitting cartridge case extraction and reloading with the conventional system.

The pressure of the spring is calculated to delay the opening of the action, which occurs after the shot has left the barrel, and to regulate the different pressures produced by cartridges of varying power, with no need for braking.

2.8.3 See also

- Benelli Raffaello
- Benelli Legacy
- Benelli Sport II
- Benelli Supersport
- Benelli Cordoba

2.8.4 External links

- Official homepage - Italy
- Official homepage - USA

2.9 Benelli Vinci

The **Benelli Vinci** is a semi-automatic shotgun manufactured and sold by the Benelli company. It uses an inertia-driven system of operation, and contains recoil-reducing features. It also features a modular design consisting of the barrel/receiver module (containing the operating system, barrel, and bolt), the trigger group/forearm module (containing the trigger assembly, safety, shell carrier and magazine), and the buttstock.[4] The shotgun was named after Leonardo da Vinci.[3] It is Benelli's first shotgun to feature an in-line inertia-driven operating system.[5] It is intended primarily for hunting, rather than combat or self-defense; the M3 and M4 shotguns are Benelli's primary contenders in the tactical shotgun market.[3] The Vinci is capable of firing 2.75 or 3 inch shells, while the "Super Vinci" model is capable of firing 3.5 inch shells as well.[6][7]

2.9.1 References

[1] Field & Stream

[2] The Firearm Blog

[3] Product page

[4] American Rifleman

[5] Benelli page on inertia system

[6] http://www.benelliusa.com/vinci-shotgun

[7] http://www.benelliusa.com/super-vinci-shotgun

2.10 Beretta 1201FP

The **Beretta 1201 FP** is a semi-automatic shotgun, developed in the late 1980s or early 1990s by the Italian arms manufacturing company Fabbrica d'Armi Pietro Beretta. It was an upgrade to the preceding model, the Beretta 1200. The 1201 was manufactured in two versions, 1201F, intended for hunting and sporting, and the 1201FP, intended for law enforcement duties.

The Beretta 1201FP shotgun uses the proven inertia drive operating system found on Benelli shotguns and is very reliable. Some models came with rifle sights and some came with ghost ring sights with a tritium "night sight" insert in the front sight.

The 1200 and 1201F and FP are no longer manufactured and the Benelli Super 90 is the current version.

2.10.1 External links

- Beretta 1201FP Owners Manual.

2.11 Beretta A303

The **Beretta A303** is a semi-automatic shotgun, developed by the Italian arms manufacturing company Fabbrica d'Armi Pietro Beretta.

2.12 Beretta AL391

The **Beretta AL391** is a semi-automatic shotgun. It is manufactured, marketed, and distributed by Fabbrica d'Armi Pietro Beretta, in Gardone Val Trompia, Italy.

The AL391 is most often used for hunting birds, and for clay target games such as trap and skeet. There are several different models, each with multiple variations. The AL391 is chambered in either 12 gauge or 20 gauge.

2.12.1 Features

The Beretta AL391 is mechanically similar to its predecessor, the AL390, but has a slimmer fore-end and a different shaped stock. It has an aluminum receiver, which reduces the weight of the gun. The magazine holds three rounds, providing a total capacity of four rounds, which can be reduced using a magazine plug. The gun has a magazine cutoff, which can be engaged to remove or replace a chambered shell without feeding a new round from the magazine.

The AL391 has a self-compensating gas-driven recoil system. This lacks the mechanical simplicity of some other recoil systems. However, it provides the advantage of automatically adjusting for shot shells with different charges and therefore different amounts of recoil. It is designed to cycle the action reliably when using a wide variety of shells, while minimizing felt recoil.

2.12.2 Models

- AL391 Urika: The standard model, available with a variety of features and finishes.

- AL391 Teknys: A more upscale version of the Urika, with upgraded finishing and fancier engraving.

- A391 Xtrema: Designed for hunting waterfowl, the Xtrema accepts shells up to 3½-inch magnums and has been produced in 12 gauge only.

2.12.3 See also

- Beretta Xtrema 2

2.12.4 References

- Simpson, Layne. "The AL 391: Beretta's Best", *Shooting Times*

- Coogan, Joe. "Beretta's A391 Xtrema 3.5 Gobbles Up The Turkeys", *Shooting Times*

- Wakeman, Randy. "Beretta AL391 Urika 2 Shotguns", ChuckHawks.com

- "20-Gauge Semis: Beretta Ekes Out Win in Competition Clash", *Gun Tests*, June 2008

- "Beretta's New AL391 Urika: A New Standard For Shotguns?", *Gun Tests*, July 2000

2.12.5 External links

- Beretta semi-automatic field guns
- Beretta AL391 Urika / Teknys Instruction Manual
- Beretta AL391 Urika 2 ratings, prices and reviews

2.13 Beretta Xtrema 2

The **Beretta AL391-Xtrema2** is a semi-automatic shotgun developed and produced by Italian firearm manufacturer Beretta. It is used by hunters and target shooters, mainly in the United States. The shotgun is commonly referred to simply as the Xtrema2. The shotgun is found in several variants, depending on barrel length, barrel type, and factory-installed camouflage exterior.

2.13.1 Overview

The Xtrema was released in mid-2004, to answer the call from hunters and target shooters for a complete do-all shotgun. Beretta's goal was to produce a shotgun that could reliably fire 2¾" loaded with light target loads all the way through the 3½" super magnum round without any modification or settings to be dealt with. They decided to take the AL391-Xtrema, and update it to fit their needs. They also wanted to add as many recoil reduction features as possible to the shotgun to increase follow-up shot accuracy while target shooting and hunting.

2.13.2 Technical advantages

The Xtrema2 had several features that were designed to increase accuracy and reliability. For one, Beretta decided to strip away as many o-rings and springs as possible for less chance of wear, and also to make easier for the weapon to be field stripped without the accidental loss of parts. They chose to go with a gas-operated action instead of inertia-driven action.

Another advantage is in the over-bored barrel design, which reduces muzzle jump and also improves shot-patterns.

Beretta also redesigned their stock choke system by increasing the length of the choke inside the barrel for a more gradual constriction, without having to add to the length of the barrel like after-market choke tubes do.

They then also chose to take the time-proven technology of hydraulic shock absorption from car-manufactures and put it in the gun's stock for up to 44% felt recoil reduction at the shoulder.

Beretta also saw the need for the gun to be protected from the elements so as to protect the gun in harsh hunting conditions such as water-fowl hunting, where salt spray can damage a gun within hours. Beretta's answer to this need was to coat the gun's working parts in a micro-thin membrane which completely protects the metal (which are not made from stainless steel, chromium, or aluminum) from corrosion while out in the field.

Other improvements include an extra long barrel tang (the part of the barrel that fits into the receiver, and is actually behind the chamber) to more accurately fix the barrel to the receiver in order to increase accuracy when using slugs with a scope fixed to the receiver.

Stock spacers are also available to change the length of pull without major modification.

2.13.3 See also

- Beretta AL391

2.13.4 References

- Beretta Xtrema2 User Manual
- A391 Xtrema2 at berettausa.com

2.14 Browning Auto-5

The **Browning Automatic 5**, most often **Auto-5** or simply **A-5**, is a recoil-operated semi-automatic shotgun designed by John Browning. It was the first successful semi-automatic shotgun design, and remained in production until 1998. The name of the shotgun designates that it is an autoloader with a capacity of five rounds, four in the magazine and one in the chamber.

2.14.1 History

The Browning Auto-5 was the first mass-produced semi-automatic shotgun. Designed by John Browning in 1898 and patented in 1900,[2] it was produced continually for almost 100 years by several makers with production ending in 1998. It features a distinctive high rear end, earning it the nickname "Humpback". The top of the action goes straight back on a level with the barrel before cutting down sharply towards the buttstock. This distinctive feature makes it easy to identify A-5s from a distance. A-5s were produced in a variety of gauges, with 12 and 20 predominating; 16 gauge (not produced between 1976 and 1987) models were also available. The gun saw military service worldwide between World War I and the Vietnam War.

Production

John Browning presented his design (which he called his best achievement)[3] to Winchester, where he had sold most of his previous designs. When Winchester refused his terms, Browning went to Remington. Tragically, the president of Remington died of a heart attack as Browning waited to offer them the gun. This forced Browning to look overseas to produce the shotgun. It was manufactured by FN (a company that had already produced Browning-designed pistols) starting in 1902. Browning would later license the design to Remington, who produced it as their Model 11 (1941–1948). The Remington Model 11 was the first auto-loading shotgun made in the USA. Savage Arms also licensed the design from Browning and produced it as their model 720 from 1930 to 1949, and their model 745 with an alloy receiver and two-shot magazine from 1941 to 1949. Browning's long-recoil design itself served as the operating system for subsequent Remington (11-48), Savage (755, 775) and Franchi (AL-48) models.[3]

Production of the Auto-5 in Belgium continued until the start of World War II, when Browning moved production to Remington Arms in the United States. The Auto-5 was produced by Remington alongside the Model 11 until FN could resume making the gun after the war.[4] Unlike the Remington Model 11, the Remington-produced Browning shotguns had magazine cutoffs. Some 850,000 Remington Model 11 shotguns were produced before production ended in 1947. In 1952, production of Browning models returned to FN, where it continued until the end. However, the majority of production moved to the Japanese company Miroku in 1975. Finally, in 1998, manufacture of A-5s ceased except for a few commemorative models created at FN in 1999. By that time, it was well established as the second-best-selling auto-loading shotgun in U.S. history, after the Remington 1100.[3]

In 2014 Browning released the A5, a recoil-operated shotgun with external resemblance to the Auto 5, which is being manufactured by Miroku in Japan.

2.14.2 Design details

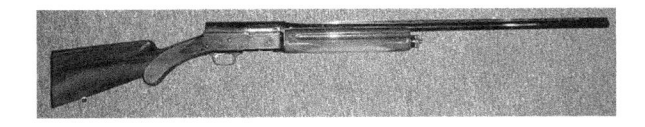

Browning Auto-5 in 20-gauge magnum (made in Japan).

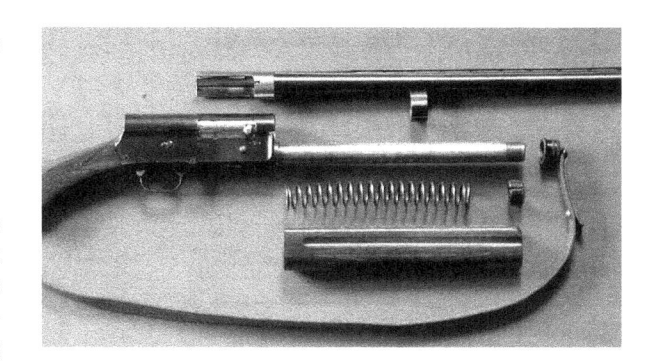

Auto-5 field stripped

The Browning Auto-5 is a long-recoil operated semi-automatic shotgun. Shells are stored in a tubular magazine under the barrel. When a chambered shell is fired, the barrel and bolt recoil together (for a distance greater than the shell length) and re-cock the hammer. As the barrel returns forward to its initial position the bolt remains behind and thus the spent shell is ejected through a port on the top of the receiver. Then the bolt returns forward and feeds another shell from the magazine into the action. This type of long recoil action was the first of its kind and patented in 1900 by John Browning.

To load the gun, shells are fed into the bottom of the action, where they are pushed into the tubular magazine. Most A-5s have removable plugs in the magazine which prevent more than three shells from being loaded (two in the magazine, plus one in the chamber) to comply with U.S. Federal migratory waterfowl laws, as well as some state hunting regulations. With the plug removed, the total capacity is five rounds. If the chamber is open (the operating handle is drawn back) the first shell loaded into the magazine tube will go directly into the chamber (there is a manual bolt closing button under the ejection port), the bolt then closes, and all further shells fed into the gun go into the magazine.

The A-5 has a system of friction rings that control the rate of recoil. Setting these rings correctly is vital to good shotgun performance and to ensure a long life to the weapon, by controlling excessive recoil. The friction rings are set based on the type of load to be fired through the gun. Different settings can be found in the owner's manual.[5]

2.14.3 References

[1] McNab, Chris (2009). *Firearms*. Queen Street House, 4th Queen Street, Bath BA1 1HE, UK: Parragon. p. 277. ISBN 978-1-4075-1607-3.

[2] Harold Murtz. *Gun Digest Treasury* (DBI Books, 1994), p.194

[3] Murtz, *Gun Digest Treasury*, pp.193–4

[4] Firearm Model History - Remington Model 11

[5] http://www.browning.com/customerservice/ownersmanuals/index.asp

2.14.4 External links

- User manual
- Model 11 Parts Diagram

2.15 FN SLP

The **FN SLP** (*Self-Loading Police*) shotgun is a semi-automatic 12-gauge shotgun designed and manufactured by FN Herstal in Belgium.[2] The SLP shotgun is gas-operated, and FN currently produces it in four different models: *SLP Standard*, *SLP Mark I*, *SLP Tactical*, and *SLP Mark I Tactical*.[2] The SLP series was introduced in 2008, and was named "2009 Shotgun of the Year" by *American Rifleman* magazine.[1]

The SLP has a MIL-STD-1913 (*Picatinny*) accessory rail and is provided with adjustable iron sights; the *SLP Standard* has a sight radius of 447 or 546 mm (17.6 or 21.5 in), while the *Mark I* has a sight radius of 457 mm (18 in).[2] SLP shotguns have a trigger pull of 28 to 33 N (6.2 to 7.3 lbF).[2] The SLP's carrier release button is located on the side of the shotgun beneath the ejection port. The shotgun's safety is located behind its trigger.[3] FN claims that the SLP is "capable of firing eight rounds in less than one second".[4]

SLP shotguns are shipped with a locking device and keys, a Standard Invector improved cylinder and modified choke tubes, a choke tube wrench, two active valve pistons (one for heavy loads and one for light loads), three interchangeable cheekpieces (with *Tactical* model only), three interchangeable recoil pads (with *Tactical* model only), and an owner's manual.[2]

2.15.1 References

[1] "FNH USA Shotguns - SLP". FNH USA. 2012. Retrieved September 7, 2012.

[2] "FNH USA SLP Autoloading Shotgun Owner's Manual" (PDF). FNH USA. 2011. Retrieved September 7, 2012.

[3] http://www.fnhusa.com/files/8913/4512/7071/2011_SLP_OMs.pdf

[4] http://www.fnhusa.com/l/products/shotguns/slp-series/slp/

2.15.2 External links

- Official website
- Official website – FNH USA
- Owner's Manual
- *FNH USA Self-Loading Police* – American Rifleman
- *FNH USA SLP MARK I 12GA* – Tactical Life
- FNH Firearms Blog

Video

- American Guardian SLP video on YouTube

2.16 Franchi AL-48

The **48 AL** is a semi-automatic shotgun manufactured by Luigi Franchi S.p.A..

The gun is available in 20 gauge and 28 gauge. Rounds are cycled through long recoil.[2] Factory models are equipped with walnut stocks and forends. Franchi offers one model with a short stock, and one model with a "Prince-of-Wales" stock.

Best known as one of the lightest semi-auto shotguns around, the Franchi 48 AL is ideal for any hunting or shooting that involves walking and carrying. The reliable action does not use gas to cycle the action but is based on John M. Browning's famous long recoil design, the Browning Auto-5.

The main advantage beside being very light is the long recoil. The barrel and bolt remain locked together during recoil, compressing the recoil spring causing the shooter to experience less recoil. Shells are stored in a tubular magazine under the barrel. When a chambered shell is fired, the barrel and bolt recoil together (for a distance greater than the shell length) and re-cock the hammer. As the barrel returns forward to its initial position the bolt remains behind and thus the spent shell is ejected through a port on the top of the receiver. Then the bolt returns forward and feeds another shell from the magazine into the action. This type of long recoil action was the first of its kind and patented in 1900 by John Browning.

2.16.1 References

[1] http://www.franchiusa.com/sites/default/files/originals/product-catalogs/2013_franchi_catalog.pdf

[2] http://www.franchiusa.com/franchi-48al-shotgun/

2.17 Franchi SPAS-12

The **Franchi SPAS-12** is a combat shotgun manufactured by Italian firearms company Franchi from 1979 to 2000. Production stopped fully in the year 2000 in favour of the newer, enhanced version, the SPAS-15, however, production of the SPAS-15 ceased in 2005, meaning there are currently no SPAS shotguns being produced. Only five percent (about 1,850) of the estimated Franchi SPAS 12 shotguns manufactured were imported into the United States. The SPAS-12 is a dual-mode shotgun, adjustable for semi-automatic or pump-action operation. The SPAS-12 was sold to military and police users worldwide on the civilian market, and has been featured in many movies, TV shows and video games.[1]

The appearance and intended purpose of the SPAS-12 initially led to its "Military" designation as a Combat Shotgun. The SPAS-12 was designed from the ground up as a rugged military shotgun and it was named the **Special Purpose Automatic Shotgun**. In 1990 Franchi renamed the shotgun to the **Sporting Purpose Automatic Shotgun**, this allowed continued sales to the United States as a limited-magazine-capacity, fixed-stock model until 1994. Following the United States Federal Assault Weapons Ban, imports of SPAS-12 shotguns were stopped into the United States. In September 2004 the ban had expired, but Franchi had ended production in 2000 of the SPAS-12 to focus on the manufacturing of the Franchi SPAS-15 model. The SPAS-12's retail price in its final year of 2000 was $1500.00 USD averaged for final sales outside the United States to non-restricted countries. Franchi S.p.A. Italy.[2]

2.17.1 Design

The SPAS-12 was designed to function primarily as a semi-automatic firearm, with the pump-action mode used to reliably fire low-pressure ammunition such as tear gas rounds or less-lethal bean bags. The firing mode is switched by depressing the button under the foregrip and also sliding the foregrip forwards or backwards until it clicks into position allowing the rotating sleeve to open or close the two gas ports.

The SPAS-12 has a magazine cut-off feature, which prevents loading a new round from the internal magazine when the gun is cycled. This allows the operator to load a specialized round into the chamber without firing the entire magazine first. A unique feature of the SPAS-12 was the hook on folding-stock variants. This hook could be rotated in 90-degree increments, so it would fit under the user's forearm when the stock was extended. With the stock supported under the forearm the gun can be fired with one hand, an example would be allowing the user to fire from a vehicle through the passenger side window while driving.

SPAS-12 models feature two safeties: (i) a lever style or push button style safety, and (ii) a "quick employment safety." Lever safeties were recalled by Franchi and were replaced through the importer American Arms in the early 1990s.[a] There are two different types of push-button safeties. The earliest version would actually release the hammer on safe up to 1/4in. of travel when the trigger was depressed. This would cause a lockup of the action that would require the user to relock the bolt assembly to the rear to reset the hammer and then reload the chamber. The later version installed a detent and machined hole in the trigger group frame to prevent an action lock. The detent would prevent the hammer from engaging when the trigger was depressed and would prevent an action lock from occurring. The quick employment safety, which is on the left side of the trigger guard, disconnects the trigger when put into safe mode. The quick employment safety can be disengaged with the trigger finger when ready to fire and is intended for competition or tactical use. A third safety type, a pistol grip safety similar to the later-developed SPAS-15, is known to have been developed by Franchi for the SPAS-12, however the pistol grip safety was not offered for sale to the general public. Examples of this safety are extremely rare, with only two known to exist in the United States.

Example of SPAS-12 pistol grip safety. The photographed gun is one of only two known examples to exist in the United States.

A B-Square rail mount for optics was available for a short time in the 1990s as an aftermarket accessory.

The Barrel of the SPAS-12 was externally threaded to accept a variety of attachments. The barrel is cylinder bored and spreads a normal shot charge to about 900mm at 40 meters range, reducing the need for precise aiming. The automatic action will fire about four shots per second, and at this rate of fire, with standard buckshot loadings, it is possible to put 48 pellets per second into a one-meter-square target at 40 meters range. At this range the pellets have about 50 percent more striking energy than a .32 pistol bullet.

There are four different Magazine Extension Tubes manufactured for the SPAS 12:

1. The 5-shell was designed for the 18" barrel.
2. The 6-shell was designed for restriction on the standard 21.5" Sporting Purpose model.
3. The 7-shell was designed for the 19 7/8in. Barrel.
4. The 8-shell was designed for the 21.5 Special purpose model.

Many different choke types both original and aftermarket exist for the SPAS-12.[3] A 44mm grenade launcher used by France was used for explosive grenades capable of a range of 150 meters.[4] A very rare factory shot diverter that spreads shot vertically or horizontally was originally included with earlier model SPAS-12's.[5]

2.17.2 SPAS-12, SAS-12 and LAW-12 Model Differences

Two of the most commonly found SPAS-12 variants: the folding-stock version (with an eight-round magazine extension) by F.I.E Corp and the fixed-stock version (with a six-round magazine extension) by American Arms Inc.

Four different stock styles exist. The first version of the SPAS-12 manufactured with the wooden detachable stock with the standard grip. Models were later available with the folding metal stock with hook. A rare aftermarket Choate skeleton stock (Approx: 150-180 Choate stocks Manufactured for the shotgun)[6] with an AR15 style grip was available for a short time in the early 1990s. After the United States imposed import restrictions on the SPAS-12 in 1989, a version was released in 1990 with the synthetic hollow fixed stock and a six shell capacity to comply with federal regulations for sporting purposes.

Four different factory barrels manufactured for the SPAS-12.

(Top) Fixed Stock 1990 Sporting Purpose SPAS-12L receiver. (Middle) A rare Choate made aftermarket AR-15 grip style skeleton stock on a 1987 SPAS-12L. (Bottom) Special Purpose Collector SPAS from 1982 with the folding stock and hook.

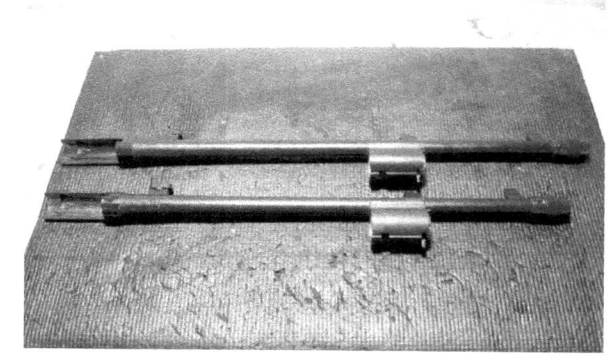

Franchi Barrel Length SPAS-12 21-1-2" Bbl VS 19-7-8" Bbl

1. (Very Rare) 18-inch (46 cm) "shorty" made for Law Enforcement/Military originally distributed mainly in France. This is the only known model to ever receive the pistol grip safety (an attribute that is extremely rare and desirable to collectors).[7]

2. (Very Rare) 19-7/8 in. found scattered on a very few of the 1983 "AL" proofed SPAS-12 Shotguns. These were made for Law Enforcement/Military originally.

3. (Common to the United Kingdom) 21-1/2" as a one piece barrel converted to a 24" UK legal barrel. This barrel adds with a 2.5-inch (6.4 cm) choke tube brazed or silver-soldered in place).[8]

4. (Most Common) The standard 21-1/2" with sight blade muzzle ended on barrel for the special purpose model or the pushed back sight blade with brazed extension for the sporting purpose model.

The **Franchi SPAS-12** came equipped with a non-adjustable circular aperture rear sight and a large, non-adjustable blade foresight integrated into the barrel. The LAW-12 was a semi-automatic only and the SAS-12 was a pump action only. These three "sister" shotguns accepted all SPAS-12 components, notably trigger groups, barrel threaded attachments and stocks. The various magazine extension tubes of the LAW-12 and SAS-12 were never designed to be interchangeable with the SPAS-12 as this would cause issues with the gas selector switch moving from Auto to Pump action on the SPAS-12 model.[9] The extensions have been known to spin off the front of the SPAS-12 during cycling if the extension was not tapered for the SPAS-12 retaining pin.

The SPAS-12 collector shotguns are wanted for certain style features.

1. The front sight blade is muzzle ended.
2. The longer extension allowing eight shells in the tubular magazine.[9]
3. The date code on the receiver is proofed 1989 or prior with F.I.E. (Firearms Import and Export) Corporation as importer.[10]
4. The barrel length is 21.5 or less and the less barrel length by factory is more sought after.
5. Attached stock is the wooden detachable with grip and or the metal folding stock with hook.

The **Franchi SAS-12** could accept 3" shells but it did not have a bolt handle cut in the bolt body. The SPAS and LAW could only accept 2¾" shells. The SAS 12 has a barrel length of 21.5" an overall length of 41.5" a weight of 7 lbs. 4 oz. and a capacity of 8 rounds in the magazine + 1 in the chamber. The Franchi SAS total numbers of import are unknown according to the BATFE, it is believed the there are fewer than 1000 total SAS-12 models imported into the United States. The SAS-12 was never under any import restrictions or assault weapon bans and yet it showed the least amount of sales between the three models from Franchi. The price of a SAS-12 shotgun was averaged at $400.00 for retail sales before its discontinuation in 2000.

The **Franchi LAW-12** Model was also restricted by importation in 1989 and banned in 1994 with the AWB. The LAW-12 has a barrel length of 21.5" a weight of 7 lbs. 4 oz. and a capacity of 8 rounds in the magazine + 1 in the chamber. The model was known to have imported with all stock styles used on the Franchi SPAS-12. Total numbers imported estimated to around 3,800 shotguns. The LAW-12 models were more common with police sales as an alternative to the more expensive SPAS-12 for departments throughout the United States. The LAW-12 was discontinued by Franchi shortly before the SPAS-12 discontinued in 2000. The LAW-12 retail price in its final year of 2000 was $470.00 averaged for final sales outside of the United States to non-restricted countries.

2.17.3 United States Importers

The United States allowed two different licensed importers for the Franchi SPAS-12 shotguns. From 1982-1989 importation of the first version known as the (Special Purpose Automatic Shotgun), SPAS-12 imported into the United States from Italy with F.I.E. Corporation. In 1989 F.I.E suffered from major losses of sales due to the importation ban restriction act of an executive order by the president under national security ruling 18 U.S.C. 925 (d)(3) on sporting restrictions. The executive order amended further the 1968 Gun Control Act.

In 1990 American Arms incorporated purchased all remaining inventories of parts and SPAS-12 shotguns from F.I.E Corp and began the re-importation of the Franchi SPAS-12 as the (Sporting Purpose Automatic Shotgun) under newly approved restrictions. From 1990-1994 American Arms incorporated two changes with the fixed stock and magazine tube extension restrictions, thus allowing Importation to continue. The ATF allowed importation of a SPAS-12 variant from American Arms because its size, weight, bulk and modified configuration were such that it was particularly suitable for traditional shooting sports.[11]

The SPAS-12 was tested by the U.S. Coast Guard and showed promising results but again was not considered cost effective for a contract over other available suppliers. The Assault Weapons Ban of September 1994 caused American Arms to stop the importation of the SPAS-12 with major losses of sales due to the legal restrictions invoked by the U.S. Assault Weapons Ban.[12]

It is important to know that both importers requested numerous additional orders for the Franchi SPAS-12 Shotguns that with both companies were never completely filled due to imposed laws by U.S. restriction throughout both importers time periods. This was the reason for such few numbers of importation into the United States.[13] Only five percent (about 1,850) of the estimated SPAS-12 shotguns manufactured were imported into the United States.[14]

2.17.4 U.S. Legal

A SPAS-12 Shotgun is not a NFA Registry item if it was imported/grandfathered into the United States between 1982-1994 bearing the import markings of F.I.E or American Arms.[b]

From 1982 to 2000, a SPAS-12L model was manufactured for law enforcement worldwide and imported in to the U.S. until the 1994 (AWB) Assault Weapons Ban. The SPAS-12L Law Enforcement model included the prior to 1990 folding stock and high capacity magazine tube extension from 1990-1994. The SPAS-12L model was later sold on the U.S. civilian market as existing (grandfathered) import.

The production year of an SPAS-12 may be identified by a two-digit letter code forward of the loading port.[15]

A SPAS-12 and SPAS-12L shotgun factory stamped by a year after 1994 is considered an illegal import violating federal importation laws with penalties for possession in the U.S. The SPAS-12 would not include Importation Markings on the side of the receiver prior to 1982 and after 1994 by the U.S. importers Firearms Import and Export (F.I.E) or American Arms.

The 1994 federal "Crime Bill," signed into law by President Clinton on Sept. 13, 1994, included the Violent Crime Control and Law Enforcement Act of 1994. That Act included provisions amending the Gun Control Act (GCA, 1968) to make it a federal crime for a private individual to possess or transfer (sell, give, etc.) an "assault weapon" manufactured after that date. [18 U.S.C. 922(v)]. "Assault weapons" manufactured on or before that date are "grandfathered," meaning that the law does not prohibit their possession or transfer. The law requires that "assault weapons" manufactured after Sept. 13, 1994 be stamped with their date of manufacture or serial number to identify with factory date of manufacturing.[16]

SPAS-12 and LAW-12 Shotguns are listed illegal for possession in states that hold a "military assault weapon style" law that identifies the shotguns by name on each states individual ban. The states may have had a registration timeline that would allow it to be grandfathered prior to each states individual ban. U.S. States and territories listed that ban the Franchi SPAS-12 and LAW-12 currently from future individual civilian possession. CA,[17] CT,[18] District of Columbia,[19] MD,[20] MA,[21] NJ,[22] NY.[23]

2.17.5 Users

- Panama: Used by Special Forces
- Argentina: Used by Special Operations.
- Australia: Used by police forces.
- Austria: Used by EKO Cobra.[24]
- Bangladesh: Special Security Force.[25]
- Bahrain: Used by the Bahrain special forces.
- Cambodia
- Croatia: Used by Croatian Army.
- India: Special forces.
- Iraq: ISOF.
- Italy: Used by military and police.
- Indonesia: *Komando Pasukan Katak* (Kopaska) tactical group and *Komando Pasukan Khusus* (Kopassus) special-forces group.[26]
- Ireland: Used by the Army Ranger Wing.[27]
- Lebanon: Lebanese Armed Forces
- Malaysia: Malaysian Special Operations Force.[28]
- Nepal: Nepal Mobile Police[29]
- Norway: Used by military
- Pakistan: Used by police and Military
- Philippines: Used by police
- Turkey: Turkish Gendarmerie.[30]
- United States: Used by police SWAT teams.[31]

2.17.6 See also

- Franchi SPAS-15
- Benelli M4
- List of shotguns
- Combat shotgun

2.17.7 Notes

^a The push-button cross bolt safety has also been known to fail and release the hammer when depressing the trigger on safe and it is recommended that the secondary Quick Employment Safety (lever tab on left side of trigger) is used on both the newer and older style trigger groups in place of the lever or cross bolt safety's to prevent accidental discharge.

^b The LAW-12 and SAS-12 models were known to have no import markings on the receiver but are actually marked by importer on the barrel itself.

2.17.8 References

[1] "Franchi SPAS-12". *imfdb.org*.

[2] Cooney, Chris (June 2002). "Introduction". Retrieved 2010-05-10.

[3] "SPAS Choke Adaptor". *spas12.com*.

[4] "Cibles #164 November 1983". *The SPAS 12 Project*.

[5] "Franchi SPAS-12 Factory Accessories". *spas12.com*.

[6] "Welcome to Choate Machine and Tool - Your Premier Source for Tactical Stocks and Accessories for Rifles, Shotguns and Submachine Guns". *riflestock.com*.

[7] "SPAS-12 -". *Guns.com*.

[8] "UK Owner's Letter". *spas12.com*.

[9] "Magazine Extension Types". *spas12.com*.

[10] "When Was My SPAS 12 Made?". *The SPAS 12 Project*.

[11] https://www.atf.gov/files/firearms/industry/january-2011-importability-of-certain-shotguns.pdf.

[12] "The Coolest Email You'll Read All Day". *The SPAS 12 Project*.

[13] "Firearms and Ammunition Technology". *atf.gov*.

[14] Lorenzo Galante per Raineri Design s.r.l. "Beretta Holding S.p.A.". *berettaholding.com*.

[15] "Untitled Document". *danddsales.com*.

[16] http://www.gpo.gov/fdsys/pkg/BILLS-110hr1022ih/html/BILLS-110hr1022ih.htm

[17] "CA Codes (pen:30500-30530)". *ca.gov*.

[18] "WEAPONS BANNED AS ASSAULT WEAPONS". *ct.gov*.

[19] "Law Center to Prevent Gun Violence". *Law Center to Prevent Gun Violence*.

[20] "Gen. 101] 101 FIREARMS May 24, 2010 Colonel Terrence B. Sheridan Superintendent, Maryland State Police You have asked for an int" (PDF). *googleusercontent.com*.

[21] "Law Center to Prevent Gun Violence". *Law Center to Prevent Gun Violence*.

[22] "S2497". *state.nj.us*.

[23] "NYSAFE Act Gun Reform - Governor Andrew M. Cuomo". *ny.gov*.

[24] http://www.bmi.gv.at/cms/BMI_EKO_Cobra/publikationen/files/LawOrder.pdf

[25] "Bangladesh Military Forces - BDMilitary.com". *Bangladesh Military Forces - BDMilitary.com*.

[26] "Kopassus & Kopaska – Specijalne Postrojbe Republike Indonezije" (in Croatian). Hrvatski Vojnik Magazine. Retrieved 2010-06-12.

[27] Matthew Hogan. "IRELAND'S ARMY RANGERS". *Tactical Life Gun Magazine: Gun News and Gun Reviews*.

[28] Thompson, Leroy (December 2008). "Malaysian Special Forces". Special Weapons. Retrieved 2010-02-10.

[29] Shotgun uses by Nepal Mobile Service police^

[30] "SÝLAHLAR". *jandarma.tsk.tr*.

[31] McManners, Hugh (2003). *Ultimate Special Forces*. DK Publishing, Inc. ISBN 0-7894-9973-8.

2.17.9 External links

- Franchi SPAS-15
- Modern Weapons—SPAS-12
- Use and Maintenance Manual
- The SPAS 12 Project
- Chris Cooney Historical Data Reference
- Carlsons
- Gun Parts Corp

2.18 Franchi SPAS-15

The **SPAS-15** is a dual-mode 12 gauge combat shotgun manufactured by the Italian company Luigi Franchi S.p.A..

2.18.1 Design

The weapon is based on the SPAS-12, and has similar pump-action/semi-automatic firing modes. In semi-automatic mode a gas piston drives a bolt carrier and rotating bolt. In pump-action mode the same components are driven by sliding the fore-end backwards. Pump-action mode is required to reliably fire low-pressure (less lethal) ammunition such as tear gas rounds or less-lethal bean bags. Switching between firing modes is done by pressing a button above the foregrip, and sliding the foregrip slightly forwards or backwards. The barrel is chrome lined and features screw-in choke tubes.[2]

Unlike its predecessor, the SPAS-15 is fed by a detachable box magazine. The gun features a folding stock and a pistol grip safety. Amongst Italian troops the weapon is known by the nickname "La Chiave dell'Incursore" (the key of the commando) because it is used to blast the locks of closed doors.

2.18.2 Legality

In 1994, the United States banned the importation of the SPAS-15 with close to 180 shotguns imported, but later abolished the relevant regulations. In Canada, the SPAS-15 is classified as a Prohibited Weapon and cannot be legally owned or imported except under very limited circumstances.[3] In Italy the SPAS-15 is not subject to any kind of restriction for sale, purchase or possession, and despite no longer being in production it is still fairly common on the civilian market.

2.18.3 Users

- Argentina: Used by Gendarmeria Nacional Argentina.[4]
- Belarus: Used by the "Almaz" anti-terrorist group.[5]
- Brazil: Used by Military Police GRT unit[6]
- Italy: 2,000 acquired in 1999 by the Italian Army.[7] Also used by the Carabinieri.[8]
- Dominican Republic: Dominican Army.
- Israel-In use with Israeli special forces [9]
- Portugal: Portuguese Army.[10]
- Serbia: Special Brigade.[11]
- Tunisia: Tunisian Armed Forces.[12]

2.18.4 See also

- List of shotguns

2.18.5 References

[1] Firearms, an illustrated guide to small arms of the world, di Chris McNab

[2] Jones, Richard (2009). *Jane's Infantry Weapons 2009-2010*. Jane's Information Group. p. 308. ISBN 0-7106-2869-2.

[3] List of Restricted and Prohibited Firearms, Canadian Firearms Centre (CFC)

[4] Juan Larrosa. "Blog de las Fuerzas de Defensa de la República Argentina". *fdra.blogspot.it*.

[5] "АЛМАЗ - антитерор". *YouTube*. 22 March 2011.

[6] "grt". *Fotolog*.

[7] http://www.asianmilitaryreview.com/upload/200712031402131.pdf

[8] Carabinieri http://www.carabinieri.it/Internet/Arma/Oggi/Armamento/Armamento+speciale/Spas15/

[9] http://www.isayeret.com/guides/weapons.shtml. Missing or empty |title= (help)

[10] http://www.exercito.pt/meios/Documents/media_MeiosOp/Armamento/ESP%20CAÇ%20SEMI-AUT%20FRANCHI-SPAS.pdf

[11] "Specijalna brigada Vojske Srbije". *Military World*.

[12] http://3.bp.blogspot.com/-JV7_JbaLQh0/TzE4ai_EtXI/AAAAAAAAOoA/HcvjumhBeJ4/s400/1image.jpg

2.18.6 External links

- Manual
- Franchi SPAS-15 at Modern Firearms
- Franchi Homepage in English
- magazine patent

2.19 Heckler & Koch HK512

The **Heckler & Koch HK 512** is a gas-operated semi-automatic shotgun, of Italian origin. It was developed and produced by Franchi at the request of Heckler & Koch, which took care of marketing and sales. The HK 512 was one of the first semi-automatic shotguns developed for law enforcement use.

2.19.1 Design

The HK 512 is a semi-automatic shotgun that uses a H&K recoil system that is also found in the later Benelli Super 90 series. The stock and forearm are made of wood and the rest of the gun is made out of metal. The smoothbore barrel is fitted with a choke that acts as a shot diverter, making it more effective against human targets. The HK512 is designed for use by police and military forces; indeed, the use of standard sporting cartridges, shells with reduced charges, or plastic training rounds will cause the HK-512 to malfunction. The muzzle of the gun incorporates a device that causes the shot to spread in an almost rectangular pattern. Because of this shot device, the HK-512 also cannot fire tear gas or signal cartridges.[1]

The HK 512 can fires 12 gauge 2.75-inch shotgun shells. The tubular magazine holds seven rounds. Only buckshot can be fired due to the muzzle device that shapes the shot horizontally in an oval pattern. The use of low powered rounds causes the HK 512 to malfunction.

2.19.2 Users

- Austria: EKO Cobra
- Germany: SEK and GSG-9
- India: National Security Guards
- Indonesia: Denjaka
- Malaysia: Royal Malaysia Police
- Spain: Grupo Especial de Operaciones

2.19.3 References

[1] German Semi-automatic Shotguns

2.19.4 External links

- Heckler & Koch HK512 WeaponsSystem.net

2.20 Ithaca Mag-10

The **Ithaca Mag-10** is a gas-operated, semi-automatic shotgun chambered in 10-gauge (3½"). The CounterCoil system built into the front of the magazine tube reduced the recoil from the round to allow easier second shots but cut the magazine size in half to 2 shells. Regular models had jeweled-finish bolts, engraved barrels and checkered stocks. It was produced until 1989, at which point Remington Arms bought the design and used it as the basis for the Remington Model SP-10.

2.20.1 Variants

RoadBlocker

The RoadBlocker, featuring a shorter 21" barrel, was designed for the law enforcement market, but met with little commercial success. It had a parkerized finish on the barrel, trigger group and bolt and plain walnut stocks. The barrel was rollmarked "RoadBlocker" and the weapon had a serial number with an RB prefix. The 1985 model could be ordered with a ribbed barrel for an extra $34.

DeerSlayer

The DeerSlayer featured a 22" barrel and rifle sights and was optimized for firing slugs. It came in a blued or parkerized finish and a plain stock.

2.20.2 References

- Wood, J.B. (2002). *The Gun Digest Book of Firearms Assembly/Disassembly, Part V: Shotguns (Second Addition)*. Krause Publications. pp. 168–169. ISBN 0-87349-400-8.
- Shideler, Dan (2010). *2010 Standard Catalog of Firearms: The Collector's Price and Reference Guide*. Gun Digest Books. p. 599. ISBN 0-89689-825-3.
- Long, Duncan (2004). *Streetsweepers: The Complete Book of Combat Shotguns*. Paladin Press. p. 140. ISBN 1-58160-436-X.

2.20.3 External links

- Ithaca Mag-10 Schematic
- NCJRS Abstract on Roadblocker

2.21 Manville gun

The **Manville gun** was a stockless, semi-automatic, revolver type gun, introduced in 1935 by Charles J. Manville.[1] The Manville Gun was a large weapon, with a heavy cylinder being rotated for each shot by a clockwork-type spring. The spring was wound manually during the reloading.

By 1938 Manville had introduced three different bore diameter versions of the gun, based on 12-gauge, 26.5-mm, or 37-mm shells. Due to poor sales, Manville guns ceased production in 1943.

2.21.1 Manville 12-Bore Gun

The original, 1935, steel-and-aluminum weapon held twenty four rounds of 12-gauge x 2.75-inch (18.5mmx70mmR) shells in a spring-driven rotary-cylinder that had to be wound counter-clockwise before firing. It consisted of a steel barrel of 11.1 inches (280 mm), a rotating aluminum-alloy ammo cylinder, a single-piece steel body and foregrip, and wooden pistol grips.

Loading and unloading were effected by unscrewing two thick, large-headed knobbed screws at the top of the weapon's cylinder that allowed the disassembly of the weapon into two halves. The forend and cylinder were the front half and the pistol-grip and cylinder backplate were the back half.

The weapon's striker was engaged by rotating and then pushing in a knob at the back of the pistol grip (reversed to disengage it - rendering it safe). Each cylinder in the weapon had its own firing pin assembly. When the trigger is pulled the striker is cocked; when the trigger "breaks", the striker is released and hits the firing pin, firing the shell.

2.21.2 26.5mm Manville Machine-Projector

In 1936, Manville introduced a version that held eighteen rounds of 26.5mm bore shells. This design fired 26.5mm x 3.15 inch Short (26.5mm x 80mmR) flare, smoke, and riot gas shells. The weapon is similar to the earlier 12-gauge version, except the barrel was either 9.5 inches (240 mm) or 9.75 inches (248 mm), and used hard rubber rear grips instead of wood.

The First Model 26.5 was a larger-bore version of the 12-gauge shotgun, using the same two securing screws.

The Second Model 26.5 differed in that it used a long, thick metal locking bar with a turned-down bolt-handle, like the metal bolt on a bolt-action rifle, which locked into a recess machined into the frame. This slid through a round sleeve atop each half of the weapon to secure the two halves. When the bolt was unlatched and pulled to the rear, the back-plate was turned to the operator's right using the rear grip, allowing access to the cylinder. The operator could then pull out the spent shells and reload fresh ones.

Barrel and cylinder inserts were available to allow it to fire 12-gauge shells or clusters of .38 Special rounds.

2.21.3 37mm Manville Gas Gun

In 1938, Manville introduced a twelve round gun with a 37mm bore. This version fired 37mm x 5.5 inch Long (37mm x 127mmR) flare, smoke, or tear gas shells and was designed for police and security use. It was meant to be used in an indirect fire mode and had its barrel mounted at the bottom of the cylinder rather than the top. Its greater weight prohibited its use by any but the strongest of men, since it was designed to be fired from a tripod or pintle mount.

2.21.4 History

The Indiana National Guard used 26.5mm Manville guns to break up mobs of strikers during the Terre Haute General Strike of 1935. They fired flare and tear gas shells at strikers until they dispersed.

Police and military forces found the Manville guns to be large and heavy, resulting in limited sales. The Manville company ceased production of the weapons in 1943, after which Charles Manville destroyed all machinery, dies, diagrams and notes.

2.21.5 Related Guns

Hawk Engineering MM-1

A gun with a similar design, the Hawk MM-1, was introduced in the 1970s.

The XM-18E1R

The 1980 film *The Dogs of War* used a 26.5mm Manville Machine-Projector as the weapon of choice for the lead protagonist, Shannon (Christopher Walken). In the film, the weapon is called a "XM-18E1R" grenade-launcher, deemed capable of firing munitions far beyond the actual Manville gun, when dialogue and literature in the film suggests that it fires fragmentation, grenade, tactical, anti-tank, anti-personnel and flashette (sic) shells. The actual "shells" used during the film were 12-gauge blanks.

2.21.6 Notes

- Machine Projector by C. J Manville

[1] **Machine Projector** United States Patent US2101148. Applied for in March 11, 1935 and granted in December 7, 1937.

2.22 MAUL (weapon)

The **Multi-shot Accessory Underbarrel Launcher**, or **MAUL**, is a semi-automatic shotgun formerly manufactured by defunct Brisbane-based company Metal Storm.[1] It is able to fire a range of loads; buckshot, slug, door-breaching slugs, and less-lethal blunt-force loads are preloaded in 5 round "stacked projectile" munition tubes. With a 12-gauge bore and weighing less than 800 grams (1.8 lb), it is designed to be used as an underslung module of a combat rifle such as M4 or M16, but may be used as a standalone[2][3]

2.22.1 Users

- Papua New Guinea: As of 3 August 2010, Metal Storm have signed a contract with the Correctional Services Minister Tony Aimo to supply 500 standalone MAULs and 10,000 less-lethal barrels for use by correctional services officers;[1] As of January 2011, this contract was awaiting ratification from the PNG government.

2.22.2 References

[1] "Metal Storm win multi-million contract". *The Sydney Morning Herald* (Fairfax Media). 3 August 2010. Retrieved 3 August 2010.

[2] "MAUL". *Metal Storm website*. Metal Storm Limited. Retrieved 3 August 2010.

[3] "MAUL – Multishot Accessory Underbarrel Launcher". *Marines magazine*. United States Marine Corps. 5 April 2010. Retrieved 3 May 2010.

2.23 Mossberg 930

The **Mossberg 930** is a 12-gauge semi-automatic shotgun designed by O.F. Mossberg & Sons.

The Mossberg 930 is one of the most popular automatic shotguns, used by hunters and skeet-shooters often.

2.23.1 Design

The Mossberg 930 is gas operated, which means that some of the hot gases from the burning gunpowder are used to push a piston that operates the action, ejecting the spent hull and chambering a fresh shell. This gas action reduces the recoil felt by the shooter. Like other Mossberg shotguns, this shotgun has an ambidextrous safety that is located on the rear of the receiver. The Mossberg 930 takes 2¾" or 3" shells and can be accessorized with shell catchers, Picatinny rails, special muzzle brakes for door breaching, etc.

2.23.2 References

[1] "930™ Autoloader Specifications". O.F. Mossberg & Sons. Archived from the original on July 12, 2012. Retrieved June 14, 2015.

[2] "930™-Special Purpose Features". O.F. Mossberg & Sons. Archived from the original on August 4, 2012. Retrieved June 14, 2015.

2.23.3 External links

- Mossberg Products Page
- Mossberg Forum
- http://www.learnaboutguns.com/2008/10/28/mossberg-930-semi-automatic-shotgun-review/

2.24 Remington Model 11-48

The **Remington 11-48** is a semi-automatic shotgun manufactured by Remington Arms as the first of the "New Generation" semi-autos produced after World War II.[1] The Model 11-48 was released as the replacement for Remington's Model 11. It was manufactured from 1949 to 1968 and was produced in 12, 16, 20 and 28 gauge and .410 variations.

2.24.1 Design

The 11-48 is a long-recoil operated semi-automatic shotgun based on the Remington Model 11. Shells are stored in a tubular magazine under the barrel. When a chambered shell is fired, the barrel and bolt recoiling together (for a distance greater than the shell length) re-cock the hammer, eject the spent shell, and feed another shell from the magazine into the action.

The 11-48 was revolutionary in that it ushered in stamped steel components for a lower cost of assembly, and featured truly interchangeable parts not requiring fitting by a gunsmith, and it was reliable in the extreme. The impact of these changes can be seen on every Remington shotgun since, and is also prevalent on competitor's models. The 11-48 differs from the Model 11 in the shape of its machined steel receiver and the use of less expensive stamped steel internal parts. The new easily removable aluminum trigger housing was to be featured on its successors, the 1100 and the 11-87.

Like the Model 11, the gun operated by way of two return springs. The first, located in the buttstock, serves as the resistance to the bolt. The second spring, located over the magazine tube, serves as the barrel recoil spring, allowing the barrel to recoil several inches into the receiver. The 11-48 differs from the Model 11 in the friction ring placed at the forward end of the barrel recoil spring. The Model 11 had a brass friction ring with one blunt end and one beveled end. The ring fit into a corresponding cut in the barrel underlug. For heavy loads, the ring was turned with the beveled end facing the lug. For lighter loads, the blunt end was turned to face the lug. The 11-48 features a similar friction ring system but is modified to be self-adjusting so as to work with all loads.

2.24.2 Sportsman '48

The Sportsman '48 is a variation introduced to comply with various US hunting laws. It came with a crimped magazine tube that allowed it to be loaded with only two shells in the magazine. One additional round placed in the chamber brought its total capacity to three shells. It came in 12, 16, and 20 gauge variations. The dimples pressed into the magazine tube can be removed with a round file from the inside, allowing the magazine to accept 4 shells instead of just 2.

2.24.3 References

[1] "Model 11-48 Autoloading Shotgun". Remington Arms. Retrieved 25 December 2012.

2.24.4 External links

- Remington 11-48 Firearm Owner's Manual

2.25 Remington Model 11-87

The **Remington 11-87** is a semi-automatic shotgun manufactured by Remington Arms. It is based on the Remington 1100 and was first announced in 1987.

The 11-87 is a gas operated semi-automatic (autoloading) shotgun, meaning that some of the high pressure gases from the burning gunpowder are diverted through two small holes in the underside of the barrel.[2] The gases force a piston (and the bolt) toward the rear of the shotgun, which in turn ejects the spent shell. A spring then forces the bolt forward, sending a new shell from the magazine into the chamber. This gas operation has the effect of reducing the recoil felt by the shooter, since the total recoil energy is spread out over a longer period of time; than would be the case with fixed breech shotguns.[2]

The 11-87 incorporates a self compensating gas system design, which allows the gun to operate with every type of load from light 2 ¾" loads up to 3" Magnum loads without any shooter adjustments. It is manufactured in two different gauges: 20 and 12, and both will cycle 2 ¾" and 3" shells. Some 11-87 shotguns, especially ones with barrels shorter than 26" or Magnum models may have issues cycling light target and birdshot loads consistently. The 12 gauge 3-1/2" SuperMag and 20 gauge Magnum models come with an extra part on the magazine tube called a "barrel seal activator" that helps cycle lighter loads. It is recommended you remove the barrel seal activator before firing 2 3/4" magnum, 3", and 3 1/2" loads; failing to do so may bring pressures to dangerous levels which could damage the gun. Recently, a Super Magnum version has been introduced to operate with the newer 3 ½" 12 gauge shells.[3] Some 11-87s have interchangeable screw-in chokes, although barrels are available with fixed chokes. Most barrels are not interchangeable between 1100 and 11-87 models. Barrel lengths range from the police 14 in (360 mm) to 30 in (760 mm).[4] The weapon was famously used in the Coen brothers' movie *No Country for Old Men*, based on the same book by Cormac McCarthy.[5]

2.25.1 Users

- United States: Used by numerous law enforcement agencies.[6]

2.25.2 External links

- Official Website

- Modern Firearms

2.25.3 References

[1] Remington firearm specifications page

[2] Remington 11-87 Semi-Automatic Shotgun Review | LearnAboutGuns.com

[3] Remington Model 11-87 Shotguns

[4] Remington Law Enforcement page

[5] http://www.nramuseum.org/the-museum/the-galleries/william-b-ruger-special-exhibits/hollywood-guns-4/no-country-for-old-men-(2007).aspx Accessed on June 27, 2014

[6] McManners, Hugh (2003). *Ultimate Special Forces*. DK Publishing, Inc. ISBN 0-7894-9973-8.

2.26 Remington Model 1100

The **Remington 1100** is a gas-operated semi-automatic shotgun, popular among sportsmen. The Remington 1100 was the first semiautomatic shotgun to feature significant improvements in felt recoil, weight and reliability.

2.26.1 History

Designed by Wayne Leek and R Kelley,[1] the Remington Model 1100 was introduced in 1963 as a successor to the Model 58 and 878 gas operated shotguns. The Model 58s had supplanted the recoil operated Model 11-48, which retained the long recoil action of John Browning's original design, present in the Remington Model 11 and the Auto-5. All models of the 1100 are gas operated with a mechanism that noticeably reduces recoil.[1] Several variations of the Model 1100, in 12, 20, and 28 gauges, and .410 bore are still in production as of 2014. The Remington Model 1100 ushered in the era of successful and reliable gas-actuated autoloading shotguns, and it is the best selling autoloading shotgun in U.S. history,[1] with over 4 million produced. The Model 1100 holds the record for the most shells fired out of an autoloading shotgun without malfunction, cleaning or parts breakage with a record of over 24,000 rounds. The record was set in 1978 with a Remington model 1100 LT-20. Breaking this record has been attempted with several other models of semi-auto shotguns but has yet to be broken. In 2011 Remington introduced the Model 1100 Competition Synthetic. A 50th Anniversary highly decorated version was introduced in 2013.

2.26.2 Design

The Model 1100 bleeds off gasses to operate the action through ports in the barrel near the end of the fore end. The gasses then drive a steel action sleeve that fits around the magazine tube and connects to the bolt carrier to the rear, ejecting the spent shell. A fresh shell is released from the magazine, which trips the carrier release, and the action spring in the stock pushes the bolt forward, picking up the fresh shell and loading it into the chamber. With modifications to the trigger group to regulate feed and firing, the design is basically a gas powered Model 870. The design team spent many hundreds of hours test firing and getting input from shooters on the design before it was released for production. The fact that plastic shotshells had come onto the scene, and even the older paper shells were carrying improved coatings, made for more reliable ammunition, which no doubt assisted the 1100 to become a true breakthrough in gas operated shotgun reliability. The design was self-compensating to an extent not seen previously, in that any 2-3/4" shell could be fired without adjustment in the standard models, and both 2-3/4" and 3" Magnum shells could be used interchangeably on the Magnum versions. The Remington 1100's carrier release is located on the underside of the firearm which is unlike a number of other semi-automatic shotguns such as the Mossberg 930 or the FN SLP whose carrier releases are located on the side.[2][3][4]

2.26.3 Use

The Remington 1100 was an immediate hit upon its introduction. It quickly became "the gun" on the Skeet ranges in the days before the over and under came to prominence. It was employed by hunters pursuing almost any game that could be pursued with a shotgun, and the 3" Magnum models found favor as waterfowling guns. The 1100 is a popular gun used in trap shooting, skeet shooting, and sporting clays; and special versions with high ribs and Monte Carlo stocks are available. The Competition Synthetic model with an adjustable carbon fibre stock set was introduced in 2012 and has been received quite favorably. As with other semi-automatic shotguns, a shell catcher can be used to avoid spent shells hitting others on the squad when shooting trap. Modified versions of the 1100 are popular in tactical three-gun shooting as well.

Model introduction

- 12 gauge (1963)
- 16 gauge (1964)
- 20 gauge (1964)
- .410 bore (1969)
- Matched Pair in .410 bore & 28 gauge (1970)
- 20 gauge Lightweight—LW (1970)
- 20 gauge Lightweight—LT (1977)

Through the years there have been numerous limited editions and Commemorative models, such as the Ducks Unlimited guns.

Nighthawk Custom offers a customized version of the Remington 1100 for police use, home defense, and competition shooting.[5]

2.26.4 Users

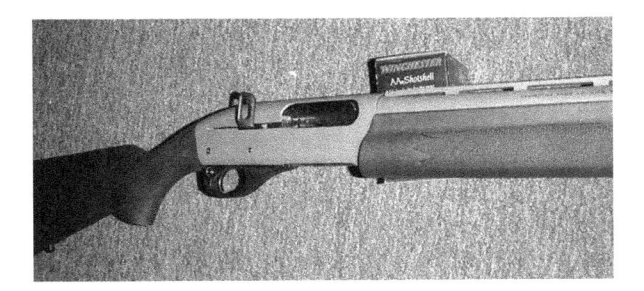

Remington 1100 Tactical Shotgun

- 🇧🇷 Brazil: Used by Military Police of Rio de Janeiro State.
- 🇨🇦 Canada: Used by Edmonton Police Service.
- 🇲🇾 Malaysia: Malaysian Special Operations Force.[6]
- 🇲🇽 Mexico: Used by Mexican Naval Infantry.
- 🇺🇸 United States: Used by some law enforcement agencies.[7]

2.26.5 Notes

[1] Murtz, Harold (1994). *Gun Digest Treasury*. DBI Books. p. 193. ISBN 978-0-87349-156-3.

[2] http://www.remington.com/pages/news-and-resources/downloads/owners-manuals.aspx

[3] http://www.gothamsurvival.com/wp-content/uploads/2012/05/Mossberg_930_935_Manual.pdf

[4] http://www.fnhusa.com/files/8913/4512/7071/2011_SLP_OMs.pdf

[5] Pridgen, D.K. (2010). "Nighthawk Tactical 1100 12 Gauge". *Guns & Weapons for Law Enforcement* **19** (10): 98.

[6] Thompson, Leroy (December 2008). "Malaysian Special Forces". Special Weapons. Retrieved 2010-02-10.

[7] McManners, Hugh (2003). *Ultimate Special Forces*. DK Publishing, Inc. ISBN 0-7894-9973-8.

2.26.6 External links

- Official Remington 1100/11-87 Manual & Schematic (.pdf)
- Remington 1100 Firearm Model History
- Dissembling and Cleaning Your Remington 1100
- Video from Viking Tactics, Inc. on the 1100 Competition Master
- Collecting Model 1100 Shotguns from Remington Society

2.27 Remington Model 58

The **Remington Model 58** also **Sportsman 58** is a semi-automatic shotgun manufactured by Remington Arms in the mid 20th century. It was Remington's first gas operated shotgun and was marketed alongside the recoil operated Model 11-48. The 58 was manufactured in 12, 16, & 20 gauge from 1956 to 1963 until it was replaced by the Model 1100.

2.27.1 Design

Being Remington's first gas-operated shotgun, the Model 58 suffered from many design shortcomings compared to the contemporary Model 11-48 with which it shared many design features and parts. The gas system was built into the front of the magazine and therefore limited capacity to two-shots. Gas was tapped from a hole in the barrel into a large chamber. A piston in this chamber drove an action bar rearward which, in turn, operated the bolt to cycle the action. The action spring was also located inside the forward end of the magazine tube.

The design proved more expensive to make than the 11-48 as well as less reliable, and heavier. Remington chose to replace the Model 58 with a model that combined the best features of the 11-48 with those of the Model 58. The resulting Model 1100 immediately replaced the Model 58 and proved so successful that it soon also replaced the model 11-48 and remains in production as of 2014, over 50 years after its introduction.

2.27.2 Versions

The Model 58 was produced in several version and grades including a 3" magnum version and one with rifle sights.

2.27.3 References

[1]

[2]

2.28 Remington Model 878

The **Remington Model 878**, also known as the **Automaster**, is a semi-automatic shotgun manufactured by Remington Arms in the mid 20th century. It is a gas operated shotgun and was marketed alongside the related Model 58 and the recoil operated Model 11-48. The 58 was manufactured in 12 gauge only from 1959 to 1963 until it was replaced by the Model 1100.

2.28.1 Design

The Model 58 suffered from many design shortcomings compared to the contemporary Model 11-48 with which it shared many design features and parts. The 878 introduced an improved "self-adjusting" gas system[2] compared to the Model 58 though it still operated similarly. Another change was in the carrier and bolt system which were now quite similar to the Model 870, thus the similar name.

While improved, Remington chose to retire the Model 58 and 878 quickly in favor of a new, more elegant design. The resulting Model 1100 immediately replaced the Model 58 and 878 and proved so successful that it soon also replaced the Model 11-48 and remains in production as of 2014, over 50 years after its introduction.

2.28.2 References

[1]

[2]

2.29 Remington Model SP-10

The **Remington Model SP-10** is a gas-operated, semi-automatic shotgun chambered in 10-gauge (3½"). The design is based on the Ithaca Mag-10.[3]

2.29.1 References

[1] "SP-10 Magnum Autoloading Shotgun". Remington Arms. Retrieved 30 December 2012.

[2] "Autoloading Model SP-10". Remington Arms. Retrieved 30 December 2012.

[3] JB Woods. *The Gun Digest Book of Firearms Assembly/Disassembly Part V - Shotguns*. p. 169. ISBN 0873494008.

2.29.2 External links

- Remington SP-10
- Manual

2.30 Remington Spartan 453

The **Remington Spartan 453** is a semi-automatic gas operated. It is a variant of a popular Russian shotgun MP-153 manufactured by Izhevsk Mechanical Plant for export under trademak "Baikal", in Izhevsk, Russia. It is marketed and distributed by Remington.[2] The Spartan 453 is inexpensive compared to other semi-automatic shotguns. It is most often used for hunting birds, and for clay target games such as trap and skeet. Remington ceased importing the shotgun in 2008.

2.30.1 Notes

[1] "SPR453 Autoloading Shotgun". Remington Arms. Retrieved 27 December 2012.

[2] SPR453 Firearm Model History on Remington.com

2.31 Safir T-14

The **Safir T-14** is a semi-automatic shotgun manufactured by AKSA int arms of Turkey. The weapon is based on the AR-15 platform[1] and is chambered in the .410 round. AKSA int arms is the only legal manufacturer and representative for all Safir Models. And, the company' R&D is currently working on the customer complaints since it overtook the Safir arms in 2014. they are planning to expose its new models after improvements first time at Prohunt istanmbul Aksa int arms is also known by its crossfire SX models.

2.31.1 See also

- Benelli M3
- Franchi SPAS-12
- Heckler & Koch FABARM FP6
- Fabarm SDASS Tactical

2.31.2 References

[1] "Safirarms T-14 shotgun (Turkey)". *Modern Firearms*. Retrieved 14 October 2014.

2.32 Saiga-12

The **Saiga-12** (/ˈsaɪɡəˈtwɛlv/) is a 12-gauge shotgun available in a wide range of configurations, patterned after the Kalashnikov series of assault rifles and named for the Saiga antelope. Like the Kalashnikov rifle variants, it is a rotating bolt, gas-operated gun that feeds from a box magazine. All Saiga-12 configurations are recognizable as Kalashnikov-pattern guns by the large lever-safety on the right side of the receiver, the optic mounting rail on the left side of the receiver and the large top-mounted dust cover held in place by the rear of the recoil spring assembly.

The Saiga-12 is manufactured by the arms division of Izhmash, in Russia. It was previously imported into the US by European American Armories, although their agreement expired in 2005 and Izhmash then began exporting through the Russian-American Armory Company. The current export import partner is Wolf Performance Arms.[2] Izhmash also manufactures Saiga 20s and Saiga 410s in 20-gauge and .410 bore, as well as the Saiga semi-automatic hunting rifles in a number of centerfire calibers.[3]

2.32.1 Modifications to the basic Kalashnikov platform

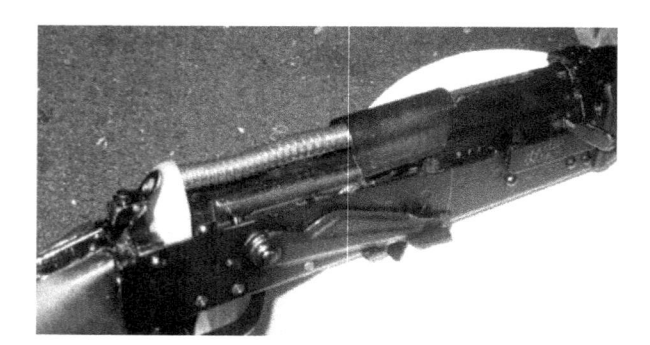

Receiver (with aftermarket recoil buffer)

The Saiga-12 incorporates several features absent on the AK-47 and similar firearms.[4]

Since shotgun shells are nearly twice as wide as 7.62×39mm cartridge, the extraction port in the side of the dust cover had to be increased in size. However, since the bolt had to remain the same length to fit inside the AK-47 sized receiver, the rear section of the bolt is covered by a sliding metal flap that rides on the recoil spring. This allows the gun to be sealed against dirt when the bolt is forward, but the compression of the recoil spring during firing moves the flap rearward to clear the extracted shells.[4]

For the likely reason of simplifying production of Izhmash's other Kalashnikov-pattern guns, the Saiga-12 extractor does not rotate, but instead delegates the bolt-locking function to a caliber-neutral lug directly behind the bolt-face.[4]

The Saiga-12 incorporates an adjustable two-position gas system, for the reason that firing high power loads such as slugs and buckshot generates so much force that the receiver will be damaged if the full power of the gas system is employed without some sort of recoil buffer. The problem is that making the gun durable with the higher power loads would make it useless with low-power loads such as beanbags and flares since the gun would fail to cycle – becoming in essence a manual straight-pull action or producing a "stovepipe" malfunction.[4]

Tactical shotgun Saiga 12K 030

2.32.2 Common Saiga 12 configurations

The Saiga-12 is manufactured in several different configurations ranging from more traditional-looking hunting models to military-style models utilizing AK or SVD hardware. All these versions are available for purchase by civilians in Russia.

Civilian barrel lengths are 17 and 23 inches. The 23" version comes with a traditional rifle stock or with an AK-style separate pistol grip and folding stock (version **S** for "skladnaya", "folding"). The 17" version (**K** for "korotkaya", "short") has an AK-style pistol grip and folding stock and a specially-designed safety, preventing operation with stock folded (due to Russian gun laws, it is illegal to own a firearm capable of firing while being less than 800 mm long). "Taktika" versions with 23" or 17" barrels feature various AK, SVD or original "Legion" furniture (handguards, folding and non-folding stocks) and AK-style open sights with high post and tangent rear. Optional screw-in chokes are available. Standard AK rail for optics may be mounted on the left side of the receiver.

Two, five, seven, eight and twelve round box magazines are available, as well as ten, twelve, and twenty round aftermarket drums. All magazines may be interchanged with all 12 gauge models (sometimes minor fitting may be necessary), although factory-original magazines from Russia only exist in 5-, 7- and 8-round box configurations.

Prior to importation to the US, all Saiga shotguns are configured with a traditional fixed "hunting-style" rifle stock and 5-round magazine. Factory 8-round box magazines are not imported in the US (though they are legal for import in other countries), making them quite rare on the civilian market.[4]

Recently, a newly configured version of the Saiga 12 was introduced. Called the Saiga Taktika mod 040, it features an extended magazine well, last round bolt hold open (recently produced very rarely and replaced with manual bolt hold), hinged dust cover with Picatinny rail for mounting optics, picatinny rail gas block, and a newly designed 8-round mag-

Saiga 12K 040 Taktika with collimator sight "Kobra"

azine (not interchangeable with other Saiga-12 models).[5]

This design seems to address deficiencies that the Saiga 12 had in function. The traditional AK "rock and lock" magazine system and the difficulties associated with magazine has been replaced by a vertical insertion system that allow the magazine to be inserted with only one hand. The hinged dustcover with picatinny rail makes mounting optics simpler, and is closer to the bore axis, making sighting of optics easier. The gas-block rail system allows for the addition of combat lights and vertical fore grips. The last round bolt hold open gives the user instant feedback that the firearm is empty and allows for a quicker magazine change.

In late September 2014 the IZ109T was released in the USA. This model featured a shortened barrel with a permanently attached brake. Barrel length was 18 inches including the brake. The IZ109T also had military style features including a rear pistol grip and 6 position stock. Various modifications were made to the trigger group, bolt, and bolt carrier that allowed loaded magazine insertion without locking the bolt back. The IZ109T also featured a fully parkerized military finish.

2.32.3 Variants

The Saiga shotgun is also available in 20-gauge and .410 calibers known as the Saiga-20 and Saiga-410, respectively.[3]

A bullpup configuration called **Kushnapup** is also available for all Saiga calibers.

2.32.4 Legal status

In Russia this shotgun can be relatively simply obtained, requiring only a "smoothbore-gun license" (which is relatively easy to obtain, compared to a "rifle license" that requires a five-year period of owning a smoothbore gun and a hunting permit).[6]

In response to the annexation of Crimea by the Russian Federation, U.S. President Barack Obama issued Executive Order 13662 on July 16, 2014 blocking the importation of all Izhmash products, including Saiga shotguns and rifles.[7][8]

2.32.5 Users

- Bangladesh Bangladesh Army.
- Kazakhstan: certified as a civilian hunting weapon.[9]
- Kyrgyzstan: Used by police forces.[10]
- Russia: "Saiga-12" used by private security companies;[11][12] **18,5 KS-K** carbine adopted by Ministry of Internal Affairs[13]
- Ukraine: in 2009 "Saiga-12K - Tactical" carbine was adopted by Ukrainian Navy[14]

2.32.6 See also

- Armsel Striker
- Atchisson Assault Shotgun
- Combat shotgun
- List of shotguns
- NeoStead 2000
- SPAS-15
- USAS-12
- VEPR-12
- List of Russian weaponry

2.32.7 References

[1] Николай Дергачев, Александр Кудряшов. "Сайга—12К" - королева самообороны // журнал "Калибр", № 6 (19), июнь 2003.

[2]

[3] Cutshaw, Charles Q. (28 February 2011). *Tactical Small Arms of the 21st Century: A Complete Guide to Small Arms From Around the World*. Iola, Wisconsin: Gun Digest Books. p. 335. ISBN 1-4402-2482-X.

[4] Lewis, Jack (1 January 2004). "Russia's Tactical Shotgun". *The Gun Digest Book of Assault Weapons*. Iola, Wisconsin: Krause Publications. pp. 237–239. ISBN 0-87349-658-2.

[5] "Saiga Taktika at the manufacturer's website". Retrieved 12 Jan 2013.

[6] "Gun Law of Russian Federation – Article 13. Acquisition of weapons by citizens" (in Russian).

[7] Chastain, Russ (July 17, 2014). "Obama Executive Order Bans Russian Rifles and Shotguns". *AllOutdoor.com*. Retrieved August 7, 2015.

[8] Wile, Rob (July 16, 2014). "Treasury Department Tells AK-47-Owning Americans They Won't Be Affected By New Russia Sanctions". *Business Insider*.

[9] "Постановление Правительства Республики Казахстан от 23 декабря 2003 года № 1304 «Об утверждении Государственного кадастра гражданского и служебного оружия и патронов к нему на 2004 год» (утратило силу)". Retrieved 25 October 2014.

[10] "Crisis in Kyrgyzstan". *Boston.com*. Retrieved 25 October 2014.

[11] Постановление Правительства РФ № 587 от 14 августа 1992 года "Вопросы частной детективной и охранной деятельности"

[12] Постановление Правительства РФ № 179 от 4 апреля 2005 года

[13] "карабин принят на вооружение МВД Российской Федерации"
"18,5 КС-К", карабин специальный / "Оружие России"

[14] Біла книга 2009. Збройні сили України. Міністерство оборони України, 2010. стор.78

2.32.8 Sources

- 18,5 мм карабин специальный с коробчатым магазином 18,5КС-К. Руководство по эксплуатации 18,5КС-К РЭ - 2008 г.

2.32.9 External links

- Izhmash – official page
- Saiga-12.com – more information
- Legion USA Inc. – Official Importer of Saiga 12 Shotguns and Rifles

2.33 Sjögren shotgun

The **Sjögren Inertia Shotgun** is a 12 gauge semi-automatic shotgun designed by the Swedish inventor Carl Axel Theodor Sjögren, manufactured in Denmark by Håndvåbenværkstederne Kjöbenhavn in 1909. It used an inertia system later revived by the Italian firm Benelli and today widely used in shotguns. It saw very limited service in World War I by both the allies & the central powers, and service with other armies and resistance groups of the interwar period and World War II.

2.33.1 References

- (1972). *Guns Review* (11).
- "Sjögren Automatic Rifles". *Hansard, Volume 198*. 10 December 1908
- material from Forgotten Weapons #1
- material from Forgotten Weapons #2
- http://www.guns.com/2012/06/16/forgotten-weapons-sjogren-shotgun-rifle/
- Marsh, Roger. (1947). "The Sjögren Shotgun and Sjögren Military Rifle". *The Weapon Series* (6).
- Peterson, Phillip. (2010). "Gun Collector's Corner - Sjögren, The First 12-Gauge Auto". *Gun Digest* (11).
- Bates, James. (1977). "Sjögren Weapons - part I". *The Gun Report* (10).
- Bates, James. (1977). "Sjögren Weapons - part II". *The Gun Report* (11).

2.34 SRM Arms Model 1216

The SRM Arms **Model 1216** is a delayed blowback semi-automatic shotgun with a 16-round detachable magazine. Designed for mobility, it is light and short and intended for home defense and law enforcement.[1]

2.34.1 Design details

The most unique feature of the M1216 is the detachable magazine. The magazine which runs parallel to the barrel is made of four tubes, each with its own spring and follower. Each tube can hold four 2 3/4" or 3" shells for a total of sixteen. When inserted into the gun, the operator can flip a switch and manually rotate the entire magazine, either clockwise or anti-clockwise, to choose which tube feeds into the receiver. In a tactical application, by loading different shells in different tubes, this would allow the operator to switch between different types of shells to adapt to a changing scenario, or it could allow rapid fire of all 16 rounds. Once the magazine is empty, pressing the release switch to drop the magazine allows it to be replaced it with a full one.

The M1216 has a polymer stock to reduce weight and a steel upper receiver. The manual safety, charging handle and ejection port can all be removed and relocated to either the left or right side of the receiver to accommodate the operators preferences. Picatinny Rails line the top and sides of the shotgun allowing a wide variety of attachments such as sights, lasers, and flashlights to be used.[2]

2.34.2 Variants

Model 1212 -
The Model 1212 is a short-barreled variant of the Model 1216. Its barrel length is 13", its overall length is 27 1/2", and the detachable magazine holds 12 rounds (4 x 3 shells). As the barrel is shorter than 16", the 1212 is regulated by the NFA as a Short-barreled shotgun.

Model 1208 -
The Model 1208 is also a short-barreled variant of the Model 1216. Its barrel length is 10", its overall length is 24 1/2", and its magazine can hold 8 rounds (4 x 2 shells). The barrel on the Model 1208 also has a barrel shorter than 16 and is therefore also regulated by the NFA as a short-barreled rifle.

2.34.3 References

[1] "SRM ARMS MODEL 1216 - American Rifleman". Retrieved 2013-05-07.

[2] "SRM Arms Model 1216 (USA) - World Guns". Retrieved 2013-05-07.

2.34.4 External links

- SRM Arms Official Website

2.35 Weatherby SA-08

The **Weatherby SA-08** is a semi-automatic shotgun marketed by Weatherby Inc. The shotgun is available in either 12 or 20 gauge. Like the Weatherby PA-08 pump action shotgun this shotgun constitutes Weatherby's low-end shotgun line. The SA-08 is manufactured in Turkey for Weatherby. This semi-automatic uses a dual valve system which require to be manually changed out when moving from light to heavy loads and vice versa.

2.35.1 Models

The SA-08 is available in six models. All 12 and 20 gauge models come with improved cylinder modified and full choke tubes. 12 gauge models weigh 6.75 lb (3.06 kg) and 20 gauge models weigh 6 lb (2.7 kg)

Upland

The Upland version comes with a walnut stock and is available in both 12 and 20 gauges and with either a 26 in (660 mm) or 28 in (710 mm) barrel. It comes with a

Synthetic

The Synthetic is offered with similar options as the Upland with the exception that it comes with an injected molded synthetic stock.

Waterfowl 3.0

The Waterfowl 3.0 is similar to the Synthetic but only comes in a 12 gauge. A special dipping process is used to adhere the Mothwing Marsh Mimicry camouflage to all metal and synthetic components of the firearm.

Synthetic Youth

The Synthetic Youth model is similar to the Synthetic except that it is available only in 20 gauge and comes with a 24 in (610 mm) barrel.

Deluxe

The Deluxe model is similar to and is available in the same options as the Upland model. The stock and metal work have a high gloss finish.

Entre Rios

The Entre Rios is a shotgun for the shooting of doves. It is available only in 28 gauge and is available with either a 26 in (660 mm) or 28 in (710 mm) barrel. Finish is similar to that of the Deluxe model. This model comes with skeet, improved cylinder and modified chokes. The Entre Rios model weigh about 5.25 lb (2.38 kg).

2.36 Winchester Model 1911

The **Winchester Model 1911 SL Shotgun** was a self-loading, recoil-operated shotgun[1] produced by the Winchester Repeating Arms Company from 1911 to 1925. It was Winchester's first autoloading shotgun, but design flaws kept it from providing competition for the autoloading shotguns made by Remington Arms and Browning Arms Company.

2.36.1 Description and development

The Model 1911 SL (for "Self-Loading") shotgun was developed in 1911 by Thomas Crossley Johnson for the Winchester Repeating Arms Corporation. At the time, Winchester lacked an autoloading shotgun in its product offering, since the company had not accepted John Browning's conditions (he wanted to be paid on a royalty basis, without giving up his rights) for taking his 1898 autoloading design in production.[2] The weapon rejected by Winchester was to become the Browning Auto-5 shotgun (also license-built as the Remington Model 11), and set the standard for autoloading shotgun designs until after World War II.

Due to patent restrictions on the 1898 design, Winchester was unable to copy the Browning design they had rejected earlier, the only autoloading shotgun design at the time, so Winchester had to adapt the design for their own production without infringing on Browning's patents; T.C. Johnson, reportedly, joked that "it took him nearly ten years to design an automatic shotgun (the Winchester 1911) which would not be an infringement on the Browning gun."[2] One of Browning's patents was for the charging handle on the bolt of the 1905 shotgun; Winchester worked around this restriction by using the barrel as the mechanism to charge the weapon.[3] In order to use the 1911 SL, a user would place the gun on safe, point the firearm in a safe direction, load the tubular magazine, and then pull back on the barrel by the checkered section. After disengaging the safety, the weapon was ready to fire.

The stock can be laminated with 3 separate lengthwise pieces glued together.

2.36.2 Design and safety flaws

The novel method of charging the 1911 could be potentially lethal if done incorrectly. Shotgun cartridges of the time were often made of paper, which could make the cartridge body vulnerable to expansion when exposed to moisture in large quantities. If this happened in the 1911, the barrel would have to be cycled in order to open the chamber so that the swelled shotgun shell could be removed. Some users mistakenly cycled the barrel by placing the butt of the weapon against the ground and forcing the barrel down. In this position, the muzzle of the weapon would be pointing towards the face of the user, and the swelled shell could fire, injuring or killing the user. This safety issue led to the Model 1911 being nicknamed "the Widowmaker".[4] This situation could be avoided with adherence to safety procedures common to handling firearms, in particular, the practice of keeping the weapon pointed in a safe direction at all times.

The potential for slam fire when clearing jams was not the only flaw in the 1911's design. The system of buffer rings used to reduce the recoil (two fiber washers[5]) when the weapon was fired often failed. The breakdown of these rings greatly increased the recoil when a round was fired. The gun's "hammering recoil" caused many a stock to split.[3]

The sales of the "mechanically ill-fated" weapon lagged significantly behind those of Remington's and Browning's autoloaders,[3] and Winchester ceased its production in 1925, after producing almost 83,000 of them.[2] As recently as 2005, four people accidentally shot themselves with the 1911 while loading or clearing the weapon.[6]

2.36.3 References

[1] Henshaw, Thomas (1993). *The History of Winchester Firearms 1866-1992*. Academic Learning Company. pp. 66–67. ISBN 978-0-8329-0503-2.

[2] Williamson, Harold Francis (1952). *Winchester: the gun that won the West*. Combat Forces Press. p. 169.

[3] Zutz, Don (2202). *The Ducks Unlimited Guide to Shotgunning*. Globe Pequot. p. 8. ISBN 978-1-57223-393-5. Check date values in: |date= (help)

[4] Shideler, Dan (December 4, 2010). "Shooting the Widowmaker: the Winchester Model 1911". *Gun Digest*. Retrieved October 16, 2013.

[5] Oliver, Doug (March 2007). "Three Questions". *American Gunsmith* **22** (3): 22.

[6] Russell, Doug (2005-12-22). "Gun goes off; four injured". *McAlester News-Capital*. Retrieved 2009-12-22.

2.37 List of semi-automatic shotguns

This list is incomplete; you can help by expanding it.

A semi-automatic shotgun is a form of shotgun that is able to fire a cartridge after every trigger squeeze, without needing to manually chamber another round. (The following list table is sortable.)

2.37.1 See also

- List of firearms
- List of assault rifles
- List of bullpup firearms
- List of machine guns
- List of multiple barrel firearms
- List of pistols
- List of revolvers
- **List of semi-automatic firearms**
    - List of semi-automatic pistols
    - List of semi-automatic rifles
- List of shotguns
- List of sniper rifles
- List of submachine guns

2.37.2 References

Chapter 3

Automatic Shotguns

3.1 Atchisson Assault Shotgun

The **Auto Assault-12** (**AA-12**), originally designed and known as the **Atchisson Assault Shotgun**, is a shotgun developed in 1972 by Maxwell Atchisson. The most prominent feature is reduced recoil. The current 2005 version has been developed over 18 years since the patent was sold to Military Police Systems, Inc. The original design was the basis of several later weapons, including the USAS-12 combat shotgun. The weapon is fully automatic only but fires at a rate of 300 rounds per minute, making it possible to fire one round at a time with brief trigger pulls. It is fed from either an 8-shell box magazine, or a 20- or 32-shell drum magazine.

3.1.1 History

In 1987, Max Atchisson sold the rights of the AA-12 to Jerry Baber of Military Police Systems, Inc., Piney Flats, Tennessee.[5] MPS in turn developed the successor simply known as Auto Assault-12, which was redesigned over a period of 18 years with 188 changes and improvements to the original blueprint, modifications included changing the AA-12 from blowback- to gas-operated with a locked breech. "When the bolt flies back after firing to cycle another round, around 80% of what would normally be felt as recoil is absorbed by a proprietary gas system. A recoil spring grabs another 10%, leaving the final recoil a remarkable 10% of the normal recoil for a 12-gauge round—so you can point the AA-12 at a target and unload the full magazine without significant loss of accuracy".[6] MPS also teamed up with Action Manufacturing Company, and Special Cartridge Company to combine the gun with FRAG-12 High-Explosive ammunition into a multifunction weapon system.

The weapon was lightened to 4.76 kg (10.5 lb) and shortened to 966 mm (38.0 in) but retained the same barrel length. The CQB model has a 13-inch barrel, and is half a pound lighter than the regular model. Uncommon in other automatic shotguns, the AA-12 fires from an open bolt, a feature more commonly found in submachine guns, as well as heavy and squad level machine guns. It uses 8-round box, 20-round drum, or 32-round drum magazines, as opposed to the original 5-round box magazine. Due to the abundant use of stainless steel and the designed clearance for fouling, MPS has claimed that the weapon requires little to no cleaning or lubrication.[7] The designer states that cleaning is required after 10,000 rounds.[8]

3.1.2 Ammunition

The AA-12 can use different types of 3" 12-gauge ammunition such as buckshot, slugs, or less-than-lethal rubber stun batons. It can also use high-explosive rounds, essentially becoming a man-portable automatic grenade launcher or autocannon.

3.1.3 Usage

In 2004, ten firing models of the AA-12 were produced and demonstrated to the United States Marine Corps.

The HAMMER unmanned defense system by More Industries uses dual-mounted AA-12s on the H2X-40 turret.[9] Neural Robotics has also mounted the weapon on their AutoCopter unmanned aerial vehicle.[10][11]

3.1.4 See also

- Automatic shotgun
- Combat shotgun
- List of shotguns
- Military technology and equipment
- Saiga-12
- Daewoo USAS-12
- Pancor Jackhammer

3.1.5 References

[1] "10 Incredible Weapons That Only America Has". *Business Insider*.

[2] http://world.guns.ru/shotgun/usa/atchisson-aa-12-e.html

[3] "Modern Firearms – Atchisson AA-12". Retrieved April 5, 2012.

[4] http://www.defensereview.com/1_31_2004/FRAG%2012.pdf

[5] Moore, Jacob; Ruble, Drew (July–August 2009). "The Automatic Warrior". *BusinessTN*.

[6] "AA-12 combat shotgun". Retrieved 29 June 2013.

[7] http://www.clcweb.net/Shooting/Military_Shotgun/military_shotgun.html Military Assault Shotgun: "During a Blackwater shoot, 5000 rounds were fired through a single weapon without cleaning or a drop of Lube."

[8] Crane, David (June 15, 2005). "Auto Assault-12 (AA-12) Full-Auto Machine Shotgun/FRAG-12 High-Explosive Round Combo/Weapon System?".

[9] Crane, David (July 19, 2006). "HAMMER Remotely-Operated Weapons System for Robotic and Manned Vehicles".

[10] Blass, Evan (1 March 2006). "Neural Robotics Incorporated equips AutoCopter with 12-gauge shotgun". Retrieved 2 September 2011.

[11] "Remote Control Helicopter With Full-Auto Shotgun". 10 January 2008. Retrieved 2 September 2011.

3.1.6 External links

- Johnson, Robert (September 10, 2014). "11 Unbelievable Weapons That Only America And Its Closest Allies Have". *Business Insider - Australia* (Allure Media). Retrieved February 26, 2015.

3.2 Daewoo Precision Industries USAS-12

The **Daewoo Precision Industries USAS-12** (Universal Sports Automatic Shotgun 12 gauge) is an automatic shotgun designed as a combat shotgun manufactured in South Korea by Daewoo Precision Industries during the 1980s.[1]

3.2.1 Design

The USAS-12 is a gas-operated, selective-fire weapon which is designed to provide sustained firepower in close-combat scenarios. It accepts detachable 10-round box magazines or 20-round drum magazines.[1] Both types of magazine are made of polymer, and drum magazines have their rear side made from translucent polymer for quick determination of the number of shot shells left. It has an effective range of 40 m.

3.2.2 History

The history of the USAS-12 dates from the 1980s vintage designs of Maxwell Atchisson. In about 1989, Gilbert Equipment Co. (USA) decided to bring up the selective fired weapon, broadly based on principles employed in Atchisson shotguns. The design of the new weapon was produced by John Trevor Jr. Since Gilbert Equipment Co. had no manufacturing capabilities, it started to look for possible manufacturers. It turned out that the only maker that agreed to produce this weapon was the South Korean company Daewoo Precision Industries, a part of the high-tech Daewoo conglomerate. Daewoo engineers adapted the new weapon to their manufacturing techniques, and mass production commenced in the early 1990s. The USAS-12 sold well to military and security forces of several (unspecified) countries in Asia, and more than 30,000 of USAS-12 shotguns were made by mid-1990s.[2]

During the same timeframe, Gilbert Equipment Co. tried to bring semi-automatic version of USAS-12 to the U.S. market, but Treasury Secretary Lloyd Bentsen classified this firearm as "having no sporting purpose", so it became a "destructive device" under the U.S. National Firearms Act of 1934.[3] This greatly restricted its civilian use. During the late 1990s, RAMO Defence Co. began to assemble USAS-12 shotguns from Korean and U.S.-made parts for sale on domestic market, but sales of this weapon were limited to government agencies only.[2] Today, this shotgun is still being manufactured by S&T Daewoo in Korea for military and law enforcement sales only.

A US firearms manufacturer, Ameetec Arms LLC of Scottsdale, Arizona, has started the manufacture of a USAS-12 semi-automatic clone, called the WM-12; it mainly differs from the USAS-12 by the lack of fixed sights and carrying handle, replaced by a Picatinny rail. The manufacturer states that the WM-12 is not a "destructive device", and is thus readily available to civilians.[4] As of January 2008, however, the WM-12 was no longer to be found on Ameetec Arms online catalogs because it was discontinued after its initial semi-production run. Only a few WM-12s were built using USAS-12 Demilled shotguns.

The semi-automatic version of the original USAS-12 is manufactured by DGN Enterprises Inc. near Martinsville, Indiana, under the store front Guns & Ordnance. The new production USAS-12 is still registered as a "destructive device".

3.2.3 See also

- Atchisson Assault Shotgun, another fully automatic shotgun
- List of shotguns
- Saiga-12

3.2.4 References

[1] Lee, Jerry (23 April 2013). *The Official Gun Digest Book of Guns & Prices 2013*. Iola, Wisconsin: Krause Publications. p. 1162. ISBN 978-1-4402-3543-6.

[2] Modern Firearms – USAS-12. Retrieved July 13, 2011.

[3] Walker, Robert E. (2013). *Cartridges and Firearm Identification*. CRC Press. p. 369. ISBN 978-1-4665-8881-3.

[4] Ameetec Arms WM-12. Retrieved on December 28, 2007.

3.2.5 External links

- Modern Firearms
- Patent
- Disassembly Video

3.3 Franchi mod .410

The **Franchi mod.410** is a fully automatic shotgun concept in the form of a bullpup. The weapon is chambered in the .410 round fed from a 15 round box magazine with the capability of firing 200 rounds per minute in full auto.[1]

3.3.1 References

[1] http://spas12.com/spas12not.htm

3.4 Gordon Close-Support Weapon System

The **Gordon Close-Support Weapon System (Gordon CSWS)** was an exotic firearm project of Australian origin.

3.4.1 Overview

A very unusual weapon system was proposed at one time by Australian Duncan Gordon. It was assumed that the basis of this family of automatic weapons constitute a belt-fed machine gun, automatic shotgun with box magazine and the double-barreled submachine gun with overhead inserted magazines (a la the Villar-Perosa SMG) in a very unusual configuration. Gordon has developed its weapons, based on personal combat experience gained in Vietnam, where he served in the forces of SEATO. Design drawings and the general conception of his ideas involved in the Australian company BSP Planning and Design Pty. Ltd. in Norwood. Led the team of engineers, Peter Chant. Work began in early 1970.

The system was developed by 1972, and drawings were accomplished by engineer Dale Evans. This system was a quick-barrel weapons, while the overall configuration has a mixture of ideas of the British EM-2, as well as WW2 platforms such as the German FG-42 and the US M1941 Johnson machine gun. Any type of weapon could be adapted to fire conventional rifle cartridges and 12 Gauge shotgun rounds. Automation system, applied in the arms of an identical pattern of patent 1.834.021 J. Destree, and used to solve problems by firing rifle bullets and shot with the same weapons sites.

3.4.2 Variants

Combat shotgun

A combat shotgun variant was fed from a magazine.

Belt fed shotgun

Fed from a belt feed.

Assault rifle

An Assault rifle variant was fed from a 30-round magazine inserted in the side.

Battle rifle/squad automatic weapon

A battle rifle/squad automatic weapon variant fed from a 30-round magazine.

Submachine gun

A twin-barrel submachine gun variant fed from overhead 32-round magazines with unusual side mounted grips and folding stock.

3.4.3 References

*

3.5 Heckler & Koch HK CAWS

The **Heckler & Koch HK CAWS** (**H&K CAWS**) is a prototype automatic shotgun—designed as a combat shotgun—co-produced by Heckler & Koch and Winchester/Olin during the 1980s. It was Heckler & Koch's entry into the U.S military's Close Assault Weapon System program.

It is a 10-round, 12-gauge, bullpup shotgun with two firing modes: semi-auto and full-auto. The gun is fully ambidextrous.

3.5.1 Development

The CAWS program started in the early 1980s in the United States. The main goal of this program was to develop a new generation personal firearm, capable of firing high-impulse, multiple projectiles with effective range of 100–150 meters. Using multiple projectiles should increase the chances of hitting the target in combat. One of the teams entered in the CAWS race was Heckler & Koch Germany, coupled with Winchester Corp. USA.[2] Heckler & Koch was responsible for developing a weapon, while Winchester was responsible for the development of new types of ammunition. Although tested by the U.S. military, the CAWS was canceled, and production, both military and civilian, has halted.[3]

3.5.2 References

[1] http://world.guns.ru/shotgun/de/hk-caws-e.html

[2] http://www.hkpro.com/index.php?option=com_content&view=article&id=101:caw&catid=11:rare-prototypes&Itemid=5

[3] http://www.militaryfactory.com/smallarms/detail.asp?smallarms_id=75

3.5.3 See also

Referenced in popular culture in the Fallout 2 video game (1998), various pen-and-paper roleplaying supplements of the early 90s (f.ex. Twilight 2000: Infantry Weapons of the World, 1991, ISBN 1558780688) and modern thrillers (f.ex. Seal Team Seven 02: Specter, Keith Douglass, ISBN 0425248178).

- List of bullpup firearms
- List of shotguns
- List of individual weapons of the U.S. Armed Forces

3.5.4 External links

- Cartridge of the Month June 2006: 12 Gauge Close Assault Weapon System (CAWS)
- HKPRO: The CAW
- Modern Firearms
- Military Factory: Heckler & Koch HK CAWS

3.6 Pancor Jackhammer

The Pancor Corporation **Jackhammer** was a 12-gauge, gas-operated automatic shotgun designed in 1984 and patented in 1987. Only a few working prototypes of the Jackhammer were built. In the late 1990s, the current owner of the design, Mark III, attempted to sell the patents, prototypes, and production rights for $350,000. Nonetheless, its distinctive appearance and futuristic design have made it a prop in action films, television programs, and video games.

3.6.1 Development

The Jackhammer was designed by John A. Anderson, who formed the company Pancor Industries in New Mexico. Reportedly, several foreign governments expressed interest in the design and even ordered initial production units once ready for delivery. However, the design was held up for production due to United States Department of Defense testing, though the design was eventually rejected. With no customers and little interest, Pancor went bankrupt. Supposed overseas orders were subject to United States Department of State approval that was not forthcoming. The assets of Pancor were sold off, including the few prototypes built.[1]

3.6.2 Design

Though unconventional, the Jackhammer can best be described as a gas-operated revolver. Many parts were constructed of Rynite polymer to reduce weight. Layout was of a bullpup configuration with a 10-round revolving cylinder that fired conventional, 12-gauge shells. The cylinder's method of rotation was very similar to the Webley–Fosbery

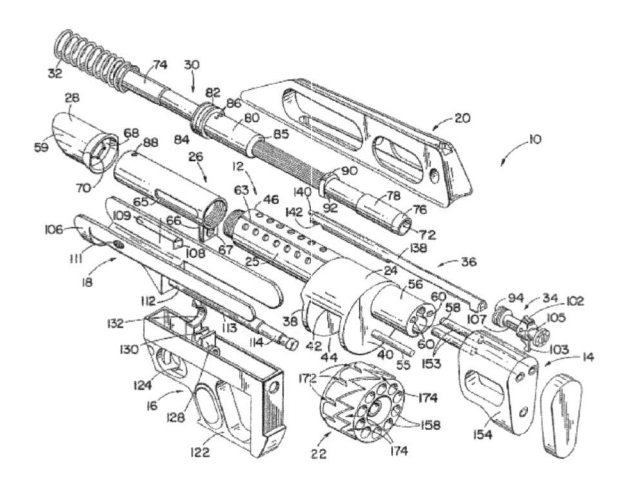

Components of the Jackhammer Machine Shotgun

Automatic Revolver, an operating rod being used to rotate the cylinder.[2]

At the moment of firing, the front of the shell sealed inside the breech of the barrel much like the Nagant M1895 revolver. Unlike the Nagant, whose cylinder moved forward to form the seal, the barrel of the Jackhammer was driven forward and away from the cylinder by a ring-piston, using gas tapped from the bore. As the barrel moved forward, the breech cleared the front of the fired cartridge and an operating rod attached to the barrel rotated the cylinder through a "zig-zag" cam arrangement. As the next shell aligned with the bore, the barrel returned under spring pressure. Spent shells were retained in the cylinder, as in a traditional revolver. For reloading, the cylinder was removed from the bottom of its housing and shells were manually extracted. Removing the cylinder required the barrel be moved and secured in the forward position.[2]

3.6.3 Related developments

- Webley–Fosbery Automatic Revolver
- Mannlicher M1894 — blow-forward barrel
- Nagant M1895 — gas seal

3.6.4 See also

- Armsel Striker (Street Sweeper)
- Atchisson Assault Shotgun
- List of bullpup firearms
- List of shotguns
- Saiga-12
- Daewoo Precision Industries USAS-12

3.6.5 References

[1] Jonathan Glazer. "The PANCOR Jackhammer". Movie Gun Services.

[2] Bishop, Chris (2006). *The Encyclopedia of Weapons: From World War II to the Present Day*. San Diego, California: Thunder Bay Press. p. 355.

3.6.6 External links

- Modern Firearms – Jackhammer
- Movie Gun Services – Pancor Jackhammer
- Pancor Jackhammer: The Real One on YouTube

Patents

- - U.S. Patent 4,709,617
  - U.S. Patent 4,856,410

3.7 Smith & Wesson AS

The **S&W AS** is a 12 gauge select-fire shotgun manufactured by Smith & Wesson. Its layout is similar to the M16 rifle and fed from a 10-round magazine.[1] The S&W AS was a rival to the Heckler & Koch HK CAWS.[2]

3.7.1 References

[1] http://www.securityarms.com/20010315/galleryfiles/1800/1864.htm

[2] The Directory of the World's Weapons, Bookmart Ltd (1996), ISBN 1-85605-348-2, ISBN 978-1-85605-348-8

3.7.2 See also

- AO-27 rifle
- Franchi SPAS-15
- Daewoo USAS-12

3.8 Special Operations Weapon

The **Special Operations Weapon** was a fully automatic[1] shotgun designed to be used by US Navy SEALs in the Vietnam War,[2] by Carroll Childers, an engineer at the Naval Special Weapons Center.

3.8.1 History

Combat experience with the Ithaca 37 and Remington Model 870 spurred experimentation with a series of fully automatic shotguns. The Remington 7188, used by SEALs, was a full-auto based on the company's Model 1100 semi-auto hunting gun. Although boasting a cyclic rate of about seven rounds per second, the gas-operated 7188 reportedly was difficult to control as well as prone to malfunction from environmental factors.

At the Naval Surface Warfare Center in Dahlgren, Va., magazine master, gun enthusiast and engineer Carroll Childers designed and patented[3] a completely different full-auto shotgun colorfully acronymed SOW for Special Operations Weapon.

A developmental SOW—called at the time the MIWS for Multipurpose Individual Weapon System—is preserved among many other one-of-a-kind artifacts in the Naval Historical Center's collection. The chunky and stubby slab-sided aluminum and steel first-generation prototype is fed from the top using one of the multi-round box mags Childers developed for the 870 shotgun. This one is apparently intended for hip fire only, featuring two pistol grips with heavily worn and deeply scratched olive drab paint giving much evidence of rough use during testing.

Development of the Childers SOW and its 12-gauge ammunition never went into full scale production due to funding being rescinded.

3.8.2 See also

- List of shotguns

3.8.3 References

[1] *Combat Guns* magazine, vol. 5, 2001

[2] http://www.thefirearmblog.com/blog/2009/12/11/full-auto-shotgun/

[3] US patent 3736839

3.8.4 External links

- "Firearms secret projects" thread at Secret Projects Forum

Chapter 4

Bolt-Action shotguns

4.1 M26 Modular Accessory Shotgun System

The **M26 Modular Accessory Shotgun System (MASS)** is a developmental under-barrel shotgun attachment for the M16/M4 family of United States military firearms. It can also be fitted with a pistol grip and collapsible stock to act as a stand-alone weapon. It is replacing the current M500 shotguns in service.[1]

Left side of M26 showing bolt handle.

4.1.1 Development

Soldier with M26 MASS.

The M26 MASS is a militarized version of the Lightweight Shotgun System, developed by C-More Systems and manufactured by Vertu Corporation[2] and originally marketed toward special operations forces. It attracted the interest of soldiers being deployed to Afghanistan who wanted to reduce the number of individual weapons they had to carry by using a shotgun as a rifle attachment instead of a discrete weapon.

The M26 has been in development at the U.S. Army's Soldier Battle Lab since the late 1990s. The idea was to provide soldiers with lightweight accessory weapons which could be mounted under the standard issue M16 rifle or M4 carbine. These would provide soldiers with additional capabilities, such as: door breaching using special slugs, very short-range increased lethality using 00 buckshot, and less-lethal capabilities using teargas shells, rubber slugs, rubber pellets, or other non-lethal rounds.

The original idea was based on the Knight's Armament Masterkey system, which dates back to the 1980s and originally comprised a shortened, tube-fed Remington 870 shotgun mounted under an M16 rifle or M4 carbine. The M26 improved upon the original Masterkey concept with a detachable magazine option and more comfortable handling, thanks to a bolt-operated system. The detachable magazine offers quicker reloading and a quicker change of ammunition types. The relatively large bolt handle is located closer to the rear rather than the slide on the Masterkey pump shotgun, and thus is easier to cycle in combat. The bolt handle can be mounted on either side of the weapon. The M26 was chosen by the U.S. Military over the Masterkey as a breaching tool.[3] At the present time, small numbers of M26 MASS shotguns have been issued to U.S. troops in

Afghanistan. The current contract calls for the delivery of 9,000 shotguns.[1] In February 2012, the first unit was fully equipped with M26s.[4]

War in Afghanistan

The shotgun is currently in low rate initial production.[5] In May 2008, the Army announced it would procure 35,000 units.[6] The first M26 shotguns were procured and fielded to military police and engineer units in 2010. However, some units in both Iraq and Afghanistan were issued the M26 in small quantities as early as 2003.[7] Full initial fielding began in 2011.[8]

4.1.2 Specifications

Stand-alone M26 MASS

- Caliber: 12 gauge
- Operation: Straight pull bolt-action.
- Capacity: 3 or 5 round detachable magazine.
- Ammunition: 2.75 and 3 in lethal, non-lethal and breaching rounds.
- Barrel length: 7.75 in (197 mm) with integral breaching stand-off adapter.
- Under-barrel version:
  - Overall length: 16.5 in (419 mm)
  - Weight: 2 lb 11 oz (1.22 kg)
- Stand-alone version:
  - Overall length: 24 in (610 mm) (stock collapsed)
  - Weight: 4 lb 3 oz (1.90 kg)

4.1.3 See also

- List of individual weapons of the U.S. Armed Forces (Shotguns)
- KAC Masterkey
- Combat shotgun
- M203 grenade launcher
- M320 Grenade Launcher Module
- Saiga-12
- MAUL (weapon)

4.1.4 References

[1] Dan Parsons (January 2013) Army, Marine Corps Succeed in Rapidly Fielding Specialized Individual Weapons (UPDATED). National Defense Magazine

[2] US Army's M26 Mass 12 Gauge. Tactical-Life.com. Retrieved on 2013-01-22.

[3] The C-MORE M26 may be available to civilians. The Firearm Blog (2010-02-16). Retrieved on 2013-01-22.

[4] 101st Airborne's 'Strike' brigade first Army unit issued M26 shotgun | Article | The United States Army. Army.mil (2012-02-17). Retrieved on 2013-01-22.

[5] Tim Chyma (2007-05-07) PM Individual Weapons Overview for the Small Arms Symposium & Exhibition. National Defense Industrial Association

[6] U.S. Army set to buy 35,000 M-26 Rifle/Shotguns. defense-update.com. Retrieved on 2013-01-22.

[7] Lance M. Bacon (30 April 2011). "Improved carbines headed your way". Gannett Government Media Corporation. Retrieved 30 April 2011.

[8] Fuller, BG Peter N.; COL Douglas A. Tamilio (18 May 2010). "Project Manager Soldier Weapons Briefing for NDIA" (PDF). *PEO Soldier*. United States Army. Retrieved 28 October 2010.

4.1.5 External links

- M26 12 Gauge Modular Accessory Shotgun System (MASS) Fact sheet
- Security Arms
- Modern Firearms
- Global Security
- patent

4.2 Marlin Model 25MG

The **Marlin Model 25MG** is a smooth bore, bolt-action, .22 WMR shotgun manufactured by Marlin firearms Company. It was designed and marketed as a "garden gun" for use in dispatching small garden and farm pests. It features a hardwood Monte Carlo stock.

4.2.1 References

- Shideler, Dan (2010). *2010 Standard Catalog of Firearms: The Collector's Price and Reference Guide.* Gun Digest Books. p. 725. ISBN 0-89689-825-3.

- Rees, Clair (March 2000). "Marlin's 'Garden Gun' - Model 25MG". Guns Magazine.

4.3 Marlin Model 55

The **Marlin Model 55** is a large, bolt-action, series of shotguns. It was produced in 20, 16, 12 and 10 gauge at various times in its production history.[1] It features a full-choke and a thumb safety. The shotgun shells are fed via a two-round, detachable, box magazine.[2][3]

4.3.1 Variants

- *Model 55 Hunter*: The original model, the Model 55 Hunter, was produced from 1954 until 1964 in 12 gauge (1956-1964 in 20 gauge and 1961-1966 in 16 gauge).[4]

- *Model 55 Goose Gun*: The Goose Gun was a 12 gauge that was produced from 1962 until 1988 and it featured a 36" barrel with an overall length of 56¾" and weighed 8 lbs.

- *Model 55 Swamp Gun*: The Swamp Gun was a 12 gauge that was only produced from 1963 to 1965.[4]

- *Model 55G (Glenfield)*: The Model 55G (Glenfield) was produced between 1961 and 1965 in 12, 16 and 20 gauges.[4]

- *Glenfield Model 50*: From 1966 until 1973, a slightly shorter variant called the Model 50 was produced. It differs in that it features a modified-choke, a 28 inch barrel (48¾" overall), and weighs 7½ pounds.[2]

- *Model 55 Slug Gun*: The Model 55 Slug Gun was a 12 gauge produced from 1973 until 1979.[4]

- *Model 5510 SuperGoose*: Another variant called the Model 5510 SuperGoose was produced and chambered for the 10-gauge (3½") cartridge. The SuperGoose was produced from 1976 to 1985.[1]

4.3.2 References

[1] Wood, JB (2002). *The Gun Digest Book of Firearms Assembly/Disassembly, Pt. V: Shotguns (2nd Edition).* Krause Publications. p. 207. ISBN 0-87349-400-8.

[2] Warner, Ken (1999). *Gun Digest 2000.* Krause Publications, Inc. ISBN 0-87341-752-6.

[3] Long, Duncan (2004). *Streetsweepers: The Complete Book of Combat Shotguns.* Paladin Press. pp. 63–64. ISBN 1-58160-436-X.

[4] Brophy, William S. (1989). *Marlin Firearms: A History of the Guns and the Company That Made Them.* Stackpole Books. p. 427. ISBN 0-8117-0877-2.

4.3.3 External links

- Exploded drawing of Model 5510 Supergoose from:

    - Murtz, Harold A. *The Gun Digest Book of Exploded Gun Drawings.* Gun Digest, 2005. ISBN 0-89689-141-0.

4.4 Mossberg 183

The **Mossberg 183** is a .410 bore bolt action shotgun, produced between 1947 and 1971 by O.F. Mossberg & Sons in New Haven, Conn.[1]

4.4.1 Variants

D

The original model produced from 1947-1948. It had a plain one-piece pistol grip stock. The gun was distributed with two choke tubes (modified and full), which mount by screwing to the outside of the barrel, as opposed to the inside, like the Remington 870 or other modern shotguns. The shotgun was shipped with a wrench for removing the choke tubes.[1]

D-A Model 183D-A Bolt Action Repeater, left hand extractor added. Made 1948-1950.[1]

D-B Model 183D-B Bolt Action Repeater, firing pin design change. Name 1950-1953.[1]

D-C Model 183D-C Bolt Action Repeater, ejector interrupter added. Made 1953-1956.[1]

D-D Model 183D-D Bolt Action Repeater, change to ejector interrupter. Made 1956-1960.[1]

D-E Model 183D-E Bolt Action Repeater, Slimmer barrel. Made 1960-1963.[1]

D-F Model 183D-F Bolt Action Repeater, change to trigger and safety lever. Made 1968-1971.[1]

D-G Model 183D-G Bolt Action Repeater, change to barrel and front sight. Made 1968-1971.[1]

K

The 183K is similar to the 183D, but had a "C-Lect-Choke", which allowed the shooter to vary the choke between four settings without changing adaptors (as with the 183D).[1][2][3] Weight 5 1/2 lbs, barrel, 25" with variable C-Lect-Choke. Genuine walnut one piece Monte Carlo stock, later models walnut finish. Made 1953-1956.[1]

K-A Model 183K-A Bolt Action Repeater, firing pin design change. Made 1956-1960.[1]

K-B Model 183K-B Bolt Action Repeater, Slimmer barrel. Made 1960-1963.[1]

K-C Model 183K-C Bolt Action Repeater, change to trigger and safety lever. Made 1963-1986.[1]

K-D Model 183K-D Bolt Action Repeater, change to barrel and front sight. Made 1968-1986.[1]

4.4.2 References

[1] "Mossberg Shotgun Models". Retrieved 2011-08-13.

[2] "C-Lect-Choke 1". Retrieved 2011-08-13.

[3] "C-Lect-Choke 2". Retrieved 2011-08-13.

4.5 Mossberg 185

The **Mossberg 185** is a 20-gauge bolt action shotgun, produced between 1948 and 1964 by O.F. Mossberg & Sons in New Haven, Conn.

4.5.1 Variants

D

The original model produced from 1947-1950. The gun was distributed with three choke tubes, which mount by screwing to the outside of the barrel, as opposed to the inside, like the Remington 870 or other modern shotguns. The shotgun was shipped with a wrench for removing the choke tubes. [1]

The shotgun will only accept 2¾-inch shotshells, and will not accept larger magnum shells.

While the magazine only holds two shells, it is possible to load three into the shotgun by first loading a shell into the chamber and then inserting a full magazine.

The stock on the shotgun, a Monte Carlo-style, also has a pistol grip shape with a black plastic trigger guard with finger ridges.

D-A

Model 185D-A Bolt Action. Produced. 1950

D-B

The Mode D-B featured a change in firing pin design. This variant was produced from 1950 – 1955[1]

D-C

The magazine floorplate was changed between the D-B and D-C models. This variant was produced from 1955 – 1958[1]

4.5.2 External links

- Mossberg Forum

4.5.3 References

[1] "Mossberg Shotgun Models". Retrieved 2007-12-21.

Chapter 5

Bullpup Shotguns

5.1 High Standard Model 10

The **High Standard Model 10** (**HS10**) is a gas operated, semi-automatic shotgun that was manufactured by the High Standard Manufacturing Company of Hamden, CT. It is easily recognized by its bullpup design, rotatable shoulder stock, and integrated flashlight.

5.1.1 History and design

The basic design of the Model 10 shotgun was developed in the late 1950s by Alferd Crouch, a Santa Monica, California police sergeant. Crouch's goal was to create the ultimate entry shotgun for SWAT and tactical units. His original design used a modified Remington semi-automatic shotgun.

In the mid 1960s, Crouch sold his design to the High Standard Manufacturing Company, who used their Flite King shotgun as the basis for the first model, the 10A. The Flite King was modified by replacing the stock, relocating the trigger assembly, and fitting a three-piece plastic shell around the receiver and first half of the barrel. The rearward piece of the shell provided an attachment point for the rotatable shoulder stock. The lower piece of the shell provided the grip. Since the trigger assembly was moved forward to accommodate the bullpup design, a rod that connected the new and original trigger locations was used to allow minimal modifications to the original Flite King receiver.

Although the standard capacity of the Model 10 is 4 shells, there was a magazine tube extension available which would increase the capacity to 6 shells.

On the early model shotgun the 10A, the upper plastic section also housed the built-in flashlight and carrying handle.

The later model shotgun the 10B was improved with a left-hand charging handle, flip-up front sight, and utilized the new flashlight mount/carrying handle mounting block (which doubles as the carrying handle mount) as the rear sight. The "Kel-Lite" branded flashlight can be removed, as it is attached to the aforementioned mounting block.

High Standard Model 10A

5.1.2 Service

Originally, the Model 10 was sold to law enforcement only. The concept of this shotgun was quite interesting to many police agencies who adopted the Model 10 in the late 1960s and early 1970s; however, most of the agencies found many shortcomings, and ultimately ceased using the Model 10.

The most common problem was the failure to cycle correctly. According to the instructions on the Model 10, only magnum or "high brass" shells were to be used. However, even with the correct shells, the action would sometimes fail to cycle reliably. Other problems that plagued the shotgun were the rough and unpredictable trigger feel, the strange rotatable shoulder stock, and the tendency of the recoil to cause the flashlight's batteries to become damaged.

Another problem was that the Model 10 could only be fired from the right arm, as the gun ejected spent cartridges from the right side of the unit with a high force. There is a warning on the right side of the shotgun reading "CAUTION - DO NOT SHOOT FROM LEFT SHOULDER."

5.1.3 Users

- Argentina Used by the Argentine Navy
- Mexico Used by the Mexican Army

- United States Used by various U.S Police Forces

5.1.4 See also

- List of bullpup firearms
- List of shotguns
- High Standard Manufacturing Company

5.1.5 External links

- Modern Firearms High Standard Model 10 Info
- Video showing operation and construction of High standard Model 10b

5.2 Kel-Tec KSG

The **Kel-Tec KSG** is a bullpup 12-gauge pump action shotgun designed by Kel-Tec. It has two tube magazines which the user of the gun can switch between manually.[2] Each tube holds a total of seven 2.75-inch (70 mm) 12-gauge shotshells or six 3-inch (76 mm) shotshells.

5.2.1 Operation

The Kel-Tec KSG shotgun is a manually operated, pump (slide) action weapon. Barrel locking is achieved by a swinging wedge, located inside the top of the bolt, which engages the barrel extension. The sliding forend is connected to the bolt by dual operating bars. The ammunition feed is from two independent tubular magazines, located below the barrel.

The user is required to manually select a magazine by switching a three-position lever, located behind the pistol grip. The middle position of the switch blocks the feed from both magazines and allows the user to chamber a single round manually. Switching the lever to one side brings the respective magazine into the feed cycle. Once one magazine is depleted, the user manually switches to the second magazine by pushing the magazine selection lever toward it.[2]

Rounds are loaded into the magazines through a large loading/ejection port, located at the bottom of the gun in the stock, behind the pistol grip. Empty shells are ejected down through the same port. A manual safety is available in the form of the cross-bolt button, located above the grip, making the gun fully ambidextrous in use. Sighting equipment (iron sights and/or red dot sights) can be installed using the standard Picatinny rail located above the barrel. A second Picatinny rail is provided at the bottom of the sliding forend, permitting installation of other Picatinny rail accessories. While not included with the stock weapon, perpendicular forward grips and back-up iron sights (BUIS) are almost always shown in photography and video demonstrations of the Kel-Tec KSG.

5.2.2 Revisions

The initial release of the KSG had a mixed reception with some having flawless experiences and others having various issues ranging from the selector switch breaking to double feeding. Kel-Tec quickly released a second generation addressing these issues while also offering to upgrade 1st generation KSGs with the second generation improvements for free. Other improvements to the KSG on the 2nd generation include a trigger reset, small shell tube peep holes, and a fix of the action release to be easier to use and ambidextrous.[3]

5.2.3 See also

- List of bullpup firearms
- List of shotguns
- Neostead 2000
- UTAS UTS-15

5.2.4 References

[1] "Kel-Tec KSG". Kel-Tec. Retrieved 28 November 2015.

[2] Paul Markel (22 August 2011), *Kel-Tec KSG: 21st Century Shotgun*, Officer.com

[3] https://www.youtube.com/watch?v=W638QRLqUyc

5.2.5 External links

- Modern Firearms
- User Manual

5.3 Neostead

The **NeoStead 2000** (**NS2000**) is a bullpup combat shotgun developed by Truvelo Armoury of South Africa.[1]

The NS2000 has been used in trial runs for a few years by special forces like the British SAS and there are hopes at NeoStead that larger weapons manufacturers will licence the production rights. Production of the shotgun began in

2001 and the first models were made available in October of that year. It is notable due to its unusual forward pump action.

5.3.1 US Debut and history

In 2002, Jerome Kunzman Jr contacted the owners of Truvelo Armory, Ann and Haynes Stead to inquire about importation of the Neostead shotgun into the United States. Eager to work together, the Stead's agreed to allow the export to the United States. Kunzman then contacted Lefty Curtis of Custom Gunstocks in Antioch, California because Curtis had a federal firearms license for manufacturing firearms. Kunzman worked successfully to get Curtis a Federal Firearms Importation License. In early 2003 Kunzman received approval from the Bureau of Alcohol, Tobacco (BATF), and Firearms to import the shotgun. By the middle of the 2003 year, Curtis and Kunzman picked up the first Neostead at the cargo area of San Francisco International Airport. Kunzman managed to import a total of three Neostead shotguns into the United States before getting a call from BATF informing him that the technical department has had a change in personnel and the new person in charge of importation held a different view regarding the importability of the Neostead. The BATF claimed that the weapon didn't meet the requirements as a sporting shotgun. This was due to the two six-round magazine tubes. In the end all three guns were voluntarily surrendered to the BATF.

5.3.2 Design and production

The NS2000 is a 12-gauge pump-action shotgun weighing just over 3 kg, designed primarily for security and civil disturbance situations.

The firearm includes a 570-millimetre barrel despite the overall weapon length of just 690 millimetres (27 in). The short length makes the weapon easier to handle in close-quarters situations; however, unlike most firearms of this type, it can still remain accurate at relatively long ranges. The long barrel length is achieved by using a bullpup configuration, with a rear-fed tubular magazine.

Another aspect of the NS2000 is its dual six-round magazines. The selector switch can be set to left, right, or alternating. In riot conditions, for example, less-lethal flexible baton rounds can be used with standard rounds in reserve.

A possible production variant of the NS2000 has a 460-millimetre barrel in a weapon with an overall length of 560 mm (22 in). The shorter length reduces the magazine capacity to 5+5 rounds and makes the weapon easier to import or licence in some countries.

Its pump mechanism operates in a forward-back motion due to its moving-barrel mechanism, instead of the traditional moving-action. This method of operation is quite rare.

The NS2000 has been available for civilian purchase since 2003, with the majority of sales in Europe.

5.3.3 Patent drawings

Patent drawings of the NeoStead 2000.

- Magazine in loading position
- Details of Magazine
- Feeding is possible only from one tube, the other is blocked
- Ejecting the empty shell
- Feeding a new shell

5.3.4 See also

- List of bullpup firearms
- List of shotguns

5.3.5 References

[1] http://world.guns.ru/shotgun/sh08-e.htm

5.3.6 External links

- Official Website
- shotgun patent
- magazine patent

Chapter 6

Double-Barreled Shotguns

6.1 Beretta 682

The **Beretta 682** (also known as the S682, 682 Gold and currently 682 Gold E)[2] is a competition grade over-under shotgun.[3] It is manufactured, marketed, and distributed by Fabbrica d'Armi Pietro Beretta, in Gardone Val Trompia, Italy.

The 682 comes in various grades for sporting clays, trap and skeet shooting.

It is distributed in the UK by GMK Ltd, and in the United States by Beretta USA.

Wide vs Narrow Beretta 682 Receivers

There are two primary versions of the action of the Beretta 682 shotgun. The first version of the action is the original version, designated by a model number such as S682305T, and made at least through 1994. These earlier models are known as "wide" or "large" frame 682s. At some point, Beretta dropped the "S" from the front of the 682 model number, narrowed the receiver, introduced a new choke system, and reduced the barrel weight as well. This new model is consistent in width (or "narrow") with the 686 and 687 lines.

It is important to know the version of the 682 in question, as the wood components from a current narrow 682/686/687 [1.525 inches, 38.7 mm] will not fit on an older S682 wide receiver [1.585 inches, 40.3 mm] shotgun; replacement stocks for wide 682 shotguns need to be custom made at this point. Other than serial number lookup for production year, measurement of the frame size is the width measured in front of the breech across the recoil shoulders.

The older and newer models share many of the same parts, and barrel sets from narrow 682 shotguns can be used without issue in the wide S682 shotgun. However, there is only a 10% chance that a new model 682 barrel with drop in place and work properly on an older wide frame S682; gunsmithing and fit checking by a professional is always recommended. Obviously, there WILL be a very small lip present where the narrow barrel doesn't exactly match the wide receiver. One of the most common issues with simply dropping an unfitted barrel into a S682 is that the ejectors may not work properly.

The primary reason given for the design changes are general thought to be related to weight savings for competition shotguns.

6.1.1 References

[1] Beretta S682 Gold on GunsReview.com

[2] Beretta 682 Gold E official web page

[3] "Beretta S682 Gold E Sporting", *Guns & Ammo*

6.1.2 External links

-
- Beretta USA Product Catalog
- Beretta Over and Unders / Side by Sides Instruction Manual
- Beretta 682 Gold E - ratings and reviews

6.2 Beretta DT-10

The **Beretta DT10** is an over and under shotgun. It is manufactured, marketed, and distributed by Fabbrica d'Armi Pietro Beretta, in Gardone Val Trompia, Italy. It is one of the few Beretta shotguns that has a trigger unit that is detachable in the field, DT standing for detachable trigger. It is a marriage between the older Beretta ASE and the newer Beretta 682 model and is targeted at their competition market.[1]

Available in Trap, Skeet and Sporting Clays variants it has found favour with several top competition shooters in recent years. It is designed on the Beretta monoblock principle with a distinctive crossbolt that emerges on the left side of the action. This crossbolt engages on either side of the barrel and provides a very strong lock up. The downside being that the action is very broad and this gives it its rather clumsy appearance.

The DT10 is available in several guises, the base DT10, a DT10L with enhanced engraving and the DT10EELL, a sideplate deluxe version. The mechanicals in each model are identical.

6.2.1 References

[1] Garden & Gun Magazine: 21st Century Southern America - Stories & Media - Game Changers

6.2.2 External links

- Beretta USA Product Catalog
- Beretta Over and Unders / Side by Sides Instruction Manual
- Beretta Japan - ????????????

6.3 Beretta Silver Pigeon

The **Beretta Silver Pigeon** is a double-barreled shotgun. It is an "over and under" gun, with one barrel above the other. It is most often used for hunting birds and for clay target games such as trap and skeet. There are several models in field and sporting, for example 682, 686, and 687, with different features and finishes, and in various gauges.[1][2][3][4][5][6][7]

The Silver Pigeon is manufactured, marketed, and distributed by Fabbrica d'Armi Pietro Beretta, in Gardone Val Trompia, Italy.

The Silver Pigeon was also produced for a short period as a pump shotgun, called the Silver Pigeon SL 2.

6.3.1 References

[1] Rawlingson, Richard. "And Then There Were Five", *Clay Shooting*. Archived from the original on September 12, 2006. Retrieved December 25, 2014.

[2] Harker, Vic (February 2, 2012). "Gun Test: Beretta Silver Pigeon Sporter", *Clay Shooting*. Retrieved December 25, 2014.

[3] Harris, Jason (July 27, 2014). "Beretta Silver Pigeon Grade 1 Sporter", Shooting UK. Retrieved December 25, 2014.

[4] "Three 20-Gauges Duke It Out on the Sporting Clays Field", *Gun Tests*, September 2007. Retrieved December 25, 2014.

[5] "Beretta Shotguns", GunsReview. Retrieved December 25, 2014.

[6] Yardley, Mike. "Beretta Silver Pigeon 1", Positive Shooting. Retrieved December 25, 2014.

[7] Anstine, Mia (November 17, 2013). "Gun Review: Beretta 686 Silver Pigeon I", *The Daily Caller*. Retrieved December 25, 2014.

6.3.2 External links

- Beretta 686 Silver Pigeon I official website

6.4 Browning Citori

The **Browning Citori** is a double-barreled shotgun of the "over and under" or "stacked-barrel" type, with one barrel above the other.

The Citori is manufactured in a wide variety of models, styles, and gauges to accommodate enthusiasts of clay target games such as trap, skeet, and sporting clays, as well as upland bird and waterfowl hunters.

The Citori is marketed and distributed by the Browning Arms Company in Morgan, Utah. It is manufactured for Browning by the Miroku Corporation in Nangoku, Japan.

6.4.1 Origin

The Browning Citori was introduced in 1973 as a more affordable version of the highly successful Browning Superposed. The Superposed, which was first sold in 1931, was the last firearm designed by the famous small arms designer John Moses Browning.

In 1977, the Browning Arms Company was acquired as a subsidiary by the FN Herstal company of Herstal, Belgium, which continues to oversee operations today.

The name "Citori" has no meaning and is an advertising construct.

6.4.2 Features

Browning Citoris come in all of the popular shotgun shell gauges, and are made in an over-under "stacked" barrel configuration, with forends and buttstocks made from high quality walnut wood. Barrel lengths can be purchased from 26 inches for skeet shooting to 32 inches for sporting clays

United States President Barack Obama firing a Browning Citori 525 on the range at Camp David.[1] The side jet of smoke is from the ported barrel.

and trap shooting. The top barrel has a vented rib attached by soldering for the entire length of the barrel tube. Newer Citori internal barrels are chrome-lined for added surface strength. All metal parts are bright blued for the standard model. "In-the-white" higher grade models with more elaborate machine-applied engraving can also be purchased. Rubber recoil butt pads (12 gauge) or plastic butt plates (sub-gauges) are standard. Citori actions are made with internal hammers and coil springs and all Citori models have shell ejectors, which expel spent shells when the breech is opened by pressing aside the top lever and bending the action fully open, which also re-cocks the internal hammers.

The Browning Citori has a single, gold-plated trigger. A barrel selector mechanism is used to choose whether the top or bottom barrel fires first. The barrel selector is combined with the manual safety and is located at the top rear of the receiver, behind the top lever. If the first shot misfires and the gun does not recoil, the trigger can be reset to fire the second shot. This is accomplished by moving the safety/barrel selector back to the "safe" position and then forward to the "fire" position, without changing the barrel selection. Opening the action does not automatically engage the safety mechanism.

Current Citoris feature screw-in Invector choke tubes to regulate shot patterns downrange and thus provide versatility for usage in hunting and target shooting. These can be used with either lead, bismuth, or steel shot. Older models had factory fixed chokes, and steel shot is not recommended for use with those.

Some newer 12 gauge and 20 gauge Citori models have back-bored barrels. These are barrels with slightly larger bore diameters. Their purpose is to improve shot patterns by reducing the friction of the shot charge on the barrel wall, while also reducing felt recoil. Models with back-bored barrels use Invector Plus choke tubes.

6.4.3 References

[1] President Barack Obama shoots clay targets on the range at Camp David, Md. White House, 2012-08-04.

- Performance test of Browning Citori Lightning Field Grade, Ruger Red Label, and Beretta Silver Pigeon, *Gun Tests*, January 1997

- "Premier Competition STS Vs.Citori XS: We Prefer Browning", *Gun Tests*, August 2007

- Field test of Browning Citori 525, *Outdoor Life*, Summer 2002

- Bourjaily, Philip. "Shotguns: The Best Guns of the Year" (2002), *Field & Stream*

- Product review of Browning Citori Ultra XS Sporting, *Shotgun Report*, August 7, 2001

- Hawks, Chuck. "Browning Citori O/U Shotguns", *chuckhawks.com*

- "What is Back-Boring?", Browning Customer Services Top Questions

6.4.4 External links

- Browning Citori official home page
- Browning Citori owner's manual

6.5 Browning Superposed

The **Browning Superposed** was one of the first over and under shotgun designs to be produced. The Superposed introduced a wide variety of innovations including the single select trigger and over-under design. This design was considered revolutionary in the 1930s, but it was later found that Browning had already made a model of this design in the 1880s.

6.5.1 History

It was the last firearm to be designed by John Browning. After Browning's death, the design work was completed by his son Val A. Browning.[1] Original production dates were 1931-1940.[2] Original production grades were Grade I (Lightning/Standard), Pigeon, Diana and Midas.

Post WWII production began in 1948 and lasted until 1960 when the model underwent major changes.[2]

6.5.2 References

[1] Hawks, Chuck. "Browning Superposed Shotguns", chuckhawks.com

[2] Superposed Shotgun dates and serial numbers on browning.com

6.6 Cynergy Shotgun

The **Browning Cynergy Over and Under Shotgun** is a firearm introduced by Browning in 2004. It is considered by most to be the first Over and under shotgun to depart from the basic design criteria that had been associated with over and unders since the early 20th century.

The Browning Company also makes the Browning Citori line of over and under shotguns. The Cynergy and the Citori are manufactured at the Miroku Firearms Manufacturing plant in Kochi, Japan. The Cynergy is substantially different in its design from the original Browning Superposed designed by John Moses Browning, and its successor the Citori (which is largely derivative in design from the Superposed.)

6.6.1 Mechanism differences

Mechanical Trigger: Based on the trigger system found in a rifle, Cynergy shotguns feature a reverse striker. The reverse striker is a mechanical trigger system that uses an actuator to reverse the direction of the impact force from the spring to the firing pin. Essentially, when the action opens up, the strikers must cock by a 'pull' rather than a 'push.'" This design offers the benefit of reduced locktime.

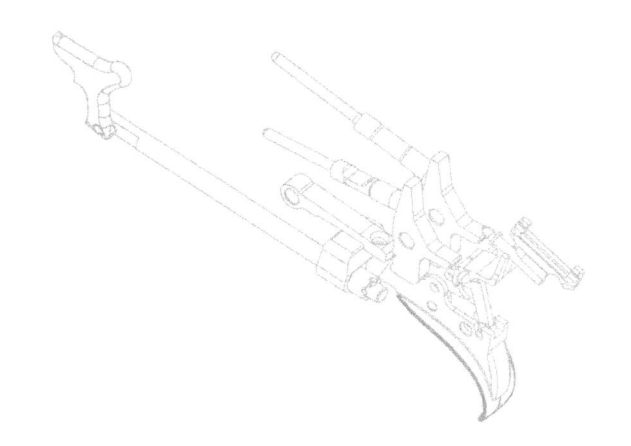

Diagram of the Browning Cynergy mechanical trigger system.

Monolock Hinge: The purpose of this design is to create a lower profile receiver. The system integrates the hinge and locking system. The MonoLock Hinge pivots on significantly more surface area than guns with conventional low profile receivers. Rectangular locking pins provide additional strength while a wear-in relief feature allows for wear without hindering lock-up.

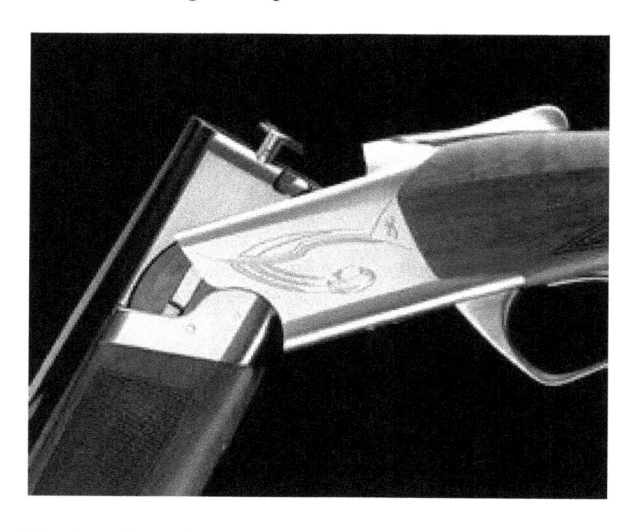

Side view of Monolock hinge system. Note large hinge radius.

6.6.2 History of the design

The beginning of the Cynergy technically begins with the original B-25 Superposed, designed by John M. Browning in 1928 and finished for production using a single trigger with barrel selector by his son Val Browning by 1939. Production continued on the Superposed until production costs hurt the Superposed in the marketplace during the late 1960s. The basic design was taken to Browning's partner, the Miroku Company in Japan, and in 1971 the Citori over and under went into production. From that point the Citori took the place of the Superposed as the primary Browning over and under shotgun.

In the early 1990s the idea of a complementary gun to the Citori was being discussed by all the Browning design teams in Belgium, Utah and in Japan. [1]

In 1994, at a management retreat in Alaska, the worldwide team determined to begin exploring ideas. Independent design projects began and in 1996 the teams came together in Belgium to discuss three basic ideas. First was a design with a reverse-type hinge system presented by Joseph Rousseau, a master Browning gun designer from Belgium, now living in Morgan, Utah. The second was a low profile receiver concept being worked on by the experienced Browning designer Joseph Mardaga, who was a member of the Browning R&D team in Herstal, Belgium. Third was a design featuring a double firing pin concept specifically created to provide exceptionally fast lock times.

About this time Dwight Potter joined Browning as a gun designer in Morgan, Utah. Potter had worked for many years prior designing robotic manipulators . . . telerobotics systems used on everything from submarine manipulators to animatronics at some of the world's most famous theme parks. [2]

By 1997 the Cynergy project became official under the code name of "Sheik" and Potter was put on the project full-time as lead designer, working closely with Master Browning gun designer, Joseph Rousseau, who was now the firm's VP of Research and Development.

The Cynergy design was to be based on the reverse hinge concept put forward by Rousseau several years earlier With the decision to proceed Potter designed all the internal mechanisms. This took over two years of design work resulting in the first prototype coming out of Browning's model shop in Morgan, Utah in 1999. Both Potter and Rousseau are listed on the patent documents for this design. [3]

Working closely with Rousseau, Potter designed the Cynergy's reverse striker system which assured very fast lock times. He created a striker type ejection system and integrated a toggle-type safety/selector. Potter's design assured good function with the mechanical triggers via a design utilizing an inertia block that prevents doubling while preserving fast lock times.

By 2001 Browning partner, Miroku, had produced the first design verification prototypes. In 2004, the new Cynergy was introduced to the public at the annual Shooting, Hunting and Outdoor Trade Show (SHOT Show) - a full decade after the original ideas were discussed in Alaska.

Many have called the Browning Cynergy "revolutionary". Ever since the invention of the Browning Superposed over and under, most manufacturers have relied on the basic principles incorporated by John M. Browning to create their own over and unders, each one adapting and evolving from previous designs. The Cynergy represents the first major rethink of the over and under concept in nearly a Century. As such, it incorporates all of the most desirable features every shooter wants. The Cynergy achieves them through forward thinking ideas and manufacturing methods, in the same manner John M. Browning did when he broke new ground with his designs starting over 125 years ago. From a historical point of view, the Cynergy shows that the innovative thinking started by John M. Browning is still alive and well at Browning today.

6.6.3 Sources

- Patent Storm
- © Browning, used with permission.
- Gun Week
- Browning
- Shooting UK
- Browning, John M., *American Gunmaker*. Browning, John & Curt Gentry. 1964.
- "American Gunmaker: The John M. Browning Story." Documentary. Written and Produced by Lee B. Groberg
- *Business Week*
- Striking shotgun designs for the 21st Century, Guns Magazine, June, 2004 by Holt Bodinson
- Browning eBlast Newsletter, June, 2008. © Browning 2008, used with permission.
- Over-and-under shotgun apparatus and method. Joseph F.N. Rousseau, Mountain Green, Morgan County; Dwight M. Potter, Liberty, Weber County. Assigned to Browning Arms Co., Morgan. Filed Jan. 5, 2005, a continuation of Patent No. 6,907,687, filed Dec. 2, 2002. Patent No. 7,207,130.

6.6.4 References

[1] Browning

[2] www.gunweek.com

[3] Patent Storm

6.6.5 External links

- Cynergy Shotgun on Browning.com

6.7 Ithaca Auto & Burglar

The **Auto & Burglar Gun** was a US-made factory-built handgun that was commercially manufactured by configuring a standard double-barrel shotgun with a pistol grip, at first engraving and later stamping "Auto & Burglar Gun" on each side of the frame, and shortening the barrels to about 10" to 12.2" in length.

6.7.1 Variants

Model A

The Auto & Burglar Gun was manufactured in two variations. Approximately 2,500 of the original variation were manufactured from 1921 to 1925 using Ithaca's standard 20 gauge Flues model shotgun, and designed to fire 2½" shells. Sometimes referred to as "Model A", its barrels were about 10" in length. These guns should only be fired with 2½" shells; firing longer shells will "bulge" the barrels.

Flues model

The Flues model was designed with a "saw handle" style grip featuring a large spur at the top to absorb recoil.

New Improved Double model

Ithaca redesigned the gun in 1925 using its New Improved Double (NID) model shotgun, which fires 2¾" shells; the barrels were lengthened to about 12.2"; and the grip was redesigned without the spur. Sometimes referred to as "Model B," about 1,500 were manufactured. Model A and Model B are not formal factory designations.[1]

6.7.2 Demise

Ithaca stopped manufacturing the Auto & Burglar Gun when it became subject to registration and a $200 transfer tax under the National Firearms Act (NFA) of 1934 (the transfer tax was reduced to $5 in 1960). Relatively few Auto & Burglar Guns were manufactured, and they are today highly prized as collector's items. Approximately 20 Auto & Burglar Guns were specially manufactured, representing .410 bore, 28 gauge, and 16 gauge, only 11 of which have been reliably documented, and all these guns are extremely rare.[2] The earliest known Ithaca Auto & Burglar Gun was manufactured about 1921, possibly as a prototype; it bears serial number 354442; is in 28 gauge with 12" barrels; "Auto & Burglar Gun" is hand-engraved on each side; and the gun is listed separately in the *Firearms Curios or Relics List* published by the Bureau of Alcohol, Tobacco, Firearms and Explosives.

While it is sometimes incorrectly identified as a "sawed-off shotgun," the Ithaca Auto & Burglar Gun is a smooth bore pistol which since 1934 has been classified as an "Any Other Weapon" (AOW)[3] under the NFA, and it must be registered with the Bureau of Alcohol, Tobacco, Firearms and Explosives (ATF). Auto & Burglar Guns that are not currently registered are contraband, and cannot be legally possessed or registered. The penalties for illegal possession include up to a $250,000 fine and 10 years in prison.

The "auto" in its name referred to "automobile"; it was intended as a self-defense weapon which could easily be carried in an automobile, but it was taken up by bank guards, police departments, watchmen and messengers.

6.7.3 See also

- Title II weapons

6.7.4 References

[1] "The Ithaca Auto and Burglar Gun," in *The World's Fighting Shotguns*, by Thomas F. Swearengen. Vol. IV. Hong Kong: Chesea, Ltd., 1978, pages 80-84.

[2] *2004 Standard Catalog of Firearms: The Collector's Price & Reference Guide*, by Ned Schwing. 14th edition. Iola, WI: Krause Publications, pages 605-607.

[3] "Any Other Weapon," as defined in 26 U.S.C., § 5845(e), means any weapon or device capable of being concealed on the person from which a shot can be discharged through the energy of an explosive, a pistol or revolver having a barrel with a smooth bore designed or redesigned to fire a fixed shotgun shell, weapons with combination shotgun and rifle barrels 12 inches or more, less than 18 inches in length, from which only a single discharge can be made from either barrel without manual reloading, and shall include any such weapon which may be readily restored to fire. Such term shall not include a pistol or revolver having a rifled bore, or rifled bores, or weapons designed, made, or intended to be fired from the shoulder and not capable of firing fixed ammunition.

6.7.5 External links

- The Ithaca Auto & Burglar by L Neil Smith

6.8 Paradox gun

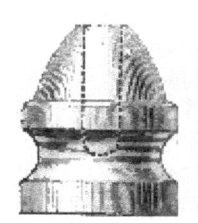

12 bore Paradox gun bullets, Hollow point (left) and Cross cut (right)

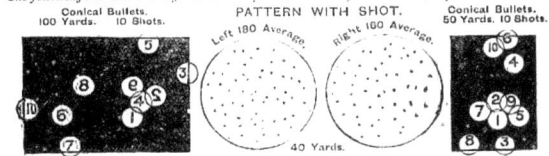

A **Paradox gun** is a firearm made by Holland & Holland with the last two to three inches (5.1 to 7.6 cm) of the muzzle rifled and the rest smooth, intended to be used as both a rifle and shotgun. Paradox guns served the needs of hunters in India and Africa who might encounter both small and large game but needed to carry only a single gun. A Paradox gun allowed the use of a shot with a specific choke for small game and Paradox bullets for large game: with the bullet engaging the rifling grooves as it swaged through the choke. This gave an advantage over a slug barrel, which could only employ cylinder bore barrels (no choke). Modern users of Paradox guns have the same advantage, especially in areas where the bird and deer hunting seasons overlap. Paradox cartridges have been loaded with either hollow-point or solid bullets of varied composition. The current Holland & Holland cartridge is loaded with the most useful of these, the 740-grain (48 g) lead solid.

6.8.1 History

Holland & Holland

Advertisement (1886)

The word "Paradox" has been used by Holland & Holland of London since 1886 to describe large-bore guns with the last few inches of the barrel rifled with a special "ratchet" style of rifling. Holland & Holland purchased the rights to the Paradox gun in 1885 from Col George Vincent Fosbery VC,[1] who also invented the Webley-Fosbery Automatic Revolver. They chose the name "Paradox" because shotguns are defined by their smoothbore barrels, and a "rifled shotgun" was thus a paradox. Over the years, Holland & Holland manufactured Paradox guns in 20, 16, 12, 10, and 8 gauge. Today they continue to manufacture Paradox guns of 12 gauge in the famous 'Royal' sidelock ejector as well as in their newer round-action sidelock gun.

Muzzle of a 12 gauge Paradox gun

Other manufacturers

Paradox-type guns were manufactured by several other firms. Other firms in Birmingham, England made them for sale under their own names and by others. For example, Westley Richards and G & S Holloway made versions. The latter made them under their own name, privately marked for and purchased for sale by high-end dealers such as P. Orr & Sons, a retailer of high-end jewellery, household items, furs, appliances and arms in Madras and Rangoon. Many had cut rifling that extended more than two inches into the muzzle(s) (3–4 inches [7.6–10.2 cm] in some cases).

6.8.2 References

[1] "Press Release - Holland & Holland re-introduce the Paradox gun after nearly 70 years.". Holland & Holland. Archived from the original on 2010-11-13. Retrieved 3 December 2008.

6.8.3 External links

- History of the Hunting Gun: The 19th Century - MyHunt.com
- What is a Paradox Gun? - ClassicShooting.com
- Notes On Shooting The Paradox Gun - ClassicShooting.com
- Paradox Bullets Against Game - ClassicShooting.com

6.9 Remington Spartan 310

The **Remington Spartan 310** is a double-barreled shotgun. It is an "over and under" gun, with one barrel above the other. There are several different models, each of them chambered in various gauges.

The Spartan 310 is marketed and distributed by Remington Arms, in Madison, North Carolina.[1] It is a variant of a classical Russian shotgun IZh-27 manufactured by Izhevsk Mechanical Plant for export under trademak "Baikal", in Izhevsk, Russia.[2] The Spartan 310 is inexpensive compared to other double barreled shotguns.[3] It is most often used for hunting birds, and for clay target games such as trap and skeet. Remington ceased importing the shotgun in 2009.

6.9.1 Features

The Spartan 310 has a walnut stock and fore-end, automatic ejectors, and a ventilated barrel rib. It uses screw-in SPR choke tubes. By default, the bottom barrel fires first, but the shooter can select the top barrel to fire first by pushing the trigger blade forward when the gun is loaded and closed.[4] Opening the action automatically engages the manual safety, which is located on the tang behind the top lever.[5]

The **SPR310** is the standard model. It has either a nickel plated or blued receiver. The barrels are 26 or 28 inches long.

The **SPR310S** is the sporting model.[6] It has ported barrels that are 29½ inches in length.

6.9.2 See also

- Remington Spartan 100

6.9.3 Notes

[1] SPR310 Over & Under Firearm Model History on Remington.com

[2] Hoots, Lee J. "Bear Simplicity", *Guns & Ammo*

[3] Workman, Dave. "Remington's 'Spartan' Shotgun: A Keeper at an Economy Price", *Gun Week*, February, 2005

[4] Mayer, Scott E. "The SPR310 Offers Pure Functionality at a Great Price", *Shooting Times*

[5] "Over/Under Shotguns for Less than $1000: Lanber is Best Buy", *Gun Tests*, October 2008

[6] Ceretto, Tom. "Spartan by Remington", *Clay Shooting USA*

6.9.4 External links

- Remington Spartan 310 official web page
- Owners manual for Remington model SPR310 and SPR320 Over/Under Shotguns

6.10 Ruger Gold Label

The **Ruger Gold Label** is a double-barreled shotgun. It is marketed and distributed by Sturm, Ruger & Company, Incorporated, a company based in Southport, Connecticut. The Gold Label is made at the Sturm, Ruger manufacturing facility in Newport, New Hampshire.

The Ruger Gold Label is a side-by-side shotgun, designed to be similar to traditional English shotguns used for upland bird hunting and for clay target games such as trap, skeet, and sporting clays.[1]

6.10.1 Features

The Gold Label has a stainless steel receiver and blued barrels. The stock and fore-end are made of AAA-grade American walnut.[2] At 6½ pounds, the Gold Label is relatively lightweight for a double barreled shotgun.

The gun has a single trigger. A barrel selector mechanism is used to choose whether the left or right barrel fires first. The second shot can be fired even if the first shot was a misfire and the gun has not recoiled. The barrel selector is combined with the manual safety and is located at the top rear of the receiver, behind the top lever. Opening the action automatically engages the safety mechanism.[3]

The Gold Label has been produced in 12 gauge only. The chambers are three inches long, to accommodate either 2¾ inch or 3 inch shells.[4] The gun uses screw-in choke tubes that are steel shot compatible.[5]

6.10.2 Models

There are two models of Gold Label. One has an American style pistol grip stock. The other has an English style straight grip stock. Both models have a splinter style fore-end.

The Gold Label was produced from 2004 to 2006 and has not been produced since. While the shotgun was still pictured in Ruger's 2008 Catalog, it was listed as "current production sold out, anticipate availability in 2009." According to most reports, including emails from Ruger customer service to customers who have asked, the Gold Label will not be produced again due to the high cost of manufacturing it.

6.10.3 Awards

In 2002, the Gold Label was named Shotgun of the Year by *Shooting Industry News*.[6] In 2005, it won the "Golden Bullseye" Shotgun of the Year award from *American Rifleman*, a magazine published by the National Rifle Association.[7]

6.10.4 Notes

[1] Bodinson, Holt. "Ruger's Elegant Game Gun", *Guns* magazine, July, 2002

[2] Hanus, Bill. "It's Time to Make Nice with Your Ruger Dealer", Bill Hanus Birdguns

[3] Ruger Gold Label Instruction Manual

[4] Miller, Payton. "Ruger Gold Label", *Guns & Ammo*, April, 2005

[5] "Ruger's Gold Label Takes On British 12-Bore Game Guns", *Gun Tests*, October, 2005

[6] "Shotgun of the Year, 1992 - 2007", *Shooting Industry News*

[7] "2005 Golden Bullseye Award Winners", nra.org

6.10.5 External links

- Ruger Gold Label official website
- Ruger Gold Label Instruction Manual

6.11 Ruger Red Label

The **Ruger Red Label** is an over and under shotgun built by Sturm, Ruger & Co.. It came about when William B. Ruger wanted to introduce an American made over and under shotgun to the US shooting public.

6.11.1 History

The Red Label was introduced in 1977 in 20 Gauge with a 26" barrel.[1] In 1979, Ruger began to offer the Red Label in 12 Gauge and eventually a scaled-down version in 28 Gauge (1994). The design was born of William B. Ruger's desire to produce a quality US made over and under shotgun. In order to achieve this and put quality on par with European hand-made shotguns, Ruger invested in expensive machinery to do most of the work.[2]

6.11.2 Design

The Red Label has a stainless steel receiver and two hammer forged barrels. The shooter can determine which barrel to fire by means of a selector mounted on the tang. The front sight is typically a brass bead. Most Red Labels are tapped to accept choke tubes for various purposes. The butt stock and forend are oil-finished American walnut with checkering on the grip and forend.[2]

The Red Label is primarily used as a sporting shotgun for waterfowling, upland game hunting as well as in skeet and sporting clays.[2]

6.11.3 Criticism

Critics of the Red Label mostly complain about the weight of the shotgun or the poor fitting of the metal to wood.[3]

6.11.4 References

[1] McNab, Chris (2007). *Sporting Guns: A Guide to the World's Rifles and Shotguns*. New York: Macmillan. p. 57. ISBN 0312368232.

[2] Wilson, R. L.; G. Allan Brown (2008). *Ruger & His Guns: A History of the Man, the Company and Their Firearms*. New York: Book Sales, Inc. ISBN 978-0785821038.

[3] Bourjaily, Phil (January 6, 2009). "Phil Bourjaily: Ruger Red Label". *Field & Stream*. Retrieved December 22, 2012.

6.12 Stoeger Coach Gun

The **Stoeger Coach Gun** is a double-barreled shotgun. It is marketed and distributed by Stoeger Industries in Accokeek, Maryland. It is manufactured by E.R. Amantino (Boito) in Veranópolis, Brazil.[1]

The Coach Gun is a side-by-side shotgun. While suitable for bird hunting, clay target shooting, or home defense, it is primarily designed for cowboy action shooting. As the name implies, it is a coach gun style shotgun, similar to those used to defend stagecoaches in the American Old West.[2]

6.12.1 Features

The Stoeger Coach Gun has been produced in 12 gauge, 20 gauge and .410 bore. The chambers are three inches long, to accommodate either 2¾ inch or 3 inch shells. barrel lengths include 18, 20 and 24 inch. The gun has a raised center rib with a brass bead front sight. The Coach Gun has dual triggers, one for each barrel. The safety mechanism is located on the tang, on the upper rear part of the receiver. Opening the action automatically engages the safety.[3] To comply with cowboy action shooting regulations, the gun does not have ejectors,[4] but it does have an extractor.[1]

6.12.2 Models

- **Coach Gun** — The standard model has fixed chokes, one Improved Cylinder and one Modified, and does not have a recoil pad. Different variations have a hardwood or walnut stock and fore-end, and a blued, matte nickel, or polished nickel receiver and barrels. Most versions have an American style pistol grip stock, but the Coach Gun has also been produced with an English style straight stock.[5]

- **Coach Gun Supreme** — The Coach Gun Supreme has screw-in choke tubes, and is equipped with a recoil pad. It features an AA-grade walnut stock and fore-end. Different versions have blued, nickel plated, stainless steel receivers and barrels.

- **Double Defense** — The recently introduced Double Defense is tactically designed for home defense. It has a black matte finish and two picatinny rails for add-on tactical accessories, such as a laser sight or flashlight. The gun has a single trigger, ported barrels, internal hammer design and a fixed Improved Cylinder choke.

6.12.3 Notes

[1] "Cowboy Doubles: Hit the Trail with the Stoeger Coachgun", *Gun Tests*, September 2001

[2] Christian, Chris. "Revival of the Coach Gun", *Popular Mechanics*, June 2004

[3] Carlson, Dan. "Guns, Game and More: Stoeger Coach Gun Review", *Black Hills Pioneer*, September 6, 2007

[4] "12-Gauge Matchup: Stoeger's Cowboy Gun Beats 870 Pump", *Gun Tests*, May 2008

[5] "Silverado Coach Gun", *Guns* magazine, August 2002

6.12.4 External links

- Stoeger Coach Gun official web page
- Stoeger Coach Gun Supreme official web page

6.13 Stoeger Condor

The **Stoeger Condor** is a double-barreled shotgun. It is an "over and under" gun, with one barrel above the other.[1]

There are several models of Condor, with different features and in various gauges. The standard model has a grade-A walnut stock and fore-end, blued receiver and barrels, a single trigger, and screw-in choke tubes. It has a vented barrel rib and a brass bead front sight. It is chambered to use either 2-¾ inch or 3 inch shells. Opening the action automatically engages the safety mechanism.[2]

The Condor is marketed and distributed by Stoeger Industries in Accokeek, Maryland, United States. It is manufactured by E.R. Amantino in Veranópolis, Brazil. The Condor is relatively inexpensive compared to other double barreled shotguns. It is most often used for hunting birds and for clay target games such as trap and skeet.

6.13.1 Condor Supreme

The Stoeger Condor Supreme is a model of Stoeger Condor. The Condor Supreme has a grade-AA walnut stock and fore-end, and high-luster bluing on the receiver and barrels. It also has automatic ejectors, and a selectable trigger that allows the shooter to choose which barrel will fire first.

6.13.2 Condor Outback

The Condor Outback model has 20-inch barrels. It has rifle style sights, with a fixed blade front sight and a notched rear sight. It is chambered in 12-gauge or 20-gauge. It has been manufactured with two different finishes — walnut stock and fore-end with blued metal, and black hardwood stock and fore-end with nickel plated metal.

6.13.3 Notes

[1] "Stoeger Condor I Over/Under Shotgun a Good Buy In 20 Gauge", *Gun Tests*, January 1998

[2] Review of Stoeger Condor Outback from *American Rifleman*

6.13.4 External links

- Stoeger Condor official web page
- Stoeger Condor Outback official web page

6.14 Ugartechea

For the Mexican general, see Domingo Ugartechea.

Armas Ugartechea is a Basque shotgun manufacturer located in Eibar, Spain. It produces several models of double-barreled shotgun.

6.14.1 Overview

Ugartechea is the last of the Big Three of Basque gunmaking from the 1960s that still exists bearing any resemblance to what it was. The Ugartechea company has survived in an unbroken line, but not without overcoming some difficulties. Today, it is no longer a mass-production company. It is mostly a custom shop, with a small workforce making high-quality guns to order.

There have been three Ignacio Ugartecheas in the history of the company; founder, son and grandson. It was founded in Eibar in 1922. The first Ignacio called his company *Casa Ugartechea* (House of Ugartechea) and set up shop in the Bidebarrieta, the first of serval locations the company occupied as it grew and diversified. After a few years it moved to San Augustín Kalea, and finally to Txonta Kalea, No. 26, which it occupies to this day.[1]

In the US market since 1996, Ugartecheas have only been imported through Lion Country Supply in Port Matilda, Pennsylvania. They're available in eight different grades in different gauges.

6.14.2 History

In addition to shotguns, Armas Ugartechea once made rifles and pistols. However, the firm is most famous for its side-by-side double-barreled shotgun, and at some point stopped manufacturing the over/under double-barreled shotgun configuration. The change in product was due in part to several different factors. After World War II, the international demand for sporting shotguns increased while the demand for pistols and rifles decreased. More importantly, Ignacio Ugartechea made his last double rifle in 1943, an 8x65R Brenneke, for the *Caudillo* himself, Generalissimo Francisco Franco and then Armas Ugartechea was passed on to the first Ignacio's son.

The second Ignacio Ugartechea was trained in the tradition of gun making at the prestigious *Escuela de Armeria* in Eibar. At one point, he was known as one of the most prominent sportsmen in Spain, developing a relationship and participating in social hunts with the likes of the king of Spain, Juan Carlos I.[2]

Armas Ugartechea builds guns based on designs and patents originating from London and Birmingham firms such as Holland & Holland and Westley Richards. When shotgun-making was in its heyday in the late nineteenth century, patents were only granted for fourteen years. After that period, advancements like the Anson & Deeley boxlock action were reproduced all over the world. When a patent that seemed efficient and easy to reproduce became available, it was not uncommon for Basque shotgun-makers to reproduce it with local components, and market it as a less-expensive alternative to the English offerings.[3]

6.14.3 Further Changes

Armas Ugartechea originally made matched-pairs of sidelocks guns for export to England. In a sidelock action, the mechanism that makes the gun function can be removed and reinserted fairly easily. At that time, the shooting of driven pheasant and partridge at large English country houses; and pigeons in Spanish pigeon rings; was very popular. These shooting sports required shotguns that could be repaired in the field. This made the sidelock very desirable (and expensive), and selling the sidelock action became a clear priority.[4]

Eventually though, the sidelock fad passed and the simpler and less expensive boxlock action gained popularity. Driven shooting and pigeon rings became less and less accessible, and sidelocks came to be considered more of a luxury. This was especially true for the rapidly growing American market after World War II. In the United States, consumers were generally looking for a gun that had the features of the traditional English shotgun, but not the corresponding steep price tag. Up until this point, Armas Ugartechea traditionally spent less time on its boxlock guns, producing mainly lower-end offerings. However, perceiving a change in the market, the company switched its focus to the boxlock, and now exports them to the United States.[5]

6.14.4 References

[1] Wieland, T. *Spanish Best*, p. 259. Countrysport Press, 2001

[2] *ibid.*, p. 261.

[3] http://www.sidebysideshotgun.com/articles/anson_deeley_article.html

[4] Wieland, T. "Ugartechea Reborn", page 27. Gray's Sporting Journal, August 1997

[5] Venters, V. "Boxlocks by Ugartechea", page 110. Shooting Sportsman, Sept./Oct. 2001

6.14.5 External links

- U.S. Importer since 1987 with further reading and availability
- U.S. Importer site with further reading
- Ugartechea - corporate site

6.15 Winchester Model 21

The **Winchester Model 21** is a deluxe side by side shotgun. The shotgun's initial production run from 1931 through 1960 yielded approximately 30,000 guns. Winchester Repeating Arms Company ceased the main production line of this shotgun in 1960 and the Model 21 was sourced to the Winchester Custom Shop until the gun's retirement in 1991. New Winchester Model 21 production continues under license to Connecticut Shotgun Manufacturing Company.[1]

The Winchester Model 21 action is of a typical breech loading shotgun, commonly called a break or hinge action. Like all quality double guns, production is time-consuming due to the laborious process of joining the barrels to produce an identical convergence of shot. The Model 21 was Winchester's effort to make a quality side by side shotgun to rival those of high-end makers such as Parker and Fox; financial troubles plagued the gun's development until the Western Cartridge Company purchased Winchester Repeating Arms in 1931. The Model 21 has a considerable collectors following as it is regarded as almost a bespoke shotgun.[2]

6.15.1 Production from 1931–1959

Model 21 grades at this time were chambered in 12, 16 and 20 gauge. .410 bore was offered in Custom Grade only and is extremely rare only exceeded by the sparse(8 known) 28 gauge guns produced. Barrel lengths were offered from 26 inches to 32 inches. The undersides of the trigger plates were typically stamped with the name of the grade.[3]

-**Standard**- This grade included barrels with a matte or vented rib, select grade walnut stocks featured in a straight or pistol grip configuration.

-**Tournament**- Produced from 1933–1944. Identical to the standard grade except with the trigger plate being stamped "TOURNAMENT."

-**Trap**- A higher grade tournament gun with higher quality wood and a stock made to a customers dimensions. The trigger plate is marked "TRAP."

-**Skeet**- Identical to Trap grade, but available in 28 gauge (8 known to exist). The trigger plate marked as "SKEET."

-**Duck/Magnum**- These grades were offered with features found in the Standard grade. The Duck variant built from 1940-1952, was chambered only for 12 gauge 3 inch shells and featured the trigger plate marked "DUCK." The Magnum version was offered from 1953–1959 in both 12 and 20 gauge, with 3 inch chambers. This Magnum grade featured no trigger plate markings.

-**Custom/Deluxe**- This particular grade included a stock which was custom fit to the customer. The top rib was marked "CUSTOM BUILT" and the bottom trigger plate was marked "DELUXE."

6.15.2 Custom Shop Production 1960–1991

Model 21 grades were offered in 12, 16, 20, 28 gauge and .410 bore with 16 gauge being the rarest. Barrels were produced in lengths from 26 inches to 32 inches. Select engraved models were available in 6 different patterns, with a higher number indicating more embellished engraving.[4]

- **Custom Grade**- Grade includes a matte center rib, a choice of a straight or pistol grip stock with fancy walnut and a checkered stock with matching forend.

- **Pigeon Grade**- Identical to the above but this grade offers a matte or ventilated center rib, a higher quality stock with custom leather recoil pad, matching forend, and a gold engraved pistol grip cap. The receiver was engraved with the number 6 pattern. This grade was dropped in 1982

- **Grand American**- Identical to the Pigeon grade, except the receiver was engraved with in the number 6 pattern with gold inlays. This grade was shipped with one extra set of barrels of the same gauge and forend in its own leather trunk case.

- **Grand American Small Gauge**- Offered starting in 1982, the firearm was shipped with both a 28 gauge and .410 bore barrel set, with matching forends.

6.15.3 Notes

[1] "Connecticut Shotgun Manufacturing Company".

[2] "Winchester Model 21 Collecting".

[3] Schider, Dan (2011). *2011 Standard Cataloge of Firearms*. Krause Publications. pp. 1333–1334. ISSN 1520-4928.

[4] Schider, Dan (2011). *2011 Standard Cataloge of Firearms*. Krause Publications. p. 1334. ISSN 1520-4928.

6.15.4 Resources

- http://www.winchestercollector.org/guns/model21.shtml

Chapter 7

Lever-Action Shotguns

7.1 Martini–Henry

Martini–Henry Mk IV

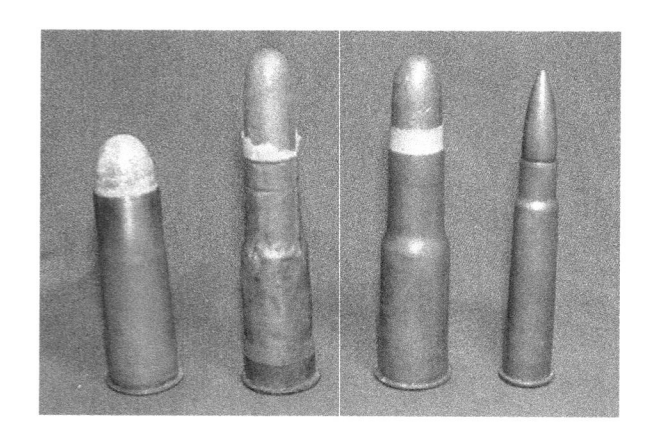

(From Left to Right): A .577 Snider cartridge, a Zulu War-era rolled brass foil .577/450 Martini–Henry Cartridge, a later drawn brass .577/450 Martini–Henry cartridge, and a .303 British Mk VII SAA Ball cartridge.

The **Martini–Henry** was a breech-loading single-shot lever-actuated rifle adopted by the British Army, combining the dropping-block action first developed by Henry O. Peabody (in his Peabody rifle) and improved by the Swiss designer Friedrich von Martini, whose work in bringing the cocking and striker mechanism all within the receiver greatly improved the operation of the rifle, which new iteration was combined with the polygonal barrel rifling designed by Scotsman Alexander Henry. It first entered service in 1871, eventually replacing the Snider–Enfield, a muzzle-loader conversion to the cartridge system. Martini–Henry variants were used throughout the British Empire for 30 years. Though the Snider was the first breechloader firing a metallic cartridge in regular British service, the Martini was designed from the outset as a breechloader and was both faster firing and had a longer range.[1]

There were four main marques of the Martini–Henry rifle produced: Mark I (released in June 1871), Mark II, Mark III, and Mark IV. There was also an 1877 carbine version with variations that included a Garrison Artillery Carbine, an Artillery Carbine (Mark I, Mark II, and Mark III), and smaller versions designed as training rifles for military cadets. The Mark IV Martini–Henry rifle ended production in the year 1889, but remained in service throughout the British Empire until the end of the First World War. It was seen in use by some Afghan tribesmen as late as the Soviet invasion. Early in 2010 and 2011, United States Marines recovered at least three from various Taliban weapons caches in Marjah.[2] In April 2011, another Martini–Henry rifle was found near Orgun in Paktika Province by United States Army's 101st Airborne Division (Air Assault).

The Martini–Henry was copied on a large scale by North-West Frontier Province gunsmiths. Their weapons were of a poorer quality than those made by Royal Small Arms Factory, Enfield, but accurately copied down to the proof markings. The chief manufacturers were the Adam Khel Afridi, who lived around the Khyber Pass. The British called such weapons "Pass-made rifles".

7.1.1 Overview

In the original chambering, the rifles fired a round-nosed, tapered-head .452-inch, soft hollow-based lead bullet, wrapped in a paper patch giving a wider diameter of .460 to .469-inch; it weighed 485 grains.[1] It was crimped in place with two cannulas (grooves on the outside neck of the case), ahead of two fibre card or mill board disks, a concaved beeswax wad another card disk and cotton wool filler. This sat on top of the main powder charge inside initially a rimmed brass foil cartridge, then made in drawn brass, The cartridge case was paper lined so as to prevent the chemical reaction between the black powder and the brass. Known today as the .577/450, a bottle-neck design with the same

The disassembled Martini–Henry action.

base as the .577 cartridge of the Snider–Enfield. It was charged with 85 grains (5.51 g) of Curtis and Harvey's No.6 coarse black powder,[1] notorious for its heavy recoil. The cartridge case was ejected to the rear when the lever was operated.

The rifle was 49 inches (124.5 cm) long, the steel barrel 33.22 inches (84 cm). The Henry patent rifling produced a heptagonal barrel with seven grooves with one turn in 22 inches (560 mm). The weapon weighed 8 pounds 7 ounces (3.83 kg). A sword bayonet was standard issue for non-commissioned officers; when fitted, the weapon extended to 68 inches (172.7 cm) and weight increased to 10 pounds 4 ounces (4.65 kg). The standard bayonet was a socket-type spike, either converted from the older Pattern 1853 (overall length 20.4 inches) or newly produced as the Pattern 1876 (overall length 25 inches). A bayonet designed by Lord Elcho was intended for chopping and other sundry non-combat duties, and featured a double row of teeth so it could be used as a saw; it was not produced in great numbers and was not standard issue.

The Mk2 Martini–Henry rifle, as used in the Zulu Wars, was sighted to 1,800 yards. At 1,200 yards (1100 m), 20 shots exhibited a mean deflection from the centre of the group of 27 inches (69.5 cm), the highest point on the trajectory was 8 feet (2.44 m) at 500 yards (450 m).

A 0.402 calibre model, the Enfield–Martini, incorporating several minor improvements such as a safety catch, was gradually phased in to replace the Martini–Henry from about 1884. The replacement was gradual, to use up existing stocks of the old ammunition.

However, before this was complete, the decision was made to replace the MartiniHenry rifles with the .303 calibre bolt-action magazine Lee–Metford, which gave a considerably higher maximum rate of fire. Consequently, to avoid having three different rifle calibres in service, the Enfield–Martinis were withdrawn, converted to 0.45 calibre, and renamed Martini–Henry "A" and "B" pattern rifles. Some 0.303 calibre black-powder carbine versions were also produced, known as the Martini–Metford, and even 0.303 calibre cordite carbines, called Martini–Enfields (as opposed to Enfield–Martinis).

During the Martini–Henry's service life the British army was involved in a large number of colonial wars, most notably the Anglo-Zulu War in 1879. The rifle was used in the Battle of Isandlwana, and by the company of the 2nd Battalion, 24th Regiment of Foot at the battle of Rorke's Drift, where 139 British soldiers successfully defended themselves against several thousand Zulus. The weapon was not completely phased out until 1904.

The rifle suffered from cartridge-extraction problems during the Zulu War, mostly due to the thin, weak, pliable foil brass cartridges used: they expanded too much into the rifle's chamber on detonation, to the point that they stuck or tore open inside the rifle's chamber. It would eventually become difficult to move the breech block and reload the rifle, substantially diminishing its effectiveness, or rendering it useless if the block could not be opened. After investigating the matter, the British Army Ordnance Department determined the fragile construction of the rolled brass cartridge, and fouling due to the black-powder propellant, were the main causes of this problem.

To correct this, the weak rolled brass cartridge was replaced by a stronger drawn brass version, and a longer loading lever was incorporated into the MK-IV to apply greater torque to operate the mechanism when fouled.[1] These later variants were more reliable in battle, although it was not until smokeless nitro powders and copper-coated bullets were tried out in these rifles in the 1920s that accuracy and 100% reliability of cartridge case extraction was finally achieved by Birmingham ammunition makers (Kynoch). English hunters on various safaris, mainly in Africa, found the Martini using a cordite charge and a 500-grain full-metal-jacketed bullet effective in stopping large dangerous game such as hippopotamus up to 80 yards away.

The nitro based/shotgun powders were used in Kynoch's .577/450 drawn-brass Martini–Henry cartridge cases well into the 1960s for the commercial market, and again were found to be very reliable and, being smokeless, eliminated fouling issues. The powder's burning with less pressure inside the cartridge case prevented the brass cases from sticking inside the rifle's chamber (because they were not expanding as much as the original black-powder loads did).

The rifle remained a popular competition rifle at National Rifle Association meetings, at Bisley, Surrey, and (NRA) Civilian and Service Rifle matches from 1872–1904, where it was used up to 1,000 yards using the standard military service ammunition of the day. By the 1880s the .577/.450

Boxer Henry round was recognised by the NRA as a 900-yard cartridge, as shooting the Martini out to 1,000 yards or (3/4 of a mile) was difficult, and took great skill to assess the correct amount of windage to drop the 485 grain bullet on the target. But by 1904 more target shooters were using the new .303 cal cartridge, which was found to be much more accurate, and thus interest in the .577/450 fell away, to the point that by 1909 they were rarely used at Bisley matches, with shooters favouring the later Lee–Enfield bolt action magazine rifles.[3]

In 1879, however, it was generally found that in average hands the .577/450 Martini–Henry Mk2, although the most accurate of the Martinis in that calibre ever produced for service life, was really only capable of hitting a man sized target out to 400 yards. This was due to the bullet going subsonic after 300 yards and gradually losing speed thereafter, which in turn affected consistency and accuracy of the bullet in flight. The 415-grain Martini Carbine load introduced in 1878 shot better out to longer ranges and had less recoil when it was fired in the rifles, with its reduced charge of only 75 grains of Curtis & Havey's. It was found that, while the rifle with its 485 grain bullet shot point of aim to 100 yards, the carbine load when fired in the rifles shot 12 inches high at the same range, but then made up for this by shooting spot-on out to 500 yards.[4] These early lessons enabled tactics to be evolved to work around the limitations of this large, slow, and heavy calibre during the Zulu War. During most of the key battles, such as Rorke's Drift and the battle of Ulundi, the order to volley fire was not given until the Zulus were at or within 400 yards.

The ballistic performance of a .577/450 is somewhat similar to that of a .45/70 American Government round, as used prolifically throughout the American Frontier West and by buffalo hunters, though the .577/450 has more power due to its extra 15 grains of black powder inside the cartridge case. It is clear from early medical field surgeons' reports that at 200 yards the rifle really came into its own, and inflicted devastating and horrific wounds on the Zulus in the Anglo–Zulu War.[5] The MK2 Martini's sights are marked to 1,800 yards, but this setting was only ever used for long-range mass volley firing on to harass an artillery position or a known massed cavalry position, prior to a main fight, and to prevent or delay infantry attacks. A similar "drop volley sight" whereby the rifle's bullets were dropped long range onto the target were employed on the later .303 Lee–Enfield rifles of WW1, which had a graduation lever sight calibrated up to 2,800 yards.

The Nepalese produced a close copy of the British Martini–Henry incorporating certain Westley Richards improvements to the trigger mechanism but otherwise very similar to the British Mark II. These rifles can be identified by their Nepalese markings and different receiver ring. A noticeably different variant incorporating earlier Westley Richards ideas for a flat-spring driven hammer within the receiver in lieu of the coil-spring powered striker of the von Martini design, known as the Gahendra rifle, was produced locally in Nepal.[6] While generally well-made, the rifles were produced substantially by hand, making the quality extremely variable. Though efforts were being made to phase out these rifles, presumably by the 1890s, some 9000 were still in service in 1906.[6]

The Martini–Henry saw service in World War I in a variety of roles, primarily as a Reserve Arm, but it was also issued (in the early stages of the war) to aircrew for attacking observation balloons with newly developed incendiary ammunition, and aircraft. Martini–Henrys were also used in the African and Middle Eastern theatres during World War I, in the hands of Native Auxiliary troops.

Greener shotgun

A shotgun variant known as the Greener Police Gun or the Greener Prison Shotgun was chambered in a special round that would make the weapon useless to anyone who stole it.[7] An example can be seen at the Royal Armouries Museum in Leeds.[8] Greener also used the Martini action for the GP single-barreled shotgun firing standard 12-bore ammunition, which was a staple for gamekeepers and rough shooters in Britain up to the 1960s.

Greener harpoon gun

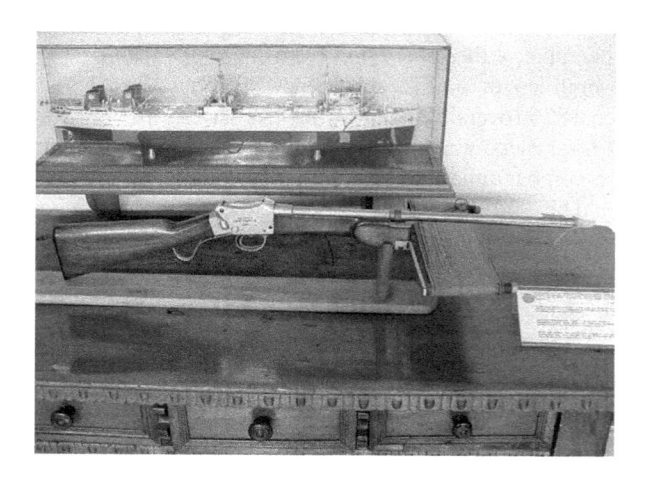

Greener-Martini Light Harpoon Gun.

W.W. Greener also used the Martini action to produce the Greener-Martini Light Harpoon Gun used for whaling, and also for commercial harvest of tuna and other large fish.[9] The gun fired a blank cartridge to propel the harpoon. A special barrel and stock were fitted to accommodate the harpoon and to lower weight. A Greener harpoon gun is used by Quint and Brody in the 1975 movie Jaws.[10]

Turkish, Romanian, and Boer Republics Peabody–Martini–Henry rifles

Unable to purchase Martini–Henry rifles from the British because their entire production was going to rearming British troops, Ottoman Turkey purchased weapons identical to the Mark I from the Providence Tool Company in Providence, Rhode Island, USA (the manufacturers of the somewhat similar Peabody rifle), and used them effectively against the Russians in the Russo-Turkish War (1877–1878).[11][12] The Ottoman Turkish outlaw and folk hero Hekimoğlu famously used the rifle during his raids on landowners.[13] The rifle is referred to as *Aynalı Martin* in Turkey and features in several famous folk songs.

A now scarce variant of the Peabody–Martini–Henry built by Steyr was adopted by Romania in 1879. Significant numbers of the basic design, with variations, were also produced for the Boer Republics, both in Belgium and, via Westley Richards, in Birmingham, as late as the late 1890s.

7.1.2 Operation of the Martini action

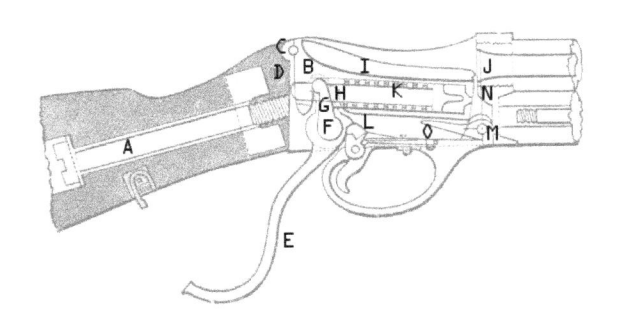

Section of Martini–Henry lock.

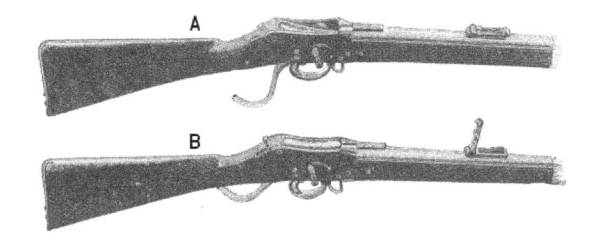

Martini–Henry rifle.
A: ready for loading.
B: loaded and ready to fire.

The lock and breech are held to the stock by a metal bolt (A). The breech is closed by the block (B) which turns on the pin (C) that passes through the rear of the block. The end of the block is rounded to form a knuckle joint with the back of the case (D) which receives the force of the recoil rather than the pin (C).

Below the trigger-guard the lever (E) works a pin (F) which projects the tumbler (G) into the case. The tumbler moves within a notch (H) and acts upon the block, raising it into the firing position or allowing it to fall according to the position of the lever.

The block (B) is hollowed along its upper surface (I) to assist in inserting a cartridge into the firing chamber (J). To explode the cartridge the block is raised to position the firing mechanism (K) against the cartridge. The firing mechanism consists of a helical spring around a pointed metal striker, the tip of which passes through a hole in the face of the block to impact the percussion-cap of the inserted cartridge. As the lever (E) is moved forward the tumbler (G) revolves and one of its arms engages and draws back the spring until the tumbler is firmly locked in the notch (H) and the spring is held by the rest-piece (L) which is pushed into a bend in the lower part of the tumbler.

After firing, the cartridge is partially extracted by the lock. The extractor rotates on a pin (M) and has two vertical arms (N), which are pressed by the rim of the cartridge pushed home into two grooves in the sides of the barrel. A bent arm (O), forming an 80° angle with the extractor arms, is forced down by the dropping block when the lever is pushed forward, so causing the upright arms to extract the cartridge case slightly and allow easier manual full extraction.

As well as British service rifles, the Martini breech action was applied to shotguns by the Greener company of Britain, whose single-shot "EP" riot guns were still in service in the 1970s in former British colonies. The Greener "GP" shotgun, also using the Martini action, was a favourite rough-shooting gun in the mid-20th century. The martini action was used by BSA and latterly BSA/Parker Hale for their series of "Small Action Martini" small bore target rifles that were in production until 1955.

7.1.3 In popular culture

- In the novel *The Man Who Would Be King*, two British adventurers use 20 Martini–Henry rifles to establish their own kingdom in Kafiristan. Rudyard Kipling also refers to the rifles in his poem *The Young British Soldier*.

- In the Dad's Army episode *A Brush with the Law* Lance-Corporal Jack Jones says he used a Martini–Henry rifle in the Mahdist War and that it was a very good rifle. He relates a rambling story about an officer who confuses the Martini–Henry with the Martini (Cocktail).

- The Martini–Henry is mentioned in Joseph Conrad's

novel "Heart of Darkness" by the main character Marlow. The helmsman later drops it overboard when he is killed, much to Marlow's chagrin.[14] "**[The pilot house] contained a couch, two camp-stools, a loaded Martini-Henry leaning in one corner, a tiny table, and the steering-wheel.**"

7.1.4 See also

- British military rifles

- Bira gun – a manually operated machine gun chambered in the same .577/450 cartridge as the Martini–Henry rifle

- Martini–Enfield – the .303 calibre version of the Martini–Henry

- Martini Cadet – Cadet target shooting rifle

- *Zulu Dawn* – shows the rifle in use at the Battle of Isandlwana

- *Zulu* – shows the rifle in use at the Battle of Rorke's Drift

- *The Man Who Would Be King*, Martini-Henry rifles used in both the story story and the 1975 film

7.1.5 References

[1] Smith-Christmas, Kenneth L. (2014). "Icon of an Empire The Martini-Henry". *American Rifleman* (National Rifle Association) **162** (November): 86–91, 108 & 109.

[2] Rifles of Advanced Age Remain in Use in Afghanistan

[3] Greener, W.W..*The Gun & its Development, 9th Edition*, 1910.

[4] Calver, Richard E.. *The Home Loader*. 2009.

[5] Grieves, Adrian. *Rourke's Drift*, 2003.

[6] Walter, John (2006). *Rifles of the World* (3rd ed.). Iola, WI: Krause Publications. pp. 147–8. ISBN 0-89689-241-7.

[7] Dave Cushman. "Greener Police Shotgun Cartridge and Weapon". Retrieved 27 November 2015.

[8] http://www.cybershooters.org/Royal%20Armoury/Greener.JPG

[9] "Lock, Stock, and History, The Greener - Martini Light Harpoon Gun, During...". Retrieved 27 November 2015.

[10] "Martini-Henry Rifle Series". Retrieved 27 November 2015.

[11] "Turkish Peabody Martini". Retrieved 27 November 2015.

[12] "The Turkish Connection: The Saga of the Peabody-Martini Rifle" by William O. Achtermeier. originally published in Man At Arms Magazine, Volume 1, Number 2, pp. 12-21, 5557, March/April 1979

[13] Yüksel, Ayhan - Eşkıya Hekimoğlu İbrahim'in 'Aynalı Martin' Tüfeği, Hürriyet Tarih 27 Kasım 2002, s. 20 - 21.

[14] "SparkNotes No Fear Literature: Heart of Darkness: Part 2: Page 9". Retrieved 27 November 2015.

- Suciu, Peter (August 2005). "The versatile Martini-Henry rifle was a mainstay of the British Empire during Queen Victoria's numerous 'little' wars". *Military Heritage* **7** (1): 24–7.

- *Small Arms Identification Series No 15: .450 & .303 Martini Rifles And Carbines* (Ian Skennerton, Arms & Militaria Press) ISBN 0-949749-44-3.

- *Encyclopædia Britannica*, "Gunmaking", 1905 edition

- Official Report of the Calcutta International Exhibition, 1883–84, Military Exhibits.

7.1.6 External links

- Martini–Henry Cavalry Carbine Mk I

- .577/.450 Martini–Henry Rifles

- martinihenry.com

- Martini Henry rifle 1881

- Martini Metford MkIV 1886

- Official Report of the Calcutta International Exhibition, 1883-84, Military Exhibits

- Rifles of Advanced Age Remain in Use in Afghanistan

7.2 Winchester Model 1887/1901

The **Winchester Model 1887** and **Winchester Model 1901** were lever-action shotguns originally designed by famed American gun designer John Browning and produced by the Winchester Repeating Arms Company during the late 19th and early 20th centuries.

7.2.1 Overview

The Model 1887 was the first truly successful repeating shotgun. Its lever-action design was chosen at the behest of the Winchester Repeating Arms Company, best known at the time as manufacturers of lever-action firearms such as the Winchester model 1873. Designer John Browning suggested that a pump-action would be much more appropriate for a repeating shotgun, but Winchester management's position was that, at the time, the company was known as a "lever-action firearm company", and felt that their new shotgun must also be a lever-action for reasons of brand recognition. Browning responded by designing a breech-loading, rolling block lever-action. To Winchester's credit, however, they later introduced a Browning designed pump-action shotgun known as the Model 1893 (an early production version of the model 1897), after the introduction of smokeless powder.

Shotgun shells at the time used black powder as a propellant, and so the Model 1887 shotgun was designed and chambered for less powerful black powder shotshells. Both 10 and 12-gauge models were offered in the Model 1887. It was soon realized that the action on the M1887 was not strong enough to handle early smokeless powder shotshells, and so a redesign resulted in the stronger Winchester Model 1901, 10-gauge only, to handle the advent of the more powerful smokeless powder. A 12-gauge chambering was not offered, as Winchester did not want the Model 1901 to compete with their successful 12-gauge Model 1897 pump-action shotgun. Other distinguishing characteristics of the Model 1901 are:

- a two piece lever

- the Winchester trademark stamp was moved to the upper tang, behind the hammer

- serial numbers between 64,856 and 79,455

Although a technically sound gun design, the market for lever-action shotguns waned considerably, as John Browning had predicted, after the introduction of the Winchester 1897 and other contemporary pump-action shotguns. Model 1887 production totaled 64,855 units between 1887 and 1901. Between 1901 and 1920, an additional 14,600 Model 1901 shotguns were manufactured before the Model 1887/1901 product line was discontinued. Serial numbers for the Model 1901 started where the serial numbers of the Model 1887 left off at 64,856 and ran through number 79,455. Thus, only 14,600 Model 1901s were produced indicating the declining demand for the lever action design.

7.2.2 Reproduction

Over the years, a number of gun companies tried to produce Model 1887/1901 shotguns that could chamber modern, smokeless shotgun shells—largely for the cowboy action shooting discipline—but with little commercial success. Recently however, three firearm companies have successfully produced viable models for the commercial firearms market:

- ADI Limited of Australia, produced a small trial run of modern Model 1887/1901 shotguns, chambered for modern smokeless 12-gauge shotshells. This was ostensibly to exploit a loophole in newer tighter gun laws in Australia which prohibited semi-automatic rifles and shotguns and pump action shotguns, amongst others, but still allowed bolt-action and lever-action rifles and shotguns. Commercial production on this firearm by ADI was anticipated for 2007, following several years of delays due to distribution issues, but this has not yet happened.

- Chinese arms manufacturer Norinco currently produces the Model 1887 shotgun chambered for modern smokeless 12-gauge shells, a version of which (featuring a 20" barrel) is manufactured for the American firearms firm Interstate Arms Corporation (IAC) and exported for sale in the United States, Canada, and Australia. As the only legal repeating shotgun (besides Mossberg bolt-action shotguns) for non-Primary Producer firearms owners in Australia, it has proven very popular with hunters and sporting shooters alike. U.S. and Canadian sales, however, have been largely focused on cowboy action shooting participants, owing to the ready availability of affordable pump-action and semi-automatic shotguns in most parts of the U.S. and Canada. In recent years, this particular firearm has become popular with regular American and Canadian firearm owners.

- The Italian firm Chiappa Firearms manufactures modern reproductions of the Winchester Model 1887 series shotguns. The shotguns appeared on the Australian and the European firearms markets in late 2008. Chiappa's replicas are offered with barrels ranging from 28 to 18.5 inches. They also offer a model with a rifled barrel and two models with pistol grips.[1]

7.2.3 Portrayals in popular culture

- The Model 1887 was prominently used by the title character in the film *Terminator 2: Judgment Day*, portrayed by Arnold Schwarzenegger. One of the guns used in the film was modified to allow one-handed use of the lever.

- The Model 1887 makes an appearance in Call of Duty: Modern Warfare 2, Call of Duty: Modern Warfare 3, Far Cry 3 and Far Cry 4

7.2.4 References

[1] http://www.chiappafirearms.com/products/69

- Madis, George (1977). *The Winchester Book*. Dallas: Taylor Publishing. OCLC 138931.

7.2.5 External links

- IAC reproduction M1887 shotgun
- SecurityArms.Com

Chapter 8

Pump-Action Shotguns

8.1 Bandayevsky RB-12

The **Bandayevsky RB-12** (Cyrillic: Ружьё Бандаевского РБ–12 – Ruzh'yo Bandayevskogo RB-12) is a shotgun of Russian origin.[1] The weapon is a slide-action (pumped forward) shotgun and comes with a folding stock.[2][3][4] The gun is designed by Aleksandr Bandayevsky, chief designer and president of JSC Uralmashproekt.

8.1.1 See also

- List of Russian weaponry
- List of shotguns

8.1.2 References

[1] http://www.bandaevskiy.com/

[2] """ -". , (,), : ,. Retrieved 14 November 2014.

[3] "–12". Retrieved 14 November 2014.

[4] "–12". ""-. , . Retrieved 14 November 2014.

8.1.3 External links

- Photos

8.2 Benelli Nova

The **Benelli Nova** is a pump action shotgun, popular for hunting and self-defense. Its most innovative and distinguishing feature is a one-piece receiver and buttstock, made of steel-reinforced polymer.[1]

8.2.1 Technical specifications

Two main models are available as well as one variant.

Hunting

This model is available with a variety of barrel and sight configurations, most intended for hunting and/or trap/skeet shooting. It is made in both Matte and camouflage finishes. Due to the polymer coated receiver and stock, along with proprietary coatings on the action and barrel, it is considered impervious to the elements. Barrels may be rifled or smoothbore, and are usually 24", 26", or 28" long. This model is available in 12 gauge or 20 gauge. Five types of chokes are available. Typically sold with improved modified and full, internal chokes. extended aftermarket chokes available.

Tactical

This model is intended for defensive purposes. With an 18½" barrel, and rifle or ghost- ring (diopter) sights, it is easier to wield and quicker to sight than hunting models. This barrel is smoothbore, and not tapped for chokes, reducing its versatility and rendering it less accurate at longer ranges. A slightly different model labeled the H2O Nova is similar, with the exception of an electroless nickel finish replacing the standard black coating, presumably with corrosion resistance in mind. This model is 12 gauge only.[1]

Supernova

Main article: Benelli Supernova

This model incorporates a number of recoil reducing features, and has a removable stock that can be replaced by a pistol-grip stock. This model has a bigger trigger set.

8.2.2 Common Features

- Synthetic Stock and Receiver Cover: for moisture resistance.

- Cross Bolt Safety

- Extendable Magazine: may optionally hold up to 7 rounds in magazine. (2.75in. 12 gauge)

- 3.5in. chamber: will fire and reliably cycle 2.75in., 3in., and 3.5in. shells. (in 12 gauge)

- Recoil Reducer: this optional mercury recoil unit is installed via a bracket that is attached to the interior of the stock. The baffled tube holds 14 oz. of mercury, which raises the length of time that the shot's impulse is spread across, thus lowering felt recoil.

- Optional Tritium Sights: for tactical units, to provide constantly illuminated sights.

- Chamber Empty Button: on the forend, allows unloading of unfired shell without releasing additional shells from the magazine. This is very useful for so-called "slug select" drills, where the user needs to quickly select a different type of ammunition (for example, a slug in order to engage a target at longer range.) The operator simply depresses the button as he cycles the action back; the chambered shell will be ejected, but the magazine will not feed another shell. The user then places the desired shell into the chamber and closes the action. On another shotgun without this feature, if the magazine were full, the user would have to cycle the shotgun to eject the chambered shell and make room in the magazine, then insert the desired shell into the magazine, then cycle the action again. This means that two shells are needlessly ejected.

8.2.3 Recoil Reducer

Recoil without the internal reducer can be harsh using the 3.5 inch shells. The shotgun is very light due to its composite/steel construction. This light weight shotgun lends itself to heavy recoil using heavy loads with high velocities. The recoil reducer helps reduce the felt recoil and allows the shooter to obtain a faster second shot. The recoil reducer is an option and must be purchased separately from a Benelli dealer or any of the more common shotgun web sites, or incorporated in the original sale/order (the recoil reducer is standard on all Benelli Supernova.)

The recoil reducer consists of two elements; the apparatus that connects to the stock via the buttstock compartment, and the mercury element that is inserted into the recoil apparatus.

8.2.4 References

[1] McNab, Chris (13 November 2007). *Sporting Guns: A Guide to the World's Rifles and Shotguns*. St. Martin's Press.

p. 54. ISBN 978-0-312-36823-4.

8.2.5 External links

- Manufacturer's Website

8.3 Benelli Supernova

The **Benelli Supernova** is a pump action shotgun, popular for hunting and self-defense. Its most innovative and distinguishing feature is a one-piece receiver and changeable stock with shim kit. The Supernova is known for its large trigger guard, extreme durability and reliability.[1]

8.3.1 Technical specifications

Three main models are available as well as one variant:

- *SUPERNOVA with ComforTech*: This model is available with a variety of barrel and sight configurations, most intended for hunting and/or trap/skeet shooting. It is made in both black and camouflage finishes. Due to the polymer coated receiver and stock, along with proprietary coatings on the action and barrel, it is considered impervious to the elements. Barrels may be rifled or smoothbore, and are usually 24", 26", or 28" in length. Five types of chokes are available.

- *SUPERNOVA with SteadyGrip*: This model is only available in a 24" barrel. The steady grip was designed for improve steadiness while taking a shot.

- *SUPERNOVA Tactical*: This model can be equipped with a rifle or Ghost Ring sight and has an 18.5" or 14" barrel with a fixed cylinder choke.[2] with either a fixed stock pistol grip or an adjustable stock pistol grip.

8.3.2 Common Features

Magazine Capacity: 4+1 Chokes: IC,M,F (Supernova Tactical: Fixed Cyl.) Length of Pull: 14-3/8" Drop at Heel: 2-1/4" Drop at Comb: 1-3/8" Recoil Reducer: this mercury recoil unit is installed via a bracket that is attached to the interior of the stock. The baffled tube holds 14 oz. of mercury, which raises the length of time that the shot's impulse is spread across, thus lowering felt recoil. Chamber Empty Button: on the forend, allows unloading of unfired shell without releasing additional shells from the magazine.[3]

8.3.3 Recoil Reducer

Recoil without the internal reducer is very harsh using the 3.5 inch shells. The shotgun is very light due to its composite/steel construction. This light weight shotgun lends itself to heavy recoil using heavy loads with high velocities. The recoil reducer helps reduce the felt recoil and allows the shooter to obtain a faster second shot.

The recoil reducer consists of two elements; the apparatus that connects to the stock via the buttstock compartment, and the mercury element that is inserted into the recoil apparatus. This unit is available as a kit for installation in regular Nova shotguns as well.

8.3.4 References

[1] Michael J. Simpson. "Benelli SuperNova". About.com. Retrieved November 20, 2013.

[2] "Supernova Tactical". Retrieved 24 January 2013.

[3] Adam Heggenstaller (October 28, 2010). "Benelli Super-Nova". Shooting Illustrated. Retrieved November 20, 2013.

8.3.5 External links

- Super Nova on Manufacturer's Website

8.4 Brixia PM-5

The **Brixia PM-5** is an Italian pump-action shotgun manufactured by Brixia Shotguns.

Shotgun, PM-5 rifle was developed by the Italian Company used by various police and military forces, including the French Navy. The PM-5 is almost unique in that it has a removable magazine, the magazine greatly improves the time and the balance of the charge.The Valtro PM-5 is available with either a fixed stock or a folding stock. The power system PM-5 is conventional, manually operated. The tube under the barrel serves as a guide for scrolling. The loader 7 rounds, plus one in the chamber.

It is unusual in that it takes a detachable box magazine. Both 7- and 10-round magazines have been manufactured, although the 7-round magazine is much more common. Renowned for their simplicity, lightweight and reliability, this pump action 12 GA shotgun has sold on the US market for as much as $1200.00. Currently PM-5 model produced by Brixia Shotgun in Italy. A company that bought Valtro Brand after it declare bankruptcy.

In Canada, Brixia Shotguns and famous PM-5, distributed by Savminter Enterprises.

8.4.1 See also

- pump-action
- shotgun

8.4.2 External links

- Modern Weapons—Valtro PM-5
- Brixia/Valtro PM-5

8.5 Ciener Ultimate Over/Under

The **Ciener Ultimate Over/Under** system is a modification of the Remington 870 shotgun by Johnathan Arthur Ciener. It is identical in purpose to the Knight's Armament Company Masterkey or the accessory weapon configuration of the Remington 870 MPS.

The system consists of a Remington 870 12 gauge pump-action shotgun mounted on a M16 or M4 assault rifle in an underbarrel configuration, much like the M203 grenade launcher. The method of attachment differs in that the Ciener system attaches to the host weapon using a yoke adaptor to join the receivers of both weapons and an adaptor to join the shotgun's barrel to the rifle's bayonet lug.

The shotgun cannot be operated independently because of the yoke adaptor. The M16's magazine well must be used as a makeshift pistol grip. Independent stocks and grips for the 870 are available for use, but they are incompatible with the M16 barrel mount.

The Ciener Ultimate has allegedly been used by Delta Force, and the design's unique mounting system is mentioned in Mark Bowden's *Black Hawk Down: A Story of Modern War*. Paul Howe was using a "CAR-15, a black futuristic-looking weapon with a pump-action shotgun attached to the bayonet lug in front."[1] The Ciener design was the only underbarreled shotgun to use the host weapon's bayonet lug as an attachment point at that time.

8.5.1 Notes

[1] in Mark Bowden, *Black Hawk Down*, Corgi Books, London, 2000 ISBN 0-552-14750-8, p.31

- "Firearm Photo Archive". Security Arms. Retrieved 2012-09-24.

8.5.2 References

- Gander, Terry & Hogg, Ian. *Jane's: Guns Recognition Guide*, 4th ed, Harper Collins publisher. 2005. ISBN 0-00-718328-3

8.5.3 See also

- Combat shotgun
- KAC Masterkey
- M26 MASS
- Remington 870

8.6 Fabarm SDASS Tactical

The **Fabarm SDASS Tactical** is a shotgun designed for police and/or security uses and has some special features such as folding front sight, built-in Picatinny rails on the top of the receiver, lengthened forearm to provide better control over the gun. SDASS shotguns are manufactured in a variety of differing styles.

8.6.1 SDASS Tactical

This is the main production variant; the others stem off of this design with slight body differences. However the internal mechanisms are the same. SDASS stands for Special Defence And Security Shotgun and is aimed for security personnel.[1]

The receiver is manufactured from Ergal 55 alloy which makes for a lightweight shotgun at only 3 kg., light compared to many other tactical shotguns such as the Franchi SPAS-12 which weighs close to 5 kg.

The bolt is locked into place by a piece of aluminum which swings into place and engages a notch in the barrel extension to lock the bolt to the barrel. This prevents a misfire from dropping as it acts as a crude safety device. Misfires from dropping are common in shotguns such as double-barreled shotguns.

The SDASS has an under-barrel tubular magazine like many other semi-automatic shotguns and holds 7 cartridges plus 1 in the chamber giving a total capacity of 8.[2]

The stock is made from a composite polymer which is the most changed structural feature among the different SDASS variants. Common changes to the stock include shortening, addition of a pistol grip and changing the material of the stock altogether like in the SDASS Trainer.

A variety of sights can be placed on the Picatinny rail above the receiver such as red dot sights. As well as sights, tactical lights and laser pointers can also be placed on this rail.

The standard Fabarm SDASS Tactical retails for $649 however its variants range in price from $600 all the way to $900.[3]

8.6.2 Variants

SDASS Composite

This is the same layout as the SDASS Tactical except it doesn't have the picatinny rail.

SDASS Heavy Combat

The Heavy Combat has a longer 61 cm barrel which is also much heavier. It also has a pistol grip like the Benelli M3 instead of a built in grip like the Mossberg 500.

SDASS Trainer

The SDASS Trainer is the lightweight version of the SDASS Composite. It is the only variant to come in more than one finish and they are black, nickel and carbon. To make the gun lighter the barrel has holes drilled into it to reduce weight and the heavier alloys are replaced with lighter alloys.

SDASS Compact

The SDASS Compact as the name suggests is a compact shotgun for close quarters combat. It has a pistol grip and no rear stock. A folding stock however can be attached onto a clip at the rear of the gun. The rest of the external and internal mechanisms are the same as the Tactical model.[4]

8.6.3 Related weapons

- Akdal MKA 1919
- Benelli M3
- Franchi SPAS-12
- Heckler & Koch FABARM FP6
- Safir T-14

8.6.4 References

[1] "Fabarm SDASS Tactical". world.guns.ru. Retrieved 2009-07-24.

[2] "Fabarm SDASS Tactical". world.guns.ru. Retrieved 2009-07-24.

[3] "Fabarm" (PDF). fabarm.com. Retrieved 2009-07-24.

[4] "SDASS Range". fabarm.com. Retrieved 2009-07-24.

8.6.5 External links

- http://world.guns.ru/shotgun/sh13-e.htm

8.7 FN P-12

The **FN P-12** shotgun is a pump-action 12-gauge shotgun designed and manufactured by FN Herstal in Belgium.[2] The weapon, which was introduced during the summer of 2012, is intended to compliment the FN SLP.[1]

The P-12 has a MIL-STD-1913 (*Picatinny*) accessory rail and comes standard with a flip-up rear sight and a fiber-optic front sight which provide a 14 in (36 cm) sight radius.[2] It also features a trigger pull of 6.2 to 7.3 lbs.[2]

8.7.1 Design

The P-12 has a receiver constructed from aircraft-grade aluminum and the matte-black synthetic stock features a non-slip recoil pad fit with steel sling swivel studs.[2]

8.7.2 References

[1] "FNH Introduces P-12 Pump Shotgun". Police Mag. Retrieved 19 December 2012.

[2] "P-12 Pump". FNH USA. Retrieved 19 December 2012.

8.7.3 External links

- Official website
- FNH Firearms Blog

8.8 FN TPS

The **FN TPS** (*Tactical Police Shotgun*) was a pump-action shotgun designed and manufactured by FN Herstal. It was based on the Winchester Model 1300 and used many similar features such as the ported barrel.[2] It also had many modern features including an adjustable stock, pistol grip, adjustable sights and, MIL-STD-1913 Picatinny rail.[2] The TPS features an M16A2 style front and rear sight. The sights are adjustable for both elevation and windage.[3]

8.8.1 References

[1] Wagner, Scott W. (2011). *Gun Digest Book of The Tactical Shotgun*. Gun Digest Books, 2011. p. 205. ISBN 1440218951.

[2] "HARDWARE - Fabrique Nationale Tactical Police Shotgun". Manhattan Shooting Excursions. Retrieved 23 December 2012.

[3] "Owner's Manual" (PDF). FN Herstal. Retrieved 23 December 2012.

8.8.2 External links

- Review
- User Manual

8.9 Heckler & Koch FABARM FP6

The **Heckler & Koch Fabarm FP6** is a pump-action combat shotgun that was manufactured by the Italian firearms company Fabbrica Bresciana Armi S.p.A. (FABARM) and merchandised by Heckler & Koch. It was intended for civilian and law enforcement use.

8.9.1 History

Upon severing business association with Benelli in 1998, Heckler & Koch replaced their entire line of shotguns with those manufactured by FABARM.[2] The line featured hunting and sport shotguns in over-and-under, side-by-side, semi-automatic autoloaders and pump shotguns including youth models. For military, law enforcement and home defense use, H&K released four variants of the FP6 model.

8.9.2 Design details

The machined receiver is manufactured from lightweight Ergal 55 alloy and is drilled and tapped for scope mounting. Three of the four variants were sold with an attached Picatinny rail for mounting optics or accessories and the bottom forward edge of the forend is also drilled to accept an accessory rail. With the exception of the short-barreled model, FABARM shotguns are sold with their Tribore barrel which is a deep-drilled, machined barrel with three separate internal bore profiles. Beginning at the chamber and forcing cone, the bore is enlarged to .7401" to soften recoil while the second profile is in the middle of the barrel gradually choking down to .7244" to emulate a cylinder bore profile to increase velocity. The final bore is the FABARM choke system which consists of standard choking followed by a cylinder profile at the muzzle which serves to improve shot patterns and distribution.[3] The muzzle is threaded to accept one of five different chokes or a muzzle brake/compensator. Some models were sold with a ventilated barrel shroud.

Features of the weapon include a chrome-plated trigger, slide release, and shell carrier. There is also an oversized triangular push-button safety. The trigger group is held in the receiver by two pins which makes removal for cleaning and maintenance very easy. Some models have a flip-up frontsight (which serves as a low-profile sight when closed) while others have a small blade sight. Other models were issued with ghost-ring sights.[1]

The forend and buttstock are synthetic black polymer with the latter having a synthetic rubber recoil pad mounted on the end. One model was issued instead with a heavy wire gauge folding stock and pistol grip. Models were available with either a black anodized protective finish, matte finish, or were finished in carbon fiber.

8.9.3 Operation

The forend is connected to dual action bars which cycle the bolt when pulled back towards the receiver. As it travels to the rear, the shell latch is pushed out of the way by a camming surface on the action bar allowing a cartridge to drop into the carrier while the remaining shells in the magazine tube are held by the cartridge retaining latch. As the forend is returned, the action bars bring the bolt forward while the carrier aligns the shell before seating it into the chamber. After the shell is fully seated, the action bars continue forward forcing the locking bolt into a recess which is on top of the barrel extension causing the action to lock into battery. Upon firing the weapon, the slide unhooking lever releases and the action is allowed to cycle, extracting and ejecting the spent shell while cocking the hammer and releasing the next round from the magazine.[4]

8.9.4 Accessories

All FP6 shotguns are sold with a choke adjustment wrench, owners manual and a hard plastic vacu-formed impact case. Additional accessories available from H&K include an assortment of chokes, muzzle brakes/compensators, magazine tube extensions, pistol grips and folding stocks. There is an adapter you can buy to put on the receiver for the FP6 to accept Remington 870 stocks such as BlackHawk and Knoxx stocks.

8.9.5 Variants

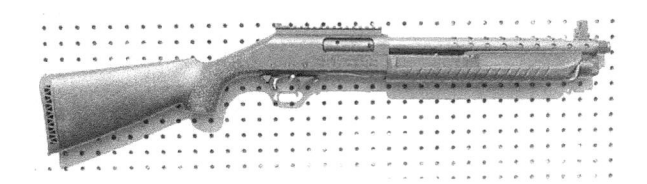

FP6 Entry - this variant features a 14" barrel and is regulated by the National Firearms Act as a Title II firearm in the United States.

H&K released four variants of the FP6.[5]

- Standard FP6 (H&K 40621HS) featuring a 20" Tribore barrel, black protective finish, perforated heatshield, small front blade sight, fixed synthetic buttstock, and a rounded forend.

- Carbon fiber finish model (H&K 40621CF) featuring a 20" Tribore barrel, no heatshield, receiver-mount Picatinny rail, small front blade sight, fixed synthetic buttstock, and a rounded forend.

- Folding stock and pistol gripped model with a 20" Tribore barrel, no heatshield, receiver-mount Picatinny rail, and a large flip-up blade sight.

- Tactical short-barreled model, the FP6 Entry (H&K 40621T), featuring a 14" barrel, matte finish, perforated heatshield, receiver-mount Picatinny rail, large flip-up blade sight, fixed synthetic buttstock, and a contoured forend. This variant has a 33.75" overall length and is regulated by the National Firearms Act as a Title II firearm in the United States.

8.9.6 Users

- France - National Gendarmerie [6]
- Germany
- Italy
- Malaysia[7]
- United States

8.9.7 See also

- Fabarm SDASS Tactical
- List of shotguns

8.9.8 Notes

[1] Ramage 2008, p. 419.

[2] Gangarosa, 2001. p. 243.

[3] Fortier 2003.

[4] H&K *FABARM Operators Instructions: FP6 Pump-action Shotgun.* (06-17-1998).

[5] Gangarosa, 2001. p. 266.

[6] Gangarosa, 2001. p. 246.

[7] http://www.malaysiandefence.com/?p=3987

8.9.9 References

- Fortier, David M. "Italian alley sweeper: pumping lead with the Fabarm FP6", *Guns Magazine*, August 2003.

- Gangarosa, Gene Jr., (2001). *Heckler & Koch— Armorers of the Free World.* Stoeger Publishing, Maryland. ISBN 0-88317-229-1.

- Ramage, Ken. (2008). *Gun Digest 2008.* Krause Publications. p. 419.

8.10 Ithaca 37

The **Ithaca 37** is a pump-action shotgun made in large numbers for the civilian, military, and police markets. It utilizes a novel combination ejection/loading port on the bottom of the gun which leaves the sides closed to the elements. Since shotshells load and eject from the bottom, operation of the gun is equally convenient for both right and left hand shooters. This makes the gun popular with left-handed shooters.

8.10.1 History

The Ithaca 37 is based on a 1915 patent by the famous firearms designer John Browning, initially marketed as the Remington Model 17. The Model 17 was a 20-gauge of trim proportions, which Remington later redesigned and refined into the popular side-ejecting Remington Model 31. The Model 31 would eventually be replaced in production by the less expensive to make Remington 870 which is still produced to this day.

Following the First World War, the Ithaca Gun Company was searching for a pump-action shotgun to produce, primarily to compete with the ubiquitous Winchester Model 1912. They settled on waiting for Remington Model 17 patents to expire. After gearing for production of the Ithaca Model 33, they discovered a Pedersen patent that would not expire until 1937; along with the introduction date, they changed the model designation from 33 to 37.

With the depression dragging on and war looming on the horizon, it was possibly the worst time to introduce a sporting arm. Many sporting arms ceased production entirely during the same period. While Ithaca did produce some shotguns for military use during the war, they also produced M1911 pistols and M3 Grease Guns.

After WW-II, Ithaca resumed production of the Model 37. Made in many different models, the Ithaca 37 has the longest production run for a pump-action shotgun in history, surpassing that of the Winchester Model 12 that had originally inspired Ithaca to produce pump-action shotguns. Ithaca has suffered many setbacks in its history, changing hands numerous times. At one time, the Ithaca 37 was renamed the Model 87, although it was soon changed back in one of many ownership changes. Production paused in 2005 when Ithaca once again changed hands. Production has resumed in Ohio.

8.10.2 Users

The largest single users outside the US Military were the New York City Police Department in 2 versions- 13" barrel with forend hand-strap for the Emergency Service Unit and 18" barrel for the Highway Patrol and the Los Angeles Police Department. Along with the Los Angeles County Sheriff's Department, numerous other users include military, police, security agencies, and prisons. The Ithaca 37 was a popular choice among civilians for both sport and personal protection. The Ithaca model 37 feather light was commonly seen in the hands of farmers in the Midwestern United States. With higher prices for new Ithacas and decreasing availability compared to the Mossberg 500 and Remington 870, use of the Ithaca 37 continues to decline. Interestingly, Ithaca's loss of market share was hastened by competition from a copy of the shotgun. Chinese copies of the Ithaca 37 have been imported recently. Additionally, the supply of used civilian and departmental shotguns has been a steady competitor.

8.10.3 Operation

Loading the Ithaca 37 involves inserting shotshells of the proper gauge through the loading/ejection port in the bottom of the receiver and pushing them forward into the magazine until retained by the shell stop. The slide release is pressed and the slide retracted completely then pushed forward. Pulling the trigger fires the gun and releases the slide for reloading. On most models up to 1975, holding the trigger down allows the gun to fire the instant a new round is cycled into the chamber without requiring the trigger to be released, a process known as slamfire. Otherwise, the model 37 operates in much the same way as other pump-action shotguns.

8.10.4 Versions

There are versions too numerous to mention. Here are some popular models:

- **S-prefix**: were manufactured for a 1962 United States military contract. S-prefixed serial numbers ran from approximately 1,000 to 23,000 with "U.S." on the receiver and "P" proof markings on the barrel and receiver. The guns have a Parkerized finish with 20 inches (51 cm) barrel and plain stocks with plastic butt plates and no sling swivels. A few later contracts produced smaller numbers of guns with sling swivels and serial numbers in the high 900,000 range. Some had "duckbill spreader" shot diverters for use by United States Navy SEALs. Others were fitted with a ventilated handguard and bayonet adopter. New bayonets were manufactured by General Cutlery, Inc. and Canada Arsenal, Ltd.[1]

- **Ultralite**: an aluminum receiver variation.

- **Deerslayer**: a version with a shortened barrel and rifle-style sighting system.

- **DSPS**: for *Deerslayer Police Special*. A military and police version

- **Stakeout**: short version with 13 inches (330 mm) barrel and pistol grip stock, which was notable for being the signature weapon for Ricardo Tubbs, Philip Michael Thomas' character on *Miami Vice* as well as being the secondary weapon of Corporal Hicks in *Aliens* (although it was technically a modified hunting variant) and *Aliens: Colonial Marines*, where it has the words "no fate" carved into the top, a reference to Michael Biehn's role in *The Terminator*.

- **28 Gauge**: 28 gauge model built on traditional size 28 gauge receiver.[2]

- **Defense**: an affordable 12 gauge model built for home defense purposes. 18.5" barrel with 5-round capacity or 20" barrel with 8-round capacity.

8.10.5 Argentine variants

The Argentine firm Industrias Marcati manufactured the Ithaca 37 under licence as the **Bataan Modelo 71**.[3][4][5]

8.10.6 Users

- Argentina: Used by the military and the police.

8.10.7 See also

- Combat shotguns
- List of shotguns
- Winchester Model 12

8.10.8 Notes

[1] Canfield, Bruce N. *American Rifleman* (March 2002) pp.44-47&92-95

[2] http://www.ithacagun.com/images/28GaFlyerWEB.jpg

[3] http://s2.postimage.org/pl14386r9/Tapa_Bataan71.jpg

[4] http://s1.postimage.org/qd05p142d/Bataan71_M.jpg

[5] http://s1.postimage.org/qd0zgpcyd/Sargento_Verdes.png

8.10.9 References

- Fawcett, Bill. Hunters & Shooters, An Oral History of the U.S. Navy SEALS in Vietnam. NY: Avon Books, 1995. ISBN 0-380-72166-X, pp. 79–80, especially.

- Snyder, Walter C. *Ithaca Featherlight Repeaters, The Best Gun Going*. NC: Cook and Uline Pub, 1998. ISBN 0-9629469-1-5

8.10.10 External links

- Official Model 37 Featherlight and Ultralight page
- Official Flyer for Special Order 28 Gauge as of Feb 2009
- American Rifleman Exploded-View Diagram for the Ithaca Model 37 Featherlight

8.11 KAC Masterkey

This article is about a shotgun. For the security key, see master key.

The **Masterkey** is a door breaching shotgun system manufactured by Knight's Armament Company.

The Masterkey project was initiated during the 1980s to provide assault rifles with a potent built-in door breaching tool. Individual soldiers were often forced to carry a breaching shotgun in addition to their standard issue rifle, but the Masterkey removes this need. The system consists of a Remington 870 12 gauge pump-action shotgun mounted on a M16 or M4 assault rifle in an underbarrel configuration, much like the M203 grenade launcher. It has a 3-round internal magazine and can carry a fourth round in the chamber.

The shotgun cannot be operated independently because it has no grip behind the trigger—when firing the Masterkey, the M16's magazine must be used as a makeshift pistol grip. Independent stocks and grips for the 870 are available for use, but they are incompatible with the M16 barrel mount. KAC makes an independent stock for the Masterkey that also can be used with the M203 grenade launcher.

The Masterkey inspired the M26 Modular Accessory Shotgun System, an attachable shotgun in use with the United States Army. The M26 was chosen by the Army over the Masterkey as a breaching tool.[1]

8.11.1 Users

- United States: Delta Force[2]

8.11.2 See also

- Ciener Ultimate Over/Under
- Combat shotgun
- M26 MASS

8.11.3 References

[1] Johnson, Steve (February 16, 2010). "The C-MORE M26 may be available to civilians". The Firearm Blog. Retrieved May 22, 2015.

[2] "Paul+Howe+Somalia+(1).jpg" Check |url= value (help). Retrieved May 22, 2015.

8.11.4 External links

- Knight's Armament Masterkey Page

8.12 KS-23

The **KS-23** is a Russian shotgun, although because it uses a rifled barrel it is officially designated by the Russian military as a carbine. KS stands for *Karabin Spetsialniy*, "Special Carbine". It is renowned for its large caliber, firing a 23 mm round, equating to 6.27 gauge using the British and American standards of shotgun gauges and approximately 4 gauge using the current European standards (based on the metric 'CIP' tables), making it the largest-bore shotgun in use today.

8.12.1 History

The KS-23 was designed in the 1970s for suppressing prison riots. It was created by TsNII-Tochmash, a key Russian weapons developer, for the Russian Ministry of Internal Affairs (MVD). The barrel for the KS-23 was made from 23 mm anti-aircraft gun barrels that were rejected due to manufacturing flaws. These rejected barrels were deemed to be acceptable for the lower stress of firing slugs and less-lethal rounds, and thus were cut down in length for use as shotgun barrels. The KS-23 began to see use during the mid-1980s by several MVD forces. During the 1990s, research was made into improving the original design to make it usable in confined indoor areas. Two prototypes were proposed, the KS-23M and KS-23K, although only the M version saw use. Today, both the standard KS-23 and the KS-23M are in use by Russian law enforcement.

8.12.2 Ammunition

The KS-23 was created with the capability to fire several different types of ammunition, listed below:

- **"Shrapnel-10"** («Шрапнель−10») buckshot round with 10-meter effective range

- **"Shrapnel-25"** («Шрапнель−25») buckshot round with 25-meter effective range

- **"Barricade"** («Баррикада») cartridge with solid steel projectile able to destroy the engine block of a car at up to 100 meters.

- **"Volna"** («Волна») - inert version of cartridge used for education and practice during training

- "**Volna-R**" («*Волна-Р*») cartridge with less-lethal rubber bullet
- "**Strela-3**" («*Стрела−3*») cartridge with less-lethal plastic bullet
- "**Bird cherry-7**" («*Черёмуха−7*») tear gas grenade with CN agent
- "**Lilac-7**" («*Сирень−7*») tear gas grenade with CS agent
- "**Zvezda**" («*Звезда*») flash-bang round
- **PV-23** (*ПВ−23*) - blank (grenade launching) cartridge

Later, two add-on muzzle mortars were produced, the 36 mm Nasadka-6 and 82 mm Nasadka-12, bringing with them several new ammunition types:

- Blank grenade launching cartridge to be used with muzzle mortars
- 36 mm "Cheremukha-6" tear gas grenade
- 82 mm "Cheremukha-12" "high-efficiency" tear gas grenade for use on open areas

8.12.3 Variants

KS-23

The original KS-23 was developed jointly by NIISpetstekhniki (MVD) and TsNIITochmash in 1971, it was accepted for use by the Soviet police in 1985.[1] The gun has a barrel length of 510 mm and an overall length of 1040 mm. The KS-23 has an underbarrel tubular magazine capable of holding three rounds, with one in the chamber giving the gun a maximum round capacity of four. The gun's effective range is 150 m.

KS-23M

The KS-23M "Thrush" (Carbine Special 23 mm modernized) was developed on the base of the KS-23. Development for it was started in October 1990. Twenty-five carbines were submitted for testing on December 10, 1991. After which the winner, then designated S-3, became the KS-23M "Thrush" and was accepted for use by the police and the Internal Troops of Russia.[2] The KS-23M includes a detachable wire buttstock and shortened barrel, as opposed to the fixed wooden stock on standard KS-23s. The gun is still chambered in 23 mm. Its overall length with the buttstock is 875 mm, without, 650 mm, and the barrel is 410 mm long. The gun's effective range is 100 m.

KS-23K

The KS-23K is a redesigned KS-23 that features a bullpup layout. The KS-23K was accepted in 1998 for the use of the Russian Ministry of Internal Affairs (MVD).[3] Development and adoption of this carbine was motivated by the fact that in the earlier accepted configurations of the KS-23 and KS-23M a major noted deficiency was that the tubular magazine did not make it possible to rapidly reload or change the type of ammunition being used, because of this a major design change for the KS-23K is that it has an extended box magazine that holds seven shells instead of the three shells seen on the other models. The gun has a mechanical safety located on the left side, above the pistol handle and open non adjustable sights. The gun's effective range is 100 m.

TOZ-123

The civilian version of the KS-23 is the TOZ-123 "Drake-4" (*ТОЗ−123 "Селезень−4"*). It is made by Tulsky Oruzheiny Zavod and features a smoothbore design, making it more similar to a traditional shotgun, and is chambered in standard 4-gauge. Since August 1996 it is allowed in Russia as civilian hunting shotgun.[4]

The gun maker's website has this as the description for the shotgun.

> The shotgun is multicharged, with a tubular underbarrel magazine of 3-cartridge capacity. Reloading is provided with a removable fore-end. The presence of the special barrel rear projection on the frame combined with the rear sight gives the possibility of mounting an optical sight. The shotgun is intended for the amateur hunting with shot cartridges.[5]

The TOZ-123 was banned from import into the United States during the Clinton administration.[6]

8.12.4 Users

- Kazakhstan - prison guards[7]
- North Korea
- Russia - used in Ministry of Internal Affairs and Border Guard Service[8]
- Soviet Union
- Uzbekistan - customs service[9]

8.12.5 See also

- List of Russian weaponry
- Zlatoust RB-12

8.12.6 References

[1] "KS-23 description in Russian". Retrieved 26 November 2014.

[2] "KS-23m description in Russian". Retrieved 26 November 2014.

[3] "KS-23K description in Russian". Retrieved 26 November 2014.

[4] "*2.3.2. ОХОТНИЧЬЕ ОГНЕСТРЕЛЬНОЕ ОРУЖИЕ ГЛАДКОСТВОЛЬНОЕ... Ружье гладкоствольное "Селезень–4"*" Распоряжение Правительства РФ № 1207-р от 3 августа 1996 г. "Перечень служебного и гражданского оружия и боеприпасов к нему, вносимых в Государственный кадастр служебного и гражданского оружия"

[5] TOZ-123 product page

[6] "eCFR — Code of Federal Regulations". Retrieved 26 November 2014.

[7] "*2. Перечень специальных средств... карабин специальный (КС–23)*" Приказ Министра юстиции Республики Казахстан № 146 от 11 декабря 2001 года "Об утверждении Инструкции по применению сотрудниками исправительных учреждений Комитета уголовно-исполнительной системы Министерства юстиции Республики Казахстан специальных средств"

[8] Перечень специальных средств, состоящих на вооружении органов и войск Федеральной пограничной службы Российской Федерации (утв. постановлением Правительства РФ № 634 от 24 июня 1998 года)

[9] "*К специальным средствам относятся: ...карабин специальный («КС–23»)*" Инструкция о порядке применения таможенными органами специальных средств (зарегистрирована Министерством юстиции Республики Узбекистан от 9 ноября 1999 года. Регистрационный № 835, 06.08.1999)

8.12.7 Further reading

- Игорь Скрылев. КС–23 - наш полицейский карабин // журнал "Мастер-ружьё", № 1, 1997. стр.48-51 (Russian)

- Карабины КС–23, КС–23М "Дрозд" // А. И. Благовестов. То, из чего стреляют в СНГ: Справочник стрелкового оружия. / под общ.ред. А. Е. Тараса. Минск, «Харвест», 2000. стр.420-424 (Russian)

- Southby-Tailyour, Ewen (2005). *Jane's Special Forces Recognition Guide.* New York: Collins. ISBN 0-00-718329-1.

8.12.8 External links

- Modern Firearms: KS-23 riot shotgun / carbine
- Security Arms: KS-23 Shotgun
- Tulsky Oruzheiny Zavod: TOZ-123

8.13 MAG-7

The **MAG-7** is a pump-action shotgun manufactured by Techno Arms PTY of South Africa since 1995.

8.13.1 History and design

MAG-7M1 modified as a short-barreled shotgun, to original design specifications.

The MAG-7 was developed as a close quarters combat (CQB) weapon, which would combine the aspects of a compact submachine gun and a pump-action shotgun.

For ease of reloading, a magazine system is ideal. With the traditional pump-action mechanism located under the barrel, there is no convenient forward location for a magazine. This leaves the bullpup layout or a pistol-like arrangement of placing the magazine within the pistol grip as possible locations. It was found that the standard 12-gauge shotgun shell at 70 mm[1] was too long to comfortably hold in the desired pistol grip mounting.

However, it was also found that at the ranges being considered for this weapon, the standard shotgun shells had too much power. This led to the development of a shorter round, 60 mm long (2.36 inch as opposed to 2.75) with both the desired power and size. The use of the MAG-7 with these cartridges yields an effective range of 45 yards (41.1 m), although they have a proven lethality to 90 yards (82 m).[2] The MAG-7 also has a detachable, top-folding sheet metal stock.

There were two models initially manufactured—the original **MAG-7**, and civilian-legal model, called the **MAG-7 M1**. The M1 features a longer barrel and fixed wooden stock to extend the barrel to 18 inches (46 cm) and the overall length to 26 inches (66 cm) to meet the requirements of the National Firearms Act, and of the gun laws of many other countries. In this NFA configuration, however, the original concept of the weapon as an extremely compact hard-hitting tool for CQB and backup is defeated.

8.13.2 Service

Although the design concept was geared towards law enforcement and military close quarters combat scenarios, there was inadequate demand for the weapon due to some problematic design issues in its conception. One such design feature was safety lever on the left side of the stamped steel receiver, above the pistol grip. The actuation of this lever is not possible without removing the left arm from the pump, and is difficult if the operator is wearing gloves. The same problem exists for the slide lock button. These problems were mainly found in the early models exported to the United States of America. The company then focused its attention on these issues and were solved by reducing the resistance of the safety lever and over-ride slide lock button. The user can now operate both levers effectively and easily without taking the left hand off the pump. Another issue that plagued the MAG-7 was the 7.7 Kgf trigger pull. It was also addressed by the manufacturer and reduced to an industry standard 3.5Kgf

8.13.3 Proprietary ammunition

Swartklip made the original 12 gauge 2.36-inch [18.5 x 60mm] shells for Techno Arms in UK No.5 shot [EU/US No.6 Birdshot], UK/EU AAA shot [US T shot], UK/EU SSG shot [US #1 Buckshot], and 12 gauge rubber slug. The original 12 gauge × 60 mm cartridges are difficult to obtain. However there are other shells that can be used instead:

- Aguila Ammunition Company of Mexico's 12 gauge 1.75-inch [18.5 x 44.5mm] "Mini-Shells" can be substituted but will not function 100% with the MAG-7 magazine. Three rounds can be usually be loaded and fired with some reliability. They come in US No.7½ Birdshot, US #1 Buckshot, and 12 gauge lead slug[3] in packs of 20 shells.

- Century International's Centurion brand 12 gauge 2-inch [18.5 x 51 mm] Mini Buckshot shells also work in the chamber as well, though not as reliably as the 60mm cartridge. They come in EU/US #00 Buck (similar to British SG or Australian 00-SG) in packs of 10 shells.

- Standard-length 12 gauge 2.75-inch [18.5 x 70mm] cartridges can have their cases modified and reloaded to reliably feed in the 60 mm chamber.

8.13.4 Current status

The manufacturer, **Techno Arms (PTY) Ltd.**, located in Modderfontein, Gauteng, South Africa, as of March 2012 is active and is marketing the MAG-7 in three versions: the standard *MAG-7*, the civilian-legal *MAG-7 M1*, and the *M7 Dual Riot*.

8.13.5 M7 *Dual Riot*

The M7 is a combination 12-gauge and 37-mm / 38-mm weapon based upon the standard MAG-7. It has a fixed metal stock and a top-mounted 37mm or 38 mm single-shot less-lethal launcher with tilting barrel. The launcher is extremely reminiscent of the widely popular South-African Milkor Stopper 37/38 mm riot gun, which Techno Arms now also manufactures.[4] It is designed as an anti-riot Law Enforcement weapon that can fire both 12 gauge rubber shot or 37-mm / 38-mm gas shells.

8.13.6 See also

- List of shotguns

8.13.7 References

[1] "Common Shotgun Shell Sizes"

[2] Techno Arms MAG-7 shotgun on Securityarms.com Retrieved on 25 March 2009.

[3] Aguila Ammo - Mini Shells

[4] Techno-Arms (PTY) Ltd. - Manufacturer's official website. Retrieved on 25 March 2009.

8.13.8 External links

- Official site

8.14 Mossberg 500

Mossberg 500 is a series of pump-action shotguns manufactured by O.F. Mossberg & Sons.[1] The 500 series comprises widely varying models of hammerless repeaters, all of which share the same basic receiver and action, but differ in bore size, barrel length, choke options, magazine capacity, and "furniture" (stock and forearm) materials. Model numbers included in the 500 series are the **500**, **505**, **510**, **535**, and **590**. The Mossberg is currently the number one selling shotgun and second in total production to the Remington 870.

8.14.1 Basic features

U.S. Marines assigned to the Commander of the Seventh Fleet's Fleet Anti-terrorism Security Team (FAST)'s Third Platoon, practice using the M590 shotgun

Introduced in 1961, all model 500s are based on the same basic concept designed by Carl Benson. Originally using a single-action bar, that was known to bind and even break, this was changed to dual- action bars in 1970, following the expiration of Remington's patent on the double-action bar design. A single large locking lug is used to secure the breech. The magazine tube is located below the barrel, and is screwed into the receiver. The slide release is located to the left rear of the trigger guard, and the safety is located on the upper rear of the receiver (often called a "tang safety").

Sights vary from model to model, from simple bead sight to a receiver mounted ghost ring or an integrated base for a telescopic sight. Most models come with the receiver drilled and tapped for the installation of a rear sight or a scope base. The factory scope base is attached to the barrel *via* a cantilever-type mount, which places the scope over the receiver but keeps it with the barrel if the barrel is removed.

Intended for use in harsh and dirty conditions, such as waterfowl hunting or combat, the Model 500 series is designed to be easy to clean and maintain. All Model 500s feature interchangeable barrels (given a particular gun's magazine capacity—a barrel designed for a five-shot tube will not fit a gun with a seven-shot tube), which may be removed without the use of tools, by loosening a screw on the end of the magazine tube, allowing the barrel to be removed.

The bolt locks into a locking lug located on the top of the barrel, ensuring a solid bolt-to-barrel connection and not relying on the receiver for any locking strength. The trigger assembly, which includes the trigger, hammer, sear, and trigger body with guard, can be removed by pushing out one retaining pin and pulling downwards on the guard (if a pistol grip is installed, it usually must be removed first as virtually all such grips obstruct the removal of the trigger body). The elevator can be removed by putting the gun on safety and squeezing the sides together, freeing the pivot pins from the receiver.

The forend can then be moved to the rear, allowing the bolt and bolt carrier to drop out, and then the forend can be removed by moving it forward. The cartridge stop and interrupter will then fall free, leaving just the ejector and the safety in the receiver, held in by screws. The magazine spring and follower may be removed by unscrewing the tube from the receiver (this may be difficult on some new 500s). This level of field stripping is sufficient to allow all components to be cleaned.

8.14.2 Model 500 options

The name "Model 500" covers an entire family of pump shotguns designed to chamber 3-inch (76 mm) "magnum" shells. The standard model holds five 2.75-inch (70 mm) or four 3-inch (76 mm) shells in the magazine and one in the chamber. The Model 500 is available in 12 gauge, 20 gauge, and .410 bore, with the 12 gauge being the most popular and having the most optional features available. A 16 gauge was offered at one time but has been discontinued.

Finishes

The standard finish for the Model 500 is an anodized aluminum alloy receiver and a polished and blued barrel. Some models come with a matte black painted receiver, and a matte blued barrel. Some 500 models are anodized to look parkerized, with parkerized barrels. This is also true of the 590 series since an aluminum receiver cannot be parkerized.

Mossberg also offers camouflage painted models, in a number of different patterns. Stocks are either wood or composite, with the composite stocks being matte black or camouflage to match the rest of the gun. A special model called the Mariner is available with the Marinecote finish, a silver finish that is highly corrosion resistant. Mariner models use the black composite stocks.

Model 500 vs. Model 590 vs. Model 590A1

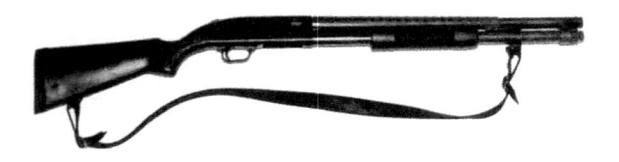

Mossberg 590 with 20-inch (510 mm) barrel

The primary difference between the Model 500 and Model 590 is in magazine tube design. The Model 500 magazines are closed at the muzzle end, and the barrel is held in place by bolting into a threaded hole at the end of the magazine tube. Model 590 magazines are designed to be opened at the muzzle end, and the barrels fit around the magazine tube and are held on by a capnut at the end. The Model 500 magazine facilitates easy barrel changes, as the barrel bolt serves no function other than holding the barrel in place. The Model 590 magazine facilitates easy cleaning and parts replacement, as removing the nut allows removal of the magazine spring and follower.

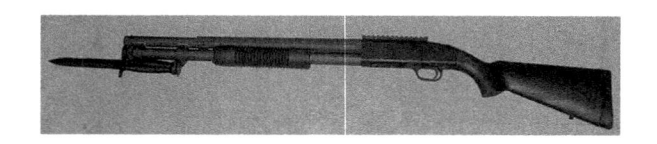

Parkerized Mossberg 590A1 with M7 Bayonet, upper picatinny rail, and modified standard 590 heat shield

The Model 500 has a plastic trigger guard and safety and a standard barrel. The Model 590A1 has an aluminum trigger guard & safety, a heavier barrel, and a bayonet lug, intended for military use under extreme conditions and rough handling; the metal trigger guard was added in response to the 3443G materials requirements, and the heavy barrel was added at the request of the Navy to prevent barrel deformation if the shotgun caught in the closing of heavy steel ship doors. Some 590A1s have a sling swivel on the back of the bayonet lug, some do not. The 590A1 usually has a swivel mount on the stock even when there is no corresponding mount on the forward end of the weapon. The 590A1 is generally sold through military and law enforcement channels, though in most jurisdictions the 18.5-inch (47 cm) and 20-inch (51 cm) models are available and may be legally purchased by any non prohibited persons. 590A1s with 14" barrels are Title II firearms, and may be purchased only by non-prohibited persons in NFA-legal states, after completing BATF transfer forms. [2][3]

The riot gun versions of the pistol grip Model 500 (Persuader, Cruiser, Road Blocker, and Mariner) are available with an 18.5-inch (47 cm) and 20-inch (51 cm) barrel depending on magazine capacity. The 590 is only available with a 20-inch (510 mm) barrel and flush-fit magazine tube. The 590A1 is available with a 14-inch (36 cm), 18.5-inch, or 20-inch (510 mm) barrel. One model sold as Model 590-SP (catalog item 51663) is technically a 590A1, as it uses the heavy barrel and military trigger group, but unlike models designated 590A1 it is sold on the civilian market.

Unlike Model 500 and 590 shotguns (with the exception of ghost-ring sight 590 models), Model 590A1 shotguns cannot be easily fitted with the common factory 500 heat shield, due to the heavier barrel. A heat shield and bayonet lug are required for military 3443G Type I riot shotguns,[2] and some 590A1s are so equipped. The 590A1 heat shield, p/n 16335P, is available for purchase from Mossberg for about the same price as the 500 heat shield.

Bantam and Super Bantam models

Mossberg 500 Bantam, with 24-inch (610 mm) barrel. Note shorter stock and forend than standard model at top.

The standard Model 500 uses a 14-inch (36 cm) length of pull (LOP) for the stock, which is suitable for adult shooters of average or greater size. The Bantam models use a 13-inch (33 cm) LOP stock and a forend that sits further back than the standard model. The Super Bantam stock includes two recoil pads and a stock spacer.

By using the short pad, the LOP can be reduced to 12 inches (30 cm); with the spacer and longer pad, the LOP is 13 inches (330 mm). A number of different models are offered with Bantam and Super Bantam stocks, or they can be ordered as accessories and fitted to any Model 500.

Model 505

The new model 505 Youth shotgun, introduced in 2005, is similar to the Bantam but scaled down further. The 505 has a 12-inch (30 cm) pull buttstock (compared to a standard model's 14 inches or 36 centimetres, or a Bantam's 13 inches or 33 centimetres), a 20-inch (51 cm) barrel, and a four-shot magazine tube. The 505 is available in 20 gauge and .410 bore. Parts are not interchangeable with other model 500 variants.

Model 535

The Model 535, new for 2005, is similar to the Model 500, but with a lengthened receiver that can fire 3.5-inch (89 mm) shells, in addition to 2.75-inch (70 mm) and 3-inch (76 mm) shells. The 535 is a less expensive alternative to the Mossberg 835 Ulti-Mag, but the 535 lacks the 835's overbored barrel. The non-overbored barrel of the 535 does, however, allow the use of slugs, which cannot be used in the overbored barrel of the 835.

Model 535 barrels are not interchangeable with Model 500 or Model 835 barrels, but 535 barrels are available in smoothbore and rifled in a variety of vent ribbed, barrel lengths and different sights. The 535 is also available in a tactical model with ghost ring sights and a collapsible pistol grip buttstock. Although Model 500 barrels can be used with Model 535 receivers, magazine tubes from the Model 500 must also be used because of the magazine tube length difference.

Magazine capacity

The Model 500 comes in a variety of different receiver configurations, whose main difference is the magazine configuration. The basic Model 500 comes with a magazine tube capable of holding five 2.75-inch (70 mm) shells, which is called a six-shot model (a full magazine plus a round in the chamber). The 500 is also available with an extended magazine tube that holds seven rounds, making an eight-shot model. The 590A1 is available with five- and eight-shot magazines, sold as six- and nine-shot models respectively.

The variants with the extended magazine tubes use different barrels, as the barrel is held in place by attaching at the end of the magazine tube. The shortest barrel length available for the eight- and nine-shot models is 20 inches (51 cm), which fits flush with the long magazine tube. A ribbed 28-inch (71 cm) modified choke field barrel was also manufactured for the 8-shot model 500. The shortest barrel for Title I six-shot models is 18.0 inches (46 cm), while military and law enforcement personnel (as well private persons in NFA states) can also get a 14-inch (36 cm) barrel (the 590 Compact), which is flush with the six-shot or eight-shot model's magazine.

8.14.3 Model 500 variants

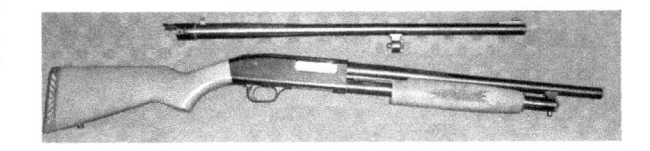

Mossberg 500 with 18.5-inch (470 mm) cylinder bore barrel installed, and a 24-inch (610 mm) cylinder bore barrel with rifle sights. (Cylinder bore means lacking any choke.)

The Model 500 is available in many variants, for a wide variety of applications. The ease of changing barrels on the Model 500 means that a single shotgun may be equipped by the owner with a number of different barrels, each for a different purpose. As sold, the Model 500 is generally classed into two broad categories: field models and special purpose models.

Field models

Field models are the basic sporting models. They are available with a variety of barrel lengths and finishes, and may be set up for waterfowl hunting, upland game hunting, turkey hunting, or shooting slugs. Most smoothbore models come with interchangeable choke tubes and vent rib barrels, while the slug models come with rifle sights or scope bases, and may have smooth cylinder bore or rifled barrels.

Special purpose models

Mossberg 590A1 Tactical, 12 Ga, 6-shot, 18.5" barrel, tactical light, and collapsible stock

Special purpose models are intended for self defense, police, or military use. The Model 590 and the eight-shot Model 500s are only sold as special purpose models. Special purpose models have short barrels, either 18.5 inches (47 cm) for the six-shot models, or 20 inches (51 cm) for the eight- and nine-shot models, but the barrels are fully interchangeable with all models of the same magazine tube length in the 500 family. Most models come with special designations like SPX, Tactical, Mariner, etc.

Special purpose models may be equipped with a variety of specialty parts which may include adjustable stock, "Speedfeed" stock that holds 4 additional rounds of ammunition, pistol grip, ghost ring and fiber optic sights, picatinny rail, forearm band, heatshield, ported barrel, muzzle brake, and even a bayonet lug. All special purpose models come only in black trim with either blued, non-glare matte blue, or parkerized finishes and come with drilled and tapped receivers for scope and optics mounting.

It should be noted that "Special Purpose" models are not the same as "Law Enforcement" models; the latter have heavier duty barrels, safeties, trigger guards, and will stand up to harder use.

Law enforcement models

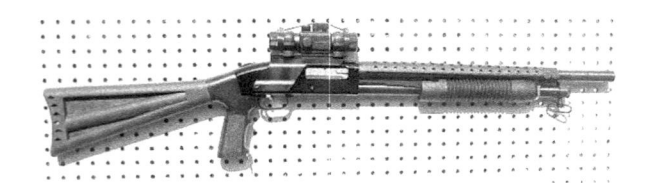

Model 500 Law enforcement combo with red-dot sight

Mossberg shotguns currently designated "law enforcement models" are 590A1s. 590A1s differ from other 500/590 shotguns, in that they have heavy barrels, metal trigger guards, and metal safeties. 590A1s are available in 14-inch (36 cm), 18.5-inch (47 cm), and 20-inch (51 cm) barrels. The 590A1 is also used by the U.S. and allied armed forces, having been designed to meet the stricter standards outlined by the U.S. Army.

Model 500s were also previously sold as law enforcement combos in 12 gauge with both 18.5-inch (47 cm) and 28-inch (71 cm) barrels, birch buttstock, pistol grip and sling.

Home security model

The model 500 HS410, or "Home Security" model, is only available in .410, and is specifically designed for defensive use. It comes with a youth-sized stock, a vertical foregrip, and a special muzzle brake and spreader choke (to help produce wider patterns when using buckshot) on an 18.5-inch (47 cm) bead sight barrel. The .410, while by far the least powerful common shotgun chambering, remains a formidable weapon. A 90-grain slug generates energy close to (and in some manufacturer claims, exceeding) a .357 Magnum when fired from a full length barrel. The HS410 is targeted at the novice user who desires a simple, easy to use, and effective defensive weapon. It is packaged with an introductory video covering use and safety, and some versions have a laser sight mounted in the foregrip.[4]

8.14.4 Accessories and combinations

The Mossberg 500 has always been marketed as a multi-purpose firearm. Mossberg sells a wide variety of accessory stocks and barrels, allowing many configurations to be made (including, in the past, a bullpup configured model 500). Mossberg is also the only company to ever offer a double-action-only model. The model 590DA offers a longer, heavier trigger pull to reduce the chance of an accidental discharge by the operator, and was targeted at the police market.

With the appropriate parts, the same Model 500 can be a field gun, a slug gun, defensive weapon for civilian, police, or military use, trap and skeet gun, or .50 caliber (12.7mm) rifled muzzleloader.

Mossberg has also sold "combination" sets, with a single receiver and more than one barrel. Common examples included a 28-inch (71 cm) field barrel packaged with an 18.5-inch (47 cm) cylinder bore barrel for defensive use, or a field barrel and a slug barrel, or a slug barrel and a .50 caliber muzzleloading rifle barrel.

A unique item offered by Mossberg for the Model 500 is a line launcher kit. It uses special blank cartridge to propel a shaft with an optional floating head and a light rope attached to it; a canister hung below the barrel to hold the line spool. A test of the Mossberg 500 with line launcher by the BoatUS Foundation showed an average range of over 330 feet (100 m) with the floating head. Distances of 700 feet (210 m) are claimed for the non-floating long distance head.[5]

All Mossberg models including the 835, 535, 500, 505 and 590 (except for Special-Purpose and Law Enforcement models) are shipped with a wooden dowel, also called a duck plug, located in the tube magazine. This is to comply with U.S. migratory bird laws. This dowel reduces and regulates the number of shells that can be loaded in the gun. This can be removed by taking off the barrel and pointing the shotgun downward and shaking it back and forth lightly until the dowel falls out. Except for the Maverick 88, all Mossberg models have a pre-drilled receiver for installation of an upper Picatinny rail for mounting various optics such as red dot sights. Some models can be bought with the rail and accessories already installed.

8.14.5 Maverick Arms subsidiary

Mossberg also markets a less expensive shotgun under the Maverick Arms name, the Mossberg Maverick 88, in blued finish with synthetic stocks, and in appearance is virtually identical to the 500 model. Maverick and Mossberg shotguns share many interchangeable parts[6][7] but Maverick shotguns differ in some ways, such as lacking sling swivel studs and having cross-bolt safeties instead of tang safeties, which makes the trigger group non interchangeable with the model 500 shotgun. The one piece forearm can be replaced with OEM or after market parts with the addition of an action slide tube, as the factory forearm has the action bars pinned into place. The Maverick series also does not come drilled and tapped for rail mounts like the 500 models. There are two basic models of the 88, the 88 field and the 88 security, with a cartridge capacity of 6 or 8 shots, and they cannot have their magazines easily extended without machining. The factory warranty on Maverick shotguns are limited to one year. Maverick Arms have many parts made in Mexico and are assembled in Eagle Pass, Maverick County, Texas rather than in Mossberg's main facility in Connecticut.

8.14.6 Model numbers

- 500A = 12 gauge
- 500AB = 12 gauge, Dual Action Bar
- 500B = 16 gauge (has been discontinued)
- 500C = 20 gauge
- 500D = 28 gauge (never went into production)
- 500E = .410 bore[8]

8.14.7 Military use

Mossberg claims the Model 500 is the only shotgun to pass the U.S. Army's Mil-Spec 3443E test, "a brutal and unforgiving torture test with 3,000 rounds of full power 12 gauge buckshot". (The updated 3443G specification requires a metal trigger guard, so only the Model 590A1 variants, which have a heavier barrel and use metal trigger groups instead of the standard Model 500's plastic trigger groups, will fit the requirements.[2]) The 500M MILS have the metal trigger group, and the heavier 20in barrel.

While the Marines officially switched to the semi-automatic M1014 Combat Shotgun in 1999, various branches of the

A U.S. soldier in Ar Ramadi, Iraq in 2004 armed with a Mossberg 500.

U.S. military are still acquiring pump shotguns. The Navy acquired several thousand Mossberg 590A1 shotguns in 2004,[9] and the U.S. Army placed an order in 2005 for 14,818 units at a price of just over US$316 each[10] (the Benelli M1014 is considerably more expensive).

In 2009, U.S. Special Forces Groups procured Military Enhancement Kits to provide a standardized shotgun configuration based on the Mossberg 500. The kits included a collapsible stock, "shotgun retention system", 1913 receiver rail, forend rail system and breaching barrels. A total of 1301 shotguns were converted with the first unit being equipped in July 2009. The majority of the kits convert the standard issue shotgun to a 14" compact model with a 16" accessory breaching barrel, H92239-09-P-0113.[11]

As of 2012, the U.S. Army is in the process of replacing the M500 with the M26 Modular Accessory Shotgun System, of which 9,000 are funded and under contract. The new shotgun is designed to be mounted in an underbarrel configuration on an M4 Carbine, similar to the M203 or M320 grenade launchers, or used as a stand-alone weapon.[12]

Users

Mossberg produced 2 U.S. military versions of the model 500, the 500 MILS and the 500M MILS, the difference being the location of the upper sling swivel.[13] The model numbers contain a U.S. prefix to the serial number. These particular models (500 MILS & 500M MILS) contain all metal parts, are parkerized with a 20-inch barrel. The magazine capacity is 6+1.[14]

- Bermuda[15][16]

- Brazil
- Dominican Republic
- Iceland: National Police of Iceland.[17]
- Iraq
- Lebanon[18]
- Malaysia: Malaysian Special Operations Force[19] and RELA Corps.
- Netherlands: *590DA1* is used by the Korps Commandotroepen, Armoured infantry and the Airmobile Brigade of the Royal Netherlands Army.[20]
- Philippines
- Poland: *50440* in use by Military Gendarmerie and *590* in use by Policja, SPAP and probably in use by Polish Troops in Afghanistan.[21]
- United States[9]

8.14.8 See also

- Mossberg Maverick
- New Haven 600
- Remington 870
- Winchester 1200
- O.F. Mossberg & Sons

General:

- List of shotguns of the U.S. Armed Forces
- List of shotguns
- Pump-action shotgun
- Combat shotgun

8.14.9 References

[1] "O.F. Mossberg & Sons, Inc. - Firearms, Shotguns, Rifles, Accessories, and Precision Machining". Mossberg.com. Retrieved 2008-09-13.

[2] "US Department of Defense specification 3443". Retrieved 2008-09-13.

[3] "U.S. military small arms today". *American Rifleman*: 77. June 2003.

[4] Scott Farrell (March 1992). "Mossberg's 410 home defender: a well-targeted shotgun". *Shooting Industry*.

[5] "Mossberg Line Launcher user manual" (PDF). Archived from the original (PDF) on 2008-04-14. Retrieved 2008-09-13.

[6] "SHOTGUN ACCESSORIES - Clips'N'Stuff Firearm Accessories". Clipsnstuff.com. Archived from the original on 2008-07-31. Retrieved 2008-09-13.

[7] "Advanced Technology Shotgun Conversion System". Allenslaw.com. Retrieved 2008-09-13.

[8] "Modern Firearms - Mossberg 500 shotgun". World.guns.ru. Retrieved 2008-09-13.

[9] "US Naval Surface Warfare Center acquisition contract for 2,200 to 7,500 Mossberg model 590A1 shotguns". 2004-08-31. Retrieved 2008-09-13.

[10] "Department of the Army Fiscal Year (FY) 2007 Budget Estimates" (PDF). US Army. 2008-02-01. pp. 278–279. Retrieved 2008-09-13.

[11] https://www.fbo.gov/index?s=opportunity&mode=form&id=37ca851363ed811af550020dab330d6c&tab=core&_cview=1

[12] "Army, Marine Corps Succeed in Rapidly Fielding Specialized Individual Weapons (UPDATED)". Retrieved 25 December 2014.

[13] http://www.mossberg.com/wp-content/uploads/2015/04/500-MILS-500M-MILS.pdf

[14] Canfield, Bruce (December 2008). "Complete Guide to United States Military Combat Shotguns". self. Retrieved 2011-08-07.

[15] "KEN_1270". *Flickr*. Retrieved 25 December 2014.

[16] "KEN_4919". *Flickr*. Retrieved 25 December 2014.

[17] "Með Glock 17 og MP5". *Fréttatíminn*. 23. 09. 2011. p. 12-14.

[18] Castelli, Christopher J. (September 2008). "Department of Defense to Equip Lebanon's Special Forces with Small Arms, Vehicles" (PDF). *DISAM Journal* (Defense Institute of Security Assistance Management) **30** (3): 123. Retrieved January 18, 2009.

[19] Thompson, Leroy (December 2008). "Malaysian Special Forces". Special Weapons. Retrieved 2010-02-10.

[20] http://www.collectie.legermuseum.nl/strategion/strategion/i007439.html - Legermuseum collections page

[21] "Serwis militarny". Retrieved 25 December 2014.

- The tactical shotgun in urban operations Infantry Magazine, Nov-Dec, 2004

8.14.10 External links

- Mossberg corporate website.
- Mossberg Owners Forum a forum dedicated to Mossberg firearms.
- Maverick Arms corporate website, a subsidiary of Mossberg.
- Mossberg's 410 home defender: a well-targeted shotgun, Scott Farrell, Shooting Industry, March, 1992.
- The Magnificent Mossberg, Guns & Ammo Magazine, April, 2007
- Knoxx Industries Sidewinder 10 rd Drum on 12 gauge Mossberg a modified Mossberg.
- Nazarian's Gun's Recognition Guide (FILM) a highly modified Mossberg 590 which includes a Cavalry Arms buttstock adapter systems and a Knoxx Industries Sidewinder Conversion Kit snail drum magazine (.wmv)

8.15 Mossberg Maverick

The **Maverick 88** is a slightly lower cost version of the pump action, 12 gauge Mossberg 500 shotgun, however in appearance it is virtually identical to the 500 model. Factory Maverick 88s feature a black, synthetic only stock and forearm, cylinder bore (although interchangeable chokes are available on some hunting models), and cross-bolt safety. Most accessories are interchangeable with a Mossberg 500 except for the forearm assembly.

8.15.1 Overview

The Maverick line of shotguns are assembled in Eagle Pass, Texas using some parts manufactured outside of the United States, mainly from Mexico; which contributes to their relatively lower price in comparison to the Mossberg 500 series of shotguns, which is entirely domestically manufactured and assembled at the O.F. Mossberg & Sons factory in Connecticut.

The trigger groups will not interchange between Maverick 88 and Mossberg 500 models, but the majority of other parts including barrels, stocks, and magazine tubes will (the barrel and magazines must be the same length). Maverick 88 do not come equipped with any sling mounts, as the Mossberg 500 series do.

Maverick 88 shotguns feature a trigger guard mounted cross-bolt safety as opposed to a top tang safety, which is used on the Mossberg 500 series.

Early Model 88s were equipped with a single slide rail, but this was updated to a dual slide rail in 1990. Also the Maverick 88 does not have a receiver top pre-drilled and tapped for a Weaver scope mount rail.

Maverick 88's are factory finished with steel bluing only, whereas Mossberg 500s have factory blued, nickel plated or parkerized (barrel/magazine) options.

There are two basic models of the 88, the 88 field and the 88 security. The 88 field comes with a longer 28" vent-rib barrel, whereas the security comes with an 18-1/2" or 20" non-vent-rib barrel. The 88's have a cartridge capacity of 5 in the tube magazine and 1 in the chamber and cannot have their magazines easily extended without machining. Magazine capacity is further limited, if loading "3 shells, to 4 in the tube magazine and 1 in the chamber.

The Mossberg Maverick comes from the factory with a black synthetic stock and forend. Sling swivels are not included, however they can be installed to allow the use of a sling.

8.15.2 See also

- Serbu Super-Shorty Compact derivative of the Mossberg Maverick

8.15.3 References

[1] "88 Field". Maverickarms.com. Retrieved 2008-09-13.

[2] "88 Security". Maverickarms.com. Retrieved 2008-09-13.

8.15.4 External links

- Official Maverick 88 product webpage
- Official Mossberg product webpage

8.16 New Haven 600

New Haven 600 is a series of pump-action shotguns manufactured by O.F. Mossberg & Sons on behalf of department stores, most notably the Montgomery Ward Company, Western Auto, and other retail stores. *New Haven* is one of O.F. Mossberg & Sons' private, promotional brands. The New Haven 600 is identical to the Mossberg 500 from O.F. Mossberg & Sons, with the addition of an anti-rattle system in the magazine tube. The 600 series comprises widely varying models of hammerless, pump action repeaters, all of which share the same basic receiver and action, but differ in bore size, barrel length, choke options, magazine capacity, and "furniture" (stock and forearm) materials.

8.16.1 Model numbers

- 600AT = 12 gauge
- 600BT = 16 gauge
- 600CT = 20 gauge
- 600ET = .410 bore

8.16.2 See also

- Mossberg 500
- O.F. Mossberg & Sons
- Pump-action shotgun

8.16.3 External links

- Mossberg corporate website.
    - Manuals in PDF format for the 500.
- Maverick Arms corporate website, a subsidiary of Mossberg.

8.17 Norinco HP9-1

The **Norinco HP9-1**, also known as the **Norinco N870-14.00**, is a short pump action shotgun made by Norinco of China. This 12 gauge smoothbore firearm has a 14-inch (36 cm) barrel and has a rust-resistant parkerized finish. It is a close copy of the Remington 870, a widely distributed design no longer under patent protection, and most parts interchange freely.

In the United States, where Norinco products are specifically non-importable, this gun is imported and sold under the names **Norinco Hawk 982** and **Interstate Hawk 982**.

8.17.1 External links

- NORINCO's Product Information page
- Canadian distributor product page
- Modern Firearms Entry

8.18 Remington Model 10

The **Remington Model 10** is a pump-action shotgun designed by John Pedersen[1] with an internal hammer and a tube magazine which loaded and ejected from a port in the bottom of the receiver.[4] An updated version, the Model 29, was introduced in 1930 with improvements made by C.C. Loomis.[2]

8.18.1 Military use

The United States military used a short-barreled version known variously as the "trench" or "riot" shotgun.[5] The Winchester Model 1897 was the major production, but Remington made 3500 of the Model 10-A version for issue to U.S. troops during World War I.[5] The Model 10 was modified by reducing barrel length to 23 inches (58 cm) and adding sling swivels, a wooden heat shield over the barrel, and an adapter with bayonet lug for affixing a M1917 bayonet.[5] These trench guns with serial numbers between 128000 and 166000 were stamped with US and the flaming bomb insignia on the left side of the receiver.[4] The United States military also purchased a number of Remington Model 10 with 20-inch (51-cm) barrels for guarding prisoners, and 26 to 30-inch (66 to 76-cm) barrels for training aerial gunners.[5] The Model 10-A was used in limited numbers by the Marine Corps through the 1930s.[5]

8.18.2 References

[1] "Model 10 Pump Shotgun". Remington Arms. Retrieved 24 December 2012.

[2] "Model 29 Pump Shotgun". Remington Arms. Retrieved 7 February 2014.

[3] Wood, J.B. (2002). *The Gun digest book of firearms assembly/disassembly.* (2nd ed.). Iola, WI: Krause Pub. ISBN 0873494008.

[4] Bruce N. Canfield "Give Us More Shotguns!" *American Rifleman* May 2004 pp.58-63

[5] Bruce N. Canfield "Remington's Model 10: The Other Trench Gun" *American Rifleman* November 2009 pp.74-107

8.19 Remington Model 17

In 1915 John Browning patented a pump-action shotgun with the following features: hammerless, under-loading, tubular-magazine, bottom-ejecting, and take-down. This design would eventually become the **Remington Model**

17.[1] Manufacturing rights were sold to Remington Arms shortly after, but due to the production efforts of World War I, Remington was unable to begin manufacturing until 1921. Before production began John Pedersen made alterations to the design, with more changes made later by G.H. Garrison. The Model 17 was a trim, 20-gauge shotgun that served as the design basis for three highly successful shotguns: the Remington Model 31, the Ithaca 37 and the Browning BPS. Additionally, features of the Model 17 were also incorporated in the later Mossberg 500 and Remington 870.

8.19.1 References

[1] Firearm Model History - Remington Model 17

8.20 Remington Model 31

The **Remington Model 31** is a pump-action shotgun that competed with the Winchester Model 1912 for the American sporting arms market.[1] Produced from 1931 to 1949, it superseded the John Pedersen designed, bottom loading and ejecting Models 10 and 29, and the John Browning designed Model 17. It was replaced by the less expensive to manufacture Remington 870 in 1951.[2]

8.20.1 History

While the Remington Model 17 enjoyed some success, a solid, 12-gauge featuring side-ejection was needed to compete with Winchester. C.C. Loomis sized up the Model 17 and adapted it for side ejection. The Model 31 was Remington's first side ejecting pump-action shotgun. Stocks were walnut with checkered walnut forend and later changed to a ribbed forend. The Model 31 was made in three gauges with 121,000 12-gauge models made and 75,000 16- and 20-gauge examples also produced. The Federal Bureau of Investigation acquired one Model 31 per office in 1935 in response to the Kansas City Massacre.[3] The model 31L was a lightweight version featuring an aluminum receiver and trigger housing.

Despite being well received, sales still lagged far behind the Winchester. Remington went back to the drawing board and designed the Model 870; this shotgun matched the durability of the Model 12 at a significantly lower cost. Despite the overwhelming success of the 870, many shotgun connoisseurs consider the Model 31 to be the *ne plus ultra* of pump shotguns with its "ball-bearing" slide action.[4]

The Model 31 was later used as a basis for the Mossberg 500 and related shotguns. The Mossberg is simplified and cheaper to produce. Notable differences are the use of a two-piece bolt with separate locking piece as well as a significantly simplified barrel mounting system. Further, the bolt locks into a barrel extension rather than directly to the receiver.

8.20.2 External links

[1] Remington's Magnificent Five - Page Two

[2] http://www.remington.com/library/history/firearm_ models/shotguns/model_31.asp Remington history page

[3] Vanderpool, Bill "Bring Enough Gun" *American Rifleman* October 2013 pp.80-85&115-116

[4] Simpson, Lane. "Remington's Magnificent Five", *Shooting Times*, May 2000

8.21 Remington Model 870

The **Remington Model 870** is a pump-action shotgun manufactured by Remington Arms Company, LLC. It is widely used by the public for sport shooting, hunting, and self-defense. It is also commonly used by law enforcement and military organizations worldwide.

8.21.1 Development

The Remington 870 was the fourth major design in a series of Remington pump shotguns. John Pedersen designed the fragile Remington Model 10 (and later the improved Remington Model 29). John Browning designed the Remington Model 17 (which was later adapted by Ithaca into the Ithaca 37), which served as the basis for the Remington 31. The Model 31 was well liked,[4] but struggled for sales in the shadow of the Winchester Model 12. Remington sought to correct that in 1951 by introducing a modern, streamlined, rugged, reliable, and relatively inexpensive shotgun – the 870.

Sales of the 870 have been steady. They reached 2 million guns by 1973 (ten times the number of Model 31 shotguns it replaced). By 1996, spurred by sales of the basic "Express" models, which were added as a lower-cost alternative to the original Wingmaster line, sales topped seven million guns. On April 13, 2009, the ten millionth Model 870 was produced; the 870 holds the record for best-selling shotgun in history.[5]

8.21.2 Design details

The 870 features a bottom-loading, side ejecting receiver, tubular magazine under the barrel, dual action bars, internal hammer, and a bolt which locks into an extension in the barrel. The action, receiver, fire control group, safety catch and slide release catch of the Remington Model 870 shotgun are similar to those used on the Remington Model 7600 series pump-action centerfire rifles and carbines. The basic fire control group design was first used in the automatic 11–48.[6][7] Twelve gauge stocks will also interchange on the older 12-gauge-sized 20-gauge receivers, although modification is needed to fit the smaller sized 20-gauge receivers employed since the late 1970s. Several parts of the 870 will interchange with the semi-automatic Remington 1100 and 11–87.

The original 870 models were offered with fixed chokes. In 1986 Remington introduced the new Remington "Rem Choke" system of screw-in chokes (also fitted to Remington model 1100 auto-loading shotguns at the same time). Initially, the Rem Chokes were offered only in 12 gauge in barrel lengths of 21", 26", and 28". The following year the availability was expanded to the 20 gauge and included other barrel lengths.[7][8]

Production 870s for over 30 years had a design whereby a user could fail to press a shell all the way into the magazine when loading such that the shell latch did not engage the shell, and such actions could tie up the gun.[7][9] This was caused by the shell which slipped out of the magazine under the bolt in the receiver to bind the action, requiring rough treatment of the action or even disassembly to clear by the uninitiated. The potential issue was resolved with the introduction of the "Flexi Tab" carrier. Guns with this modification can be identified by the "U"-shaped cut-out on the carrier, visible from below the gun. The cut-out, combined with a modified machining on the underside of the slide assembly, allows the action to be opened with a shell on the carrier.

8.21.3 Variants

There are hundreds of variations of the Remington 870 in 12, 16, 20, 28 gauges and .410 bore. In 1969 Remington introduced 28 gauge and .410 bore models on a new scaled down receiver size, and in 1972 a 20 gauge Lightweight version was introduced on the same sized receiver, and all of the smaller gauges today are produced on that size receiver. From the original fifteen models offered, Remington currently produces dozens of models for civilian, law enforcement, and military sales. 870 variants can be grouped into:

- **Express** – Matte blue/black bead-blasted with hardwood, laminated hardwood or synthetic stocks and chambered for 2 3/4" and 3" 12 or 20 gauge shotshells. All Expresses have been chambered in 3" in 12 and 20 gauge, but markings have varied.

- **Marine** – Nickel plated with synthetic stocks.

- **Mark 1** – adopted by the United States Marine Corps in the late 1960s and saw service into the 21st century. The Model 870 Mark 1 has a 21 inches (53 cm) barrel with an extended magazine increasing total capacity to 8 rounds, and was fitted with an adapter allowing use of the standard M7 bayonet for the M16 rifle.[7][10]

- **MCS** (**M**odular **C**ombat **S**hotgun) – A new modular version of the M870 which can be quickly modified with different barrels, magazine tubes, and stocks for different purposes, such as urban combat and door breaching.

- **Police** – Chambered in 12 gauge only with a 3" magnum chamber. Blued or Parkerized steel finish. These models feature a stronger sear spring, carrier latch spring, and a forged steel extractor (as opposed to the MIM extractor found on Express models). Receivers are stamped "Remington 870 Police Magnum" as of 2014.

They are equipped with Police-specific walnut or synthetic stocks which are fitted with sling mounts. Walnut stocks lack checkering as found on the Express/Wingmaster models. 870P models come with matching walnut or synthetic forends that are shortened to prevent interference with most vehicle-mounted rack systems. The shortened forend also allows quick visual inspection of the magazine regardless of what position the forend is in, whereas the lengthened sport-type forend on other models partially blocks the loading port when pulled to the rear.

Police models are available with 18" or 20" barrels, with or without rifle sights, and have a standard capacity of four rounds. They can be ordered with a two or three round extended magazine tube from the factory, bringing total capacity to 6+1 (18" barrel) or 7+1 (20" barrel). All police barrels come with an Improved Cylinder choke unless specially ordered.

- **Super Mag** – Chambered for 3½" 12 gauge shotshells.

- **Wingmaster** – Blued steel with high gloss or satin walnut stocks. They have been offered in Skeet, Trap, and field configurations. Originally the basic Wingmaster was chambered for 2 3/4" rounds and came with a fixed choke, and the 3" chambered versions were designated Magnum models. Models built after 1986 offer the RemChoke Interchangeable choke tube system, and the 12 and 20 gauge versions are chambered in 3" for either 2 3/4" or 3" shells. Prior to the introduction of the "Police" model 870, altered Wingmasters were popular among law enforcement.

Chinese versions

Arms manufacturer, Norinco, of the People's Republic of China has made unlicensed copies of the Remington 870 as the design is no longer under patent protection. The most common of these designs are the Norinco HP9-1 and M-98, the difference being that the HP9-1 has either a 12.5" or 14" barrel, whereas the M-98 has an 18.5" barrel.[11] In the United States, where most Norinco products are specifically non-importable,[12] this shotgun was imported and sold under the names Norinco Hawk 982 and Interstate Hawk 982.[13]

8.21.4 Users

A U.S. Coast Guard petty officer from Maritime Safety and Security Team 91106 armed with an Mk870P fitted with a Trijicon reflex sight and a Speedfeed stock.

8.21.5 See also

- Combat shotgun
- KAC Masterkey
- List of individual weapons of the U.S. Armed Forces

8.21.6 References

[1] Remington model history

[2] Remington product page*dead link*]

[3] "Remington Model 870 Shotguns". Remington Arms Company, Inc. Retrieved 2008-06-10.

The Remington 870 12-gauge shotgun loaded with pyrotechnical shells (blanks) is seen here used as a last resort to scare off unwanted birds in flight from the vicinity of Incirlik Air Base.

[4] "The Five Most Popular Remington Rifles and Shotguns – Page Two". Retrieved 25 December 2014.

[5] Harold Murtz. *Gun Digest Treasury* (DBI Books, 1994), p.193

[6] Michalowski, Kevin (2005). *The Gun Digest Book of Sporting Shotguns*. Gun Digest Books. p. 152. ISBN 0-89689-173-9.

[7] "Remington Model 870 (M870) Combat / Game Pump Action Shotgun (1950)". Military Factory. August 7, 2014. Retrieved 2015-04-12.

[8] *Remington Firearms Catalogs*. Remington Arms. 1986&1987. Check date values in: |date= (help)

[9] "An Uncommon Remington 870 Review". Shooters' Journal. 2010-11-05. Retrieved 2011-01-22.

[10] Canfield, Bruce N. "Combat Shotguns of the Vietnam War" *American Rifleman* March 2002 pp.44–47&92–95

[11] Cutshaw, Charles Q. (28 February 2011). *Tactical Small Arms of the 21st Century: A Complete Guide to Small Arms From Around the World*. Iola, Wisconsin: Gun Digest Books. p. 327. ISBN 978-1-4402-2709-7. Retrieved 24 September 2013.

[12] Peterson, Phillip (2008). "Norinco". *Gun Digest Buyer's Guide To Assault Weapons*. Iola, Wisconsin: Gun Digest Books. p. 178. ISBN 978-1-4402-2672-4. Retrieved 24 September 2013.

8.21. REMINGTON MODEL 870

A U.S. Air Force Security Forces Marine Patrol airman from MacDill AFB with an M870.

[13] Lee, Jerry (11 April 2012). *The Official Gun Digest Book of Guns & Prices 2012*. Iola, Wisconsin: Gun Digest Books. p. 747. ISBN 978-1-4402-2927-5.

[14] "870P Shotgun". Royal Australian Navy. 2010-09-09. Retrieved 2011-01-22.

[15] "Weapons : Royal Australian Air Force". Airforce.gov.au. 2009-09-07. Retrieved 2011-01-22.

[16] http://www.bmi.gv.at/cms/BMI_EKO_Cobra/publikationen/files/LawOrder.pdf

[17] "Remington Model 870 (M870) – Combat / Game Pump-Action Shotgun – History, Specs and Pictures – Military, Security and Civilian Guns and Equipment". Retrieved 25 December 2014.

[18] "Dhaka Metropolitan Police SWAT – Overview". bdmilitary. Retrieved 22 February 2009.

[19] "Belgian Defence Remington 870 technical sheet". Retrieved 14 January 2015.

[20] Remington 870 Shotgun makes a comeback

[21] "Report to the Attorney General – Public inquiry into the deaths of Connie and Ty Jacobs". Alberta Justice. 2000-05-18. Retrieved 2011-01-22.

[22] "Pumppuhaulikko 12 HAUL REM 870". Mil.fi. Retrieved 2013-10-17.

[23] "TRANSIT-Informationsseite: www.denic.de". Rkneckarzimmern.de. 2007-02-11. Retrieved 2011-01-22.

[24] "Greece Ministry of Public Order Press Office: Special Anti-Terrorist Unit" (PDF). Official Website of the Hellenic Police. July 2004. Retrieved 2009-10-13.

[25] Janq Designs. "Special Operations.Com". Special Operations.Com. Retrieved 2011-01-22.

[26] "isayeret.com – The world's leading Israeli Special Forces resource". Retrieved 25 December 2014.

[27] url=http://blue-paper.tistory.com/901

[28] "Unofficial Pistols Page, Equipment". http://USP.lu – Unofficial Website of Unité Spéciale, Officially Endorsed. Retrieved 2009-10-06. External link in |publisher= (help)

[29] "L'Unite d'Intervention de la Police Luxembourgeoise" (PDF) (in French). RAIDS Magazine. March 2006. Retrieved 2009-09-23.

[30] Lasterra, Juan Pablo (2004). "UPS Unidad Especial de la Policia Luxembourguesa" (PDF) (in Spanish). ARMAS Magazine. Retrieved 2009-09-23.

[31] Thompson, Leroy (December 2008). "Malaysian Special Forces". Special Weapons. Retrieved 2009-11-29.

[32] Högkvarteret Informationsstaben (February 2011). "Försvarsmakten". Högkvarteret Informationsstaben. Retrieved 2011-02-26.

[33] "El equipo de los tiradores de precisión de las fuerzas armadas suizas | Armas – Revista Armas | Reportajes de armas cortas, rifles, armamento policial/militar, armas blancas, competiciones". Revista Armas. Retrieved 2011-01-22.

[34] http://thediplomat.com/2015/08/taiwans-coast-guard-conducts-armed-raid-to-reclaim-hostages-taken-Missing or empty |title= (help)

[35] Skennerton, Ian D. (2005). "L-prefix Nomenclature". Arms & Militaria Press. Retrieved 6 January 2010.

[36] "Guns of the United States Border Patrol". Human Events. Retrieved 2011-01-22.

[37] "Remington Shotguns – Federal Business Opportunities: Opportunities". Retrieved 2010-03-17.

[38] Clancy, Tom (1996). *Marine: A Guided Tour of a Marine Expeditionary Unit*. Berkeley, California: Berkeley Trade. pp. 64, 79–80. ISBN 978-0-425-15454-0.

[39] Jones, Richard D. *Jane's Infantry Weapons 2009/2010*. Jane's Information Group; 35 edition (January 27, 2009). ISBN 978-0-7106-2869-5.

[40] "TIRWR-10-Q-00023". https://www.fbo.gov – Federal Business Opportunities. February 2, 2010. Retrieved 2010-06-10. External link in |publisher= (help)

[41] http://www.chp.ca.gov/features/pdf/perspectives.pdf

[42] "On the Range". The Sparta Independent. June 2, 2010. Retrieved 2010-06-03.

[43] Diez, Octavio (2000). *Armament and Technology*. Lema Publications, S.L. ISBN 84-8463-013-7.

[44] NRA Staff. "Pennsylvania State Police Select Remington 870". American Rifleman. Retrieved 26 December 2012.

8.21.7 External links

- Remington page for 870
- A guide to Collecting Remington 870 Shotguns from Remington Society
- Remington page for 870 Tactical
- Remington Military MCS page
- Important differences between Remington 870 Police and 870 Express shotguns
- KAC Masterkey page
- Model 870P MAX Police
- Blog and forum about Remington 870

8.22 Remington Model 887

The **Remington Model 887 Nitro Mag** is a pump-action shotgun manufactured by Remington Arms Company, Inc. It is noted for using a polymer finish called ArmorLokt,[1] which is designed to survive any type of weather condition and leaves no exterior surfaces to rust.[4] This gives the 887 a "space age" look which is one of the gun's more defining features.[5]

8.22.1 Design and Features

As the name suggests, the 887 Nitro Mag can chamber 3 ½″ magnum shells. In this way, it competes with the Mossberg 835 Ulti-Mag, which is designed specifically for firing 3 ½″ magnum shells.[6] The look of the 887 is also frequently compared to that of the Benelli Nova.[7] The Remington 887's brochure confirms this by comparing itself to the Mossberg 835 and the Benelli Nova.[2]

ArmorLokt Finish

The 887's most striking feature is the ArmorLokt finish. The entire receiver and barrel of the 887 is coated with a glass-filled nylon material which protects the steel interior of the gun. In this way, the steel provides the strength for the gun while the polymer protects the inner workings from the elements, including inclement weather and resulting corrosion. Manufacturers have come up with several ways to help protect a gun's metal surface, but overmolding the gun with a polymer is a unique concept.[4]

Remington claims that the ArmorLokt finish is impenetrable, and has several tests to help back up this claim. Company engineers subjected the 887 to salt-corrosion and submersion tests and checked for leaks and separation in the polymer, and none were found.[2] A second test was conducted, where over 10,000 rounds were discharged through a single 887 barrel, and the barrel's coating showed no signs of separation. Smaller tests have been conducted by reviewers which somewhat verify these results.[4]

Several key parts of the weapon are not treated with the ArmorLokt process. Noted on several sites are issues with the fore end tube assembly having rust directly from the factory.

The surface of the barrel, receiver, and synthetic fore-end has a tire-tread pattern to make a non-slip surface. It also gives the gun a unique look, which is often criticized.[5]

8.22.2 Remington Model 870 Comparison

These two actions are completely different. The 870 uses a lifting lug to lock the action and the 887 uses a rotating bolt head.

The core design, specifically, the action, the receiver, and the barrel, is based upon that of the famous Remington 870. These make up the steel "core" of the 887.[3] However, besides this, the 887 actually differs fairly significantly from the 870, and is not designed to replace the 870.[4]

The 887 offers several improvements over the 870's design, usually in the name of user-friendliness. The slide release, for example, is a large, triangular button located on the top half of the trigger guard's face which is easy to use, even with gloves on or with numb hands. This is in contrast to the 870, where the slide release was located to the left of a trigger guard and was a small metal tab.[4]

The 887 is also much easier to strip down and clean than the 870. Stripping down the 887 does not require any tools (with the exception of the Tactical Model which does require a hex wrench and screwdriver to remove the barrel/magazine clamp), unlike the 870,[4] and stripping down the 887 is much quicker; it only takes two minutes to field strip an 887 and reassemble.

8.22.3 Variations

Remington is initially marketing two versions of the 887, the **887 Nitro Mag**[1] and the **887 Nitro Mag Waterfowl**.[3] Remington has released several new models including **887 Nitro Mag Tactical**, **887 Nitro Mag Bone Collector**, and **887 Nitro Mag Camo Combo**.

The Tactical model is similar to the base model, but with an 18.5 inch barrel, a magazine extension tube, and 2 Picatinny mounting rails. The 887 Nitro Mag Waterfowl is very similar to the base version, with the main difference being the finish. The waterfowl version includes a finish covered in Mossy Oak's Break-Up Infinity and also Realtree Advantage Max-4 HD camo, which makes it ideal for hunting, as per its namesake.[8][4] The 887 Waterfowl is also slightly heavier than the 887.[2]

8.22.4 See also

- Remington Model 10
- Remington 870
- Mossberg 835 Ulti-Mag
- Benelli Nova

8.22.5 Notes

[1] "Model 887 Nitro Mag". Remington Arms Company, Inc. Retrieved January 20, 2010.

[2] "887 Brochure". Remington Arms Company, Inc. Retrieved January 22, 2010.

[3] "Model 887 Nitro Mag Waterfowl". Remington Arms Company, Inc. December 20, 2008. Retrieved January 22, 2010.

[4] Adam Heggenstaller. "Up-Armored Pump: Remington's 887 Nitro Mag" (PDF). American Rifleman. Retrieved January 22, 2010.

[5] Adam Heggenstaller (December 19, 2008). "New Pump From Remington". Incoming. Retrieved January 10, 2010.

[6] "New pump shotgun from Remington: Model 887 Nitro-Mag". The Firearm Blog. December 20, 2008. Retrieved January 22, 2010.

[7] Randy Wakeman. "Preview: Remington's 2009 887 Nitro Mag Pump Action". Retrieved January 23, 2010.

[8] http://www.outdoorwriter.net/?p=357

8.23 RMB-93

The **RMb-93** is a pump-action shotgun designed and manufactured by the KBP Instrument Design Bureau of Tula, Russia. It is the baseline model of the *Rys* ("Lynx") series of shotguns, taking the modelname of **Rys-K**. The RMb-93 has been conceived as a combat weapon for Special Forces and Police units that might face Close Quarters Battle situations. The weapon is thus engineered to reduce size and encumbrance as much as possible. The working system of the RMb-93 is itself an odd slide-action operation called "Inverted Cycle", similar in concept to the one used in the South-African Truvelo Armoury Neostead shotgun (the only other mass-produced firearm to be based upon this system). The feeding tube is placed over the barrel rather than under it, and tilts upwards for loading. Once the weapon is loaded, a shell is chambered by pushing the slide forward-then-backward, instead of the standard backward-then-forward motion of the forend found on most pump-action weapons. Having the RMb-93 a fixed breech face and movable barrel, the operation moves the entire barrel assembly. Once a round is fired and another is chambered, the empty shell falls downwards to the ground, pushed by its own weight. The design of the RMb-93 "Rys-K" carries several advantages: the ejection system makes the gun fully ambidextrous, and the magazine located over the barrel gives the shotgun a low center of mass and reduces upward recoil. The main drawback of the overall design stands in the fact that the weapon has a pistol grip with upfolding metal stock, which when folded finds itself right up the feeding tube. The RMb-93 thus can not be reloaded without extending or removing the stock, a disadvantage if it is being used tactically with a folded stock.

8.23.1 Variants and commercial availability

The RMb-93 "Rys-K" shotgun is commercially available to civilians in Canada, Russia, Italy and possibly in other Countries. For the civilian distribution in Russia and Canada, the shotgun is provided with a stock disconnector that prevents it from firing if the stock is not extended, so to comply with local laws and regulation about the minimum legal length for civilian firearms.

Additionally, KBP manufactures several variants of the "Rys" shotgun series for the civilian distribution. The RMb-93 "Rys-K" itself is manufactured with Phosphatized finish to resist salt corrosion (for use in maritime environments). The **RMO-93** *"Rys"* is a purely sporting variant with wooden thumbhole stock and either wooden or synthetic slide-forend; very similar to it is the *"Rys-OT"* variant with longer barrel, synthetic or wooden slide-forend and standard wooden shotgun stock. The **RMf-96** *"Rys-F"* shotgun is instead a longer-barrel variant of the RMb-93 "Rys-K", plus equipped with the above-mentioned stock disconnector.

8.23.2 Users

- Russia - used in private security companies until 1 March 2006[1]

8.23.3 See also

- List of Russian weaponry

8.23.4 References

[1] *"3. Установить, что огнестрельное оружие, приобретенное в соответствии с законодательством Российской Федерации негосударственными (частными) охранными предприятиями до вступления в силу настоящего постановления и не включенное в перечень видов вооружения охранников, утвержденный постановлением Правительства Российской Федерации от 14 августа 1992 г. N 587 (с изменениями, внесенными настоящим постановлением), может находиться на вооружении охранников до 1 марта 2006 г."*
Постановление Правительства РФ № 179 от 4 апреля 2005

8.23.5 Sources

- Cutshaw, Charlie (1998). *The New World of Russian Small Arms & Ammo*. Boulder, CO: Paladin Press. ISBN 0-87364-993-1.

8.23.6 External links

- KBP: RMB-93 "Rys-K" 12-Gauge Magazine Shotgun
- "Rys" 12-Gauge Hunting and Sporting Shotguns
- Enemy Forces: RMB-93 Smoothbore Shotgun
- Nazarian's Gun Recognition Guide: RMB-93
- Modern Firearms: RMB-93

8.24 Serbu Super-Shorty

The **Super-Shorty** is a compact, stockless, pump-action AOW chambered in 12-gauge (2¾ and 3").[1] The basic architecture of most of the production models is based on the Mossberg Maverick 88 shotgun, with Mossberg 500 and Remington 870 receivers also available.[2][3] The shotgun features a spring-loaded, folding foregrip.[4] A 20-gauge model is available on special order.[4][5]

In the United States, civilian ownership transfers of the shotgun require a $5 tax stamp and registration as an Any Other Weapon (AOW) to be in compliance with the National Firearms Act.[6][7] As the weapon is originally manufactured without a shoulder stock, it is considered a smooth-bore handgun, and thus an AOW, rather than a short-barrelled shotgun.[7]

8.24.1 Users

- United States: United States Army.[8]

8.24.2 See also

- Title II weapons

8.24.3 References

[1] David Crane. "SUPER-SHORTY 12-Gauge Mini-Shotgun by Serbu Firearms, Inc.". Defense Review. Retrieved 2010-10-02.

[2] "Serbu Super Shorty Remigton 870 12 gauge". Retrieved 2010-10-02.

[3] "Super Shorty (official site)". Retrieved 2010-10-02.

[4] Long, Duncan (2004). *Streetsweepers: The Complete Book of Combat Shotguns*. Paladin Press. p. 103. ISBN 1-58160-436-X.

[5] "SUPER-SHORTY 20". Retrieved 2014-02-16.

[6] "Buying NFA Items". Retrieved 2010-10-02.

[7] "BATFE National Firearms Handbook" (PDF). BATFE. Retrieved 2010-10-02.

[8] *Serbu Firearms, Inc. Promotional Video* (Tampa, Florida). Serbu Firearms, Inc. August 11, 2012. Retrieved February 10, 2015.

8.24.4 External links

- Official Site
- SBSReview.Net: Super-Shorty Review & Videos

8.25 Stevens Model 520/620

The **Stevens Model 520** was a pump-action shotgun developed by John Browning and originally manufactured by the J Stevens Arms & Tool Company between 1909 and 1915.[1] Savage Arms Corporation purchased Stevens out of bankruptcy in 1920 and changed their name to the J Stevens Arms Company. Stevens, under Savage ownership, continued to produce the Model 520 until 1939 when it was replaced by the Model 520A which ended production in 1947.[2] Stevens also further modified the design when they introduced the streamlined Model 620 in 1927.[3] The Model 620 is internally similar to the Model 520 and was produced until 1939[4] when it was replaced by the Model 620A which ended production in 1955.[5] This shotgun is a hammerless, pump action, take-down design with a tubular magazine which holds 5 shells. All models can also be slam fired: the shotgun has no trigger disconnector and shells can be fired one after the other simply by working the slide if the trigger is held down.

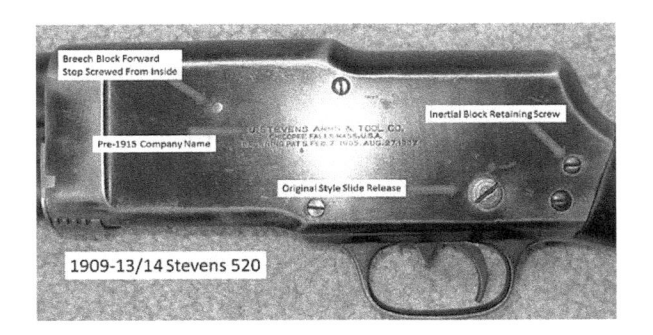

8.25.1 Background

John Browning filed a patent for a "hammerless" shotgun with a unique take-down barrel and locking breech block on 10 Jul 1903, it was approved on 7 Feb 1905 and along with a separate 27 Aug 1907 patent, that applies to the connection between the slide arm and the fore end, became what would be the Stevens Model 520. Browning eventually sold this design to the J Stevens Arms & Tool Company in Chicopee Falls MA.

8.25.2 Model 520

The first Stevens 520 appeared in Stevens' 1909 Catalog #52[1] and was also offered for sale in the Fall 1909 Sears & Roebuck catalog.[2] It is easily recognizable by its "Humpback" double hump receiver. It has a round slide release knob on the left side of the receiver, a visible breech locking bolt on the top of the receiver, and base models have a rounded pistol grip on the butt stock. The fore grip is ringed and uniform in size. The trigger housing is retained with three screws and the safety is a lever located inside the trigger guard in front of the trigger. The cartridge stop is a rocker design with a set screw on front right side of the

Stevens Model 520 (1909-1913)

Stevens Catalog No. 53 (1911)

receiver. There are other models including a Model 522 trap gun and the 525, 530, and 535 with increasing levels of engraving and stock quality (some straight grip) and fore grips.[6] Internally there is an inertial slide release block that is affixed to the inside of the receiver. This inertial release uses the recoil of a discharged round to unlock the breech. The action is designed to only unlock after firing or with use of the slide release and not by dry firing like many modern shotguns. All model 520s are only offered in 12 gauge until 1928.[7]

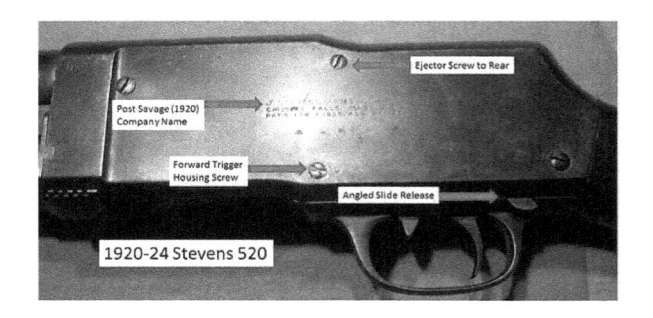

Stevens Model 520 (1920-1924)

Stevens halts civilian gun production in 1915 and teams up with New England Westinghouse to make Mosin-Nagant rifles for the Russian Czar during WWI. When the czar was deposed, the communists didn't pay the bill and Stevens went bankrupt. Around 1918 Stevens provided a 520 trench gun prototype to the US military. Supposedly several examples were made but no known examples survive. It had a unique two piece heat shield/bayonet lug.[8] Savage Arms buys them in 1920 and changes the company name from "J Stevens Arms & Tool Co" to "J Stevens Arms Company".

Production of the Model 520 resumes in 1920 incorporating several design changes that were emerging prior to 1915. These include a relocated slide release button, moved from the left side of the receiver to the left side of the trigger plate, and a redesigned inertial slide release, incorporated into the design of the trigger plate.

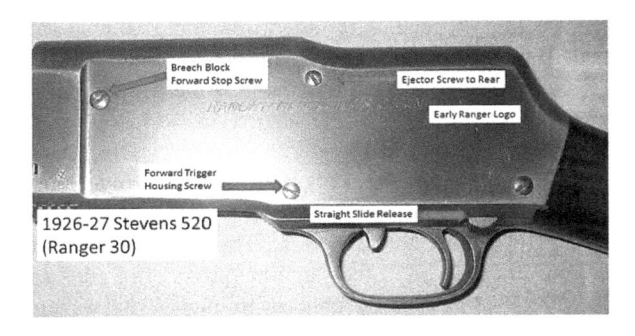

Stevens Model 520 (1926-1927)

In 1925 the Model 520 appears as a store branded gun when it is sold as the Ranger Repeater Model 30 by Sears[9] and the Western Field Model 30 by Montgomery Wards. Around this time the inertial slide release blocks are removed and replaced with a spring that provides forward pressure on the slide release. Guns made after this time can be unlocked after a dry fire with forward pressure on the slide.

In 1928 the first sub-gauge Model 520 is introduced when a 16 gauge option is offered.[10] It is followed in 1930 by a 20 gauge Model 520.[11]

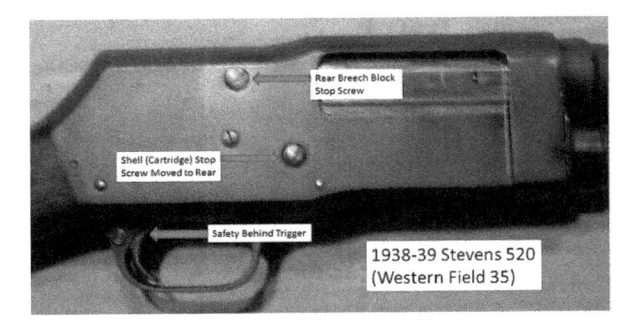

Stevens Model 520 (1938-1939)

The Model 520 last appears in a Stevens sales publication in 1928 and 1929 (Catalog #57)[3] but remains in full production until 1939.[12] During this time it is sold as a store branded gun and under Stevens' budget line Riverside Arms. The shotgun goes through several design changes during this period. Most notably is a redesign of the cartridge stop in 1932 and the relocation of the safety, from inside the trigger guard to behind the trigger in 1937.

Model 520 production ends in 1939 and it is replaced by the improved Model 520A in 1940.[13]

8.25.3 Model 520A

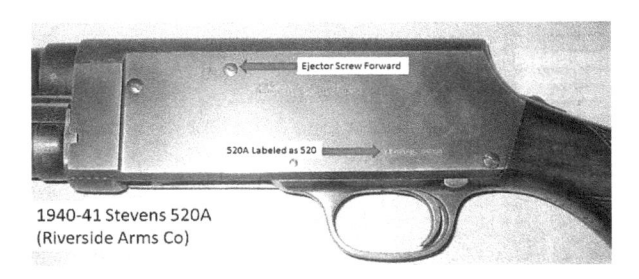

Stevens Model 520A (1940-1941)

The redesigned Model 520A is closely related to the Model 520, utilizing the same takedown action and locking breech block. The receiver looses the distinctive double hump and has a flat top and squared-off back end. The safety is moved to the receiver tang and the trigger housing is redesigned to use a coil mainspring instead of a flat bar mainspring. The 520A continues to be sold as a store branded gun and under Stevens' budget line Riverside Arms (stamped Model 520). The 520A is never shown in a Stevens sales publication, it only appears in Sears & Roebuck and Montgomery Wards catalogs and in Stevens component parts catalogs (the only source where it is identified as a 520A).[14]

Stevens halts civilian production in 1942 to make weapons for use by the US military during World War II (see Model 520-30 below). Civilian Model 520A production resumed after WWII, again as store branded guns, and continued until 1947.[15]

8.25.4 Model 620

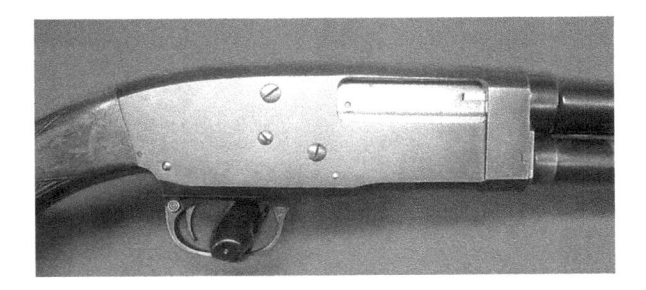

Stevens Model 620 (1938-39) 20Ga

The Model 620 was introduced in 1927 and is a streamlined version of the original 520. The safety was initially located inside the trigger housing just like the Model 520 but by 1929 it had been changed to a cross-bolt located behind the trigger. The stock is attached by a bolt connecting the receiver and trigger tangs through the grip of the stock. Initially the 620 is only offerd in 12 gauge but a 16 gauge follows in 1928 and a 20 gauge is introduced in 1930.

8.25.5 Model 620A

The Model 620A began production in 1940. The main difference between the 620 and the 620A is how the stock attaches. The 620A uses a long draw blot through the end of the stock and does away with the receiver and trigger plate tangs used on the 620. Without the trigger tang, a flat main spring has no place to attach and the 620A has a shortened trigger housing using a coil main spring. Civilian production of the Model 620A halts during World War II but continues afterwards until 1955.

8.25.6 Model 520-30 and 620A (US Military)

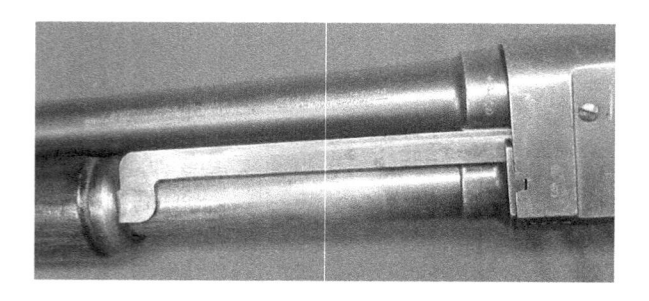

Stevens WWII Riot Gun Markings (M620A)

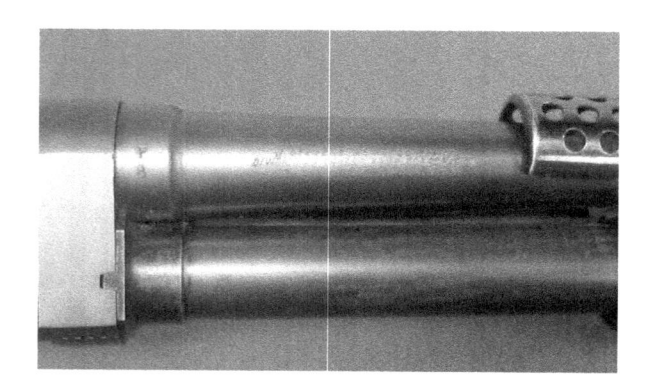

Stevens WWII Trench Gun Markings (M520-30)

During World War II, Stevens began producing both the Model 520A (renamed the Model 520-30) and the Model 620A (labeled as the Model 620) as trench guns, riot guns, and long-barreled training guns for the US military. Trench guns were produced with 20 inch barrels (cylinder bore) and had a heat shield with a unique pinkish anodized bayonet lug attached to the front of the barrel (late war examples have a small "S" stamped on the left side). The receivers of both models were stamped on the left side (from front to back) with a small "P" and ordnance bomb, "Model 520-30" or "Model 620", and a small "U.S." over the trigger. Model 520-30 trench gun barrels are marked "Proof Tested--12 Gauge -–2 3/4 Inch Chamber--" on the **left** side and have another small "P" and ordnance bomb and the "J Stevens Arms Company" address on the **right** side of the barrel. This was done so that all the markings could be read with the heat shield installed. Some Model 620 trench gun barrels are marked in the same manner as the Model 520-30 trench guns and some have all the barrel markings on the left side. Trench guns are also fitted with a sling swivel in the stock. Riot guns also have 20 inch barrels (cylinder bore) and have all the same martial markings, except that all the barrel markings are on the left side. The long barreled training guns are marked in the same manner as riot guns and were mainly used for aerial gunnery training. Total wartime production of all Model 520-30 shotguns was 33,306 and all Model 620 shotguns was 12,174.[16] After the war the US military standardized both the Model 520-30 and the Model 620 and kept them in the inventory. They were used in the Korean War and as late as the Vietnam War.[17]

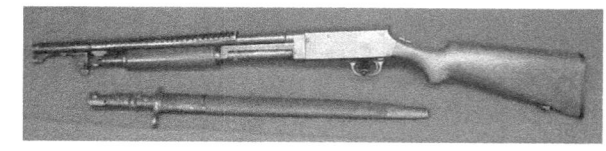

Stevens WWII M520-30 Trench Gun with M1917 Bayonet

8.25.7 References

[1] *Catalog No.52 (Revised Edition)*. J. Stevens Arms & Tool Co. 1909. pp. 91–98.

[2] *Sears & Roebuck Catalog*. Sears & Roebuck. 1909–1947. pp. Multiple pages spanning 38 years and 76 editions (Spring/Fall).

[3] *Stevens No. 57*. J. Stevens Arms Company. 1928. p. 29.

[4] *Stevens Rifles and Shotguns*. J. Stevens Arms Company. 1940. p. 7.

[5] *Savage, Stevens and Fox, Shotguns and Rifles*. Savage Arms Corporation. 1955. p. 11.

[6] *Stevens Firearms General Catalog No. 53*. J. Stevens Arms & Tool Company. 1911. pp. 4–8.

[7] *Stevens Catalogs 1909-1930*. J. Stevens Arms & Tool Company/J. Stevens Arms Company. 1909–1930. pp. Multiple.

[8] Canfield, Bruce (2007). *Complete Guide to US Military Combat Shotguns*. Mowbray Publishers Inc. pp. 47–48. ISBN 1-931464-28-6.

[9] *Sears & Roebuck Fall Catalog 1925*. Sears & Roebuck. p. 956.

[10] *Sears & Roebuck Catalog Fall 1928*. Sears & Roebuck. 1928. p. 587.

[11] *Sears & Roebuck Catalog Fall 1930*. Sears & Roebuck. 1930. p. 571.

[12] *Sears & Roebuck Catalog Fall 1939*. Sears & Roebuck. 1939. p. 950.

[13] *Sears & Roebuck Catalog Fall 1940*. Sears & Roebuck. 1940. p. 1064.

[14] *Component Parts List for Savage, Stevens, Fox Shotguns and Rifles 1951-52*. Savage Arms Corporation. 1951. p. 37.

[15] *Sears & Roebuck Catalog Fall 1947*. Sears & Roebuck. 1947. p. 584.

[16] Canfield, Bruce (2007). *Complete Guide to US Military Combat Shotguns*. Mowbray Publishers Inc. pp. 94–95, 117, 134–139. ISBN 1-931464-28-6.

[17] *Complete Guide to US Military Combat Shotguns*. p. 163.

8.26 Stevens Model 77E

The **Stevens Model 77E** was the most widely used shotgun of the Vietnam War. The Model 77E was a short-barreled pump-action shotgun known variously as the "trench" or "riot" shotgun. The Model 77E had noticeably shorter stocks than similar United State military shotguns built by Ithaca Gun Company, Remington Arms, and Winchester Repeating Arms Company. These short stocks were intended to accommodate South Vietnamese soldiers, and the Model 77E was the first United States combat shotgun equipped with a rubber recoil pad. Model 77E shotguns were Parkerized with sling swivels and wooden stocks. Receivers were marked "U.S." and "p" proofmarks appeared on both barrels and receivers.[1]

A few prototypes were fitted with bayonet adapters, but none are known to have been issued. A few Stevens Model 69R shotguns also saw service during the Vietnam War. The Model 77E gave satisfactory service, but proved less durable than the Ithaca Model 37. Breakage at the point of attachment of the buttstock to the receiver was the most common complaint.[1]

8.26.1 References

[1] Canfield, Bruce N. "Combat Shotguns of the Vietnam War" *American Rifleman* March 2002 pp.44-47&92-95

[2] DK Publishing (Dorling Kindersley) *Gun* Penguin (2012) ISBN 146540354X p.253

8.27 TOZ-194

The **TOZ-194** is a 12 Gauge, pump-action shotgun manufactured by the Tula Arms Plant.[2] Designed during the later years of the Soviet Union, the production of this firearm has started after the Soviet era in Russia, and since then it has gained a certain popularity within civilian shooters in Russia itself and in Europe, and is reported to be in use with some Russian Security forces.

The TOZ-194 is a conventional pump-action shotgun that feeds from a 7-rounds tube and chambers 70 mm shotgun shells ("Standard" $2^3/_4$" 12-gauge, therefore the use of 76 mm (3 inches) "Magnum" shells is strongly counterindicated). Its main feature is its 540 mm (21.2 inches approx.) barrel, which is oddly long for a combat shotgun; this was done to reach an overall length of 805 mm (31.6 inches approx.) which makes it legal for civilian ownership in Russia.

8.27.1 Variants

Four variants of the TOZ-194 shotgun are available on the market: the **TOZ-194M** with sole pistol grip; the **TOZ-194-01M** with pistol grip and upfolding metal stock, and muzzle adapters available for tactical applications; the **TOZ-194-02M** and **TOZ-194-03M**, both with standard fixed stock, the latter one also available with muzzle adapter.

8.27.2 Notes

[1] BELLUM - TOZ-194

[2] Tulsky Oruzheiny Zavod

[3] without muzzle adapters

[4] length with stock

8.27.3 See also

- List of Russian weaponry

8.27.4 External links

- Tulsky oruzheiny zavod (TOZ - Tula Armory)
- (TOZ-194 shotgun page in English on the manufacturer's website)

8.28 UTAS UTS-15

The **UTAS UTS-15** is a bullpup 12 gauge pump-action shotgun with two 7-round magazine tubes that can feed in an alternating or selecting pattern. The UTS-15 has a 28.3" overall length with an 18.5" barrel, chambered for 2½", 2¾", and 3" magnum ammunition. Constructed primarily of fiber reinforced injection molded polymer, the UTS-15 weighs 6.9 lbs. Additionally, there is a top mounted picatinny rail for the mounting of a wide variety of both iron and optical sights, coupled with Beretta style barrel threading for choke tubes.[1]

8.28.1 Background

The UTS-15 was developed as a result of a request to UTAS made by Smith & Wesson in 2006 to develop "the ultimate police shotgun". Smith & Wesson's criteria for the shotgun were: 12 Gauge, pump-action, less than 30" overall length, and 13-round minimum capacity.[2]

8.28.2 Features

The following features are standard on all UTS-15 models:

- **Bullpup design:** pistol grip and trigger are located forward of the barrel breech and action assembly. This allows for the same barrel length as a traditional shotgun but shortens the overall length of the weapon.[3]
- **Top mounted picatinny rail:** allows for the mounting of a wide variety of iron and optical sights.
- **Twin magazine tubes:** set above the barrel to allow for easy access to the loading ports.
- **Alternating or select tube feed:** a selector switch located on the top of the tube/barrel assembly allows for use of multiple ammo types (i.e.: buckshot and birdshot; buckshot and rubber pellets; etc.).
- **Built-in laser/light controls:** the right side of the grip is reserved for controls (a button) for controlling the optional light and laser assembly.
- **Threaded barrel:** Beretta-style barrel threading for choke tubes allows the UTS-15 to be adapted for any situation and a range of attachments.[4]

Accessories and optional equipment for the UTS-15 (as listed by UTAS USA):

- **Front and rear sight assembly:** machined from a solid billet of 7000 series ordinance aluminium with matte black anodized finish these sights are elevation and windage adjustable.[5]
- **Tactical Choke Tube:** machined from 4140 ordinance grade steel and matte black oxide finished. This choke features muzzle spikes and gas ports for breeching. Also considered a choked cylinder it can be used for firing slugs as well as buck shot.[6]
- **7.5" Barrel Extension:** machined from 4140 ordnance grade steel with a matte black oxide finish. This attachment is threaded to screw into the UTS-15 barrel (like the Tactical Choke Tube).[7]
- **Red Laser/Flashlight Unit:** the laser/flashlight unit is specially designed for the UTS-15 shotgun. The flashlight casts a 200 lumen lens focused beam when switched on (using the integrated control button on the grip). The laser is high-intensity and adjustable for both windage and elevation. The machined aluminum housing for the laser/flashlight holds two lithium batteries and is specifically designed to slide into the barrel retaining tube in the lower stock below the barrel where it is held in place by the barrel retaining cap. The UTAS provided set comes with the necessary equipment for mounting the assembly into the shotgun.[8]

8.28.3 Variants

- **UTS-15 Desert**: features a digitized camo pattern used by both American and NATO forces. Incorporates a desert sand base coat over which the two-color non-glare digital camouflage pattern is applied.[9]
- **UTS-15 Marine**: features a digitized camo pattern which incorporates a marine blue base coat over which the black and gray non-glare digital camouflage pattern is applied. The springs have a corrosion resistant coating and all exposed metal parts are satin nickel plated to be resistant to saltwater. All other metal parts, such as the barrel are black chromed or similarly treated to further increase saltwater corrosion resistance.[10]
- **UTS-15 Hunting**: features a hunting-style camouflage pattern.[11]

8.28.4 Critical Reception and Malfunctions

Due to its unique design the UTS 15 became an easily recognizable weapon within the firearms culture and was reviewed by several different sources. However, over time the UTS 15 became the subject of harsh criticism in the firearms industry developing a reputation for being plagued by numerous malfunctions (primarily failure to feed and failure to extract). UTAS attempted to correct these issues by developing a generation 2 and generation 3 variant of the UTS 15 that were supposed to correct the reliability issue.

8.28.5 See also

- List of bullpup firearms
- List of shotguns
- Kel-Tec KSG
- Neostead

8.28.6 In popular culture

In Jurassic World, ACU(Asset Containment Unit) trooper Miller fires his UTS-15 at escaped *Indominus rex* to cover other troopers, but eventually was eaten. It was also in the popular first-person-shooter video game Call of Duty Ghosts by Activision. As well as the popular first-person-shooter Battlefield 4 by EA DICE. It's also in the Walking Dead.

8.28.7 References

[1]

[2] 2012 NRA Annual Meetings: UTS-15 Polymer Tactical Shotgun

[3] http://world.guns.ru/shotgun/tr/shotgun-utas-uts-15-e.html\char"0022\relax{}WorldGuns".

[4] http://utas-usa.com/product.aspx?id=12

[5] http://utas-usa.com/product.aspx?id=5

[6] http://utas-usa.com/product.aspx?id=7

[7] http://utas-usa.com/product.aspx?id=8

[8] http://utas-usa.com/product.aspx?id=10

[9]

[10]

[11]

8.29 Valtro PM-5/PM-5-350

The **Valtro PM-5** is an Italian pump-action shotgun manufactured by Valtro.

Shotgun, PM-5 rifle was developed by the Italian company Valtro used by various police and military forces, including the French Navy. The PM-5 is almost unique in that it has a removable magazine, the magazine greatly improves the time and the balance of the charge.The Valtro PM-5 is available with either a fixed stock or a folding stock. The power system PM-5 is conventional, manually operated. The tube under the barrel serves as a guide for scrolling. The loader 7 rounds, plus one in the chamber.

They are reportedly actually manufactured by Benelli. Import has been banned for several years now but are used in Europe by numerous Security forces. It is unusual in that it takes a detachable box magazine. Both 7- and 10-round magazines have been manufactured, although the 7-round magazine is much more common.

Renowned for their simplicity, lightweight and reliability, this pump action 12 GA shotgun has sold on the US market for as much as $1200.00. Currently PM-5 model produced by Brixia Shotgun in Italy. A company that bought Valtro Brand after it declare bankruptcy. In Canada, Brixia Shotguns and famous Valtro PM-5, distributed by Savminter Enterprises.

8.29.1 See also

- pump-action
- shotgun

8.29.2 External links

- Modern Weapons—Valtro PM-5
- Brixia/Valtro PM-5

8.30 Winchester Model 1200

The **Model 1200** and **Model 1300** are two pump-action shotguns that are manufactured by the Winchester-Western Division of Olin Corporation. It was produced in 12-, 16- and 20-gauge. The military version of the 1200 has the ability to have a bayonet fixed on the end of the barrel to be used in close quarter combat. It is a takedown type shotgun which means it has the capability of being taken apart for easy transportation and storage.[1]

8.30.1 History

The Winchester Model 1200 was introduced in 1964 as a low-cost replacement for the venerable Model 12.[2] A small number of these weapons were acquired by the United States Army in 1968 and 1969.[3] The military style Model 1200 was essentially the same weapon as the civilian version, except it had a ventilated handguard, sling swivels, and a bayonet lug.[3] The Model 1200 was succeeded by the Winchester Model 1300 in 1983 when U.S. Repeating Arms Company became the manufacturer of Winchester firearms.[1] Production of the Model 1300 ceased in 2006, when USRAC went bankrupt.[4]

8.30.2 Description

The Winchester Model 1200 came in barrel lengths of 30-inch, and 28-inch with a fixed choke or the Win-choke screw in choke tubes system and is a 12, 16, or 20-gauge, manually operated, slide action shotgun. The slide action, also known as a pump-action, means that the shotgun has a moving bolt system which is operated by a "wooden or composite slide called the fore-end".[5] The fore-end is located on the underside of the barrel and moves front to back. The weapon can hold a maximum of five rounds total with four in the tubular magazine and one in the chamber. It has a hammerless action which means that there is no external hammer spur. There is only a firing pin which strikes the primer on the shell to ignite the powder in the round. The Model 1200 is a takedown type of shotgun; it can be taken apart for easy storage and transportation.[6]

The Model 1200 was the first shotgun to utilize a rotary bolt with four locking lugs secured within the barrel extension. The 1200 was Winchester's first shotgun to incorporate the company's patented Winchoke system, a quick change tube to allow the easy replacement of chokes.[1]

8.30.3 Bayonet

A bayonet could be attached to the front end of the barrel of the Military version of the Model 1200. The primary uses of the bayonet on the model 1200 are for close combat, guarding prisoners, and riot duty.[6] The most commonly used bayonet with the Model 1200 was the M1917 bayonet. After World War I ended, there was a large surplus of the M-1917 bayonets because the Army decided to keep the M1903 Springfield as the standard issued rifle. The M-1917 bayonet did not fit the Springfield rifles so instead of just getting rid of them, the Army decided to make newer shotguns compatible with the bayonets.[7]

8.30.4 Variants

- **Model 1200**: Standard capacity model with four-shell tubular magazine
- **Model 1200 Defender**: Increased capacity model with six-shell tubular magazine (Six 3" Shells or seven 2&3/4" Shells).
- **Model 1200 Police**: Increased capacity variant of the Model 1200 Defender with an electrolysis nickel plated satin barrel and magazine tube.
- **Model 1200 Marine**: Increased capacity variant of the Model 1200 Defender with an electrolysis nickel plated polished barrel and magazine tube.
- **Model 1200 Riot**: Standard capacity model with 18.5" barrel and rifle sights. Blued steel barrel and magazine. Marked "Riot" on barrel.
- **Ted Williams Model 200**: Standard Model 1200 marketed by Sears
- **Model 1200 Hunting**: 28-inch barrel with a built-in choke and a five-shell tubular magazine.
- **Model 1300**: Slightly updated version with five-shell tubular magazine
- **Model 1300 Defender**: Increased capacity variants of the Model 1300 with a seven-shell tubular magazine.
- **Model 1300 Marine**: Increased capacity variant of the Model 1300 with an electroless nickel plated barrel and magazine tube.
- Various Model 1300 variants[8][9]
- **Model 2200**: Model 1200 with full length stock and barrel, produced for the Canadian firearms market.
- **Model 120**: Budget version marketed at various department stores, such as K-Mart. Birch stock, fixed choke, etc.
- **Ranger Model 120**: Budget version marketed at sporting goods stores, such as K-Mart. Plain stock, Winchoke, etc.

8.30.5 Users

- Czech Republic: The Model 1300 Defender is used in small numbers by the Czech Armed Forces.[10]
- Peru - The Model 1300 Defender is used by special forces[11]

- 🇷🇺 Russia - since 14 August 1992[12] until March 2006[13] Winchester 1300 shotguns were used in private security companies[14]
- 🇺🇸 United States[15]

The Model 12 Ranger (note correction in name order) is a smaller/youth version of the Model 120.

8.30.6 See also

- List of shotguns

8.30.7 References

[1] Wilson, R. L. (2008). *Winchester: An American Legend*. Book Sales, Inc. pp. 223–265. ISBN 978-0-7858-1893-9.

[2] Criss, Chuck (2008-05-28). "Winchester Repeating". olive-drab.com. Retrieved 2010-04-16.

[3] Criss, Chuck (2008-05-22). "WINCHESTER 1200 SHOTGUN". Olive-drab.com. Retrieved 2010-04-16.

[4] Hunter, Stephen (2006-01-21). "Out With A Bang". Washington Post. Retrieved 2010-04-05.

[5] Coustan, Dave. "How Shotguns Work". HowStuffWorks.com. Retrieved 2010-04-17.

[6] Westmoreland, William (1970-03-11). "Winchester Model 1200 Riot Shotgun Manual". U.S. Government Printing Office. Retrieved 2010-04-16.

[7] Criss, Chuck (2008-05-22). "M-1917 BAYONET". Olive-drab.com. Retrieved 2010-04-16.

[8] Winchester Repeating Firearms. "IWinchester Firearms timeline". Winchester Repeating Arms. Retrieved 2010-04-15.

[9] Winchester Repeating Firearms. "IWinchester 1200 and Model 130 comparison". Winchester Repeating Arms. Retrieved 2010-04-15.

[10] "zbrane.indd" (PDF). Retrieved 2010-04-16.

[11] Julio A. Montes. Peruvian Small Arms Gunning for the Shining Path // "Small Arms Defence Journal", № 8, 2011

[12] Постановление Правительства Российской Федерации № 587 от 14 августа 1992 года "Вопросы частной детективной и охранной деятельности"

[13] "3. Установить, что огнестрельное оружие, приобретенное в соответствии с законодательством Российской Федерации негосударственными (частными) охранными предприятиями до вступления в силу настоящего постановления и не включенное в перечень видов вооружения охранников, утвержденный постановлением Правительства Российской Федерации от 14 августа 1992 г. N 587 (с изменениями, внесенными настоящим постановлением), может находиться на вооружении охранников до 1 марта 2006 г."
Постановление Правительства РФ № 179 от 4 апреля 2005

[14] "в 1995 году... охранники московского охранного бюро "Алекс" В. Смирнов и А. Утехин, возвращаясь из служебной командировки, распили спиртные напитки с неизвестными лицами. В результате, были утрачены пистолет ПМ ье "Winchester-1300""
Виктор Микляев. Не верьте "Грифону"! // "Частный сыск. Охрана. Безопасность" № 10, 1995, стр.10-11

[15] Canfield, Bruce N. *American Rifleman* (March 2002) pp.44-47&92-95

8.30.8 External links

- Model 1200 Field Strip Guide on BATTLETONE.com

8.31 Winchester Model 1897

The **Winchester Model 1897**, also known as the **Model 97**, **M97**, or **Trench Gun**, was a pump-action shotgun with an external hammer and tube magazine manufactured by the Winchester Repeating Arms Company. The Model 1897 was an evolution of the Winchester Model 1893 designed by John Browning. From 1897 until 1957, over one million of these shotguns were produced. The Model 1897 was offered in numerous barrel lengths and grades, chambered in 12 and 16 gauge, and as a solid frame or takedown. The 16-gauge guns had a standard barrel length of 28 inches, while 12-gauge guns were furnished with 30-inch length barrels. Special length barrels could be ordered in lengths as short as 20 inches, and as long as 36 inches. Since the time the Model 1897 was first manufactured it has been used by American soldiers,[1] police departments,[2] and hunters.[2]

8.31.1 History

The Winchester Model 1897 was designed by the famous American firearms inventor John Moses Browning. The Model 1897 was first listed for sale in the November 1897 Winchester catalog as a 12 gauge solid frame. However, the 12 gauge takedown was added in October 1898, and the 16 gauge takedown in February 1900.[3] Originally produced as a tougher, stronger and more improved version of the Winchester 1893, itself a takeoff on the early Spencer pump gun, the 1897 was identical to its forerunner, except that the receiver was thicker and allowed for use of smokeless powder shells, which were not common at the time. The 1897 introduced a "take down" design, where the barrel could be taken off; a standard in pump shotguns made today, like the Remington 870 and Mossberg 500 series. Over time, "the model 97 became the most popular shotgun on the American market and established a standard of performance by which other kinds and makes of shotguns were judged, including the most expensive imported articles".[2] The Winchester Model 1897 was in production from 1897 until 1957. It was in this time frame that the "modern" hammerless designs became common, like the Winchester Model 1912 and the Remington 870 and the Model 1897 was superseded by the Winchester Model 1912.[4] However, the gun can still be found today in regular use.

Improvements From the 1893

In the new Model 1897, many of the weaknesses that were present in the Model 93 were taken into account and remedied.[3] These improvements included:

- The frame was strengthened and made longer to handle a 12 gauge 2¾-inch shell, as well as the 2⅝-inch shell.[3]

- The frame at the top was covered so that the ejection of the fired shell was entirely from the side.[3] This added a great amount of strength to the frame of the gun and it allowed the use of a 2¾ inch shell without the danger of the gun constantly jamming.[5]

- The gun could not be opened until a slight forward movement of the slide handle released the action slide lock. In firing, the recoil of the gun gave a slight forward motion to the slide handle and released the action slide lock which enabled immediate opening of the gun. In the absence of any recoil, the slide handle had to be pushed forward manually in order to release the action slide lock.[3]

- A movable cartridge guide was placed on the right side of the carrier block to prevent the escape of the shell when the gun was turned sideways in the act of loading.[3]

- The stock was made longer and with less drop.[3]

Of the improvements, the slide lock is the one that really made the gun safer. This improved slide lock kept the gun locked until actual firing occurred which prevented the gun from jamming in the case of a misfire. The slide lock "stands in such a relation to the body of the firing pin as will prevent the firing pin reaching the primer until the pin has moved forward a sufficient distance to insure locking of the breech bolt."[6] This prevents the action sleeve "from being retracted by the hand of the gunner until after firing, and hence rendering the fire arm more safe"[7]

8.31.2 Description

Open action on an 1897 portraying the long slide that projects from the receiver.

The Winchester Model 1897 evolved from the Winchester Model 1893. The Model 1897 and 1893 were both designed by John Browning. The Model 1897 is an external hammer shotgun lacking a trigger disconnector. This means that the user can hold the trigger down while cycling the shotgun and once the action is returned to battery the gun fires.[8] The gun itself is classified as a slide action pump shotgun. It was the first truly successful pump-action shotgun produced. Throughout the time period the Model 1897 was in production, over a million of the type were produced in various grades and barrel lengths. 16-gauge guns had a standard barrel length of 28 inches, while 12-gauge guns were furnished with 30-inch length barrels. Special length barrels could be ordered in lengths as short as 20 inches, and as long as 36 inches. Along with various grades and barrel lengths, the Model 1897 came in two different chamberings. One was the 12 gauge and the other was the 16 gauge.[8] The shells should be of the 2-¾ inch or 2-⅝ inch model.[3] Any shells larger are not recommended. An average Model 1897 held 5 shotgun shells in the magazine tube. After including the one shell that could be held in the chamber, the average Model 1897 held a total of 6 shotgun shells. However, this would vary from grade to grade.[9] When working the action of the Model 1897 the fore end is racked and a long slide comes out of the receiver and ejects the spent shell while simultaneously cocking the external hammer. This is why the gun is classified as a slide action pump shotgun.

The Chinese company Norinco has made an effort to reproduce this firearm. The Norinco 97 is an almost exact copy of the Winchester 1897, produced in both Trench and Riot grades, yet lacking in the fit and finish of the originals.[1]

Model 1897 (trench grade) and the reproduced Norinco (riot grade)

Grades of the Model 97

Original Prices

When the Model 1897 was first introduced, the price depended upon what grade was being purchased and what features were being added to that specific gun. To purchase a plain finished shotgun would cost the buyer $25. Whereas to have an engraved receiver with checkered and finer wood included, it would cost $100.[8] The more expensive grades of the Model 1897 were the standard, trap, pigeon, and tournament grades. These were the grades that were normally equipped with an engraved receiver and with checkered, finer wood.[4][14] The less expensive and plainer grades were the Brush, Brush Takedown, Riot, and Trench. These grades were not given the higher valued wood or special designs.[4][14] This is because these guns were designed and built for hard abuse. These grades stood a higher chance of being badly damaged so there was no need to put extra money into them for appearance purposes. As the functions that were performed with these grades required them to be lightweight it was not beneficial to use heavy and expensive wood when designing them. Most often, when these grades were purchased, they were purchased in high numbers. By designing these grades with standard wood and finish, it kept the prices at a lower level.[4][14]

8.31.3 Military use

The Model 1897 was popular before World War I, but it was after the war broke out that sales of the Model 1897 picked up. This was because many were produced to meet the demands of the Military. When the United States entered World War I, there was a need for more service weapons to be issued to the troops. It became clear to the United States just how brutal trench warfare was, and how great the need was for a large amount of close-range firepower while fighting in a trench, after they had observed the war for the first three years.[1] The Model 1897 Trench grade was an evolution of this idea. The pre-existing Winchester Model 1897 was modified by adding a perforated steel heat shield over the barrel which protected the hand of the user from the barrel when it became over-heated,[15] and an adapter with bayonet lug for affixing an M1917 bayonet.[1]

Winchester Model 1897 Trench Gun

Model 1897 adapter that allowed the attachment of the M1917 bayonet

This model was ideal for close combat and was efficient in trench warfare due to its 20 inch cylinder bore barrel. Buckshot ammunition was issued with the trench grade during the war. Each round of this ammunition contained nine 00 (.33-caliber) buckshot pellets. This gave considerable firepower to the individual soldier by each round that was fired.[2] This shorter barrel and large amount of firepower is what made this grade ideal for trench warfare. The Model 1897 was used by American troops for other purposes in World War I other than a force multiplier. American soldiers who were skilled at trap shooting were armed with these guns and stationed where they could fire at enemy hand grenades in midair.[2] This would deflect the grenades from falling into the American trenches and therefore protect American soldiers.[2]

Unlike most modern pump-action shotguns, the Winchester Model 1897 (versions of which were type classified as the Model 97 or M97 for short) fired each time the action closed with the trigger depressed (that is, it lacks a trigger disconnector). Coupled with its six-shot capacity made it effective for close combat, such that troops referred to it as a "trench sweeper". This characteristic allowed troops to fire the whole magazine with great speed. The Model 1897 was so effective, and feared, that the German government protested (in vain) to have it outlawed in combat.[16] The Model 1897 was used in limited numbers during World War II by the United States Army and Marine Corps, although it was largely superseded by the similarly militarized version of the hammerless Model 1912.

Other military uses of the shotgun included "the execution of security/interior guard operations, rear area security operations, guarding prisoners of war, raids, ambushes, military operations in urban terrain, and selected special operations."[16]

8.31.4 World War I protests

Although the Model 1897 was popular with American troops in World War I, the Germans soon began to protest its use in combat. "On 19 September 1918, the German government issued a diplomatic protest against the American use of shotguns, alleging that the shotgun was prohibited by the law of war."[16] A part of the German protest read that "[i]t is especially forbidden to employ arms, projections, or materials calculated to cause unnecessary suffering" as defined in the 1907 Hague Convention on Land Warfare.[2] This is the only known occasion in which the legality of actual combat use of the shotgun has been raised.[16] However, the United States interpreted their use of the shotgun differently than Germany. The Judge Advocate General of the Army, Secretary of State Robert Lansing carefully considered and reviewed the applicable law and promptly rejected the German protest.[16] France and Britain considered using shotguns as trench warfare weapons during World War I. The shotgun in question was a double-barreled shotgun, which was not used because they were unable to obtain high powered ammunition and that type of gun is slow to reload in close combat.[16]

German Response

The rejection of their protest greatly upset the German forces, because they believed they were treated unjustly in the war. Shortly after the protest was rejected, Germany issued threats that they would punish all captured American soldiers that were found to be armed with a shotgun.[2] This led to the United States issuing a retaliation threat, stating that any measures unjustly taken against captured American soldiers would lead to an equal act by the United States on captured German soldiers.[17]

8.31.5 Other uses

After the war, a shorter-barrelled version of the Model 1897 was marketed by Winchester as a riot gun. Messengers of The American Express Company were armed with this weapon as were various police departments throughout the US.[2] The differences between this riot version and the trench version were the riot version lacked the heat shield and bayonet lug,[1] and all trench guns were equipped with sling swivels, whereas most riot guns were not.[8]

8.31.6 See also

- List of individual weapons of the U.S. Armed Forces
- List of shotguns

8.31.7 References

[1] Davis (2006)

[2] Williamson (1952) p. 158.

[3] Henshaw (1993) p. 49.

[4] Miller (2005) p. 694, Miller.

[5] Farrow (1904) p. 335

[6] Smith (1911) p. 5

[7] Smith (1911) p. 4

[8] Hager (2005)

[9] Farrow (1904) p. 337

[10] Wilson (2008) pp.214-219

[11] Miller (2006) p. 98

[12] Miller (2006) p. 99

[13] Wilson(2008). p.220

[14] Carmichel (1986) p. 78-79

[15] Lewis (2007) p. 162

[16] Parks (1997)

[17] Williamson (1952) p. 159.

8.31.8 Bibliography

- Boorman, Dean K. (2001). *History of Winchester Firearms*. The Lyons Press. ISBN 978-1-58574-307-0.

- Carmichel, Jim (1986). *Guns and Shooting, 1986*. Times Mirror Magazines, Incorporated, Book Division. pp. 78–79. ISBN 978-0-943822-58-7.

- Lewis, Jack; Robert K. Campbell; David Steele (2007). *The Gun Digest Book of Assault Weapons* (7th ed.). Krause Publications. p. 162. Retrieved 2010-04-20.

- Miller, David (2006). *The History of Browning Firearms*. First Lyons Press Edition. pp. 98–99. Retrieved 2010-04-19.

- Miller, David (2005). *The Illustrated Directory of Guns*. Collin Gower Enterprises Ltd. p. 694. ISBN 0-681-06685-7.

- Davis, Phil (2006-08-07). "Sangamon County Rifle Association Winchester Model 1897". Retrieved 2010-01-23.

- Farrow, Edward S. (1904). *American Small Arms*. New York: The Bradford Company. pp. 335–337. Retrieved 2010-04-20.

- Henshaw, Thomas. *The History of Winchester Firearms* (6th ed.). Winchester Press, 1993. pp. 48–50.

- Parks, W. Hays (1997). "October 1997 The Army Lawyer". Retrieved 2010-04-10.

- Smith, Morris F. (1911-12-14). "United States Patent Office". PIBEABM Patent Search. pp. 4–5. Retrieved 2010-03-20.

- Williamson, Harold F. (1952). *Winchester* (1st ed.). Washington DC: Combat Forces. pp. 158–159.

- Wilson, R. L. (2008). *Winchester: An American Legend*. New York: Book Sales, Inc. pp. 214–220. ISBN 978-0-7858-1893-9.

8.31.9 External links

- Olive-Drab: Winchester Model 97 Shotgun

8.32 Winchester Model 1912

The **Winchester Model 1912** (also commonly known as the **Model 12**, or **M12**) is an internal-hammer, pump-action, shotgun with an external tube magazine. Popularly-named the *Perfect Repeater* at its introduction, it largely set the standard for pump action shotguns over its 51 year high-rate production life. From August 1912 until first discontinued by Winchester in May 1964, nearly two million Model 12 shotguns were produced in various grades and barrel lengths. Initially chambered for 20 gauge only, the 12 and 16 gauge versions came out in 1913 (first listed in the 1914 catalogs), and the 28 gauge version came out in 1934. A .410 version was never produced; instead, a scaled-down version of the Model 12 known as the **Model 42**, directly derived from scaled drawings of the Model 12, was produced in .410 .

8.32.1 Description

The Model 1912 (shortened to Model 12 in 1919) was the next step from the Winchester Model 1897 hammer-fired shotgun, which in turn had evolved from the earlier Winchester Model 1893 shotgun. The Model 12 was designed by Winchester engineer T.C. Johnson, and was based in part on the M1893/97 design by John M. Browning, in that it used a sliding forearm or "pump action" to cycle the mechanism. It was initially available in 20 gauge only (12 and 16 gauge guns were not sold until late 1913). The Model 12 was the first truly successful internal hammer pump-action shotgun ever produced. Its tubular magazine was loaded through the bottom of the gun. Empty shotgun shells ejected to the right. Depending on the particular wooden plug installed in the magazine, two, three, or four shells could be stored in the tubular magazine. The magazine holds six 2¾-inch 12 ga. shells, when no plug is installed, unlike most shotguns of today which hold four or five shells. With forged and machined steel parts, the ultimate reason for discontinuation in 1964 was that it was too expensive to produce at a competitive price. The primary competition at this time came from the much less expensive Remington Model 870, which had been introduced in 1950. The majority of "modern" Model 12 shotguns manufactured after 1927 were chambered for 2¾-inch shotgun shells only, although some specialized models such as the Heavy Duck Gun Model 12 were chambered for 3" Super Speed and Super X shells (basically a 3" magnum). The early 20 gauge Model 12 guns had chambers that were 2½", and the 16 gauge Model 12's were chambered for a 2 9/16-inch shotgun shell. To add further confusion, some of these early Model 12's have subsequently been modified, with their chambers lengthened to accept 2¾-inch shotgun shells, while others remain in their factory-stock chamber lengths. Careful inspection by a gunsmith is always recommended to determine whether or not it is safe to fire a modern 2¾-inch shotgun shell in older Model 12's.

Special production examples were produced by Winchester, the U.S. Repeating Arms Company, and Miroku after 1964 through 2006 through specialized gun collector purchase programs, but the Perfect Repeater shotgun was never mass-produced after 1964. The U.S. Repeating Arms Company (a subsidiary of F.N.) announced a complete closing of the New Haven, Connecticut factory facility in January 2006, thus ending the Model 12's long and illustrious career at the age of 95 years.

8.32.2 Military use

The United States armed forces used various versions of the Model 12 in World War I, World War II, Korea, and in the early part of the Vietnam War, until inventory was exhausted after the Model 12's initial production ceased in 1964. Versions of the Model 12 were type classified as the **Model 12** or **M12** for short. Approximately 20,000 Model 12 trench guns were purchased by the US Army in World War I, differing from the civilian version by having a shorter barrel, a perforated steel heat shield, and a M1917 bayonet adapter.

Winchester Model 12 Trench Gun

More than 80,000 Model 12 shotguns were purchased during World War II by the United States Marine Corps, Army Air Forces, and Navy, mostly for use in the Pacific theater. Riot gun versions of the Model 12, lacking the heat shield and bayonet, were purchased by the Army for use in defending bases and in protecting Air Forces aircraft against saboteurs when parked. The Navy similarly purchased and used the riot gun version for protecting Navy ships and personnel while in foreign ports. The Marine Corps used the trench gun version of the Model 12 to great success in taking Japanese-occupied islands in the Pacific. The primary difference in Model 12 shotguns between the World War II trench gun version versus the World War I trench gun version was that the original design, containing six rows of holes in the perforated heat shield, was reduced to only four rows during 1942.

During the Korean War, the Marines used the Model 12 extensively. Likewise, the Marines and Army used the Model 12 during the early part of the Vietnam War, until, due to the Model 12's production ending in 1963, and the high rate of wartime use, the Model 12 shotguns in inventory were consumed. The Ithaca 37 soon filled the void caused by the end of the Model 12's production, especially among U.S. Navy SEALS.

Unlike most modern pump-action shotguns, the Winchester Model 12 had no trigger disconnector. Like the earlier Model 1897, it too fired each time the action closed with the trigger depressed. That and its 6-shot capacity made it effective for close-combat. As fast as one could pump the action, another shot would be fired.

See List of individual weapons of the U.S. Armed Forces

8.32.3 See also

- Combat shotgun
- Riot shotgun
- List of shotguns
- Winchester Model 1897

8.32.4 References

- Fawcett, Bill. *Hunters & Shooters: An Oral History of the U.S. Navy SEALS in Vietnam*. NY: Avon Books, 1995. ISBN 0-380-72166-X, pp. 79–80, especially.
- "Give Us More Shotguns!" by Bruce N. Canfield, *American Rifleman*, May 2004
- "Sequence of Take-down and Assembly Operations Model 12 Slide Action Repeating Shotgun", A. A. Arnold, Olin, Winchester-Western Division, New Haven, CT, October 1957

8.32.5 External links

- GlobalSecurity.org – Military use of shotguns

Chapter 9

Revolver Shotguns

9.1 Armsel Striker

The **Armsel Striker** also known as the **Sentinel Arms Co Striker-12**, **Protecta** and **Protecta Bulldog** is a 12-gauge shotgun with a revolving cylinder that was designed for riot control and combat.

9.1.1 History

The Armsel Striker was designed by a Rhodesian national, Hilton R. Walker, in 1981. Walker subsequently emigrated to South Africa, bringing with him the design for the Striker shotgun. His shotgun became a success, and was exported to various parts of the world. Even though it was successful, the shotgun still had its flaws. The rotary cylinder-type magazine was bulky, had a slow reload time, and the basic action was not without certain flaws.[2]

Walker redesigned his weapon in 1989, removing the cylinder rotation mechanism, and adding an auto cartridge ejection system. The new shotgun was named the *Protecta*.[3][4]

A copy of the Striker was made by US gunmaker, Cobray and marketed as the SWD Street Sweeper from 1989 through 1993.[5]

9.1.2 Design and features

The weapon's action is similar to that of a revolver, using a rotating magazine. Since the Striker uses a conventional double action only trigger and a very large and heavy cylinder (compared to handguns), Walker added a pre-wound clock-work spring to revolve the magazine which proved to make loading the weapon slow. The design was changed into having a cocking lever on the right side of the barrel.[2][6]

The first designs were criticized as having a slow and cumbersome firing mechanism. The shells had to be individually loaded and then the drum wound by a clockwork mechanism. Shell ejection was by an ejector rod along the right hand side of the barrel. The last version has the clockwork winding mechanism removed, the ejector rod has been replaced by an automatic ejection system and in the rod's place is a cocking lever that winds the drum automatically. The Striker design has a twelve round magazine capacity and short overall length. Compact variants have 7 rounds.[2][6][7]

9.1.3 Availability in the USA

The Striker and Streetsweeper were declared destructive devices under the National Firearms Act with no sporting purpose by Treasury Secretary Lloyd Bentsen in 1994 and their transfer and ownership is regulated by the Bureau of Alcohol, Tobacco, Firearms and Explosives (ATF).[8]

9.1.4 Variants

- Armsel Striker—this is Hilton Walker's first design.

- Armsel Protecta—An improved version of the Armsel Striker. Readying the weapon for firing was simplified and the weapon's reliability was improved.[3]

- Armsel Protecta Bulldog—An extremely shortened, stockless version of the Armsel Protecta. It is intended for building entry and vehicular duties.[3]

- Sentinel Arms Striker-12—A fully licensed and improved copy of the Armsel Striker for the American market made by Sentinel Arms Co. It was available with an 18 inch barrel and a 7 inch stockless version.[5]

- Cobray/SWD Streetsweeper—A lower-end clone of the Armsel Striker, having a limited parts commonality to the original weapons system.[5]

- Cobray/SWD Ladies Home Companion—A reduced caliber version of the Streetsweeper. The triggergroup is attached to a .410 bore or .45/70 Government drum and barrel.[9]

9.1.5 See also

- Automatic shotgun
- Combat shotgun
- List of combat shotguns
- List of shotguns
- Riot shotgun
- Semi-automatic shotgun

9.1.6 References

[1] "patent". Retrieved 1 May 2014.

[2] Wood, J B (2002). *The Gun Digest Book of Firearms Assembly/Disassembly Part V - Shotguns*. Iola, Wisconsin: Krause Publications. p. 474. ISBN 978-0-87349-400-7.

[3] Cutshaw, Charles Q. (28 February 2011). *Tactical Small Arms of the 21st Century: A Complete Guide to Small Arms From Around the World*. Iola, Wiosconsin: Gun Digest Books. pp. 338–339. ISBN 978-1-4402-2709-7.

[4] Jones, Richard D.; White, Andrew (27 May 2008). *Jane's Guns Recognition Guide 5e*. HarperCollins. p. 355. ISBN 978-0-06-137408-1.

[5] Walker, Robert E. (2013). *Cartridges and Firearm Identification*. CRC Press. p. 369. ISBN 978-1-4665-8881-3.

[6] Lee, Jerry (2011). *Standard Catalog of Rifles & Shotguns*. Iola, Wisconsin: Gun Digest Books. p. 1403. ISBN 978-1-4402-3014-1.

[7] United States. Bureau of Alcohol, Tobacco, and Firearms (2000). *Your guide to federal firearms regulation*. Dept. of the Treasury, Bureau of Alcohol, Tobacco, and Firearms. p. 109.

[8] Smith, Al (November 2007). *American Cultures: Readings in Social and Cultural History*. Lulu Enterprises Incorporated. p. 167. ISBN 978-1-4357-0160-1.

[9] Larson, Erik (27 July 2011). *Lethal Passage: The Story of a Gun*. Knopf Doubleday Publishing Group. p. 196. ISBN 978-0-307-80331-3.

9.1.7 External links

- Image of the Cobray/SWD Ladies Home Companion
- Combined Systems— Current manufacturer of Striker Shotguns in the US.

9.2 ENARM Pentagun

The **Pentagun** is a semi automatic revolver action shotgun manufactured by the Brazilian firm ENARM. The layout is very similar to the LAPA FA-03 bullpup rifle.

9.2.1 References

- Security Arms webpage
- Armas de Fogo e Municoes blog

9.3 MTs255

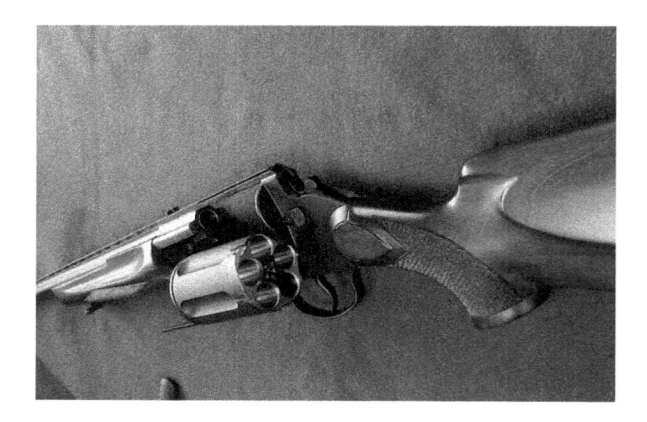

With action open

The **MTs255** (Russian: **МЦ255**) is a shotgun fed by a 5-round internal revolving cylinder. It is produced by the TsKIB SOO Central Design and Research Bureau of Sporting and Hunting Arms. The Russian-made guns are available in 12, 20, 28 and 32 gauges, and .410 bore.

The MTs255 is unique in that the forearm extends nearly all the way back to the cylinder. The shotgun is reloaded in a manner consistent with that of most modern revolvers, by unlocking the cylinder, and swinging it away from the frame to the left and down.

9.3.1 See also

- Colt Revolving Rifle
- List of Russian weaponry

9.3.2 External links

Media related to MTs-255 at Wikimedia Commons

- МЦ255 Revolver-Type Shotguns - KBP Instrument Design Bureau
- MTs-255 - TsKIB SOO

9.4 RGA-86

The **RGA-86** is a Polish 26 mm revolver shotgun, developed (along with proprietary ammunition) between 1983 and 1986 at the *Wojskowa Akademia Techniczna* state research institute by a team consisting of: S. Ciepielski, M. Czaladzki, S. Derecki, H. Głowicki, W. Koperski, J. Pawłowski and R. Wójcik.

9.4.1 See also

- List of shotguns
- RG-6 grenade launcher

Chapter 10

Text and image sources, contributors, and licenses

10.1 Text

- **Shotgun** *Source:* https://en.wikipedia.org/wiki/Shotgun?oldid=691672131 *Contributors:* TwoOneTwo, Jimbo Wales, Bryan Derksen, Stephen Gilbert, Rmhermen, Maury Markowitz, Heron, Edward, Bdesham, Michael Hardy, Modster, Ixfd64, Karada, Ellywa, CatherineMunro, Jay-Tau, TUF-KAT, Angela, BigFatBuddha, Error, Evercat, [212], Charles Matthews, JeffTL, Daniel Quinlan, Selket, Furrykef, Tempshill, SD6-Agent, Riddley, Phil Boswell, ZimZalaBim, Nurg, Romanm, Ojigiri~enwiki, Hcheney, GreatWhiteNortherner, Carnildo, Buster2058, Fabiform, Werbwerb, Smjg, Oberiko, Cobaltbluetony, Tom harrison, Ds13, Leonard G., Dav4is, Iota, Finn-Zoltan, Mboverload, Bobblewik, Tagishimon, Ryanaxp, Chowbok, Utcursh, Antandrus, Kilogulf59, ThC, Andy Christ, Trevor MacInnis, Gest, AliveFreeHappy, DanielCD, Jiy, Discospinster, Twinxor, Rich Farmbrough, Avriette, FT2, Fluzwup, Mani1, Night Gyr, ESkog, Mashford, Calair, El C, Tom, Sietse Snel, Sajt, Bobo192, Tronno, Sasquatch, Sukiari, Hooperbloob, Alansohn, Anthony Appleyard, Free Bear, Primalchaos, Great Scott, Stillnotelf, Snowolf, RPellessier, RainbowOfLight, Sumergocognito, Gene Nygaard, Netkinetic, Dan100, Pekinensis, Firsfron, Interslice, Mindmatrix, Blackeagle, Camw, Jeff3000, MONGO, Kmg90, BlaiseFEgan, Crazysunshine, Yesukai, MikeWilson, Mtloweman, GraemeLeggett, Marudubshinki, Ashmoo, Graham87, NCdave, BD2412, Kbdank71, Bdrewery, FreplySpang, Jorunn, Rjwilmsi, Dimitrii, Hitssquad, Quale, Seraphimblade, AliasXIII, Ligulem, Gilesmorant, DickClarkMises, FlaBot, Ian Pitchford, RexNL, LeCire~enwiki, Coolhawks88, Chobot, Knife Knut, Writer-Hound, RobotE, Hairy Dude, RussBot, Filippof, Hydrargyrum, Shell Kinney, Gaius Cornelius, CambridgeBayWeather, Toecutter, SEWilcoBot, Greenlead, Mipadi, Mike18xx, Howcheng, Dr. R, Matnkat, Shotgunlee, Kyle Barbour, DeadEyeArrow, .marc., Decromin, Haemo, CLW, Asams10, Slaarti, Deeday-UK, Deville, Closedmouth, Derek1G, Dspradau, TheQuaker, ArielGold, SodiumBenzoate, Mebden, Kstingily, Luk, Sacxpert, Blastwizard, Wulfila, User24, SmackBot, Prodego, Gigs, Pgk, KocjoBot~enwiki, ScaldingHotSoup, DrStrangeLove, Jongpil Yun, Vilerage, Boris Barowski, Kintetsubuffalo, Geoff B, Shai-kun, Septegram, Xaosflux, Canonblack, Peter Isotalo, Hmains, Chris the speller, Persian Poet Gal, Crashmasterd, Snori, Droll, Adpete, Jgrabbs, Sbharris, Colonies Chris, Trekphiler, Yaf, Can't sleep, clown will eat me, DéRahier, Chlewbot, OrphanBot, KaiserbBot, Daleraby, Scottie theNerd, BRCConsultations, Nahum Reduta, Flyguy649, Fuhghettaboutit, Cybercobra, Davptb, T-borg, Funky Monkey, RaCha'ar, Bubby the Tour G, Dreadstar, Orion Minor, Derek R Bullamore, Wacki, DMacks, Kukini, Kuru, Carnby, Dialecticas, Hotspur23, LWF, AllStarZ, Warfire, Doobuzz, PseudoSudo, Pikipiki, Svippong, MarkSutton, The Bread, Mushmush123, 2T, Moretz, Haveronjones, Btillman, Blue eyed writer, Yes0song, Krispos42, Levineps, OnBeyondZebrax, Iridescent, Michaelbusch, Teddings, Mikehelms, Blackhawk charlie2003, Haystacker, Ewulp, Arto B, Az1568, Ggarfield, Mcwatson, Tawkerbot2, Penguincornguy, Xcentaur, Twipie, CmdrObot, Escaper7, Ale jrb, Apfox, Mattbr, Fieldmarshal Miyagi, IceColdKilla, Makeemlighter, Cautaro, Im.a.lumberjack, Jesse Viviano, Pgr94, Orca1 9904, Cahk, A876, Trasel, Erik E., Mortus Est, Flowerpotman, A Softer Answer, Tawkerbot4, Drrobertdecker, Chuto, JCO312, Bugsbunny86, Cancun771, Hippapaflagapapedal, Epbr123, Skyfire.michael, Cosmi, CynicalMe, Commander Zulu, Sukisuki, Legaiaflame, Tapir Terrific, Nslsmith, Universe Man, Cverlo, Cool Blue, VaneWimsey, Philippe, Nick Number, Wikidenizen, Siggis, I already forgot, AntiVandalBot, Luna Santin, Vic226, Alphachimpbot, Cynic2, Benmwah, Kagrenak, JAnDbot, Hmaag, Instinct, Andonic, Hut 8.5, Matthew Husdon, Ryan4314, Boris B, Magioladitis, VoABot II, Aberhow, Kuyabribri, Slayerment, WODUP, Avicennasis, Nick Cooper, Thernlund, Heliac, Memotype, Ahmad87, DerHexer, Patstuart, Calltech, IvoShandor, CeeWhy2, S3000, Giblets, Katana314, MartinBot, Fedfan0001, Pupster21, UnfriendlyFire, Tholly, SouthernStang93, Bjørn som tegner, CommonsDelinker, Johnsomb, J.delanoy, Kimse, Goldfishsoldier, Garnett F, Bejammin, Rrostrom, Silverxxx, Jerry, Omfgtehpwnage, Tonyrenploki, New Hampshirite, Davandron, AntiSpamBot, Jo7hs2, Robertgreer, SlightlyMad, Flatscan, Jaimeastorga2000, Red Thrush, Inwind, S, Adam Zivner, Xiahou, Sooner Dave, Lights, Vranak, Atexhoffman, ABF, ShienYang, Mudwater, Blindboy22, Noware7, DOHC Holiday, Nburden, Aicchalmers, TXiKiBoT, Weapons, Eddiehimself, Kritikos99, ElinorD, Tinkerer, Someguy1221, Liko81, Kempires1111, Sintaku, John michael bibbings, Mzmadmike, Jeremy Bolwell, Quindraco, Mray1, Telecineguy, SQL, Grsz11, Lawless101, Thinkcentrenoob, Onceonthisisland, Kyle112, Mroduner, Solicitr, Alucard365, Burgercat, Are2dee2, Ratsbew, SaltyBoatr, BonesBrigade, ToePeu.bot, Dawn Bard, Caltas, Letter 7, Alucard51717, Barliner, Andersmusician, Robbie999, Keilana, Radon210, BirdHunters, ZombieWacker, Faradayplank, Lightmouse, Jarrodhollinger, ZH Evers, Squizzyfish, Anchor Link Bot, Georgette2, Latics, Witchkraut, Maralia, Dabomb87, Jons63, BHenry1969, Hoplon, Ironman1104, ClueBot, GorillaWarfare, TableManners, Tos42, Quackiv, Wysprgr2005, Chessy999, Rawness, Uncle Milty, CounterVandalismBot, Epsilon60198, Blanchardb, Daredavil, Malomaboy06, Neverquick, Razvanjr, Boneyard90, Tackdriver, Monkeytree, Excirial, Gbrims, John Nevard, Raptor2k7, Gwguffey, Niteshift36, Jacksly, DeltaQuad, Gcdonaldson, Dmxx99, La Pianista, Fungusdookie, Thingg, Fordag, Versus22, Hahayoya, Callinus, MrDeodorant, Berean Hunter, SoxBot III,

Apparition11, DumZiBoT, Jackhelm93, Thomasplutapl, Hahayoyo, Mifter, Nukes4Tots, Kace7, MatthewVanitas, Birdman1138, Marshdog, Hoplophile, Addbot, American Eagle, Yousou, Wvonkessler, Rj734, MartinezMD, CanadianLinuxUser, Fixit23, Fabi666, The Wings of UK, Patton123, Lightbot, Totorotroll, Gail, Ontask, Luckas-bot, Yobot, Onetwo345, Eric-Wester, Tempodivalse, NuBz Banyai, AnomieBOT, Galoubet, Piano non troppo, AdjustShift, Csigabi, Mogdonazia, Rocketpeacock, Citation bot, Onesius, Quebec99, Sionus, Karagamber, Winged Brick, Boots1120, TracyMcClark, Muscat0, Gigemag76, Tyrol5, FlashHawk4, Ute in DC, Amendola90, DoomScooper, Acranney, Thehelpfulbot, Elcochan, Captain Weirdo the Great, TerraHikaru, FrescoBot, Surv1v4l1st, Tobby72, Krj373, DJEFFER, Keserman, Endofskull, Full-date unlinking bot, Miguel Escopeta, FoxBot, Mercy11, Felis domestica, Vrenator, Begoon, DARTH SIDIOUS 2, Kory207, Nutarama, Jackehammond, Beyond My Ken, PoorRichard22, EmausBot, John of Reading, WikitanvirBot, Tnt1984, Fly by Night, Faceless Enemy, Bears9086, K6ka, Terribleidea, Dffgd, AvicAWB, L1A1 FAL, L Kensington, Marrune, MALLUS, ChuispastonBot, JohnLloydScharf, Doctor Ruud, Catlemur, Primergrey, Ose\fio, Helpful Pixie Bot, I donotwork, Regulov, BG19bot, AfroThundr3007730, AvocatoBot, Godzilladude123, BattyBot, Historyphysics, Cyberbot II, Mogism, Kbog, Smohammed2, Gatitbat, Monkbot, Rezin, Orduin, Truniper and Anonymous: 589

- **Semi-automatic shotgun** *Source:* https://en.wikipedia.org/wiki/Semi-automatic_shotgun?oldid=674850225 *Contributors:* Vroman, Riddley, Chris Roy, Buster2058, AliveFreeHappy, Monkeyleg, Hohum, Vegaswikian, Beerslurpy, Quuxplusone, Swartzer, O^O, Shiroi Hane, Sacxpert, Hydrogen Iodide, Thumperward, Moshe Constantine Hassan Al-Silverburg, Oatmeal batman, Yaf, Z-d, Cabez, Avicennasis, KTo288, McSly, Robertgreer, Mudwater, LeaveSleaves, Lightbreather, Bracton, Scalhotrod, AnomieBOT, ArthurBot, Locobot, Arandomlogin, Anonymous.translator, Surv1v4l1st, Pinethicket, TJFadness, Ose\fio, I donotwork, Penrijames and Anonymous: 31

- **Automatic shotgun** *Source:* https://en.wikipedia.org/wiki/Automatic_shotgun?oldid=673798186 *Contributors:* YUL89YYZ, Rjwilmsi, Sus scrofa, Hairy Dude, Innocentmind, Chris the speller, Thumperward, TwistOfCain, Ale jrb, Cydebot, Gogo Dodo, Matthew Proctor, TAnthony, Lightbreather, Brooklynxman, ClueBot, MatthewVanitas, Addbot, The Bushranger, Yobot, The Banner, Arandomlogin, FrescoBot, Zaqq, AvicBot, Pageman234567, Skrunyak, ChuispastonBot, Jac98, Whoop whoop pull up, ClueBot NG, Ts7946, Ose\fio, Helpful Pixie Bot, MPS-Doomsday, ChrisLee77, Hidden12, Green547 and Anonymous: 31

- **Double-barreled shotgun** *Source:* https://en.wikipedia.org/wiki/Double-barreled_shotgun?oldid=689278338 *Contributors:* Jimbo Wales, Bryan Derksen, Charles Matthews, RichiH, Securiger, Tobias Bergemann, Buster2058, Mackeriv, Icairns, Acad Ronin, AliveFreeHappy, Fluzwup, Neurophyre, Monkeyleg, Geo Swan, TaintedMustard, RainbowOfLight, Graham87, Martin-C, RussBot, Spaully, Gaius Cornelius, O^O, DonaldDuck, Grafen, Gilliam, LinguistAtLarge, Jumping cheese, LWF, Chrisch, Neelix, Epbr123, Jedibob5, Commander Zulu, Escarbot, QuiteUnusual, Thernlund, Symbolt, Robertgreer, Vanished user 39948282, Philip Trueman, CelestialSpore, Jeremy Bolwell, Alucard365, Mikemoral, Qblik, Jarrodhollinger, ClueBot, The Thing That Should Not Be, John Nevard, Mlaffs, Berean Hunter, Ratbertovich~enwiki, Facts707, HexaChord, MatthewVanitas, Mdnahas, Jarble, Legobot, Luckas-bot, AnomieBOT, A More Perfect Onion, Capricorn42, Winged Brick, Harmphrey, Earlypsychosis, Amaury, Silverije, Some standardized rigour, Griffinofwales, Raniero Supremo, Surv1v4l1st, Daram.G, Finalius, Glass spiders, Pinethicket, Miguel Escopeta, Stroppolo, EmausBot, Faceless Enemy, Mr little irish, Wingman4l7, Skrunyak, ClueBot NG, Mrxtreme2, Wbm1058, BattyBot, Arr4, Mogism, No1inparticularhere and Anonymous: 93

- **Lever action** *Source:* https://en.wikipedia.org/wiki/Lever_action?oldid=685708561 *Contributors:* Olivier, Zoicon5, Riddley, Altenmann, Philwelch, Everyking, Leonard G., Meswiss, Oneiros, Stepp-Wulf, Fluzwup, Alansohn, Monkeyleg, Geo Swan, RPellessier, Ianblair23, Dan East, Dmol, MikeWilson, Gewhere, Chobot, Fabartus, O^O, Ospalh, Shotgunlee, DeadEyeArrow, Asams10, Stiletto Null, Kahonas, Groyolo, SmackBot, Septegram, Hmains, Chris the speller, Oatmeal batman, Trekphiler, Sawran~enwiki, Lox, Savidan, Keyesc, Atirador, Cosmoline, AllStarZ, Robofish, Vaarok, Dr. Rondart, Naaman Brown, Jaksmata, Neoking, Andkore, Trasel, Commander Zulu, Top Gunn, Jeff dean, Avicennasis, Thernlund, RebDrummer61, STBot, Arjun01, J.delanoy, Uncle Dick, Morphinea, Nothingofwater, Robertgreer, TXiKiBoT, Jakedaniel, Cerebellum, MCTales, Solicitr, Motorrad-67, Fratrep, Hamiltondaniel, ClueBot, King Ghidora, John Nevard, MatthewVanitas, Addbot, Tide rolls, Lightbot, Luckas-bot, AnomieBOT, Materialscientist, Xqbot, Richillinois, Yhljjang, FrescoBot, Surv1v4l1st, Pinethicket, Faceless Enemy, ClueBot NG, Cmccluskey33, Ose\fio, Obsfucate again, Ed in North Texas, Hornsignal, BattyBot, Jimw338, MountainRail, Nuohr, Pktlaurence, Humaag, Wiki13565, SQMeaner and Anonymous: 78

- **Pump action** *Source:* https://en.wikipedia.org/wiki/Pump_action?oldid=693673008 *Contributors:* Riddley, Dmol, K6ka, ClueBot NG, Hornsignal, Oursmili, Melonkelon, Dorkmax, Keydet92 and Anonymous: 5

- **Akdal MKA 1919** *Source:* https://en.wikipedia.org/wiki/Akdal_MKA_1919?oldid=645542553 *Contributors:* YUL89YYZ, CeeGee, Woohookitty, BD2412, Uncle Bubba, Mranostay, Cydebot, Postcard Cathy, Anaxial, Robertgreer, Thomas.W, TXiKiBoT, Falcon8765, SieBot, Canglesea, TheTranc, Yozer1, Addbot, AnomieBOT, Xqbot, Ajpralston1, D'ohBot, Akjar13, Sdafhgh, SporkBot, L1A1 FAL, KazekageTR, Poizzin, DrunkSquirrel, StarkeySuper64, Makecat-bot, Nabaker, Rezin and Anonymous: 16

- **Baikal MP-153** *Source:* https://en.wikipedia.org/wiki/Baikal_MP-153?oldid=667344890 *Contributors:* Rjwilmsi, BiH, FrescoBot, SporkBot, BG19bot and Penrijames

- **Benelli M1** *Source:* https://en.wikipedia.org/wiki/Benelli_M1?oldid=689449184 *Contributors:* Brianhe, Mani1, Miguelfp1, GregorB, Vegaswikian, FlaBot, TonicBH, SmackBot, K-Swift, Gurklurk, Lkegley9, RangerHAAF, Cydebot, Consequentially, Thijs!bot, Gwern, R'n'B, CommonsDelinker, Robertgreer, DanMP5, Philip Trueman, PianoKeys, CEOMao, ImageRemovalBot, Scartboy, Alexbot, Mlaffs, EpicDream86, Frankandjesse, Addbot, Debresser, Tassedethe, Xqbot, GrouchoBot, A Werewolf, Hell in a Bucket, Emediarifleman, ROG5728, Faceless Enemy, ClueBot NG, YFdyh-bot, JYBot, Jamesallain85, Addonexus, Sashkarossiya and Anonymous: 14

- **Benelli M2** *Source:* https://en.wikipedia.org/wiki/Benelli_M2?oldid=693025788 *Contributors:* Brianhe, K-Swift, Cydebot, Mr kitehead, Mike Searson, R'n'B, CommonsDelinker, Gene93k, Niceguyedc, Addbot, Jojhutton, Luckas-bot, Shadowjams, A Werewolf, ROG5728, Faceless Enemy, ClueBot NG, Helpful Pixie Bot, BG19bot, Sashkarossiya and Anonymous: 3

- **Benelli M3** *Source:* https://en.wikipedia.org/wiki/Benelli_M3?oldid=689449176 *Contributors:* Nufy8, AliveFreeHappy, Marblespire, Alansohn, PaulHanson, TaintedMustard, Daveydweeb, The JPS, Miq, Rjwilmsi, Gurch, Jpfagerback, YurikBot, Welsh, Asams10, Closedmouth, Ybbor, Nick-D, SmackBot, Ominae, Deon Steyn, Snori, Oatmeal batman, UNHchabo, JoeBot, Sanandros, Wilhelm Wiesel, Orca1 9904, Jader-Vason, Ka3ak, Cydebot, Thijs!bot, Chico75, Benmwah, Bahar, Catgut, Thernlund, CommonsDelinker, Grim Revenant, SU Linguist, Robertgreer, DanMP5, Matthew craigge, McM.bot, Francis Flinch, Koalorka, Phe-bot, PianoKeys, Hyperionsteel, Berean Hunter, XLinkBot, WikHead, Shotgun71, Yaik9a, Addbot, Boksi, AnomieBOT, GrouchoBot, Mark Schierbecker, Arikama1, BornInLeningrad, FrescoBot, A Werewolf, Macgyver-bd 896, Kartamm, Draco demonicus, ROG5728, JenVan, Anpeq, John of Reading, Faceless Enemy, ArmordHawk 001, Skrunyak,

10.1. TEXT

Dean amx, Dinoflagellate, BattyBot, Isä Apotti, Jamesallain85, Albert777MAX, Addonexus, Dairhead, YiFeiBot, IrishSpook, Tpats90028 and Anonymous: 68

- **Benelli M4** *Source:* https://en.wikipedia.org/wiki/Benelli_M4?oldid=689449171 *Contributors:* Jonadab~enwiki, Riddley, Rholton, Christopher Parham, Tom harrison, Wwoods, Brockert, Bobblewik, Christopherlin, Maclyn611, AlexanderWinston, Klemen Kocjancic, Kevin Rector, Guanabot, Pmsyyz, YUL89YYZ, Xezbeth, Fluzwup, Pauli133, Kelly Martin, Woohookitty, D.E. Watters, LOL, Kralizec!, Vegaswikian, Wouter-Bot, Chobot, Lightsup55, Toecutter, Ve3, CKHideki, Asams10, Searchme, Jolb, Hayden120, Nick-D, SmackBot, Hanchi, Ominae, Eskimbot, Moshe Constantine Hassan Al-Silverburg, Oatmeal batman, Deenoe, Jumping cheese, Williamsonj, Kefra™, Saxbryn, Hellogoodsir, Blackhawk charlie2003, LSX, DangerousPanda, Micah hainline, Orca1 9904, Cydebot, Fnlayson, Kevin23, JamesAM, Thijs!bot, Deathbunny, I already forgot, Mutt Lunker, Benmwah, Ribonucleic, Jacce, I JethroBT, Thernlund, Rettetast, CommonsDelinker, Pharaoh of the Wizards, Robertgreer, DanMP5, STBotD, Czarbender, Gothbag, VolkovBot, SQL, Kimber1911, Bahamut0013, Koalorka, AlleborgoBot, BonesBrigade, Mothmolevna, PianoKeys, Usdiver, Spartan198, ZH Evers, Phykyloman~enwiki, ClueBot, Blemo 23, EpicDream86, Berean Hunter, Nukes4Tots, Addbot, CL, LaaknorBot, Lightbot, VFDguy, Sammt2600, The Bushranger, Yobot, TaBOT-zerem, AnomieBOT, Citation bot, Xqbot, Hitman-Hood, Ocelotl10293, WotWeiller, Ohmygod766, FrescoBot, Surv1v4l1st, Anthrax2525, D'ohBot, A Werewolf, PrincessofLlyr, TheMighty-General, ROG5728, Reach Out to the Truth, Kory207, Reedo302, EmausBot, John of Reading, Faceless Enemy, Ps3master34, Universeis42, SemperFi1775, Illegitimate Barrister, H3llBot, Eamonnslattery, MIDFTheBlink, MIDFThe Blink, Wayne Slam, L1A1 FAL, Gehrgolesl, TyA, ChuispastonBot, VADemon, Chikupakas, Roughbeak, Zackaback, BG19bot, Turfreak, Albi888, DeTermit, Alexander.kvasa, ArsA-92, BattyBot, Tomh903, MilitaryNut, Superxoki, YFdyh-bot, Jamesallain85, Cerabot~enwiki, Kcgunesq, Tsengy1, M11rtinb, Black houk, Tekogi, Shkvoz, Robmyman97, IrishSpook and Anonymous: 194

- **Benelli Raffaello** *Source:* https://en.wikipedia.org/wiki/Benelli_Raffaello?oldid=689449187 *Contributors:* OrphanBot, Cydebot, CommonsDelinker, Robertgreer, SieBot, CultureDrone, Alexbot, Addbot, Lawyer2bee, LilHelpa, A Werewolf, Jamesallain85, Sashkarossiya and Anonymous: 1

- **Benelli Raffaello CrioComfort** *Source:* https://en.wikipedia.org/wiki/Benelli_Raffaello_CrioComfort?oldid=689449186 *Contributors:* Nikkimaria, OrphanBot, Cydebot, JaGa, Robertgreer, SieBot, Eeme, Alexbot, Addbot, Lawyer2bee, LilHelpa, A Werewolf, AJCrabbe1980 and Anonymous: 1

- **Benelli Vinci** *Source:* https://en.wikipedia.org/wiki/Benelli_Vinci?oldid=689449195 *Contributors:* Cydebot, CommonsDelinker, Gene93k, Addbot, A Werewolf, FoxBot, Faceless Enemy, Jamesallain85, Addonexus, Sashkarossiya and Anonymous: 2

- **Beretta 1201FP** *Source:* https://en.wikipedia.org/wiki/Beretta_1201FP?oldid=639592955 *Contributors:* Riddley, Chowbok, AliveFreeHappy, BroadArrow, Stemonitis, Woohookitty, Vegaswikian, Bluewave, SmackBot, Oatmeal batman, K-Swift, ApolloCreed, Radagast83, Saxbryn, Silicon Wolverine, Neurillon, Aldis90, JustAGal, Alphachimpbot, CommonsDelinker, Robertgreer, Matthew craigge, Gooly, Wilhelmina Will, Berean Hunter, Gaulinmp, Erik9bot, 777sms, Catlemur, Helpful Pixie Bot, Sashkarossiya and Anonymous: 6

- **Beretta A303** *Source:* https://en.wikipedia.org/wiki/Beretta_A303?oldid=438604951 *Contributors:* MJ94, Salvio giuliano and Rajaerry

- **Beretta AL391** *Source:* https://en.wikipedia.org/wiki/Beretta_AL391?oldid=659557000 *Contributors:* DocWatson42, Gadget850, Robertgreer, Mudwater, TXiKiBoT, ImageRemovalBot, Berean Hunter, Addbot, Yobot, 777sms, EmausBot, Mauromeli, Catlemur, Hair and Anonymous: 3

- **Beretta Xtrema 2** *Source:* https://en.wikipedia.org/wiki/Beretta_Xtrema_2?oldid=625607126 *Contributors:* DocWatson42, Chowbok, AliveFreeHappy, Ynhockey, Ywong137, Ground Zero, CWenger, CSWarren, Weggie, Alaibot, Thernlund, CommonsDelinker, J.delanoy, Plankton5005, Adamdaley, Robertgreer, Mudwater, SQL, Fenderfiend, Koalorka, Chinese3126, ImageRemovalBot, ClueBot, Grainman, Berean Hunter, 777sms, Mauromeli, MauchoEagle, The1337gamer, Khazar2, Jamesallain85, Addonexus and Anonymous: 13

- **Browning Auto-5** *Source:* https://en.wikipedia.org/wiki/Browning_Auto-5?oldid=681261684 *Contributors:* DocWatson42, Phil1988, Trevor MacInnis, AliveFreeHappy, PatrickFisher, Ashley Pomeroy, Woohookitty, Ketiltrout, Rjwilmsi, Ground Zero, Nemo5576, VolatileChemical, Asams10, Natmaka, SmackBot, Dangerous~enwiki, Gjs238, Trekphiler, Yaf, LWF, Courcelles, CmdrObot, Cydebot, Aldis90, Thijs!bot, Hmaag, ElComandanteChe, Thernlund, C1010, Robertgreer, DanMP5, Rantingmadhare, Hugo999, Gothbag, Phyrkrakr, SQL, Sf46, VoidPoint, Powermugu, EoGuy, Cfarinella, DumZiBoT, Nukes4Tots, MatthewVanitas, Addbot, CL, LaaknorBot, Yobot, Wiki15Pedia, LilHelpa, Xqbot, GrouchoBot, Slyaskiw, Surv1v4l1st, Macgyver-bd 896, ScottEMayer, DeusImperator, John of Reading, Gary7even, ZéroBot, SporkBot, Wingman4l7, L1A1 FAL, Zackmann08, Trinjac, MilitaryNut, Soni, Marcus22gunpro, Chassafrass, The2niro and Anonymous: 46

- **FN SLP** *Source:* https://en.wikipedia.org/wiki/FN_SLP?oldid=639690668 *Contributors:* The RedBurn, Cydebot, Francis Flinch, Plasticspork, ROG5728, EmausBot, Zackmann08, Gsg-9 and Anonymous: 1

- **Franchi AL-48** *Source:* https://en.wikipedia.org/wiki/Franchi_AL-48?oldid=694369940 *Contributors:* Fluzwup, Tronno, Woohookitty, SmackBot, Oatmeal batman, RCopple, ElComandanteChe, BJ Axel, Robertgreer, Yobot, Erik9bot, Floraguns, MilitaryNut, Lemnaminor and Anonymous: 11

- **Franchi SPAS-12** *Source:* https://en.wikipedia.org/wiki/Franchi_SPAS-12?oldid=693417314 *Contributors:* Andrewman327, Jni, Altenmann, Yosri, DocWatson42, Chowbok, Quadell, AlexanderWinston, Brian0918, Thunderbrand, Tronno, RPellessier, Coolgamer, Nuno Tavares, Woohookitty, Hailey C. Shannon, Kralizec!, Nemo5576, Chobot, YurikBot, Witan, NawlinWiki, Merman, Ve3, Banes, Shultz, Wknight94, Pegship, Georgewilliamherbert, Patto, Some guy, NiTenIchiRyu, SmackBot, Ominae, Deon Steyn, Eskimbot, Boris Barowski, Anthonzi, Thumperward, Moshe Constantine Hassan Al-Silverburg, Oatmeal batman, OrphanBot, Solar Powered Toaster, Er Komandante, Arctic-Editor, Veritas Panther, Tythesly, Wilhelm Wiesel, Billyfishzwei, ShelfSkewed, Orca1 9904, Cydebot, Besieged, Metal Snake, After Midnight, Aldis90, N5iln, Drmemory, Judenovak, Nakedjuice, Fusionmix, Thernlund, Zikol, MartinBot, Anaxial, CommonsDelinker, Kguirnela, Qat727, J.delanoy, Robertgreer, DanMP5, SOCAR, STBotD, Ariobarzan, VolkovBot, Dom Kaos, Eddiehimself, GDonato, Fredrick day, Don4of4, Feliza the noobhunter7, Koalorka, Planet-man828, Glennklockwood, Crserrano, OldBlack, Toddst1, Flyer22 Reborn, Oxymoron83, Miniapolis, Mockmaster2009, Hyperionsteel, RobertLeBlais, ImageRemovalBot, ClueBot, Alien NL, Bensci54, Jcreek201, Berean Hunter, DumZiBoT, Josh Woolstenhulme, Nukes4Tots, Thatguyflint, MatthewVanitas, Addbot, Twca, Sadkjos, CanadianLinuxUser, LaaknorBot, Glane23, Herr Gruber, Tide rolls, Lightbot, Luckas-bot, Yobot, TaBOT-zerem, AnomieBOT, Deadman01, LilHelpa, Xqbot, Digiphi, DSisyphBot, Ajpralston1, Mark Schierbecker, BornInLeningrad, Dominick1283, FrescoBot, Surv1v4l1st, Pigplucker, Pinethicket, I dream of horses, Joguwa86, Supreme Deliciousness, Rbrausse, Macgyver-bd 896, LeutenantKD, Thegunkid, Aoidh, FX19, ROG5728, EmausBot, John of Reading, WikitanvirBot,

Immunize, ZéroBot, Doddy Wuid, TyA, KazekageTR, Ocean82, ClueBot NG, Byjinkung, Helpful Pixie Bot, Calabe1992, Kenny12345, Mastanerfma2117, Mark Arsten, ConCelFan, MilitaryNut, Gladius123p, Webclient101, Redalert2fan, Black houk, Camyoung54, Stan-ens, Tekogi, Filip Sivák, SoLongSidekick, Tbessler, Monkbot, KitFistoPL, IrishSpook, HellsXgunsmith, Rezin, Amortias, DawnGuardWolf, Ohsosexybrit, ModicumofKnowledge and Anonymous: 217

- **Franchi SPAS-15** *Source:* https://en.wikipedia.org/wiki/Franchi_SPAS-15?oldid=689498087 *Contributors:* Edward, Rlandmann, Andrewman327, Riddley, Yosri, Bobblewik, Tronno, RPellessier, Gene Nygaard, Coolgamer, Woohookitty, Knife Knut, Albrozdude, Megapixie, Grafikm fr, Asams10, Ominae, Boris Barowski, Thumperward, Oatmeal batman, Operatique, Arctic-Editor, Wilhelm Wiesel, Cydebot, K61824, Thernlund, R'n'B, Martinf550, TheTrojanHought, Robertgreer, DanMP5, Paulwharton, VolkovBot, SieBot, Hyperionsteel, Alexbot, Salud101, Carriearchdale, Berean Hunter, Josh Woolstenhulme, Nukes4Tots, MatthewVanitas, Addbot, Luckas-bot, Boksi, AnomieBOT, Xqbot, Digiphi, Mark Schierbecker, Amendola90, BornInLeningrad, Surv1v4l1st, Jonesey95, Plasticspork, Mouath14, ROG5728, RjwilmsiBot, Altes2009, WikitanvirBot, ZéroBot, Coolcatlols, Caturday2, ClueBot NG, BG19bot, Jwandbt, Andriel duran, Kevin12xd, Miratvorac 151271, Hedermacedo7, KitFistoPL, Rezin and Anonymous: 45

- **Heckler & Koch HK512** *Source:* https://en.wikipedia.org/wiki/Heckler_%26_Koch_HK512?oldid=683742530 *Contributors:* Ominae, Rizuan, Yobot and AnomieBOT

- **Ithaca Mag-10** *Source:* https://en.wikipedia.org/wiki/Ithaca_Mag-10?oldid=681365498 *Contributors:* Woohookitty, Hotspur23, Surv1v4l1st, RjwilmsiBot, Helpful Pixie Bot and Soni

- **Manville gun** *Source:* https://en.wikipedia.org/wiki/Manville_gun?oldid=588263166 *Contributors:* Kingturtle, Tabletop, GregorB, Rjwilmsi, Hotspur23, Cydebot, Jmg38, Robertgreer, StAnselm, Foofbun, Yobot, Dethlock99, 3family6, WotWeiller, Jonathon A H, Seekadet, Snotbot, Soni and Anonymous: 3

- **MAUL (weapon)** *Source:* https://en.wikipedia.org/wiki/MAUL_(weapon)?oldid=689771579 *Contributors:* Arthena, David Woodward, Bobamnertiopsis, Cuneas, Nick Number, Nono64, Robertgreer, Bahamut0013, Dolphin51, MatthewVanitas, Herr Gruber, Lightbot, AnomieBOT, ThaddeusB, Amendola90, Cod1337, Erik9bot, JohnLloydScharf, LTInvestor, 220 of Borg, Arigoldberg, BattyBot, ChrisGualtieri, Trim02 and Anonymous: 14

- **Mossberg 930** *Source:* https://en.wikipedia.org/wiki/Mossberg_930?oldid=666854718 *Contributors:* DocWatson42, Malcolma, Dv82matt, SmackBot, Orca1 9904, Bobbfwed, Robertgreer, Fbifriday, Lightbot, Aaronb121, Juno, ROG5728, Burmiester, ClueBot NG, ⁇⁇⁇ and Anonymous: 3

- **Remington Model 11-48** *Source:* https://en.wikipedia.org/wiki/Remington_Model_11-48?oldid=655902367 *Contributors:* DocWatson42, Yellowking, Woohookitty, Ratagonia, SmackBot, Gjs238, Boris Barowski, Virginian, Cydebot, Thernlund, Robertgreer, SQL, LtcOliverNorth, Yobot, AnomieBOT, FrescoBot, DrilBot, DeusImperator, Acather96, Madara100, ClueBot NG, SpikeTorontoRCP, Zackmann08, Hilltoppa101, Lemnaminor and Anonymous: 9

- **Remington Model 11-87** *Source:* https://en.wikipedia.org/wiki/Remington_Model_11-87?oldid=646236477 *Contributors:* Rlandmann, Dysprosia, DocWatson42, Chowbok, AliveFreeHappy, Talldean, Sietse Snel, Bobo192, Woohookitty, Rjwilmsi, Jaxl, Dmakatra, SmackBot, Gjs238, Boris Barowski, Oatmeal batman, Kefra™, Virginian, ShelfSkewed, Cydebot, Thernlund, CommonsDelinker, Dp cameron, Robertgreer, DanMP5, Philip Trueman, Matthew craigge, SQL, CEOMao, ZH Evers, Alexbot, Darkhelmet322, BOTarate, Mlaffs, DumZiBoT, Kelleroid, Nukes4Tots, Addbot, Hockeyrockcars, Lightbot, Yobot, Ptbotgourou, PMLawrence, FrescoBot, DeusImperator, ROG5728, WikitanvirBot, Helpful Pixie Bot, CSBurksesq, SunsetLimited and Anonymous: 10

- **Remington Model 1100** *Source:* https://en.wikipedia.org/wiki/Remington_Model_1100?oldid=653053463 *Contributors:* DocWatson42, Chowbok, AliveFreeHappy, Yellowking, RPellessier, Woohookitty, Jivecat, Shawnc, SmackBot, Gjs238, Boris Barowski, Chris the speller, Moshe Constantine Hassan Al-Silverburg, Oatmeal batman, Trekphiler, Silent Tom, Pauldstubbs, Fissionfox, LWF, Virginian, ShelfSkewed, Cydebot, CynicalMe, Geckzilla, Thernlund, Mike Searson, Davidwiz, CommonsDelinker, Goldfishsoldier, H8jd5, Dp cameron, Robertgreer, DanMP5, TXiKiBoT, Matthew craigge, Meszi, BwDraco, Polarloch, ZH Evers, Mlaffs, Berean Hunter, Nukes4Tots, Addbot, Leeroy73, Lightbot, Yobot, AnomieBOT, Winged Brick, Dtaylor05, FrescoBot, A Werewolf, Costcutter, DeusImperator, ROG5728, EmausBot, WikitanvirBot, Wingman4l7, Quake44, ClueBot NG, Helpful Pixie Bot, BG19bot, Markm84, MilitaryNut, Wedgebuster53, Lemnaminor, Crystallizedcarbon and Anonymous: 44

- **Remington Model 58** *Source:* https://en.wikipedia.org/wiki/Remington_Model_58?oldid=598902114 *Contributors:* Winged Brick

- **Remington Model 878** *Source:* https://en.wikipedia.org/wiki/Remington_Model_878?oldid=598943309 *Contributors:* Winged Brick

- **Remington Model SP-10** *Source:* https://en.wikipedia.org/wiki/Remington_Model_SP-10?oldid=644634279 *Contributors:* Chowbok, Woohookitty, MystBot, Addbot, Yobot, AnomieBOT, Obersachsebot, Surv1v4l1st, HRoestBot, DeusImperator, ROG5728, EmausBot, Orphan Wiki, Helpful Pixie Bot, Zackmann08 and Anonymous: 1

- **Remington Spartan 453** *Source:* https://en.wikipedia.org/wiki/Remington_Spartan_453?oldid=670813221 *Contributors:* ImageRemovalBot, Addbot, JackieBot, BornInLeningrad, Dinamik-bot, Zackmann08 and Anonymous: 1

- **Safir T-14** *Source:* https://en.wikipedia.org/wiki/Safir_T-14?oldid=686736562 *Contributors:* CeeGee, Tabletop, Cydebot, Nick Number, Avicennasis, BilCat, Patar knight, Robertgreer, KylieTastic, SirBob42, John Nevard, SchreiberBike, Degen Earthfast, Akjar13, Sdafhgh, Ts7946, Kungfu2187, DrunkSquirrel, BattyBot, Rezin, Yasinozcurcu and Anonymous: 4

- **Saiga-12** *Source:* https://en.wikipedia.org/wiki/Saiga-12?oldid=683462038 *Contributors:* Everyking, DO'Neil, Klemen Kocjancic, Night Gyr, Sukiari, Ashley Pomeroy, Ahruman, Denniss, Hohum, Kelly Martin, GregorB, Scottanon, Rjwilmsi, Valentinejoesmith, Ian Pitchford, Beerslurpy, BabyNuke, Albrozdude, Sus scrofa, Joel7687, Asams10, SamuelRiv, Closedmouth, Hayden120, SmackBot, Vbrtrmn, Chris the speller, Thumperward, Klichka, Modest Genius, Lenin and McCarthy, OrphanBot, Zazpot, Rwjohnst, Neo3DGfx, Atirador, Attys, John, LWF, Arctic-Editor, Atakdoug, CP\M, Wilhelm Wiesel, Henrickson, CmdrObot, Daniel J. Leivick, BetacommandBot, CynicalMe, Dawkeye, TimVickers, BADMINton, General Bob, Kent Witham, CaptainColon, Geniac, Mike Searson, CeeWhy2, Climax Void, CommonsDelinker, GarrettJL, C1010, Dlegros, Tatrgel, Robertgreer, DanMP5, STBotD, Idioma-bot, Duchamps comb, Paulwharton, VolkovBot, Thomas.W, Rsweens, One half 3544, Francis Flinch, Koalorka, Jessesellers, French Stick, Not home, Joelrod47, John Nevard, Tnxman307, Nwilde, Berean Hunter, Eik

10.1. TEXT

Corell, SilvonenBot, Addbot, MartinezMD, Cst17, Glane23, HandThatFeeds, Cyberlogicx, AnomieBOT, Wikieditoroftoday, Materialscientist, Amendola90, ArikamaI, BornInLeningrad, Surv1v4llst, ThiagoRuiz, Digital22on, Random Checkhead, Bldi7, Rbrausse, MastiBot, DonDawson, Mstroev, ROG5728, Tnt1984, Faceless Enemy, Mrolemiss, Ὁ οἶστρος, Quantumor, Terraflorin, ClueBot NG, Ts7946, Catlemur, Sinodov, Roughbeak, MerlIwBot, Zombiegristle, Tempac3, Maadog80, BattyBot, MilitaryNut, Redalert2fan, SoTotallyAwesome, Miratvorac 151271, G PViB, SpetsnazAlpha, Infinitus Potentia, Nexus mk.7, Asdaven, Elucidator121, XANTHO GENOS, AK Builder, Felsic, Anipad68 and Anonymous: 149

- **Sjögren shotgun** *Source:* https://en.wikipedia.org/wiki/Sj%C3%B6gren_shotgun?oldid=619100098 *Contributors:* Woohookitty, Mandarax, Mais oui!, Robertgreer, Falcon8765, WotWeiller, FrescoBot, BG19bot, ☒☒☒, KitFistoPL and Anonymous: 7
- **SRM Arms Model 1216** *Source:* https://en.wikipedia.org/wiki/SRM_Arms_Model_1216?oldid=689247016 *Contributors:* Hotspur23, Nick Number, KTo288, Drmies, Niceguyedc, Materialscientist, Digital RNG, Delija Do Groba, EpicFX, LowProfileStudios and Anonymous: 4
- **Weatherby SA-08** *Source:* https://en.wikipedia.org/wiki/Weatherby_SA-08?oldid=656217069 *Contributors:* Eeekster, Yobot, DeusImperator, John of Reading, Gurt Posh and Anonymous: 3
- **Winchester Model 1911** *Source:* https://en.wikipedia.org/wiki/Winchester_Model_1911?oldid=640932698 *Contributors:* AliveFreeHappy, Woohookitty, Zchris87v, Robertgreer, Solicitr, Drmies, Diaa abdelmoneim, Chamal N, ChildofMidnight, Shubinator, FrescoBot, Cijjag, 777sms, DeusImperator, RjwilmsiBot, Fæ, Luigibastardo, Helpful Pixie Bot, Lerret, Lemnaminor and Anonymous: 4
- **List of semi-automatic shotguns** *Source:* https://en.wikipedia.org/wiki/List_of_semi-automatic_shotguns?oldid=694270733 *Contributors:* Lightbreather, CorenSearchBot, Faceless Enemy and Crow
- **Atchisson Assault Shotgun** *Source:* https://en.wikipedia.org/wiki/Atchisson_Assault_Shotgun?oldid=688816084 *Contributors:* Michael Reiter, Riddley, DocWatson42, Tom harrison, Kross, Denniss, Mikeo, Woohookitty, LOL, Mangojuice, J M Rice, BD2412, Chris Capoccia, DWizzy, RadioFan, Kvn8907, Allens, Elepsis, SmackBot, Boris Barowski, Hmains, Chris the speller, Bluebot, Thumperward, Frap, Jacob Poon, Jumping cheese, Wizardman, Khazar, John, Hotspur23, LWF, Arctic-Editor, Naaman Brown, Iridescent, Cydebot, Fnlayson, Myscrnnm, Thijs!bot, Davewho2, Avicennasis, SunSw0rd, CommonsDelinker, Malone23kid, Clintiam, DanMP5, Nikthestunned, Philip Trueman, TXiKiBoT, Eddiehimself, Olea, Reptilecobra13, Nazgul02, Koalorka, Monty845, Lightbreather, Cehlon, Grnadier, Bakemaster, Benjabenn, Explicit, ImageRemovalBot, ClueBot, Drphallus, Chessy999, Wikijens, Blanchardb, Alexbot, Jusdafax, SoxBot, PotentialDanger, Berean Hunter, XLinkBot, Bonsaiguy13, Samuelkowal906, Addbot, Kongr43gpen, MartinezMD, Hayden1Grayson, Akyoyo94, HandThatFeeds, Lightbot, Luckas-bot, Yobot, Ptbotgourou, AnomieBOT, Jim1138, Quebec99, Xqbot, Nesaverde, CultArmorer, Griz45acp, KoreanSentry, DSisyphBot, Monkeyduke, Ohmygod766, Cod1337, Arandomlogin, Palermobull, FrescoBot, Surv1v4llst, LucienBOT, D'ohBot, Rui769, BenzolBot, Ub3rname, Jaros428, RedBot, Macgyver-bd 896, Wikked Flashlight, Lotje, MilitaryHistoryFan, ROG5728, Mrfencey, TGCP, Az29, Sumsum2010, Byron the punk, Thecheesykid, Nicolo4567, ZéroBot, JAK0723, Spacemancer, Ὁ οἶστρος, AManWithNoPlan, Kalgsto, Arman Cagle, Skrunyak, Avatar9n, Elite Brigade, Libbmaster, ClueBot NG, Jam3shook, Rich459, Ryan Vesey, Helpful Pixie Bot, USDesign, KT-TIZZLE4, Bmusician, Tohoeg, Dan653, Lazy613, RedheadsWin, The1337gamer, EpicMusicGeniusMan0, MilitaryNut, GoShow, Epic-fatty, Jamesallain85, Uatrhg, Black houk, SoTotallyAwesome, Awesomeness00000, Monkbot, Themasterisback, Sciophobiaranger, Borealeum and Anonymous: 133
- **Daewoo Precision Industries USAS-12** *Source:* https://en.wikipedia.org/wiki/Daewoo_Precision_Industries_USAS-12?oldid=694179933 *Contributors:* Bloodshedder, Robbot, Wmahan, Tamman2000, Avriette, Pmsyyz, Mecanismo, Night Gyr, Martey, Evil Monkey, Magister Mathematicae, Miq, Ground Zero, Gurch, Chobot, Albrozdude, Kjlewis, Coltius, TonicBH, NawlinWiki, Asams10, Digitalguru, Some guy, SmackBot, Asgard01, Chris the speller, Thumperward, Sadads, Cassivs, LWF, CenozoicEra, Shadowspirit216, Andypandy.UK, Arctic-Editor, Veritas Panther, CmdrObot, Timothylord, Cydebot, Hydraton31, Aldis90, Indy muaddib, PaperTruths, Jhsounds, DagosNavy, Thernlund, Mike Searson, Olegvolk, MartinBot, Ginsengbomb, Stultus juventus, EPIC X, DanMP5, Num1dgen, Specter01010, Paulwharton, DOHC Holiday, TXiKiBoT, Wepsexpert, Cycloptic, Koalorka, MrChupon, SieBot, ToePeu.bot, ZH Evers, Ecthelion83, ClueBot, PixelBot, TheTranc, Berean Hunter, DumZiBoT, WikHead, Nukes4Tots, Addbot, Nohomers48, Lightbot, Luckas-bot, Yobot, Desertfox2001, ArmyRangerSniper, Kadrun, Citation bot, GrouchoBot, Arandomlogin, Surv1v4llst, DrilBot, Pilot850, ROG5728, Mztourist, EmausBot, Armypilot, Wingman4l7, Skrunyak, Zeta1127,89thLegion, Widr, Testtesthax, RedheadsWin, Roachtech, Editorhulk, Redalert2fan, Recon Apache, Ironborn99, ArmbrustBot, Stormmeteo, KitFistoPL and Anonymous: 81
- **Franchi mod .410** *Source:* https://en.wikipedia.org/wiki/Franchi_mod_.410?oldid=647000788 *Contributors:* Bgwhite, Cydebot, Berean Hunter, MatthewVanitas, Yobot, Sdafhgh, Skrunyak, DrunkSquirrel and Anonymous: 1
- **Gordon Close-Support Weapon System** *Source:* https://en.wikipedia.org/wiki/Gordon_Close-Support_Weapon_System?oldid=652736392 *Contributors:* DocWatson42, Tabletop, Hairy Dude, SmackBot, Chris the speller, Cydebot, Magioladitis, R'n'B, Berean Hunter, Yobot, AnomieBOT, Diannaa, Skrunyak, ClueBot NG, Moneywagon, DrunkSquirrel, RedheadsWin, Wukkawakka and Anonymous: 7
- **Heckler & Koch HK CAWS** *Source:* https://en.wikipedia.org/wiki/Heckler_%26_Koch_HK_CAWS?oldid=693870603 *Contributors:* Finlay McWalter, Riddley, DocWatson42, Axeman, DragonflySixtyseven, Titanium Dragon, GregorB, GraemeLeggett, Vegaswikian, Dar-Ape, FlaBot, Sus scrofa, Wavelength, Cplbeaudoin, Ve3, Zzuuzz, Bluebot, Thumperward, Wizardman, KG200, LWF, Accurizer, Arctic-Editor, BSI, Ken Gallager, Cydebot, Daniel J. Leivick, MoogleDan, TXiKiBoT, Jschager, SieBot, Cehlon, Hyperionsteel, Mlaffs, Berean Hunter, Nukes4Tots, Kbdankbot, MatthewVanitas, Addbot, Lightbot, Htews, Yobot, Xqbot, Arandomlogin, Surv1v4llst, Anthrax2525, HJ Mitchell, Darkman IV, Cvuxton, 777sms, Tnt1984, Sdafhgh, CrimsonBot, Skrunyak, Zackmann08, MatteoNL97, Rezin, Eteethan and Anonymous: 25
- **Pancor Jackhammer** *Source:* https://en.wikipedia.org/wiki/Pancor_Jackhammer?oldid=682261422 *Contributors:* D, [212], Riddley, Naddy, Axeman, Gracefool, Chowbok, Geni, Sam Hocevar, Gest, Poccil, Mecanismo, Xezbeth, Phrost, El C, Sajt, Smalljim, Interiot, InShaneee, Ebz123, Cal 1234, Drat, Gene Nygaard, Coolgamer, Scienda, D.E. Watters, Mathmo, MarkTBSc, QuaestorXVII, A Train, 25~enwiki, Ud terrorist, Kallemax, Nemo5576, CoolFox, Chobot, DVdm, Albrozdude, Koveras, Hairy Dude, Hydrargyrum, Tastemyhouse, Asams10, Simmemann, Wilzo, Dutch-Bostonian, TheJesse, DisambigBot, SmackBot, ZS, Crondeemon, Peter Isotalo, Gilliam, Chris the speller, Thumperward, Deuxhero, The Rogue Penguin, Oatmeal batman, Trekphiler, UNHchabo, Cernen, Thomasyen, Mistress Selina Kyle, Xen 1986, JohnnyBatina, KG200, Rambo23, LWF, Arctic-Editor, Izaakb, Cabez, Dp462090, Henrickson, JForget, Cydebot, Peripitus, Thijs!bot, Jedibob5, Tachikoma22, Hmrox, Ingolfson, HanzoHattori, Cyclonius, Mike Searson, Gwern, CommonsDelinker, KTo288, Skepticus, Wil101, DanMP5, Ariobarzan, VolkovBot, Anynobody, TXiKiBoT, Robert1947, Curlycrouton, CanadrianUK, Hyperionsteel, Martarius, Happynoodleboycey, ClueBot, PipepBot, Mild

140   CHAPTER 10. TEXT AND IMAGE SOURCES, CONTRIBUTORS, AND LICENSES

Bill Hiccup, Infocalypse~enwiki, Berean Hunter, XLinkBot, Stickee, Kbdankbot, MatthewVanitas, Addbot, Ronhjones, SpBot, Herr Gruber, Lightbot, Luckas-bot, AnomieBOT, Winged Brick, SassoBot, Arandomlogin, Surv1v4l1st, D'ohBot, Degen Earthfast, ROG5728, WikitanvirBot, Tommy2010, Melissa1995, Sahurst123, Skrunyak, One.Ouch.Zero, ClueBot NG, Vjvjfjnbhvnvfnfv, Roughbeak, Helpful Pixie Bot, MilitaryNut, Hoppi8, Redalert2fan, M11rtinb, Uoayo, Kingrhem, MatteoNL97, Martin Cold Mans and Anonymous: 139

- **Smith & Wesson AS** *Source:* https://en.wikipedia.org/wiki/Smith_%26_Wesson_AS?oldid=652734582 *Contributors:* Axeman89, Tabletop, Od Mishehu, Chris the speller, Cydebot, Logan, Drmies, Niceguyedc, Addbot, Yobot, AnomieBOT, VernoWhitney, Wehw, Helpful Pixie Bot, MilitaryNut, Nabaker and Anonymous: 1

- **Special Operations Weapon** *Source:* https://en.wikipedia.org/wiki/Special_Operations_Weapon?oldid=680774918 *Contributors:* DocWatson42, Sarrica, Richwales, Tabletop, Mandarax, Ahpook, Felixmeister, Chris the speller, Snori, Wilhelm Wiesel, Cydebot, Rep07, Thorncrag, John Nevard, Arjayay, Yobot, 8GAUGE, Skrunyak, Vjvjfjnbhvnvfnfv, Shotoku64, DrunkSquirrel, ArmbrustBot and Anonymous: 6

- **M26 Modular Accessory Shotgun System** *Source:* https://en.wikipedia.org/wiki/M26_Modular_Accessory_Shotgun_System?oldid=661078394 *Contributors:* Riddley, Xanzzibar, Brianhe, Fluzwup, El C, Tronno, Thatguy96, Anthony Appleyard, Gene Nygaard, Woohookitty, D.E. Watters, Pol098, Nemo5576, WouterBot, Chobot, YurikBot, Hairy Dude, Ve3, Asams10, Thethinredline, SmackBot, Hanchi, Ominae, Chris the speller, LWF, Arctic-Editor, Sanandros, Orca1 9904, Cydebot, Myscrnnm, Thijs!bot, Deathbunny, Legaiaflame, Kronnang Dunn, A-Nottingham, Trusilver, Zero Serenity, Paulwharton, Ondundozonananandana, Bahamut0013, Koalorka, AlleborgoBot, Solicitr, ToePeu.bot, Whiporwill, Spartan198, Hyperionsteel, Ficbot, Berean Hunter, Nukes4Tots, Addbot, LaaknorBot, Herr Gruber, Lightbot, Delta 51, Luckas-bot, Yobot, Materialscientist, Xqbot, Amyl5869, Mark Schierbecker, Surv1v4l1st, MastiBot, EME44, Fallschirmjägergewehr 42, BattyBot, America789, MilitaryNut, TheOneHonkingAntelope, Monkbot, KitFistoPL, Rezin and Anonymous: 48

- **Marlin Model 25MG** *Source:* https://en.wikipedia.org/wiki/Marlin_Model_25MG?oldid=589616580 *Contributors:* Robofish, Berean Hunter, Yobot, Surv1v4l1st, Helpful Pixie Bot, BattyBot and Anonymous: 2

- **Marlin Model 55** *Source:* https://en.wikipedia.org/wiki/Marlin_Model_55?oldid=647337555 *Contributors:* Alan Liefting, Vegaswikian, Cydebot, Robertgreer, Berean Hunter, Surv1v4l1st, RjwilmsiBot, Helpful Pixie Bot and Anonymous: 2

- **Mossberg 183** *Source:* https://en.wikipedia.org/wiki/Mossberg_183?oldid=678526015 *Contributors:* KylieTastic, Berean Hunter, Juno, Talbot mike, Buttguy123 and Anonymous: 6

- **Mossberg 185** *Source:* https://en.wikipedia.org/wiki/Mossberg_185?oldid=678402893 *Contributors:* Hydrargyrum, SmackBot, Xx236, Cydebot, Robertgreer, SQL, Brewcrewer, Berean Hunter, Surv1v4l1st, Juno, DrilBot, Drumminor2nd, Helpful Pixie Bot, Chubblybunny124 and Anonymous: 7

- **High Standard Model 10** *Source:* https://en.wikipedia.org/wiki/High_Standard_Model_10?oldid=686757819 *Contributors:* Charles Matthews, Cmdrjameson, Anthony Appleyard, Babajobu, Spangineer, Gene Nygaard, Woohookitty, Icey, The Deviant, Grafikm fr, Oatmeal batman, Yaf, KaiserbKot, UVnet, Ohconfucius, LWF, Thernlund, STBot, Ana Nim, Thomas.W, Quindraco, Koalorka, Flyer22 Reborn, TubularWorld, Berean Hunter, Nukes4Tots, MatthewVanitas, Addbot, Al Jazeera Geezer, Lightbot, Luckas-bot, FrescoBot, BotdeSki, Sdafhgh, ZéroBot, Avatar9n, ClueBot NG, Catlemur, Piast93, Captwhale, Sabre ball, JosueRyan, CECrouch, MilitaryNut, Tbessler, MatteoNL97 and Anonymous: 22

- **Kel-Tec KSG** *Source:* https://en.wikipedia.org/wiki/Kel-Tec_KSG?oldid=692801041 *Contributors:* DocWatson42, Tabletop, BD2412, WriterHound, PhilKnight, Mike Searson, CommonsDelinker, Dbooksta, Niceguyedc, Darkhelmet322, John Nevard, SchreiberBike, Berean Hunter, Hoplophile, Addbot, Dreg102, Surv1v4l1st, Aoidh, Shosh3333, Reaper Eternal, ROG5728, ZéroBot, Wingman4l7, Thewolfchild, ClueBot NG, Andrewnius, Enfcer, Geornn, Helpful Pixie Bot, Kungfu2187, Wzrd1, Zackmann08, MilitaryNut, YFdyh-bot, PCondon45, Faizan, Shadowgun master, LegendRazgriz, TropicAces, MatteoNL97, Wcin2001 and Anonymous: 39

- **Neostead** *Source:* https://en.wikipedia.org/wiki/Neostead?oldid=655028209 *Contributors:* The Anome, JayTau, [212], Rogor, Zoicon5, Riddley, Orthogonal, DocWatson42, Axeman, Sam Hocevar, Gest, Tronno, Mark, Gene Nygaard, Coolgamer, D.E. Watters, Tabletop, SmackBot, Thumperward, Gmw, Arctic-Editor, Viperine, Thijs!bot, C6H12O6, Fallschirmjäger, Moses6533, CommonsDelinker, Adavidb, Robertgreer, Hammersoft, Quindraco, Koalorka, Maox, Dodger67, ImageRemovalBot, Happynoodleboycey, ClueBot, Mild Bill Hiccup, Berean Hunter, XLinkBot, Nukes4Tots, Kbdankbot, MatthewVanitas, Addbot, Deus257, Nohomers48, Wiki-Chris~enwiki, Tide rolls, Yobot, Legobot II, AnomieBOT, Xqbot, Arandomlogin, TobeBot, ROG5728, Tonoros7, Pokemon36, Sdafhgh, ClueBot NG, Yowanvista, MilitaryNut, KAF 314, Thescaredshadow, Filedelinkerbot, KitFistoPL, MatteoNL97, Jerry Kunzman and Anonymous: 37

- **Beretta 682** *Source:* https://en.wikipedia.org/wiki/Beretta_682?oldid=687186466 *Contributors:* DocWatson42, Old Moonraker, DrKay, Robertgreer, Mudwater, SieBot, CEOMao, Niceguyedc, Arjayay, Berean Hunter, Addbot, EdgeNavidad, LaaknorBot, Hidrobyte, Nototter, 777sms, EmausBot, GBMaryland and Anonymous: 9

- **Beretta DT-10** *Source:* https://en.wikipedia.org/wiki/Beretta_DT-10?oldid=645127573 *Contributors:* DocWatson42, RJFJR, Jtrainor, GregorB, Rjwilmsi, SmackBot, CSWarren, LessHeard vanU, CmdrObot, Alaibot, Fisherjs, Thernlund, Robertgreer, Jan Powell, Lucamaori, CEOMao, ClueBot, Berean Hunter, DumZiBoT, Yobot, Smoore102, 777sms, 英雄少年ревверон, SkateTier and Anonymous: 9

- **Beretta Silver Pigeon** *Source:* https://en.wikipedia.org/wiki/Beretta_Silver_Pigeon?oldid=639601897 *Contributors:* DocWatson42, CommonsDelinker, Robertgreer, Mudwater, ImageRemovalBot, SchreiberBike, Berean Hunter, Tim1357, 777sms, Catlemur, Addonexus and Anonymous: 6

- **Browning Citori** *Source:* https://en.wikipedia.org/wiki/Browning_Citori?oldid=660445911 *Contributors:* O'Dea, Tarc, Gadget850, NeilN, Chris the speller, AndrewHowse, DumbBOT, Ekabhishek, Thernlund, Robertgreer, Mudwater, JamesBHunt, Dawn Bard, CEOMao, Greatrobo76, ImageRemovalBot, Dataproducts, ShadowPeo, Berean Hunter, Locobot, Weedwhacker128, Thediyhunter, Jack Greenmaven, Lowercase sigmabot, TexGEOas and Anonymous: 16

- **Browning Superposed** *Source:* https://en.wikipedia.org/wiki/Browning_Superposed?oldid=649390960 *Contributors:* RJFJR, Woohookitty, Adamdaley, Robertgreer, Mudwater, JamesBHunt, CEOMao, Berean Hunter, PMLawrence, Locobot, Tim1357, Jamesallain85, Lemnaminor and Anonymous: 12

- **Cynergy Shotgun** *Source:* https://en.wikipedia.org/wiki/Cynergy_Shotgun?oldid=615229337 *Contributors:* RJFJR, Rjwilmsi, Avalon, Accurizer, CmdrObot, Tirkfl, Robertgreer, ImageRemovalBot, Excirial, Berean Hunter, Paulmnguyen, Rich jj, Rogerstitt and Anonymous: 3

10.1. TEXT

- **Ithaca Auto & Burglar** *Source:* https://en.wikipedia.org/wiki/Ithaca_Auto_%26_Burglar?oldid=663722977 *Contributors:* Asams10, Salmanazar, SmackBot, Boris Barowski, Cydebot, Nadal Kenlyl, Thijs!bot, Darklilac, StudierMalMarburg, Degenret01, Robertgreer, Berean Hunter, Addbot, Tassedethe, Lightbot, Yobot, Surv1v4l1st, HRoestBot, Yowzemz, Quake44, Lemnaminor and Anonymous: 6
- **Paradox gun** *Source:* https://en.wikipedia.org/wiki/Paradox_gun?oldid=653091147 *Contributors:* Shyamal, Pol098, Tabletop, Jimp, SmackBot, O keyes, Can't sleep, clown will eat me, Dl2000, Gil Gamesh, Amalas, Lesqual, Wikid77, Thernlund, NJR ZA, Robertgreer, S, Clmckelvie, Nothernug, Addbot, OlEnglish, Luckas-bot, Linsboat, Secahtah, Jonesey95, Lord Mountbatten, Bill Bryant, Hmainsbot1, Geckcgt and Anonymous: 20
- **Remington Spartan 310** *Source:* https://en.wikipedia.org/wiki/Remington_Spartan_310?oldid=503673569 *Contributors:* Gjs238, Cydebot, Robertgreer, Mudwater, SQL, ImageRemovalBot, Berean Hunter, LuK3, BornInLeningrad, Egill masson and Anonymous: 4
- **Ruger Gold Label** *Source:* https://en.wikipedia.org/wiki/Ruger_Gold_Label?oldid=551193328 *Contributors:* Gjs238, Deathsythe, Cydebot, Robertgreer, Mudwater, ImageRemovalBot, Berean Hunter and Anonymous: 4
- **Ruger Red Label** *Source:* https://en.wikipedia.org/wiki/Ruger_Red_Label?oldid=682174221 *Contributors:* Graeme Bartlett, BD2412, Delldot, John, Mike Searson, Malik Shabazz, Fluffernutter, AnomieBOT, Tyrol5, Plasticspork, GoingBatty, Cf collins, Zackmann08, Monkbot and Anonymous: 2
- **Stoeger Coach Gun** *Source:* https://en.wikipedia.org/wiki/Stoeger_Coach_Gun?oldid=587973456 *Contributors:* Nyttend, Craxd, Robertgreer, Mudwater, ImageRemovalBot, Berean Hunter, DumZiBoT, Winged Brick, Professor Storyteller and Anonymous: 11
- **Stoeger Condor** *Source:* https://en.wikipedia.org/wiki/Stoeger_Condor?oldid=557637040 *Contributors:* MassGalactusUniversum, Welsh, SmackBot, Danethebrown, MarshBot, Wiki Raja, Robertgreer, Mudwater, Mzmadmike, ImageRemovalBot, Berean Hunter, Emediarifleman, ClueBot NG and Anonymous: 12
- **Ugartechea** *Source:* https://en.wikipedia.org/wiki/Ugartechea?oldid=666824581 *Contributors:* Woohookitty, BD2412, Rjwilmsi, SmackBot, Hmains, Chris the speller, Ntsimp, Robertgreer, Maile66, Jarrodhollinger, YSSYguy, Berean Hunter, Yobot, Kartano, Kostas 03, Faceless Enemy, RedheadsWin, Lcsupply and Anonymous: 3
- **Winchester Model 21** *Source:* https://en.wikipedia.org/wiki/Winchester_Model_21?oldid=694431377 *Contributors:* Discospinster, Woohookitty, Vegaswikian, Bgwhite, SmackBot, Ohconfucius, Kent Witham, Nitro308, Thernlund, CommonsDelinker, Robertgreer, Matthew craigge, Andy Dingley, SQL, Solicitr, Montanakennedy, Berean Hunter, Kartano, LilHelpa, FrescoBot, Keserman, Jonesey95, 777sms, DeusImperator, AvicAWB, RedheadsWin, Flynn lives shotguns, DaWulf2013, Dylan395 and Anonymous: 7
- **Martini–Henry** *Source:* https://en.wikipedia.org/wiki/Martini%E2%80%93Henry?oldid=692691955 *Contributors:* TwoOneTwo, The Anome, Maury Markowitz, Kchishol1970, Llywrch, Fred Bauder, Jll, Wik, Riddley, Altenmann, DocWatson42, Crimson30, Average Earthman, Neilc, Dunks58, AliveFreeHappy, Rich Farmbrough, Pavel Vozenilek, Kross, Polylerus, Grutness, Max rspct, BanyanTree, Lkinkade, Woohookitty, Pol098, Before My Ken, Dmol, GregorB, MikeWilson, GraemeLeggett, Tradnor, Pmj, Josh Parris, Jivecat, Leithp, Nemo5576, Chris Capoccia, Gaius Cornelius, Ve3, Adamrush, Grafikm fr, HLGallon, SmackBot, Deon Steyn, JohnMac777, Hmains, ChrisPer, Chris the speller, Bluebot, Rcbutcher, Modest Genius, Trekphiler, Yaf, KaiserbBot, Zazpot, Atirador, Zeppfan, Khazar, Мико, Gungho, Wilhelm Wiesel, Kevin Murray, Mattbr, Cydebot, Aodhdubh, Dennette, Lugnuts, Aldis90, Thijs!bot, Commander Zulu, Petecarney, SupremeDalek~enwiki, Geniac, Faizhaider, Thernlund, Raoulduke47, Rettetast, Jetwave Dave, Ja 62, Vkt183, Thomas.W, Kyle the bot, Bigyaks, Jeff 8, Nedrutland, Tttom, Koalorka, Paul J Williams, Lightmouse, KeithDoyon, TinyMark, Parkwells, Nick19thind, PixelBot, Rhododendrites, Eddaido, Thewellman, Berean Hunter, GPS73, Kintaro, MatthewVanitas, Addbot, Yobot, PMLawrence, AnomieBOT, LilHelpa, Chilicheez, WickerWiki, J appleseed2, Padres Hana, Gürgli, LucienBOT, Johnco50, John of Reading, Faceless Enemy, Sdafhgh, K6ka, ZéroBot, L1A1 FAL, Mongoosander, SSDGFCTCT9, Whoop whoop pull up, Catlemur, MarcusBritish, Helpful Pixie Bot, KLBot2, Apachedave, Oblivionisathand, RedheadsWin, Conorman123, Irondome, KingQueenPrince, Miratvorac 151271, Collection77, Ithinkicahn, Crow, Abattoir666, Monkbot, Diffish, Zortwort, ProprioMe OW and Anonymous: 86
- **Winchester Model 1887/1901** *Source:* https://en.wikipedia.org/wiki/Winchester_Model_1887/1901?oldid=694178809 *Contributors:* Netsnipe, Evercat, David3565, DocWatson42, Tom harrison, AliveFreeHappy, Ianblair23, Pauli133, Tierlieb, Martyr~enwiki, Erebus555, Vegaswikian, Chobot, Cornellrockey, Rowan Moore, Jakash, D. Wu, ColdFusion650, Asams10, Lani12, Groyolo, Ominae, Bluebot, Cloj, Dual Freq, Rrburke, Kukini, Evenios, Omnedon, Courcelles, Tawkerbot2, Gogo Dodo, Commander Zulu, JustAGal, Not Diablo, Thernlund, CeeWhy2, Robertgreer, DanMP5, Thomas.W, JamesBHunt, Matthew craigge, SQL, SieBot, Pacoseguro, Martarius, ClueBot, SuperHamster, Sun Creator, Scalhotrod, Berean Hunter, Jovianeye, Quickload, Nukes4Tots, SireMarshall, King Pickle, Addbot, 1525amo, Ronhjones, LaaknorBot, Luckasbot, Yobot, Thegunslinger99, 5infBrig, AnomieBOT, Xqbot, Bryce264, Winged Brick, FrescoBot, Surv1v4l1st, LucienBOT, Kingkong0192, Ceraniic, Tetraedycal, Noelmaguire, Pinethicket, 777sms, Diiscovery, DeusImperator, Bradosh, ROG5728, Seanl42, Minimanpo, Zaqq, WikitanvirBot, CorneiliusIII, Model1887, Gary7even, Jpearce63, Daonguyen95, Hitmage, FinalRapture, LukeQuietus, XNUMB4H THR33x, ClueBot NG, Pies tiki chicken, RedheadsWin, Survivalist27, MilitaryNut, Cerabot~enwiki, Isarra (HG), Nabaker, AKS.9955, Codyminer1, NicktheSlick870, Bu193 and Anonymous: 166
- **Bandayevsky RB-12** *Source:* https://en.wikipedia.org/wiki/Bandayevsky_RB-12?oldid=633796480 *Contributors:* DocWatson42, Woohookitty, Whpq, CommonsDelinker, Yobot, AnomieBOT, Catlemur, Zenithfel, Ose\fio, Sdhslajhdj, MilitaryNut, G PViB, Nikvonbond and Anonymous: 4
- **Benelli Nova** *Source:* https://en.wikipedia.org/wiki/Benelli_Nova?oldid=689449173 *Contributors:* Chowbok, Discospinster, Xezbeth, CDN99, Ricky81682, Woohookitty, SmackBot, LWF, Cydebot, Hit bull, win steak, Thernlund, Mike Searson, CommonsDelinker, Skier Dude, Robertgreer, Nburden, Matthew craigge, Daveosok, PianoKeys, Berean Hunter, XLinkBot, SilvonenBot, Addbot, Sportpro448, LaaknorBot, דוד55, Yobot, Ukman123, A Werewolf, Jericovb, GoingBatty, ZéroBot, ClueBot NG, 220 of Borg, TheCascadian, Jamesallain85, Addonexus, Thejoj and Anonymous: 23
- **Benelli Supernova** *Source:* https://en.wikipedia.org/wiki/Benelli_Supernova?oldid=689449191 *Contributors:* SmackBot, Scottwrites, Archangelmr, Cydebot, Mike Searson, Skier Dude, Robertgreer, DanMP5, Mpeylo, Berean Hunter, Yobot, Quebec99, LilHelpa, A Werewolf, Jericovb, ClueBot NG, 220 of Borg, Alexander.kvasa, Jamesallain85 and Anonymous: 9

- **Brixia PM-5** *Source:* https://en.wikipedia.org/wiki/Brixia_PM-5?oldid=684547545 *Contributors:* Niceguyedc, XLinkBot, Jbhunley, Bobby quite and Martabrixia

- **Ciener Ultimate Over/Under** *Source:* https://en.wikipedia.org/wiki/Ciener_Ultimate_Over/Under?oldid=660727790 *Contributors:* Woohookitty, Rjwilmsi, Warreed, SmackBot, Hmains, Thumperward, Lfstevens, GurchBot, Robertgreer, Paulwharton, NickResonance, K1ng l0v3, Ketas, Nohomers48, Yobot, Novaseminary, PigFlu Oink, City52, Helpful Pixie Bot, BattyBot and Anonymous: 6

- **Fabarm SDASS Tactical** *Source:* https://en.wikipedia.org/wiki/Fabarm_SDASS_Tactical?oldid=694245229 *Contributors:* BD2412, Rjwilmsi, Valentinejoesmith, Bgwhite, CommonsDelinker, Robertgreer, Mockingbus, Irving17, Berean Hunter, MatthewVanitas, LilHelpa, Ajpralston1, FrescoBot, H3llBot, Sashkarossiya and Anonymous: 5

- **FN P-12** *Source:* https://en.wikipedia.org/wiki/FN_P-12?oldid=639690655 *Contributors:* The RedBurn, Cydebot, Plasticspork, ROG5728 and Zackmann08

- **FN TPS** *Source:* https://en.wikipedia.org/wiki/FN_TPS?oldid=639690675 *Contributors:* The RedBurn, Cydebot, Plasticspork, Zackmann08, Mogism and ???

- **Heckler & Koch FABARM FP6** *Source:* https://en.wikipedia.org/wiki/Heckler_%26_Koch_FABARM_FP6?oldid=640506823 *Contributors:* Chowbok, The RedBurn, Woohookitty, Gadget850, Hebrides, CommonsDelinker, Robertgreer, Gokevgo, Jumbo Walrus, Berean Hunter, MatthewVanitas, Yobot, Ulric1313, Ajpralston1, Darkman IV, Macgyver-bd 896, Braden 0.0, 777sms, Moloko ogog, Ts7946, Carrera 3.2, Sashkarossiya and Anonymous: 8

- **Ithaca 37** *Source:* https://en.wikipedia.org/wiki/Ithaca_37?oldid=692842054 *Contributors:* Choster, Mike Rosoft, PaulHanson, Hohum, RPellessier, SchuminWeb, Ground Zero, Kjlewis, Wavelength, Asams10, Garion96, GMan552, SmackBot, Yaf, OrphanBot, Zonedar, Keyesc, Jjjjjjjjjj, Hotspur23, Arctic-Editor, J Milburn, Cydebot, Aldis90, Thijs!bot, Ulfrikr, Deathbunny, HHWhitePony, MartinBot, Robertgreer, DanMP5, Ana Nim, Kilmer-san, SQL, BMHBrown, MOOOOOPS, Martarius, ClueBot, Shentosara, Excirial, PixelBot, John Nevard, Niteshift36, Thewellman, Berean Hunter, Josh Woolstenhulme, Nukes4Tots, Chiefops, Addbot, Cuaxdon, Tide rolls, Lightbot, Teles, Zorrobot, Yobot, TaBOT-zerem, Tony0Maxwell, 5infBrig, Ulric1313, LilHelpa, DSisyphBot, Amendola90, Surv1v4l1st, A Werewolf, DrilBot, Guncrank, Emediarifleman, Ace Oliveira, WikitanvirBot, Ose\fio, Dastare, Metricopolus, MilitaryNut, TheFlarbar, Jamesallain85, Gr8bald1, ArmbrustBot, Thescaredshadow, DAVFUR, Johnmacintosh14, RiotheFixer and Anonymous: 63

- **KAC Masterkey** *Source:* https://en.wikipedia.org/wiki/KAC_Masterkey?oldid=688257516 *Contributors:* JohnOwens, DocWatson42, Fluzwup, Tronno, D.E. Watters, WouterBot, Chobot, Ve3, Grafikm fr, SmackBot, MalafayaBot, Woodrow Buzard, Hotspur23, Orca1 9904, Deathbunny, Thernlund, CommonsDelinker, Robertgreer, Paulwharton, Yvori, Koalorka, Spartan198, MystBot, Addbot, Yobot, Ulric1313, Surv1v4l1st, Reaper Eternal, Ben H Wong, Sverigekillen, EmausBot, Writ Keeper, America789, MilitaryNut, Tyrotrus, Treaduuue and Anonymous: 15

- **KS-23** *Source:* https://en.wikipedia.org/wiki/KS-23?oldid=653851961 *Contributors:* Rlandmann, Jouster, Altenmann, DocWatson42, Bobblewik, Avriette, CanisRufus, Wendell, TaintedMustard, Miq, Rjwilmsi, Nemo5576, Arima, Groyolo, SmackBot, Edgar181, OrphanBot, AndrewHowse, MarshBot, Gdo01, Bobby Boulders the Merciful, CommonsDelinker, Robertgreer, Thomas.W, Cerebellum, ClueBot, Mlaffs, Berean Hunter, MatthewVanitas, Zeberwood, Addbot, Nohomers48, LaaknorBot, Lightbot, Robmcmahan, Yobot, Xqbot, FrescoBot, Surv1v4l1st, EmausBot, WikitanvirBot, Tnt1984, L1A1 FAL, -xwingsx-, Catlemur, Ose\fio, Terrance123, Juubelimies, TimeScorpion, BG19bot, MilitaryNut, Maverick chile86, Kanadskaja Kazarka and Anonymous: 45

- **MAG-7** *Source:* https://en.wikipedia.org/wiki/MAG-7?oldid=692848902 *Contributors:* Maury Markowitz, DocWatson42, Bobblewik, Discospinster, Goldom, Gene Nygaard, GregorB, Mayumashu, The Deviant, Grafikm fr, Ospalh, SmackBot, Ohconfucius, Hotspur23, AllStarZ, Arctic-Editor, Marshaul, Aldis90, STBot, Robertgreer, DanMP5, TXiKiBoT, Addbot, Materialscientist, Surv1v4l1st, HRoestBot, Techno Arms, ROG5728, Widr, BendelacBOT, Sb4220, MilitaryNut, Aliwal2012, NS777, Sergei Brukovskyi, CounterStroke, Lttlefoot, SSB Ratchet and Anonymous: 25

- **Mossberg 500** *Source:* https://en.wikipedia.org/wiki/Mossberg_500?oldid=693915245 *Contributors:* Edward, Taxman, Riddley, DocWatson42, Everyking, Leonard G., Chowbok, AliveFreeHappy, Stepp-Wulf, Wcrowe, Blanchette, Wrp103, Xezbeth, Fluzwup, El C, Keron Cyst, Cmdrjameson, Anthony Appleyard, Spangineer, RPellessier, Docboat, Kenyon, Mmarkley, Woohookitty, Tabletop, GregorB, Macaddct1984, GraemeLeggett, Rjwilmsi, Vary, 25~enwiki, FlaBot, RedSoxFan, Nemo5576, Alhutch, Innotminkus, Jimp, RussBot, Hydrargyrum, Gaius Cornelius, Toecutter, Ve3, TDogg310, Ospalh, Asams10, PGPirate, Natmaka, Hayden120, SmackBot, Hanchi, Boris Barowski, Chris the speller, Bluebot, Trekphiler, Yaf, Lox, Wayneh, Caim, LWF, Pikipiki, Beetstra, TastyPoutine, Neddyseagoon, Neoking, JForget, CmdrObot, Virginian, Gunny01, Orca1 9904, Cydebot, Aodhdubh, Jmaynard, Pennstump, Chuto, Dromoli, Epbr123, Rhrad, Corwin MacGregor, I already forgot, Doc Tropics, Alexselkirk1704, BatteryIncluded, Mike Searson, Frotz, Bowingo, Jawatech, MartinBot, Rettetast, R'n'B, Anas Salloum, Dakirw8, New Hampshirite, Robertgreer, Mangotang, DanMP5, ArcticTundra, John2510, Ana Nim, Gothbag, Mudwater, Soliloquial, Dbooksta, TXiKiBoT, Liko81, Delk, Zaher1988, Cerebellum, Ultratone85, Andy Dingley, SQL, Kimber1911, Freebiegrabber, Bahamut0013, Koalorka, S.Örvarr.S, Crserrano, Grimitar, Apple farmer, Jmp98251, Abramsgavin, ClueBot, EoGuy, PixelBot, Sun Creator, Mlaffs, Berean Hunter, Nukes4Tots, Hoplophile, Addbot, Kelly, Jessaveryja, Leszek Jańczuk, Boltaction338sniper, SpBot, Delta 51, Yobot, Boksi, AnomieBOT, Jim1138, JackieBot, Unara, Materialscientist, Aneah, Capricorn42, LucienBOT, A Werewolf, Juno, ROG5728, RjwilmsiBot, Misconceptions2, Kenmiller7883, Akjar13, Faceless Enemy, 1brettsnyder, Illegitimate Barrister, Sbninja, H3llBot, Ewa5050, L1A1 FAL, Thewolfchild, ClueBot NG, Catlemur, MeFr, Ose\fio, PeturW, KLBot2, BG19bot, Jwandbt, Viperjody, 556A2, StrangeApparition2011, Dainomite, Glacialfox, Andriel duran, Mossy500, MilitaryNut, JonyDAG, Bluebasket, Wywin, Black houk, Kenny199955, Lemnaminor, Shkvoz, Monkbot, George Pattern, Coppz46, XFullxMetalxWolfx and Anonymous: 191

- **Mossberg Maverick** *Source:* https://en.wikipedia.org/wiki/Mossberg_Maverick?oldid=632194928 *Contributors:* AliveFreeHappy, PoccilScript, Mandarax, NawlinWiki, SmackBot, Moez, Nawsum526, Hardyplants, Boris Barowski, MiroslavPragl, Halo Storm, Cydebot, JustAGal, Robertgreer, DanMP5, SQL, Websterphreaky, Grainman, Fugi187, Addbot, JimVC3, Surv1v4l1st, Juno, Djlipsy, ClueBot NG, Jack Greenmaven, Imthatbigboy, MilitaryNut, JasonA19 and Anonymous: 34

- **New Haven 600** *Source:* https://en.wikipedia.org/wiki/New_Haven_600?oldid=632194956 *Contributors:* Woohookitty, Pennstump, Vipinhari, Juno, ClueBot NG, Justinclarke and Anonymous: 4

10.1. TEXT

- **Norinco HP9-1** *Source:* https://en.wikipedia.org/wiki/Norinco_HP9-1?oldid=567674703 *Contributors:* Ds13, Woohookitty, BlaiseFEgan, Chris the speller, MGlosenger, Octane, Matt714, Cydebot, Hydraton31, Kevin23, Thernlund, LindaWarheads, CommonsDelinker, Robertgreer, VolkovBot, RagnarokEOTW, One half 3544, EnviroGranny, Denisarona, ImageRemovalBot, ClueBot, Chessy999, Addbot, EZ1234, Lightbot, Delta 51, AnomieBOT, 22Rimfire, Surv1v4l1st, RedBot and Anonymous: 24

- **Remington Model 10** *Source:* https://en.wikipedia.org/wiki/Remington_Model_10?oldid=674767982 *Contributors:* Robertgreer, Drmies, Thewellman, Yobot, AnomieBOT, Ulric1313, Winged Brick, FrescoBot, A Werewolf, Plasticspork, DeusImperator, Zackmann08, BattyBot, MilitaryNut, RainbowDash 21 and Anonymous: 6

- **Remington Model 17** *Source:* https://en.wikipedia.org/wiki/Remington_Model_17?oldid=568667047 *Contributors:* Vegaswikian, Asams10, Gjs238, IronGargoyle, Cydebot, Robertgreer, Skipweasel, Nukes4Tots, Lightbot, Yobot, Tony0Maxwell, Ulric1313, Gary7even, ??? and Anonymous: 4

- **Remington Model 31** *Source:* https://en.wikipedia.org/wiki/Remington_Model_31?oldid=694348576 *Contributors:* Luis Dantas, Geni, Pol098, Vegaswikian, Asams10, SmackBot, Gjs238, Cydebot, CommonsDelinker, Robertgreer, SQL, Thewellman, Berean Hunter, DumZiBoT, Nukes4Tots, Yobot, Tony0Maxwell, Ulric1313, Winged Brick, Macgyver-bd 896, Gary7even, ClueBot NG, Jamesalfred009, ???, DaWulf2013, Brian2759 and Anonymous: 10

- **Remington Model 870** *Source:* https://en.wikipedia.org/wiki/Remington_Model_870?oldid=693836324 *Contributors:* Riddley, DocWatson42, Luis Dantas, Ds13, Gamaliel, Mike Rosoft, AliveFreeHappy, Avriette, Night Gyr, Bender235, El C, Bobo192, Tronno, Monkeyleg, TheParanoidOne, Andrew Gray, Fat pig73, Wtmitchell, Deacon of Pndapetzim, Gene Nygaard, Woohookitty, Tabletop, Vegaswikian, Jmajonis, FlaBot, Coolhawks88, Chobot, Bgwhite, Junky, Gaius Cornelius, Los688, TonicBH, Ve3, Dr Debug, Asams10, Wknight94, Koblentz, Hayden120, Waterj2, Nick-D, SmackBot, Hanchi, Ominae, Deon Steyn, C.Fred, Eskimbot, Gjs238, KingRaptor, Ohnoitsjamie, Winterheart, Manuelomar2001, Chris the speller, Zsinj, Trekphiler, Yaf, Sawran~enwiki, OrphanBot, Shadow1, Michael clements, Zahid Abdassabur, LWF, Mark-Sutton, Clementsm, DouglasCalvert, Rkosh, Tawkerbot2, Virginian, Timothylord, Tbq, Hga, Cydebot, Kevin23, DumbBOT, RottweilerCS, PKT, Mattisse, CosineKitty, Thernlund, Dili, Mike Searson, Yhinz17, Climax Void, Rettetast, CommonsDelinker, FLJuJitsu, It Is Me Here, New Hampshirite, Dp cameron, Ndunruh, Robertgreer, Heero Kirashami, DanMP5, Pistolspete, Gyrel, Signalhead, Paulwharton, Gothbag, Thomas.W, Mudwater, Refuto Nefandus, Urbancore, SQL, Bahamut0013, Koalorka, Wixteria, SieBot, Crserrano, K1ng l0v3, Mockingbus, PraetorianD, Sf46, KoshVorlon, ZH Evers, ClueBot, Hutcher, Chessy999, CounterVandalismBot, PixelBot, Niteshift36, Fugi187, Thewellman, Berean Hunter, GPS73, 1scruffy1, Nukes4Tots, MystBot, HexaChord, Addbot, Raymond88824, Kyle E. Coyote, Download, Lightbot, LuK3, Luckas-bot, Yobot, Kadrun, PMLawrence, 5infBrig, AnomieBOT, RandyWakeman, 22Rimfire, Jim1138, Piano non troppo, Ulric1313, Mks86, Aneah, Xqbot, Terrortank, Cureden, Capricorn42, Winged Brick, WotWeiller, Amendola90, SCΛRECROW, Maddog07, Surv1v4l1st, LyndsySimon, A Werewolf, Mrzeppolainen22, Brody Kennen, Godblessamerica1, PvsKllKsVp, RedBot, Pikiwyn, MKFI, Plasticspork, Macgyver-bd 896, Felis domestica, TheOriginalFlavor, DeusImperator, ROG5728, BuckeyeDentite, Ben H Wong, Med358, EmausBot, WikitanvirBot, Akjar13, IiDarKStaR, Tommy2010, ZéroBot, L1A1 FAL, Donner60, Puffin, ChuispastonBot, EdoBot, ClueBot NG, Catlemur, Ose\fio, Helpful Pixie Bot, Lowercase sigmabot, BG19bot, Mark Arsten, Dainomite, Crh23, Tahiatt1, CensoredBiscuit, Ices2Csharp, Zackmann08, Gulosten, BattyBot, Spencer2012, MilitaryNut, Rickdrick, Khan trav, Redalert2fan, Lindeman4m, Lemnaminor, Shkvoz, SamTheClam, IrishSpook, Hrqa, George Pattern, ColonialGrid, FrontRangeFuzz and Anonymous: 268

- **Remington Model 887** *Source:* https://en.wikipedia.org/wiki/Remington_Model_887?oldid=628851298 *Contributors:* Golbez, Chowbok, BD2412, ChewyLSB, SmackBot, Widefox, VAcharon, Czr88, Robertgreer, Roarshocker, ImageRemovalBot, Piledhigheranddeeper, Berean Hunter, Lightbot, Yobot, Metalhead94, Surv1v4l1st, DeusImperator, ClueBot NG, Markm84, Drew Sheily, MichaelGScarn and Anonymous: 13

- **RMB-93** *Source:* https://en.wikipedia.org/wiki/RMB-93?oldid=635544821 *Contributors:* Tabletop, SmackBot, AndrewHowse, Robertgreer, VolkovBot, Cerebellum, SieBot, Dodger67, Addbot, Luckas-bot, Yobot, ROG5728, Zaqq, Tnt1984, Catlemur, Helpful Pixie Bot, MilitaryNut and Anonymous: 6

- **Serbu Super-Shorty** *Source:* https://en.wikipedia.org/wiki/Serbu_Super-Shorty?oldid=675321178 *Contributors:* Rich Farmbrough, GregorB, Rjwilmsi, Hairy Dude, Mike Searson, Robertgreer, Bluejames19, Precision40, Hoplophile, Stanislao Avogadro, The real Marcoman, Surv1v4l1st, Miguel Escopeta, Trappist the monk, Helpful Pixie Bot, StolenBlueBox, MilitaryNut, Monkbot and Anonymous: 11

- **Stevens Model 520/620** *Source:* https://en.wikipedia.org/wiki/Stevens_Model_520/620?oldid=694720300 *Contributors:* Delta13C, Cordless Larry, Oshwah, Yobot, Winged Brick, Faceless Enemy, BG19bot, Rezin and Keydet92

- **Stevens Model 77E** *Source:* https://en.wikipedia.org/wiki/Stevens_Model_77E?oldid=680878127 *Contributors:* Chris the speller, CommonsDelinker, Thewellman, Djbaird95 and Anonymous: 3

- **TOZ-194** *Source:* https://en.wikipedia.org/wiki/TOZ-194?oldid=646341257 *Contributors:* Altenmann, Herbee, Chowbok, BD2412, Rjwilmsi, Nautilator, Jonathen snake, Rettetast, Robertgreer, Cyfal, Nn123645, Explicit, TheTranc, Cold Phoenix, DumZiBoT, MatthewVanitas, Addbot, Yobot, Madara100, MilitaryNut, G PViB, TheGFishs and Anonymous: 7

- **UTAS UTS-15** *Source:* https://en.wikipedia.org/wiki/UTAS_UTS-15?oldid=691667502 *Contributors:* DocWatson42, Nick Number, KylieTastic, Thomas.W, Wachholder, Yobot, Surv1v4l1st, ROG5728, John of Reading, Shadowgun master, Nabaker, LegendRazgriz, MatteoNL97 and Anonymous: 16

- **Valtro PM-5/PM-5-350** *Source:* https://en.wikipedia.org/wiki/Valtro_PM-5/PM-5-350?oldid=650058196 *Contributors:* Chris the speller, ChrisCork, Nyttend, Ferics, Addbot, RANDREWF7777, Yobot, ZéroBot, MilitaryNut, Bobby quite and Anonymous: 3

- **Winchester Model 1200** *Source:* https://en.wikipedia.org/wiki/Winchester_Model_1200?oldid=689400364 *Contributors:* Kainaw, AliveFreeHappy, Koavf, Vegaswikian, FlaBot, SchuminWeb, TexasAndroid, Asams10, Hayden120, Hmains, LinguistAtLarge, Open-box, OrphanBot, SMasters, Naaman Brown, Dl2000, NativeForeigner, CumbiaDude, Alaibot, Aldis90, PaZuZu, Mike Searson, Robertgreer, VolkovBot, TXiKiBoT, Albinoballpython, SQL, Molotovnight, Solicitr, Hutcher, Excirial, Thewellman, Berean Hunter, Addbot, WikiDreamer Bot, Ptbotgourou, AnomieBOT, Ulric1313, Xqbot, Ohmygod766, RibotBOT, Septuater, Auntieruth55, 777sms, DeusImperator, ROG5728, Phoenix ICR, Zaqq, EmausBot, Ruby38, Ragfin, Mzwhiz21, TheXenomorph1, Jill Orly, Ose\fio, Helpful Pixie Bot, Cyberpower678, Shanethoms, ArmbrustBot and Anonymous: 44

- **Winchester Model 1897** *Source:* https://en.wikipedia.org/wiki/Winchester_Model_1897?oldid=692420060 *Contributors:* Ahoerstemeier, Steinsky, Bloodshedder, Riddley, Fredrik, DocWatson42, Oberiko, Pettifogger, Phil1988, Kross, Mdd, Evil Monkey, Fdewaele, Rjwilmsi, Koavf, Vegaswikian, Nemo5576, Agamemnon2, Uew, YurikBot, Gaius Cornelius, RandallJones, Wiki alf, Megapixie, Ve3, JdwNYC, Asams10, Jacklee, KaHOnas, Allens, Tom Morris, SmackBot, Hux, Eskimbot, Srnec, Chris the speller, Bluebot, Yaf, OrphanBot, Rhkramer, Calvados~enwiki, SMasters, Hawf wit, NativeForeigner, Drlegendre, Dlohcierekim, Heqs, Elf242, JohnCD, Cydebot, Lovemachine~enwiki, Thijs!bot, Commander Zulu, Deathbunny, James086, Jack Bethune, JustAGal, Parsecboy, Thernlund, Mike Searson, Robertgreer, STBotD, 1337Intellect, Dorftrottel, Thomas.W, SQL, AlleborgoBot, MrChupon, Solicitr, Alucard365, ClueBot, XPTO, Drmies, Boing! said Zebedee, Jusdafax, John Nevard, Sun Creator, DumZiBoT, Dawnsky24, Josh Woolstenhulme, Nukes4Tots, MatthewVanitas, Addbot, Magus732, LaaknorBot, AndersBot, Zorrobot, Weaseloid, Yobot, AnomieBOT, Rubinbot, Ulric1313, LilHelpa, Xqbot, GrouchoBot, James1902004, FrescoBot, Surv1v4l1st, A Werewolf, Pinethicket, RedBot, Macgyver-bd 896, Trappist the monk, DeusImperator, NameIsRon, EmausBot, Dr Aaij, Rubyt38, Weepy89, JohnnyJohnny, ClueBot NG, Widr, Ose\fio, CHRMCX, Helpful Pixie Bot, CJ Madsen, MilitaryNut, Jamesallain85, XXzoonamiXX, Epicgenius, Nabaker, Jhe888, Monkbot, Nick Ferrara A. and Anonymous: 75

- **Winchester Model 1912** *Source:* https://en.wikipedia.org/wiki/Winchester_Model_1912?oldid=643001309 *Contributors:* DocWatson42, Kross, Jakew, Ashley Pomeroy, Woohookitty, GregorB, Vegaswikian, Hellbus, TDogg310, Asams10, SmackBot, Yaf, LWF, Stanlekub, Cydebot, Fnlayson, Deathbunny, James086, Jack Bethune, Dybdal~enwiki, Thernlund, Robertgreer, Jamesofur, Chuckotte, Kilmer-san, SQL, Solicitr, Bald Zebra, Nukes4Tots, MatthewVanitas, Addbot, Magus732, LaaknorBot, Luckas-bot, Yobot, AnomieBOT, Winged Brick, FrescoBot, A Werewolf, Miguel Escopeta, DeusImperator, Gary7even, ZéroBot, Michael Essmeyer, L1A1 FAL, Ose\fio, MilitaryNut, Lemnaminor, ArmbrustBot and Anonymous: 32

- **Armsel Striker** *Source:* https://en.wikipedia.org/wiki/Armsel_Striker?oldid=679508838 *Contributors:* Skysmith, DocWatson42, Greenwave75, Anirvan, Neale Monks, GreenReaper, Rich Farmbrough, Xezbeth, B0at, Holloluke, Anthony Appleyard, Alyeska, Mikeo, Gene Nygaard, Angr, Alvis, Mathmo, SDC, BD2412, RadioActive~enwiki, Mobius Soul, Agamemnon2, WriterHound, Albrozdude, Xerstau, Enigmatick, Kyle Barbour, JLaTondre, That Guy, From That Show!, CompuHacker, K-UNIT, Ominae, Deon Steyn, RlyehRising, Septegram, Bluebot, TheDarkArchon, Moshe Constantine Hassan Al-Silverburg, CWesling, Thomasyen, Atirador, Holocron, Hotspur23, LWF, AllStarZ, PEiP, Hargle, Arctic-Editor, JoeBot, Yendor33, Sanandros, CP\M, Henrickson, CmdrObot, Kylu, Thijs!bot, CynicalMe, Z10x, Chairman Meow, Greenhelm, VoABot II, Prestonmcconkie, Thernlund, Mike Searson, Shorttail, Moses6533, CommonsDelinker, Vietminh, Robertgreer, DanMP5, Jimmy C.Corn, Paulwharton, VolkovBot, TXiKiBoT, Hickboy91, Chris9086, Koalorka, EnviroGranny, Lightbreather, Azazyel, Flyer22 Reborn, BALIBOY2007, Sanya3, Dodger67, Hyperionsteel, Vanilla2, HistOry neRd 3850, The 888th Avatar, Socrates2008, John Nevard, Wiccawill420, Berean Hunter, Life of Riley, Bilsonius, Jovianeye, SilvonenBot, Nukes4Tots, MystBot, Addbot, Ronhjones, FrysUniverse, Lightbot, Luckas-bot, AadaamS, Yobot, Reenem, AnomieBOT, Rubinbot, The Banner, IHelpWhenICan, GrouchoBot, Surv1v4l1st, A Werewolf, Armsnut, Pilot850, ROG5728, ClueBot NG, Roughbeak, General Electric Engines, Katangais, Chip123456, MilitaryNut, ChrisGualtieri, Outland19, LadyBeardJohnson, Dustysniper, Addonexus, ArmbrustBot, KitFistoPL, Fishfoot614 and Anonymous: 140

- **ENARM Pentagun** *Source:* https://en.wikipedia.org/wiki/ENARM_Pentagun?oldid=692033599 *Contributors:* Klemen Kocjancic, Robertgreer, Ost316, Yadayadayaday, ROG5728, John of Reading, Catlemur, Лукас Фокс and Anonymous: 4

- **MTs255** *Source:* https://en.wikipedia.org/wiki/MTs255?oldid=682342788 *Contributors:* Adamrush, SmackBot, Boris Barowski, Snori, Lenin and McCarthy, Breversa, Fedallah, Wilhelm Wiesel, Alaibot, Robertgreer, Rowdy yates, FPS Tony, Kernel Saunters, PixelBot, XLinkBot, Addbot, Surv1v4l1st, Tnt1984, Faceless Enemy, ClueBot NG, Ts7946, MilitaryNut, ScullyTime69 and Anonymous: 12

- **RGA-86** *Source:* https://en.wikipedia.org/wiki/RGA-86?oldid=627008973 *Contributors:* Piotrus, Cydebot, Robertgreer, TXiKiBoT, Koalorka, Truthanado, MatthewVanitas, Addbot, Nohomers48 and Lightbot

10.2 Images

- **File:1894_mannlicher6.sized.jpg** *Source:* https://upload.wikimedia.org/wikipedia/commons/c/ce/1894_mannlicher6.sized.jpg *License:* CC-BY-SA-3.0 *Contributors:* ? *Original artist:* ?

- **File:3-Gun-PosterLogo.jpg** *Source:* https://upload.wikimedia.org/wikipedia/commons/b/b5/3-Gun-PosterLogo.jpg *License:* CC BY-SA 3.0 *Contributors:* Own work *Original artist:* Gibraltar Arms

- **File:590a1_001.jpg** *Source:* https://upload.wikimedia.org/wikipedia/commons/b/b3/590a1_001.jpg *License:* Public domain *Contributors:* Transferred from en.wikipedia to Commons. *Original artist:* Jawatech at English Wikipedia

- **File:6_SFS_marine_patrol_airmans_magazine.jpg** *Source:* https://upload.wikimedia.org/wikipedia/commons/f/fa/6_SFS_marine_patrol_airmans_magazine.jpg *License:* Public domain *Contributors:* http://www.flickr.com/photos/usairforce/6166833010 *Original artist:* Tech. Sgt. Bennie J. Davis III

- **File:97_and_Norinco.JPG** *Source:* https://upload.wikimedia.org/wikipedia/commons/0/0e/97_and_Norinco.JPG *License:* Public domain *Contributors:* Own work *Original artist:* Rubyt38

- **File:AA-12.jpg** *Source:* https://upload.wikimedia.org/wikipedia/commons/7/75/AA-12.jpg *License:* CC BY-SA 3.0 *Contributors:* Own work *Original artist:* Mulhollant

- **File:AK47map.svg** *Source:* https://upload.wikimedia.org/wikipedia/commons/7/7e/AK47map.svg *License:* CC BY-SA 3.0 *Contributors:* AK47map.png *Original artist:* Original work: Gimme moaR

- **File:AUG_A1_508mm_04.jpg** *Source:* https://upload.wikimedia.org/wikipedia/commons/3/39/AUG_A1_508mm_04.jpg *License:* CC BY 2.0 *Contributors:* http://www.steyr-arms.at/index.php?id=80 *Original artist:* Steyr Mannlicher

- **File:Action_open.JPG** *Source:* https://upload.wikimedia.org/wikipedia/commons/3/31/Action_open.JPG *License:* Public domain *Contributors:* Own work *Original artist:* Rubyt38

10.2. IMAGES

- **File:Akdal_MKA-1919.JPG** *Source:* https://upload.wikimedia.org/wikipedia/commons/b/bf/Akdal_MKA-1919.JPG *License:* CC-BY-SA-3.0 *Contributors:* Transferred from en.wikipedia to Commons. *Original artist:* TheTranc at English Wikipedia
- **File:Ambox_important.svg** *Source:* https://upload.wikimedia.org/wikipedia/commons/b/b4/Ambox_important.svg *License:* Public domain *Contributors:* Own work, based off of Image:Ambox scales.svg *Original artist:* Dsmurat (talk · contribs)
- **File:Barack_Obama_shooting.jpg** *Source:* https://upload.wikimedia.org/wikipedia/commons/d/dd/Barack_Obama_shooting.jpg *License:* Public domain *Contributors:* White House (P080412PS-0464) *Original artist:* Pete Souza
- **File:Bayonet_Mount.JPG** *Source:* https://upload.wikimedia.org/wikipedia/commons/5/51/Bayonet_Mount.JPG *License:* Public domain *Contributors:* Own work *Original artist:* Rubyt38
- **File:Beanbag_shotgun.jpg** *Source:* https://upload.wikimedia.org/wikipedia/commons/4/4e/Beanbag_shotgun.jpg *License:* CC BY-SA 2.0 *Contributors:* http://www.flickr.com/photos/2010observers/4354268939/in/photostream/ *Original artist:* 2010 Legal Observers
- **File:Benelli_M3_Super_90.jpg** *Source:* https://upload.wikimedia.org/wikipedia/commons/3/37/Benelli_M3_Super_90.jpg *License:* CC-BY-SA-3.0 *Contributors:* http://www.imagestation.com/album/pictures.html?id=2127173051 *Original artist:* Unknown<a href='//www.wikidata.org/wiki/Q4233718' title='wikidata:Q4233718'><img alt='wikidata:Q4233718' src='https://upload.wikimedia.org/wikipedia/commons/thumb/f/ff/Wikidata-logo.svg/20px-Wikidata-logo.svg.png' width='20' height='11' srcset='https://upload.wikimedia.org/wikipedia/commons/thumb/f/ff/Wikidata-logo.svg/30px-Wikidata-logo.svg.png 1.5x, https://upload.wikimedia.org/wikipedia/commons/thumb/f/ff/Wikidata-logo.svg/40px-Wikidata-logo.svg.png 2x' data-file-width='1050' data-file-height='590' /></a>
- **File:Benelli_m4_2.jpg** *Source:* https://upload.wikimedia.org/wikipedia/commons/0/03/Benelli_m4_2.jpg *License:* Public domain *Contributors:* 2nd Battalion, 25th Marine Regiment, 4th Marine Division website. [1] *Original artist:* United States Marine Corps
- **File:Beretta_92_FS.gif** *Source:* https://upload.wikimedia.org/wikipedia/commons/6/6c/Beretta_92_FS.gif *License:* CC BY 2.5 *Contributors:* Originally from it.wikipedia; description page is/was here. Transfer was stated to be made by User:Peter Benjamin. *Original artist:* Original uploader was Stefab at it.wikipedia
- **File:Browning_Auto-5_20g_Mag.jpg** *Source:* https://upload.wikimedia.org/wikipedia/commons/1/19/Browning_Auto-5_20g_Mag.jpg *License:* CC-BY-SA-3.0 *Contributors:* Own work *Original artist:* Arthurrh
- **File:Browning_Auto_5_zerlegt.JPG** *Source:* https://upload.wikimedia.org/wikipedia/commons/a/a2/Browning_Auto_5_zerlegt.JPG *License:* CC BY-SA 3.0 *Contributors:* Own work *Original artist:* Hmaag
- **File:Browningcynergytrigger.jpg** *Source:* https://upload.wikimedia.org/wikipedia/commons/3/3c/Browningcynergytrigger.jpg *License:* CC BY 3.0 *Contributors:* Own work *Original artist:* Rogerstitt
- **File:Browningmonohinge.jpg** *Source:* https://upload.wikimedia.org/wikipedia/commons/e/e0/Browningmonohinge.jpg *License:* CC BY 3.0 *Contributors:* Own work *Original artist:* Rogerstitt
- **File:Catalog_No._53_(1911)_pg_5.jpeg** *Source:* https://upload.wikimedia.org/wikipedia/commons/7/71/Catalog_No._53_%281911%29_pg_5.jpeg *License:* Public domain *Contributors:* This work is in the **public domain** in the United States because it was published (or registered with the U.S. Copyright Office) before January 1, 1923. *Original artist:* Keydet92
- **File:Commons-logo.svg** *Source:* https://upload.wikimedia.org/wikipedia/en/4/4a/Commons-logo.svg *License:* ? *Contributors:* ? *Original artist:* ?
- **File:Confederateshotgun.jpg** *Source:* https://upload.wikimedia.org/wikipedia/commons/c/c3/Confederateshotgun.jpg *License:* Public domain *Contributors:* Transferred from en.wikipedia to Commons by Sreejithk2000 using CommonsHelper. *Original artist:* The original uploader was Primalchaos at English Wikipedia
- **File:Edit-clear.svg** *Source:* https://upload.wikimedia.org/wikipedia/en/f/f2/Edit-clear.svg *License:* Public domain *Contributors:* The *Tango! Desktop Project*. *Original artist:*
  The people from the Tango! project. And according to the meta-data in the file, specifically: "Andreas Nilsson, and Jakub Steiner (although minimally)."
- **File:Fiocchi_rubber_buckshot.jpg** *Source:* https://upload.wikimedia.org/wikipedia/commons/c/cb/Fiocchi_rubber_buckshot.jpg *License:* Public domain *Contributors:* Transferred from en.wikipedia to Commons by Amendola90. *Original artist:* Fluzwup at English Wikipedia
- **File:Flag_of_Argentina.svg** *Source:* https://upload.wikimedia.org/wikipedia/commons/1/1a/Flag_of_Argentina.svg *License:* Public domain *Contributors:* Here, based on: http://manuelbelgrano.gov.ar/bandera/creacion-de-la-bandera-nacional/ *Original artist:* Government of Argentina
- **File:Flag_of_Australia.svg** *Source:* https://upload.wikimedia.org/wikipedia/en/b/b9/Flag_of_Australia.svg *License:* Public domain *Contributors:* ? *Original artist:* ?
- **File:Flag_of_Austria.svg** *Source:* https://upload.wikimedia.org/wikipedia/commons/4/41/Flag_of_Austria.svg *License:* Public domain *Contributors:* Own work, http://www.bmlv.gv.at/abzeichen/dekorationen.shtml *Original artist:* User:SKopp
- **File:Flag_of_Bahrain.svg** *Source:* https://upload.wikimedia.org/wikipedia/commons/2/2c/Flag_of_Bahrain.svg *License:* Public domain *Contributors:* http://www.moci.gov.bh/en/KingdomofBahrain/BahrainFlag/ *Original artist:* Source: Drawn by User:SKopp, rewritten by User:Zscout370
- **File:Flag_of_Bangladesh.svg** *Source:* https://upload.wikimedia.org/wikipedia/commons/f/f9/Flag_of_Bangladesh.svg *License:* Public domain *Contributors:* http://www.dcaa.com.bd/Modules/CountryProfile/BangladeshFlag.aspx *Original artist:* User:SKopp
- **File:Flag_of_Belarus.svg** *Source:* https://upload.wikimedia.org/wikipedia/commons/8/85/Flag_of_Belarus.svg *License:* Public domain *Contributors:* http://www.tnpa.by/ViewFileText.php?UrlRid=52178&UrlOnd=%D1%D2%C1%20911-2008 *Original artist:* Zscout370
- **File:Flag_of_Belgium_(civil).svg** *Source:* https://upload.wikimedia.org/wikipedia/commons/9/92/Flag_of_Belgium_%28civil%29.svg *License:* Public domain *Contributors:* ? *Original artist:* ?

- **File:Flag_of_Bermuda.svg** *Source:* https://upload.wikimedia.org/wikipedia/commons/b/bf/Flag_of_Bermuda.svg *License:* Public domain *Contributors:* Own work *Original artist:* **Version 1:** Made by Caleb Moore from the Open Clip Art website and uploaded by Nightstallion **Version 2:** Made by Nameneko from version 1 of Image:Flag of Bermuda.svg and version 2 of Image:Coa Bermuda.svg by Cronholm144.
- **File:Flag_of_Brazil.svg** *Source:* https://upload.wikimedia.org/wikipedia/en/0/05/Flag_of_Brazil.svg *License:* PD *Contributors:* ? *Original artist:* ?
- **File:Flag_of_Cambodia.svg** *Source:* https://upload.wikimedia.org/wikipedia/commons/8/83/Flag_of_Cambodia.svg *License:* CC0 *Contributors:* File:Flag_of_Cambodia.svg *Original artist:* Draw new flag by User:???_?????
- **File:Flag_of_Canada.svg** *Source:* https://upload.wikimedia.org/wikipedia/en/c/cf/Flag_of_Canada.svg *License:* PD *Contributors:* ? *Original artist:* ?
- **File:Flag_of_Croatia.svg** *Source:* https://upload.wikimedia.org/wikipedia/commons/1/1b/Flag_of_Croatia.svg *License:* Public domain *Contributors:* http://www.sabor.hr/Default.aspx?sec=4317 *Original artist:* Nightstallion, Elephantus, Neoneo13, Denelson83, Rainman, R-41, Minestrone, Lupo, Zscout370, <a href='//commons.wikimedia.org/wiki/User:MaGa' title='User:MaGa'>Ma</a><a href='//commons.wikimedia.org/wiki/File:Croatian_squares_Ljubicic.png' class='image'><img alt='Croatian squares Ljubicic.png' src='https://upload.wikimedia.org/wikipedia/commons/thumb/7/7f/Croatian_squares_Ljubicic.png/15px-Croatian_squares_Ljubicic.png' width='15' height='15' srcset='https://upload.wikimedia.org/wikipedia/commons/thumb/7/7f/Croatian_squares_Ljubicic.png/23px-Croatian_squares_Ljubicic.png 1.5x, https://upload.wikimedia.org/wikipedia/commons/thumb/7/7f/Croatian_squares_Ljubicic.png/30px-Croatian_squares_Ljubicic.png 2x' data-file-width='202' data-file-height='202' /></a><a href='//commons.wikimedia.org/wiki/User_talk:MaGa' title='User talk:MaGa'>Ga</a> (based on Decision of the Parliament)
- **File:Flag_of_Denmark.svg** *Source:* https://upload.wikimedia.org/wikipedia/commons/9/9c/Flag_of_Denmark.svg *License:* Public domain *Contributors:* Own work *Original artist:* User:Madden
- **File:Flag_of_Estonia.svg** *Source:* https://upload.wikimedia.org/wikipedia/commons/8/8f/Flag_of_Estonia.svg *License:* Public domain *Contributors:* http://www.riigikantselei.ee/?id=73847 *Original artist:* Originally drawn by User:SKopp. Blue colour changed by User:PeepP to match the image at [1].
- **File:Flag_of_Finland.svg** *Source:* https://upload.wikimedia.org/wikipedia/commons/b/bc/Flag_of_Finland.svg *License:* Public domain *Contributors:* http://www.finlex.fi/fi/laki/ajantasa/1978/19780380 *Original artist:* Drawn by User:SKopp
- **File:Flag_of_France.svg** *Source:* https://upload.wikimedia.org/wikipedia/en/c/c3/Flag_of_France.svg *License:* PD *Contributors:* ? *Original artist:* ?
- **File:Flag_of_Georgia.svg** *Source:* https://upload.wikimedia.org/wikipedia/commons/0/0f/Flag_of_Georgia.svg *License:* Public domain *Contributors:* Own work based on File:Brdzanebuleba 31.pdf *Original artist:* User:SKopp
- **File:Flag_of_Germany.svg** *Source:* https://upload.wikimedia.org/wikipedia/en/b/ba/Flag_of_Germany.svg *License:* PD *Contributors:* ? *Original artist:* ?
- **File:Flag_of_Greece.svg** *Source:* https://upload.wikimedia.org/wikipedia/commons/5/5c/Flag_of_Greece.svg *License:* Public domain *Contributors:* own code *Original artist:* (of code) cs:User:-xfi- (talk)
- **File:Flag_of_Hong_Kong.svg** *Source:* https://upload.wikimedia.org/wikipedia/commons/5/5b/Flag_of_Hong_Kong.svg *License:* Public domain *Contributors:* http://www.protocol.gov.hk/flags/chi/r_flag/index.html *Original artist:* Tao Ho
- **File:Flag_of_Iceland.svg** *Source:* https://upload.wikimedia.org/wikipedia/commons/c/ce/Flag_of_Iceland.svg *License:* Public domain *Contributors:* Islandic National Flag *Original artist:* Ævar Arnfjörð Bjarmason, Zscout370 and others
- **File:Flag_of_India.svg** *Source:* https://upload.wikimedia.org/wikipedia/en/4/41/Flag_of_India.svg *License:* Public domain *Contributors:* ? *Original artist:* ?
- **File:Flag_of_Indonesia.svg** *Source:* https://upload.wikimedia.org/wikipedia/commons/9/9f/Flag_of_Indonesia.svg *License:* Public domain *Contributors:* Law: s:id:Undang-Undang Republik Indonesia Nomor 24 Tahun 2009 (http://badanbahasa.kemdiknas.go.id/lamanbahasa/sites/default/files/UU_2009_24.pdf) *Original artist:* Drawn by User:SKopp, rewritten by User:Gabbe
- **File:Flag_of_Iraq.svg** *Source:* https://upload.wikimedia.org/wikipedia/commons/f/f6/Flag_of_Iraq.svg *License:* Public domain *Contributors:*
- This image is based on the CIA Factbook, and the website of Office of the President of Iraq, vectorized by User:Militaryace *Original artist:* Unknown, published by Iraqi governemt, vectorized by User:Militaryace based on the work of User:Hoshie
- **File:Flag_of_Ireland.svg** *Source:* https://upload.wikimedia.org/wikipedia/commons/4/45/Flag_of_Ireland.svg *License:* Public domain *Contributors:* Drawn by User:SKopp *Original artist:* ?
- **File:Flag_of_Israel.svg** *Source:* https://upload.wikimedia.org/wikipedia/commons/d/d4/Flag_of_Israel.svg *License:* Public domain *Contributors:* http://www.mfa.gov.il/MFA/History/Modern%20History/Israel%20at%2050/The%20Flag%20and%20the%20Emblem *Original artist:* "The Provisional Council of State Proclamation of the Flag of the State of Israel" of 25 Tishrei 5709 (28 October 1948) provides the official specification for the design of the Israeli flag.
- **File:Flag_of_Italy.svg** *Source:* https://upload.wikimedia.org/wikipedia/en/0/03/Flag_of_Italy.svg *License:* PD *Contributors:* ? *Original artist:* ?
- **File:Flag_of_Japan.svg** *Source:* https://upload.wikimedia.org/wikipedia/en/9/9e/Flag_of_Japan.svg *License:* PD *Contributors:* ? *Original artist:* ?
- **File:Flag_of_Kazakhstan.svg** *Source:* https://upload.wikimedia.org/wikipedia/commons/d/d3/Flag_of_Kazakhstan.svg *License:* Public domain *Contributors:* own code, construction sheet *Original artist:* -xfi-

10.2. IMAGES

- **File:Flag_of_Kyrgyzstan.svg** *Source:* https://upload.wikimedia.org/wikipedia/commons/c/c7/Flag_of_Kyrgyzstan.svg *License:* Public domain *Contributors:* Drawn by User:SKopp, construction sheet. Redo by: cs:User:-xfi- *Original artist:* Made by Andrew Duhan for the Sodipodi SVG flag collection, and is public domain.
- **File:Flag_of_Lebanon.svg** *Source:* https://upload.wikimedia.org/wikipedia/commons/5/59/Flag_of_Lebanon.svg *License:* Public domain *Contributors:* ? *Original artist:* Traced based on the CIA World Factbook with some modification done to the colours based on information at Vexilla mundi.
- **File:Flag_of_Libya.svg** *Source:* https://upload.wikimedia.org/wikipedia/commons/0/05/Flag_of_Libya.svg *License:* Public domain *Contributors:* File:Flag of Libya (1951).svg *Original artist:* The source code of this SVG is <a data-x-rel='nofollow' class='external text' href='//validator.w3.org/check?uri=https%3A%2F%2Fcommons.wikimedia.org%2Fwiki%2FSpecial%3AFilepath%2FFlag_of_Libya.svg,,&,,ss=1'>valid</a>.
- **File:Flag_of_Lithuania.svg** *Source:* https://upload.wikimedia.org/wikipedia/commons/1/11/Flag_of_Lithuania.svg *License:* Public domain *Contributors:* Own work *Original artist:* SuffKopp
- **File:Flag_of_Luxembourg.svg** *Source:* https://upload.wikimedia.org/wikipedia/commons/d/da/Flag_of_Luxembourg.svg *License:* Public domain *Contributors:* Own work http://www.legilux.public.lu/leg/a/archives/1972/0051/a051.pdf#page=2, colors from http://www.legilux.public.lu/leg/a/archives/1993/0731609/0731609.pdf *Original artist:* Drawn by User:SKopp
- **File:Flag_of_Malaysia.svg** *Source:* https://upload.wikimedia.org/wikipedia/commons/6/66/Flag_of_Malaysia.svg *License:* Public domain *Contributors:* Create based on the Malaysian Government Website (archive version)
Original artist: SKopp, Zscout370 and Ranking Update
- **File:Flag_of_Malta.svg** *Source:* https://upload.wikimedia.org/wikipedia/commons/7/73/Flag_of_Malta.svg *License:* CC0 *Contributors:* ? *Original artist:* ?
- **File:Flag_of_Mexico.svg** *Source:* https://upload.wikimedia.org/wikipedia/commons/f/fc/Flag_of_Mexico.svg *License:* Public domain *Contributors:* This vector image was created with Inkscape. *Original artist:* **Alex Covarrubias**, 9 April 2006
- **File:Flag_of_Moldova.svg** *Source:* https://upload.wikimedia.org/wikipedia/commons/2/27/Flag_of_Moldova.svg *License:* Public domain *Contributors:* vector coat of arms image traced by User:Nameneko from Image:Moldova gerb large.png. Construction sheet can be found at http://flagspot.net/flags/md.html#const *Original artist:* Nameneko and others
- **File:Flag_of_Nepal.svg** *Source:* https://upload.wikimedia.org/wikipedia/commons/9/9b/Flag_of_Nepal.svg *License:* Public domain *Contributors:* Constitution of The Kingdom of Nepal, Article 5, Schedule 1 [1] *Original artist:* Drawn by User:Pumbaa80, User:Achim1999
- **File:Flag_of_New_Zealand.svg** *Source:* https://upload.wikimedia.org/wikipedia/commons/3/3e/Flag_of_New_Zealand.svg *License:* Public domain *Contributors:* http://www.mch.govt.nz/files/NZ%20Flag%20-%20proportions.JPG *Original artist:* Zscout370, Hugh Jass and many others
- **File:Flag_of_North_Korea.svg** *Source:* https://upload.wikimedia.org/wikipedia/commons/5/51/Flag_of_North_Korea.svg *License:* Public domain *Contributors:* Template:?? ???? ?? ???? *Original artist:* Zscout370
- **File:Flag_of_Norway.svg** *Source:* https://upload.wikimedia.org/wikipedia/commons/d/d9/Flag_of_Norway.svg *License:* Public domain *Contributors:* Own work *Original artist:* Dbenbenn
- **File:Flag_of_Pakistan.svg** *Source:* https://upload.wikimedia.org/wikipedia/commons/3/32/Flag_of_Pakistan.svg *License:* Public domain *Contributors:* The drawing and the colors were based from flagspot.net. *Original artist:* User:Zscout370
- **File:Flag_of_Panama.svg** *Source:* https://upload.wikimedia.org/wikipedia/commons/a/ab/Flag_of_Panama.svg *License:* Public domain *Contributors:* ? *Original artist:* ?
- **File:Flag_of_Papua_New_Guinea.svg** *Source:* https://upload.wikimedia.org/wikipedia/commons/e/e3/Flag_of_Papua_New_Guinea.svg *License:* Public domain *Contributors:* Own work, FOTW *Original artist:* User:Nightstallion
- **File:Flag_of_Peru.svg** *Source:* https://upload.wikimedia.org/wikipedia/commons/c/cf/Flag_of_Peru.svg *License:* Public domain *Contributors:* Peru *Original artist:* David Benbennick
- **File:Flag_of_Poland.svg** *Source:* https://upload.wikimedia.org/wikipedia/en/1/12/Flag_of_Poland.svg *License:* Public domain *Contributors:* ? *Original artist:* ?
- **File:Flag_of_Poland_2.svg** *Source:* https://upload.wikimedia.org/wikipedia/commons/4/40/Flag_of_Poland_2.svg *License:* Public domain *Contributors:* Own work *Original artist:* Kuba_G, Nux
- **File:Flag_of_Portugal.svg** *Source:* https://upload.wikimedia.org/wikipedia/commons/5/5c/Flag_of_Portugal.svg *License:* Public domain *Contributors:* http://jorgesampaio.arquivo.presidencia.pt/pt/republica/simbolos/bandeiras/index.html#imgs *Original artist:* Columbano Bordalo Pinheiro (1910; generic design); Vítor Luís Rodrigues; António Martins-Tuválkin (2004; this specific vector set: see sources)
- **File:Flag_of_Russia.svg** *Source:* https://upload.wikimedia.org/wikipedia/en/f/f3/Flag_of_Russia.svg *License:* PD *Contributors:* ? *Original artist:* ?
- **File:Flag_of_Serbia.svg** *Source:* https://upload.wikimedia.org/wikipedia/commons/f/ff/Flag_of_Serbia.svg *License:* Public domain *Contributors:* From http://www.parlament.gov.rs/content/cir/o_skupstini/simboli/simboli.asp. *Original artist:* sodipodi.com
- **File:Flag_of_Singapore.svg** *Source:* https://upload.wikimedia.org/wikipedia/commons/4/48/Flag_of_Singapore.svg *License:* Public domain *Contributors:* The drawing was based from http://app.www.sg/who/42/National-Flag.aspx. Colors from the book: *(2001). The National Symbols Kit. Singapore: Ministry of Information, Communications and the Arts. pp. 5. ISBN 8880968010* Pantone 032 shade from http://www.pantone.com/pages/pantone/colorfinder.aspx?c_id=13050 *Original artist:* Various

- **File:Flag_of_Slovakia.svg** *Source:* https://upload.wikimedia.org/wikipedia/commons/e/e6/Flag_of_Slovakia.svg *License:* Public domain *Contributors:* Own work; here, colors *Original artist:* SKopp
- **File:Flag_of_Slovenia.svg** *Source:* https://upload.wikimedia.org/wikipedia/commons/f/f0/Flag_of_Slovenia.svg *License:* Public domain *Contributors:* Own work construction sheet from http://flagspot.net/flags/si%27.html#coa *Original artist:* User:Achim1999
- **File:Flag_of_South_Africa_(1928-1994).svg** *Source:* https://upload.wikimedia.org/wikipedia/commons/2/2a/Flag_of_South_Africa_%281928-1994%29.svg *License:* Public domain *Contributors:* SVG based on this image *Original artist:* Parliament of South Africa
- **File:Flag_of_South_Korea.svg** *Source:* https://upload.wikimedia.org/wikipedia/commons/0/09/Flag_of_South_Korea.svg *License:* Public domain *Contributors:* Ordinance Act of the Law concerning the National Flag of the Republic of Korea, Construction and color guidelines (Russian/English) ← This site is not exist now.(2012.06.05) *Original artist:* Various
- **File:Flag_of_Spain.svg** *Source:* https://upload.wikimedia.org/wikipedia/en/9/9a/Flag_of_Spain.svg *License:* PD *Contributors:* ? *Original artist:* ?
- **File:Flag_of_Sweden.svg** *Source:* https://upload.wikimedia.org/wikipedia/en/4/4c/Flag_of_Sweden.svg *License:* PD *Contributors:* ? *Original artist:* ?
- **File:Flag_of_Switzerland.svg** *Source:* https://upload.wikimedia.org/wikipedia/commons/f/f3/Flag_of_Switzerland.svg *License:* Public domain *Contributors:* PDF Colors Construction sheet *Original artist:* User:Marc Mongenet

Credits:

- **File:Flag_of_Thailand.svg** *Source:* https://upload.wikimedia.org/wikipedia/commons/a/a9/Flag_of_Thailand.svg *License:* Public domain *Contributors:* Own work *Original artist:* Zscout370
- **File:Flag_of_Tunisia.svg** *Source:* https://upload.wikimedia.org/wikipedia/commons/c/ce/Flag_of_Tunisia.svg *License:* Public domain *Contributors:* http://www.w3.org/ *Original artist:* entraîneur: BEN KHALIFA WISSAM
- **File:Flag_of_Turkey.svg** *Source:* https://upload.wikimedia.org/wikipedia/commons/b/b4/Flag_of_Turkey.svg *License:* Public domain *Contributors:* Turkish Flag Law (Türk Bayrağı Kanunu), Law nr. 2893 of 22 September 1983. Text (in Turkish) at the website of the Turkish Historical Society (Türk Tarih Kurumu) *Original artist:* David Benbennick (original author)
- **File:Flag_of_Ukraine.svg** *Source:* https://upload.wikimedia.org/wikipedia/commons/4/49/Flag_of_Ukraine.svg *License:* Public domain *Contributors:* ДСТУ 4512:2006 - Державний прапор України. Загальні технічні умови

    SVG: 2010

Original artist: України
- **File:Flag_of_Uzbekistan.svg** *Source:* https://upload.wikimedia.org/wikipedia/commons/8/84/Flag_of_Uzbekistan.svg *License:* Public domain *Contributors:* Own work *Original artist:* O'zbekiston Respublikasining Davlat bayrog'i. The officially defined colours are Pantone 313C for blue and 361C for green (source: [1], [2]). Drawn by User:Zscout370.
- **File:Flag_of_the_Czech_Republic.svg** *Source:* https://upload.wikimedia.org/wikipedia/commons/c/cb/Flag_of_the_Czech_Republic.svg *License:* Public domain *Contributors:*
    - -xfi-'s file
    - -xfi-'s code
    - Zirland's codes of colors

Original artist:
(of code): SVG version by cs:-xfi-.
- **File:Flag_of_the_Dominican_Republic.svg** *Source:* https://upload.wikimedia.org/wikipedia/commons/9/9f/Flag_of_the_Dominican_Republic.svg *License:* Public domain *Contributors:* Own work *Original artist:* User:Nightstallion
- **File:Flag_of_the_Netherlands.svg** *Source:* https://upload.wikimedia.org/wikipedia/commons/2/20/Flag_of_the_Netherlands.svg *License:* Public domain *Contributors:* Own work *Original artist:* Zscout370
- **File:Flag_of_the_People'{}s_Republic_of_China.svg** *Source:* https://upload.wikimedia.org/wikipedia/commons/f/fa/Flag_of_the_People%27s_Republic_of_China.svg *License:* Public domain *Contributors:* Own work, http://www.protocol.gov.hk/flags/eng/n_flag/design.html *Original artist:* Drawn by User:SKopp, redrawn by User:Denelson83 and User:Zscout370
- **File:Flag_of_the_Philippines.svg** *Source:* https://upload.wikimedia.org/wikipedia/commons/9/99/Flag_of_the_Philippines.svg *License:* Public domain *Contributors:* The design was taken from [1] and the colors were also taken from a Government website *Original artist:* User:Achim1999
- **File:Flag_of_the_Republic_of_China.svg** *Source:* https://upload.wikimedia.org/wikipedia/commons/7/72/Flag_of_the_Republic_of_China.svg *License:* Public domain *Contributors:* [1] *Original artist:* User:SKopp
- **File:Flag_of_the_Soviet_Union.svg** *Source:* https://upload.wikimedia.org/wikipedia/commons/a/a9/Flag_of_the_Soviet_Union.svg *License:* Public domain *Contributors:* http://pravo.levonevsky.org/ *Original artist:* CCCP
- **File:Flag_of_the_United_Kingdom.svg** *Source:* https://upload.wikimedia.org/wikipedia/en/a/ae/Flag_of_the_United_Kingdom.svg *License:* PD *Contributors:* ? *Original artist:* ?
- **File:Flag_of_the_United_States.svg** *Source:* https://upload.wikimedia.org/wikipedia/en/a/a4/Flag_of_the_United_States.svg *License:* PD *Contributors:* ? *Original artist:* ?

10.2. IMAGES

- **File:Flickr_-_~{}Steve_Z~{}_-_870.jpg** *Source:* https://upload.wikimedia.org/wikipedia/commons/f/f7/Flickr_-_~{}Steve_Z~{}_-_870.jpg *License:* CC BY-SA 2.0 *Contributors:* 870 *Original artist:* Stephen Z
- **File:Folder_Hexagonal_Icon.svg** *Source:* https://upload.wikimedia.org/wikipedia/en/4/48/Folder_Hexagonal_Icon.svg *License:* Cc-by-sa-3.0 *Contributors:* ? *Original artist:* ?
- **File:Franchi_Barrel_Length_SPAS-12_21-1-2\char"0022\relax{}_Bbl_VS_19-7-8\char"0022\relax{}_Bbl.jpg** *Source:* https://upload.wikimedia.org/wikipedia/commons/b/bd/Franchi_Barrel_Length_SPAS-12_21-1-2%22_Bbl_VS_19-7-8%22_Bbl.jpg *License:* CC BY-SA 3.0 *Contributors:* Own work
  Previously published: photobucket [URL=http://s30.photobucket.com/user/catacombshadows1/media/IMG_2104_zps714b5ac4.jpg.html][IMG]http://i30.photobucket.com/albums/c325/catacombshadows1/IMG_2104_zps714b5ac4.jpg[/IMG][/URL] *Original artist:* HellsXgunsmith
- **File:Franchi_SPAS_12_Grip_Safety.jpeg** *Source:* https://upload.wikimedia.org/wikipedia/en/4/4d/Franchi_SPAS_12_Grip_Safety.jpeg *License:* CC-BY-SA-4.0 *Contributors:*

Own work;

Original artist:

ModicumofKnowledge (talk) (Uploads)

- **File:Fusilier_Commando_de_l'Air_et_un_membre_de_l'USAF_sur_l'aéroport_de_Kandahar.JPG** *Source:* https://upload.wikimedia.org/wikipedia/commons/b/bf/Fusilier_Commando_de_l%E2%80%99Air_et_un_membre_de_l%27USAF_sur_l%27a%C3%A9roport_de_Kandahar.JPG *License:* Public domain *Contributors:* http://www.usafe.af.mil/news/story.asp?id=123308864 http://www.afcent.af.mil/shared/media/photodb/photos/2012%5C07%5C120620-F-JO436-026.JPG *Original artist:* Sgt. Clay Lancaster, USAF
- **File:Greener-Martini_Light_Harpoon_Gun.JPG** *Source:* https://upload.wikimedia.org/wikipedia/commons/5/5e/Greener-Martini_Light_Harpoon_Gun.JPG *License:* CC BY-SA 4.0 *Contributors:* Own work *Original artist:* Catlemur
- **File:Gurkha_IOC_1.jpg** *Source:* https://upload.wikimedia.org/wikipedia/commons/4/4a/Gurkha_IOC_1.jpg *License:* CC BY-SA 2.5 *Contributors:* ? *Original artist:* ?
- **File:H&KFabarmFP6entry.jpg** *Source:* https://upload.wikimedia.org/wikipedia/commons/d/d1/H%26KFabarmFP6entry.jpg *License:* CC BY-SA 3.0 *Contributors:* Own work *Original artist:* Berean Hunter
- **File:HK_512'{}s_PDRM.jpg** *Source:* https://upload.wikimedia.org/wikipedia/commons/9/9d/HK_512%27s_PDRM.jpg *License:* CC BY 3.0 *Contributors:* Own work *Original artist:* Rizuan
- **File:HK_CAWS.jpg** *Source:* https://upload.wikimedia.org/wikipedia/commons/b/bc/HK_CAWS.jpg *License:* CC BY-SA 3.0 *Contributors:* Own work *Original artist:* Mulhollant
- **File:High_Standard_10A.jpg** *Source:* https://upload.wikimedia.org/wikipedia/commons/c/c2/High_Standard_10A.jpg *License:* CC BY-SA 3.0 *Contributors:* Own work *Original artist:* Tim Bessler
- **File:Hs10b-1.jpg** *Source:* https://upload.wikimedia.org/wikipedia/commons/6/69/Hs10b-1.jpg *License:* BSD *Contributors:* Own work *Original artist:* User The Deviant on en.wikipedia
- **File:Ithaca-auto-burglar.jpg** *Source:* https://upload.wikimedia.org/wikipedia/commons/2/20/Ithaca-auto-burglar.jpg *License:* Public domain *Contributors:* http://www.atf.gov/firearms/guides/identification-of-nfa-firearms.html *Original artist:* ATF
- **File:Ithaca_37.jpg** *Source:* https://upload.wikimedia.org/wikipedia/commons/d/d2/Ithaca_37.jpg *License:* Public domain *Contributors:* Own work *Original artist:* Rooster
- **File:Ithaca_Mag-10_Shotgun.jpg** *Source:* https://upload.wikimedia.org/wikipedia/commons/5/55/Ithaca_Mag-10_Shotgun.jpg *License:* Public domain *Contributors:* (Original text: *I (Surv1v4l1st $^{(Talk|Contribs)}$) created this work entirely by myself.*) *Original artist:* Surv1v4l1st $^{(Talk|Contribs)}$. Original uploader was Surv1v4l1st at en.wikipedia
- **File:Jackhammer_blow.jpg** *Source:* https://upload.wikimedia.org/wikipedia/commons/4/46/Jackhammer_blow.jpg *License:* Public domain *Contributors:* http://world.guns.ru/shotgun/sh10-e.htm *Original artist:* John Andersen
- **File:Jackhammer_draw.jpg** *Source:* https://upload.wikimedia.org/wikipedia/commons/d/d0/Jackhammer_draw.jpg *License:* Public domain *Contributors:* http://world.guns.ru/shotgun/sh10-e.htm *Original artist:* John Andersen
- **File:JohnBrowning.jpeg** *Source:* https://upload.wikimedia.org/wikipedia/commons/f/f1/JohnBrowning.jpeg *License:* Public domain *Contributors:* ? *Original artist:* ?
- **File:KAC_MasterKey.jpg** *Source:* https://upload.wikimedia.org/wikipedia/commons/3/36/KAC_MasterKey.jpg *License:* Public domain *Contributors:* http://www.m4carbine.net/showthread.php?t=29771 *Original artist:* DrBaker of M4Carbine.net
- **File:KS-23M-01.jpg** *Source:* https://upload.wikimedia.org/wikipedia/commons/c/c2/KS-23M-01.jpg *License:* CC BY-SA 3.0 *Contributors:* Vitalykuzmin.net *Original artist:* Vitaly V. Kuzmin
- **File:Kel-Tec_KSG_(2).jpg** *Source:* https://upload.wikimedia.org/wikipedia/commons/6/6e/Kel-Tec_KSG_%282%29.jpg *License:* CC BY-SA 3.0 *Contributors:* http://weapon-planet.ru/droboviki/usa/item/57-kel-tec-ksg *Original artist:* Не указан
- **File:Lupara.jpg** *Source:* https://upload.wikimedia.org/wikipedia/commons/3/30/Lupara.jpg *License:* CC-BY-SA-3.0 *Contributors:* Own work *Original artist:* Bluedog
- **File:M&Prevolver.jpg** *Source:* https://upload.wikimedia.org/wikipedia/commons/b/bf/M%26Prevolver.jpg *License:* CC BY 2.5 *Contributors:* Transferred from en.wikipedia to Commons by OhanaUnited. *Original artist:* The original uploader was Olegvolk at English Wikipedia

- **File:M16_operators_of_the_world.svg** *Source:* https://upload.wikimedia.org/wikipedia/commons/d/dc/M16_operators_of_the_world.svg *License:* Public domain *Contributors:* SVG map: BlankMap-World6.svg *Original artist:* Original: Canuckguy and others

- **File:M1887_LH.JPG** *Source:* https://upload.wikimedia.org/wikipedia/commons/5/5e/M1887_LH.JPG *License:* Attribution *Contributors:* Transferred from en.wikipedia to Commons by Common Good using CommonsHelper. *Original artist:* The original uploader was Commander Zulu at English Wikipedia

- **File:M1895_diagram.jpg** *Source:* https://upload.wikimedia.org/wikipedia/commons/b/bf/M1895_diagram.jpg *License:* Public domain *Contributors:* ? *Original artist:* ?

- **File:M870wingmaster.JPEG** *Source:* https://upload.wikimedia.org/wikipedia/commons/6/66/M870wingmaster.JPEG *License:* Public domain *Contributors:* http://www.dodmedia.osd.mil/Assets/Still/1993/Navy/DN-ST-93-01524.JPG *Original artist:* DoD photo by: PHAN MILNE/PHAN DILLON

- **File:MAUL_shotgun.PNG** *Source:* https://upload.wikimedia.org/wikipedia/commons/a/aa/MAUL_shotgun.PNG *License:* Public domain *Contributors:* Marines magazine: http://marinesmagazine.dodlive.mil/2010/04/05/maul/ *Original artist:* USMC employee

- **File:MC255-2.jpg** *Source:* https://upload.wikimedia.org/wikipedia/commons/4/4f/MC255-2.jpg *License:* Public domain *Contributors:* Own work *Original artist:* Sillymike

- **File:MKV-Ultramark.jpg** *Source:* https://upload.wikimedia.org/wikipedia/commons/4/4d/MKV-Ultramark.jpg *License:* CC BY 3.0 *Contributors:* Own work *Original artist:* Weatherby

- **File:Mag7-m1.jpg** *Source:* https://upload.wikimedia.org/wikipedia/commons/c/c7/Mag7-m1.jpg *License:* BSD *Contributors:* Self *Original artist:* User The Deviant on en.wikipedia

- **File:Mag7-sbs.PNG** *Source:* https://upload.wikimedia.org/wikipedia/commons/9/9d/Mag7-sbs.PNG *License:* BSD *Contributors:* Own work *Original artist:* User The Deviant

- **File:Marines_raid_Fallujah_garage.jpg** *Source:* https://upload.wikimedia.org/wikipedia/commons/e/e5/Marines_raid_Fallujah_garage.jpg *License:* Public domain *Contributors:*

  This Image was released by the United States Marine Corps with the ID 060528-M-3312R <a class='external text' href='//commons.wikimedia.org/w/index.php?title=Category:Files_created_by_the_United_States_Marine_Corps_with_known_IDs,,&,,filefrom=060528-M-3312R#mw-category-media'>(next)</a>.

  This tag does not indicate the copyright status of the attached work. A normal copyright tag is still required. See Commons:Licensing for more information.

  Original artist: Cpl. Brain Reimers

- **File:Maritime_Safety_&_Security_Team_(MSST)_91106.jpg** *Source:* https://upload.wikimedia.org/wikipedia/commons/c/ca/Maritime_Safety_%26_Security_Team_%28MSST%29_91106.jpg *License:* Public domain *Contributors:* http://cgvi.uscg.mil/media/main.php?g2_itemId=93385 *Original artist:* USCG photo by PO Milke Lutz

- **File:Marlin39receiver.jpg** *Source:* https://upload.wikimedia.org/wikipedia/commons/3/3f/Marlin39receiver.jpg *License:* CC BY-SA 3.0 *Contributors:* Own work *Original artist:* MatthewVanitas

- **File:Martini-Henry_m1871_-_England_-_AM.032017.jpg** *Source:* https://upload.wikimedia.org/wikipedia/commons/0/0c/Martini-Henry_m1871_-_England_-_AM.032017.jpg *License:* Public domain *Contributors:* Armémuseum (The Swedish Army Museum) through the Digital Museum (http://www.digitalmuseum.se) *Original artist:* Armémuseum (The Swedish Army Museum)

- **File:Martini_Henry_Action_Parts.jpg** *Source:* https://upload.wikimedia.org/wikipedia/commons/4/40/Martini_Henry_Action_Parts.jpg *License:* CC BY-SA 3.0 *Contributors:* Own work *Original artist:* SupremeDalek

- **File:Martini_Henry_Mk_IV.jpg** *Source:* https://upload.wikimedia.org/wikipedia/commons/5/5c/Martini_Henry_Mk_IV.jpg *License:* CC BY-SA 2.0 *Contributors:* originally posted to **Flickr** as Martini Henry Mk IV *Original artist:* Antique Military Rifles

- **File:Martini_henry_lock_section.png** *Source:* https://upload.wikimedia.org/wikipedia/commons/1/1b/Martini_henry_lock_section.png *License:* Public domain *Contributors:* ? *Original artist:* ?

- **File:Martini_henry_rifle_0213.png** *Source:* https://upload.wikimedia.org/wikipedia/commons/3/30/Martini_henry_rifle_0213.png *License:* Public domain *Contributors:* ? *Original artist:* ?

- **File:Maverick_88_Pragl.jpg** *Source:* https://upload.wikimedia.org/wikipedia/commons/6/62/Maverick_88_Pragl.jpg *License:* CC-BY-SA-3.0 *Contributors:* ? *Original artist:* ?

- **File:Moss185.png** *Source:* https://upload.wikimedia.org/wikipedia/commons/e/e3/Moss185.png *License:* CC BY 3.0 *Contributors:* Transferred from en.wikipedia to Commons by Giggy. *Original artist:* SQL at English Wikipedia

- **File:Mossberg500LawCombo.jpg** *Source:* https://upload.wikimedia.org/wikipedia/commons/3/3f/Mossberg500LawCombo.jpg *License:* CC BY-SA 3.0 *Contributors:* Own work *Original artist:* Berean Hunter

- **File:Mossberg930_SPX.jpg** *Source:* https://upload.wikimedia.org/wikipedia/commons/d/d1/Mossberg930_SPX.jpg *License:* CC BY-SA 3.0 *Contributors:* Own work *Original artist:* Bobbfwed

- **File:Mossberg_500AL.jpg** *Source:* https://upload.wikimedia.org/wikipedia/commons/9/9e/Mossberg_500AL.jpg *License:* CC-BY-SA-3.0 *Contributors:* Transferred from en.wikipedia *Original artist:* Original uploader was Chuto at en.wikipedia

- **File:Mossberg_500_2_barrels.png** *Source:* https://upload.wikimedia.org/wikipedia/commons/0/09/Mossberg_500_2_barrels.png *License:* CC-BY-SA-3.0 *Contributors:* ? *Original artist:* ?

- **File:Mossberg_500_Bantam.png** *Source:* https://upload.wikimedia.org/wikipedia/commons/2/25/Mossberg_500_Bantam.png *License:* CC-BY-SA-3.0 *Contributors:* ? *Original artist:* ?

10.2. IMAGES

- **File:Mossberg_M590A1.JPG** *Source:* https://upload.wikimedia.org/wikipedia/commons/7/7e/Mossberg_M590A1.JPG *License:* CC BY-SA 3.0 *Contributors:* Own work *Original artist:* BatteryIncluded
- **File:My_Serbu.jpg** *Source:* https://upload.wikimedia.org/wikipedia/commons/0/08/My_Serbu.jpg *License:* Public domain *Contributors:* Own work *Original artist:* Bluejames19 (talk)
- **File:Nuvola_apps_kaboodle.svg** *Source:* https://upload.wikimedia.org/wikipedia/commons/1/1b/Nuvola_apps_kaboodle.svg *License:* LGPL *Contributors:* http://ftp.gnome.org/pub/GNOME/sources/gnome-themes-extras/0.9/gnome-themes-extras-0.9.0.tar.gz *Original artist:* David Vignoni / ICON KING
- **File:PEO_M26_MASS_Stand-alone.jpg** *Source:* https://upload.wikimedia.org/wikipedia/commons/8/87/PEO_M26_MASS_Stand-alone.jpg *License:* Public domain *Contributors:* http://www.flickr.com/photos/peosoldier/4639651790/in/set-72157621946887368/ *Original artist:* Photo Courtesy of PEO Soldier
- **File:PEO_M26_MASS_on_M4_Carbine.jpg** *Source:* https://upload.wikimedia.org/wikipedia/commons/9/98/PEO_M26_MASS_on_M4_Carbine.jpg *License:* Public domain *Contributors:* http://www.flickr.com/photos/peosoldier/3880647910/in/set-72157621946887368/ *Original artist:* Photo Courtesy of PEO Soldier
- **File:PEO_Mossberg_590A1.jpg** *Source:* https://upload.wikimedia.org/wikipedia/commons/d/dd/PEO_Mossberg_590A1.jpg *License:* Public domain *Contributors:* http://www.flickr.com/photos/peosoldier/4639041243/in/set-72157621946887368/ *Original artist:* Photo Courtesy of PEO Soldier
- **File:ParadoxGunAdvert.jpg** *Source:* https://upload.wikimedia.org/wikipedia/commons/3/3a/ParadoxGunAdvert.jpg *License:* Public domain *Contributors:* Colonial and Indian exhibition 1886 *Original artist:* Unknown<a href='//www.wikidata.org/wiki/Q4233718' title='wikidata:Q4233718'><img alt='wikidata:Q4233718' src='https://upload.wikimedia.org/wikipedia/commons/thumb/f/ff/Wikidata-logo.svg/20px-Wikidata-logo.svg.png' width='20' height='11' srcset='https://upload.wikimedia.org/wikipedia/commons/thumb/f/ff/Wikidata-logo.svg/30px-Wikidata-logo.svg.png 1.5x, https://upload.wikimedia.org/wikipedia/commons/thumb/f/ff/Wikidata-logo.svg/40px-Wikidata-logo.svg.png 2x' data-file-width='1050' data-file-height='590' /></a>
- **File:Paradox_gun-bullets-001.jpg** *Source:* https://upload.wikimedia.org/wikipedia/commons/b/b8/Paradox_gun-bullets-001.jpg *License:* Public domain *Contributors:* Big game shooting (1894), page 400 - http://www.archive.org/details/biggameshooting02philiala *Original artist:* Sir Clive Phillipps-Wolley
- **File:Paradox_muzzle.JPG** *Source:* https://upload.wikimedia.org/wikipedia/commons/2/21/Paradox_muzzle.JPG *License:* CC BY-SA 3.0 *Contributors:* Own work *Original artist:* Lord Mountbatten
- **File:Protecta-shotgun-p1030163.jpg** *Source:* https://upload.wikimedia.org/wikipedia/commons/8/8b/Protecta-shotgun-p1030163.jpg *License:* CC BY-SA 2.0 fr *Contributors:* Own work *Original artist:* Rama
- **File:Queen_Victoria_by_Bassano.jpg** *Source:* https://upload.wikimedia.org/wikipedia/commons/e/e3/Queen_Victoria_by_Bassano.jpg *License:* Public domain *Contributors:* Scanned from the book *The National Portrait Gallery History of the Kings and Queens of England* by David Williamson, ISBN 1855142287, p. 153. *Original artist:* Alexander Bassano
- **File:Question_book-new.svg** *Source:* https://upload.wikimedia.org/wikipedia/en/9/99/Question_book-new.svg *License:* Cc-by-sa-3.0 *Contributors:*
  Created from scratch in Adobe Illustrator. Based on Image:Question book.png created by User:Equazcion *Original artist:*
  Tkgd2007
- **File:RMB-93_Engineering_technologies_2010.jpg** *Source:* https://upload.wikimedia.org/wikipedia/commons/3/30/RMB-93_Engineering_technologies_2010.jpg *License:* CC BY-SA 3.0 *Contributors:* Vitalykuzmin.net *Original artist:* Vitaly V. Kuzmin allow to use this picture in Copyright Policy
- **File:RemingtonMd11.JPG** *Source:* https://upload.wikimedia.org/wikipedia/commons/6/6f/RemingtonMd11.JPG *License:* Public domain *Contributors:* http://en.wikipedia.org/wiki/File:RemingtonMd11.JPG *Original artist:* Sf46
- **File:Remington_11-87_NFM.JPG** *Source:* https://upload.wikimedia.org/wikipedia/commons/3/37/Remington_11-87_NFM.JPG *License:* CC BY-SA 3.0 *Contributors:* Transferred from en.wikipedia; transfer was stated to be made by User:ArikamaI. *Original artist:* Original uploader was Darkhelmet322 at en.wikipedia
- **File:Remington_1100_Tactical_8_Rounds.jpg** *Source:* https://upload.wikimedia.org/wikipedia/commons/0/02/Remington_1100_Tactical_8_Rounds.jpg *License:* CC-BY-SA-3.0 *Contributors:* Own work *Original artist:* Arthurrh
- **File:Remington_1100_Tactical_Action.jpg** *Source:* https://upload.wikimedia.org/wikipedia/commons/1/15/Remington_1100_Tactical_Action.jpg *License:* CC-BY-SA-3.0 *Contributors:* Own work *Original artist:* Arthurrh
- **File:Remington_Model_700.JPG** *Source:* https://upload.wikimedia.org/wikipedia/commons/c/cb/Remington_Model_700.JPG *License:* CC BY-SA 3.0 *Contributors:* English Wikipedia, self made by the author *Original artist:* User:M855GT
- **File:Ruger_mkiii_bull.jpg** *Source:* https://upload.wikimedia.org/wikipedia/commons/9/9e/Ruger_mkiii_bull.jpg *License:* CC-BY-SA-3.0 *Contributors:* http://en.wikipedia.org/wiki/Image:Ruger_mkiii_bull.jpg *Original artist:* Bobbfwed
- **File:SIG220-Morges.jpg** *Source:* https://upload.wikimedia.org/wikipedia/commons/0/0b/SIG220-Morges.jpg *License:* CC BY-SA 2.0 fr *Contributors:* Own work *Original artist:* Rama
- **File:SPAS-12_Variants..png** *Source:* https://upload.wikimedia.org/wikipedia/commons/b/ba/SPAS-12_Variants..png *License:* CC BY-SA 4.0 *Contributors:* Own work *Original artist:* HellsXgunsmith
- **File:SPAS-12_stock_folded.jpg** *Source:* https://upload.wikimedia.org/wikipedia/commons/0/09/SPAS-12_stock_folded.jpg *License:* CC BY-SA 3.0 *Contributors:* Own work *Original artist:* Tekogi

- **File:SPAS15.jpg** *Source:* https://upload.wikimedia.org/wikipedia/commons/4/4d/SPAS15.jpg *License:* CC BY 2.5 *Contributors:* http://www.esercito.difesa.it/root/equipaggiamenti/armi_legg.asp#individuali *Original artist:* italian army
- **File:SPAS_12_Fixed_Stock_and_Folding_Stock.JPG** *Source:* https://upload.wikimedia.org/wikipedia/commons/4/47/SPAS_12_Fixed_Stock_and_Folding_Stock.JPG *License:* Public domain *Contributors:* Photo taken by uploader. *Original artist:* Joguwa86
- **File:Saiga-12K-040-02-with_Cobra.jpg** *Source:* https://upload.wikimedia.org/wikipedia/commons/1/10/Saiga-12K-040-02-with_Cobra.jpg *License:* CC BY-SA 3.0 *Contributors:* My Canon EOS 400D *Original artist:* Serguei S. Dukachev 16:40, 12 January 2008 (UTC)
- **File:Saiga_12_shotgun.jpg** *Source:* https://upload.wikimedia.org/wikipedia/commons/0/02/Saiga_12_shotgun.jpg *License:* CC BY-SA 3.0 *Contributors:* Own work *Original artist:* SpetsnazAlpha
- **File:Saiga_dust_cover_flap.jpg** *Source:* https://upload.wikimedia.org/wikipedia/commons/5/57/Saiga_dust_cover_flap.jpg *License:* CC-BY-SA-3.0 *Contributors:* Transferred from en.wikipedia; transferred to Commons by User:Commonsnoop using CommonsHelper. *Original artist:* Original uploader was Beerslurpy at en.wikipedia
- **File:Shotgun-shot-sequence-1g.jpg** *Source:* https://upload.wikimedia.org/wikipedia/commons/f/f4/Shotgun-shot-sequence-1g.jpg *License:* CC BY 3.0 *Contributors:* http://people.rit.edu/andpph/exhibit-3.html *Original artist:* Andrew Davidhazy
- **File:Shotgun.jpg** *Source:* https://upload.wikimedia.org/wikipedia/commons/d/da/Shotgun.jpg *License:* Public domain *Contributors:* http://web.archive.org/web/http://www4.army.mil/armyimages/armyimage.php?photo=1507 *Original artist:* United States Army photo by Staff Sergeant Joseph Roberts
- **File:ShotgunAction.JPG** *Source:* https://upload.wikimedia.org/wikipedia/commons/a/a4/ShotgunAction.JPG *License:* Attribution *Contributors:* Transferred from en.wikipedia to Commons. Transfer was stated to be made by User:evers. *Original artist:* The original uploader was Commander Zulu at English Wikipedia
- **File:Shotgun_Mossberg_590.jpg** *Source:* https://upload.wikimedia.org/wikipedia/commons/d/dc/Shotgun_Mossberg_590.jpg *License:* Public domain *Contributors:* ? *Original artist:* ?
- **File:Shotgun_in_training_US_military.jpg** *Source:* https://upload.wikimedia.org/wikipedia/commons/b/b5/Shotgun_in_training_US_military.jpg *License:* Public domain *Contributors:* U.S. Department of Defense U.S. Navy Photo. *Original artist:* Eric A. Clement (U.S. Navy)
- **File:Shotgunammo.jpg** *Source:* https://upload.wikimedia.org/wikipedia/commons/b/ba/Shotgunammo.jpg *License:* Public domain *Contributors:* ? *Original artist:* ?
- **File:Snider-Martini-Enfield_Cartridges.JPG** *Source:* https://upload.wikimedia.org/wikipedia/commons/9/99/Snider-Martini-Enfield_Cartridges.JPG *License:* Attribution *Contributors:* Transferred from en.wikipedia to Commons. Original uploader was Commander Zulu at en.wikipedia 2006-12-17 (original upload date) *Original artist:* Image taken by Commander Zulu, December 2006.
- **File:Stevens_520-30_Trench_Gun.JPG** *Source:* https://upload.wikimedia.org/wikipedia/commons/6/68/Stevens_520-30_Trench_Gun.JPG *License:* CC BY-SA 4.0 *Contributors:* Own work *Original artist:* Keydet92
- **File:Stevens_520-30_Trench_Gun_R.JPG** *Source:* https://upload.wikimedia.org/wikipedia/commons/3/35/Stevens_520-30_Trench_Gun_R.JPG *License:* CC BY-SA 4.0 *Contributors:* Own work *Original artist:* Keydet92
- **File:Stevens_520_09-13_L.jpg** *Source:* https://upload.wikimedia.org/wikipedia/commons/e/ea/Stevens_520_09-13_L.jpg *License:* CC BY-SA 4.0 *Contributors:* Own work *Original artist:* Keydet92
- **File:Stevens_520_20-24_L.jpg** *Source:* https://upload.wikimedia.org/wikipedia/commons/d/dd/Stevens_520_20-24_L.jpg *License:* CC BY-SA 4.0 *Contributors:* Own work *Original artist:* Keydet92
- **File:Stevens_520_26-27_L.JPG** *Source:* https://upload.wikimedia.org/wikipedia/commons/7/75/Stevens_520_26-27_L.JPG *License:* CC BY-SA 4.0 *Contributors:* Own work *Original artist:* Keydet92
- **File:Stevens_520_38-39_R.JPG** *Source:* https://upload.wikimedia.org/wikipedia/commons/2/24/Stevens_520_38-39_R.JPG *License:* CC BY-SA 4.0 *Contributors:* Own work *Original artist:* Keydet92
- **File:Stevens_520_40-41_L.JPG** *Source:* https://upload.wikimedia.org/wikipedia/commons/0/0f/Stevens_520_40-41_L.JPG *License:* CC BY-SA 4.0 *Contributors:* Own work *Original artist:* Keydet92
- **File:Stevens_620_1938-39.JPG** *Source:* https://upload.wikimedia.org/wikipedia/commons/4/43/Stevens_620_1938-39.JPG *License:* CC BY-SA 4.0 *Contributors:* Own work *Original artist:* Keydet92
- **File:Stevens_WWII_Riot_Gun_Markings.JPG** *Source:* https://upload.wikimedia.org/wikipedia/commons/d/d5/Stevens_WWII_Riot_Gun_Markings.JPG *License:* CC BY-SA 4.0 *Contributors:* Own work *Original artist:* Keydet92
- **File:Text_document_with_red_question_mark.svg** *Source:* https://upload.wikimedia.org/wikipedia/commons/a/a4/Text_document_with_red_question_mark.svg *License:* Public domain *Contributors:* Created by bdesham with Inkscape; based upon Text-x-generic.svg from the Tango project. *Original artist:* Benjamin D. Esham (bdesham)
- **File:Trench_Shotgun_win12_800.jpg** *Source:* https://upload.wikimedia.org/wikipedia/commons/3/32/Trench_Shotgun_win12_800.jpg *License:* Public domain *Contributors:* ? *Original artist:* ?
- **File:USAF_870_Shotgun.JPEG** *Source:* https://upload.wikimedia.org/wikipedia/commons/4/44/USAF_870_Shotgun.JPEG *License:* Public domain *Contributors:* Defenseimagery.mil, VIRIN 020612-F-OK231-010 *Original artist:* SRA James Harper, USAF
- **File:USAF_logo.png** *Source:* https://upload.wikimedia.org/wikipedia/commons/6/69/USAF_logo.png *License:* Public domain *Contributors:* http://www.dobbins.afrc.af.mil/shared/media/ggallery/hires/AFG-060112-014.jpg *Original artist:* USAF
- **File:USAS12shotgun4104.jpg** *Source:* https://upload.wikimedia.org/wikipedia/commons/6/62/USAS12shotgun4104.jpg *License:* CC BY 2.5 *Contributors:* Transferred from en.wikipedia to Commons. *Original artist:* The original uploader was Olegvolk at English Wikipedia

10.2. IMAGES

- **File:USMC-05459.jpg** *Source:* https://upload.wikimedia.org/wikipedia/commons/6/6e/USMC-05459.jpg *License:* Public domain *Contributors:* http://www.marines.mil/unit/basecamppendleton/PublishingImages/2007/focus1high.jpg *Original artist:* ?

- **File:US_Navy_041102-N-4649C-001_U.S._Marines_assigned_to_Commander,_Seventh_Fleet,_Fleet_Anti-terrorism_Security_Team_(FAST),_Third_Platoon,_familiarize_themselves_with_the_M500_shotgun.jpg** *Source:* https://upload.wikimedia.org/wikipedia/commons/0/0a/US_Navy_041102-N-4649C-001_U.S._Marines_assigned_to_Commander%2C_Seventh_Fleet%2C_Fleet_Anti-terrorism_Security_Team_%28FAST%29%2C_Third_Platoon%2C_familiarize_themselves_with_the_M500_shotgun.jpg *License:* Public domain *Contributors:*
This Image was released by the United States Navy with the ID 041102-N-4649C-001 <a class='external text' href='//commons.wikimedia.org/w/index.php?title=Category:Files_created_by_the_United_States_Navy_with_known_IDs,,&,,filefrom=041102-N-4649C-001#mw-category-media'>(next)</a>.
This tag does not indicate the copyright status of the attached work. A normal copyright tag is still required. See Commons:Licensing for more information.
Original artist: U.S. Navy Photo by Photographer's Mate Second Class Chantel M. Clayton

- **File:US_flag_45_stars.svg** *Source:* https://upload.wikimedia.org/wikipedia/commons/8/8e/US_flag_45_stars.svg *License:* Public domain *Contributors:* No machine-readable source provided. Own work assumed (based on copyright claims). *Original artist:* No machine-readable author provided. Jacobolus assumed (based on copyright claims).

- **File:Utas-15-bitmap.png** *Source:* https://upload.wikimedia.org/wikipedia/commons/c/c1/Utas-15-bitmap.png *License:* CC BY-SA 3.0 *Contributors:* Own work *Original artist:* Luk

- **File:Vepr-12_ARMS_&_Hunting_2012_01.jpg** *Source:* https://upload.wikimedia.org/wikipedia/commons/8/87/Vepr-12_ARMS_%26_Hunting_2012_01.jpg *License:* CC BY-SA 3.0 *Contributors:* Vitalykuzmin.net *Original artist:* Vitaly V. Kuzmin

- **File:Vincent_Hancock_at_2008_Summer_Olympics_men'{}s_skeet_finals_2008-08-16.JPG** *Source:* https://upload.wikimedia.org/wikipedia/commons/9/90/Vincent_Hancock_at_2008_Summer_Olympics_men%27s_skeet_finals_2008-08-16.JPG *License:* Public domain *Contributors:* http://www.defenseimagery.mil/imagery.html#guid=d7e950e78ab77932dbe8b711eff4b4b9747d34 *Original artist:* Tim Hipps

- **File:Wiki_letter_w.svg** *Source:* https://upload.wikimedia.org/wikipedia/en/6/6c/Wiki_letter_w.svg *License:* Cc-by-sa-3.0 *Contributors:* ? *Original artist:* ?

- **File:Wiki_letter_w_cropped.svg** *Source:* https://upload.wikimedia.org/wikipedia/commons/1/1c/Wiki_letter_w_cropped.svg *License:* CC-BY-SA-3.0 *Contributors:* This file was derived from Wiki letter w.svg: <a href='//commons.wikimedia.org/wiki/File:Wiki_letter_w.svg' class='image'><img alt='Wiki letter w.svg' src='https://upload.wikimedia.org/wikipedia/commons/thumb/6/6c/Wiki_letter_w.svg/50px-Wiki_letter_w.svg.png' width='50' height='50' srcset='https://upload.wikimedia.org/wikipedia/commons/thumb/6/6c/Wiki_letter_w.svg/75px-Wiki_letter_w.svg.png 1.5x, https://upload.wikimedia.org/wikipedia/commons/thumb/6/6c/Wiki_letter_w.svg/100px-Wiki_letter_w.svg.png 2x' data-file-width='44' data-file-height='44' /></a>
Original artist: Derivative work by Thumperward from:

- **File:Winchester1200Def-1.jpg** *Source:* https://upload.wikimedia.org/wikipedia/commons/b/bb/Winchester1200Def-1.jpg *License:* CC-BY-SA-3.0 *Contributors:* Own photo work *Original artist:* Shotgun

- **File:Winchester_1897.jpg** *Source:* https://upload.wikimedia.org/wikipedia/commons/9/98/Winchester_1897.jpg *License:* Public domain *Contributors:* Transferred from en.wikipedia to Commons by Amendola90. *Original artist:* Asams10 at English Wikipedia

- **File:Winchester_1911.jpg** *Source:* https://upload.wikimedia.org/wikipedia/commons/2/23/Winchester_1911.jpg *License:* Public domain *Contributors:* Own work *Original artist:* Luigibastardo

- **File:Winchester_Model_1873_Short_Rifle_1495.jpg** *Source:* https://upload.wikimedia.org/wikipedia/commons/1/11/Winchester_Model_1873_Short_Rifle_1495.jpg *License:* Attribution *Contributors:* ? *Original artist:* ?

- **File:Winchester_Model_1912.JPG** *Source:* https://upload.wikimedia.org/wikipedia/commons/6/67/Winchester_Model_1912.JPG *License:* Public domain *Contributors:* Transferred from en.wikipedia to Commons by SreeBot. *Original artist:* Yaf at en.wikipedia

- **File:Winchester_Repeating_Arms_Company_advertisement,_1898.jpg** *Source:* https://upload.wikimedia.org/wikipedia/commons/3/3f/Winchester_Repeating_Arms_Company_advertisement%2C_1898.jpg *License:* Public domain *Contributors:* Google Books - (1898). "Advertisements". *The American Monthly Review of Reviews*: p. 49. New York: The Review of Reviews Co.. *Original artist:* Unknown<a href='//www.wikidata.org/wiki/Q4233718' title='wikidata:Q4233718'><img alt='wikidata:Q4233718' src='https://upload.wikimedia.org/wikipedia/commons/thumb/f/ff/Wikidata-logo.svg/20px-Wikidata-logo.svg.png' width='20' height='11' srcset='https://upload.wikimedia.org/wikipedia/commons/thumb/f/ff/Wikidata-logo.svg/30px-Wikidata-logo.svg.png 1.5x, https://upload.wikimedia.org/wikipedia/commons/thumb/f/ff/Wikidata-logo.svg/40px-Wikidata-logo.svg.png 2x' data-file-width='1050' data-file-height='590' /></a>

- **File:WncsterCatMod97trench.jpg** *Source:* https://upload.wikimedia.org/wikipedia/commons/7/7b/WncsterCatMod97trench.jpg *License:* Public domain *Contributors:* ? *Original artist:* ?

- **File:Ww2marineshotgun.jpg** *Source:* https://upload.wikimedia.org/wikipedia/commons/c/cd/Ww2marineshotgun.jpg *License:* Public domain *Contributors:* ? *Original artist:* ?

- **File:XM-26_Shotgun.JPG** *Source:* https://upload.wikimedia.org/wikipedia/commons/f/f1/XM-26_Shotgun.JPG *License:* Attribution *Contributors:* ? *Original artist:* ?

- **File:XM26_0126_highRes.jpg** *Source:* https://upload.wikimedia.org/wikipedia/commons/d/dd/XM26_0126_highRes.jpg *License:* Public domain *Contributors:* ? *Original artist:* ?

- **File:Сайга_12К_030.jpg** *Source:* https://upload.wikimedia.org/wikipedia/commons/b/b7/%D0%A1%D0%B0%D0%B9%D0%B3%D0%B0_12%D0%9A_030.jpg *License:* CC BY-SA 3.0 *Contributors:* Transferred from ru.wikipedia to Commons by ArikamaI. *Original artist:* Sinodov at Russian Wikipedia

10.3 Content license

- Creative Commons Attribution-Share Alike 3.0

CPSIA information can be obtained
at www.ICGtesting.com
Printed in the USA
LVHW021356250821
696067LV00010B/1078